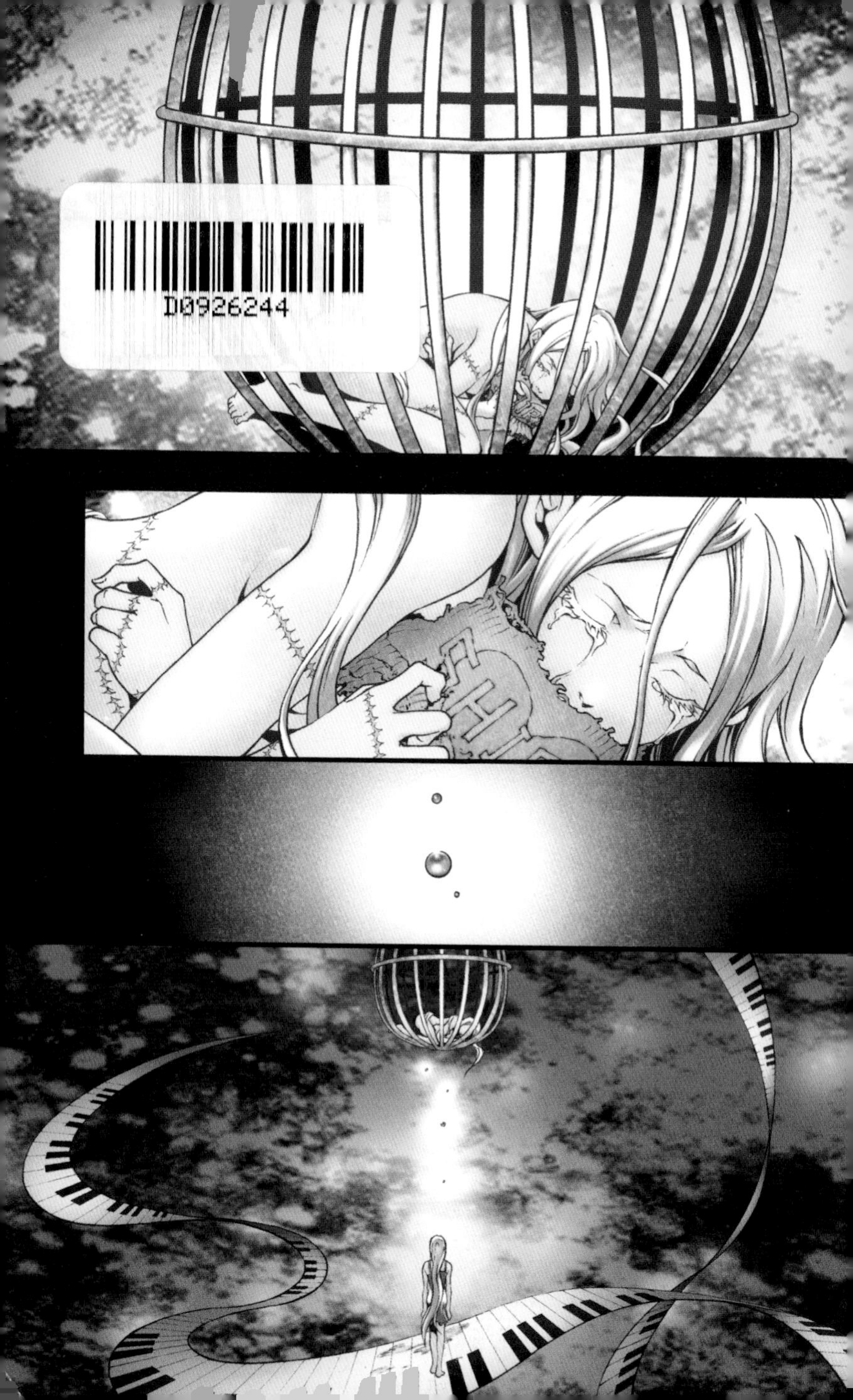

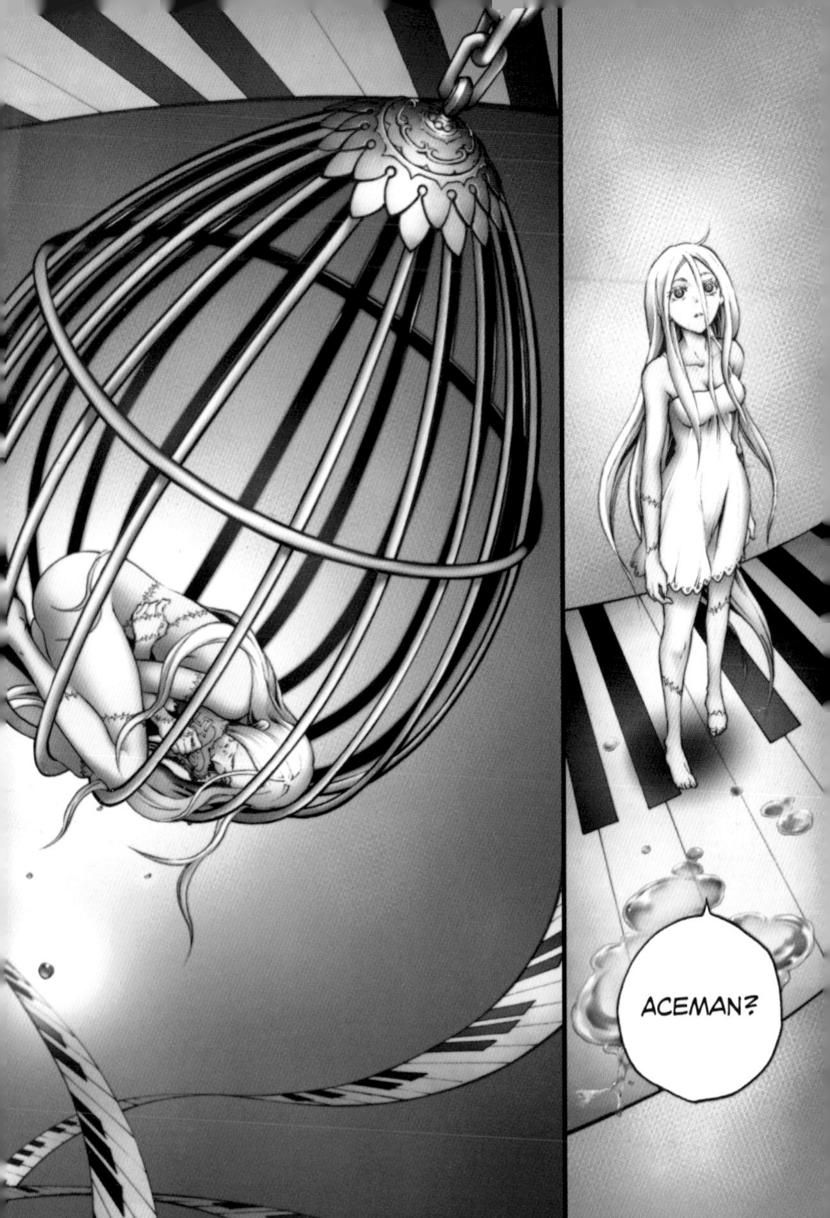
ACEMAN?

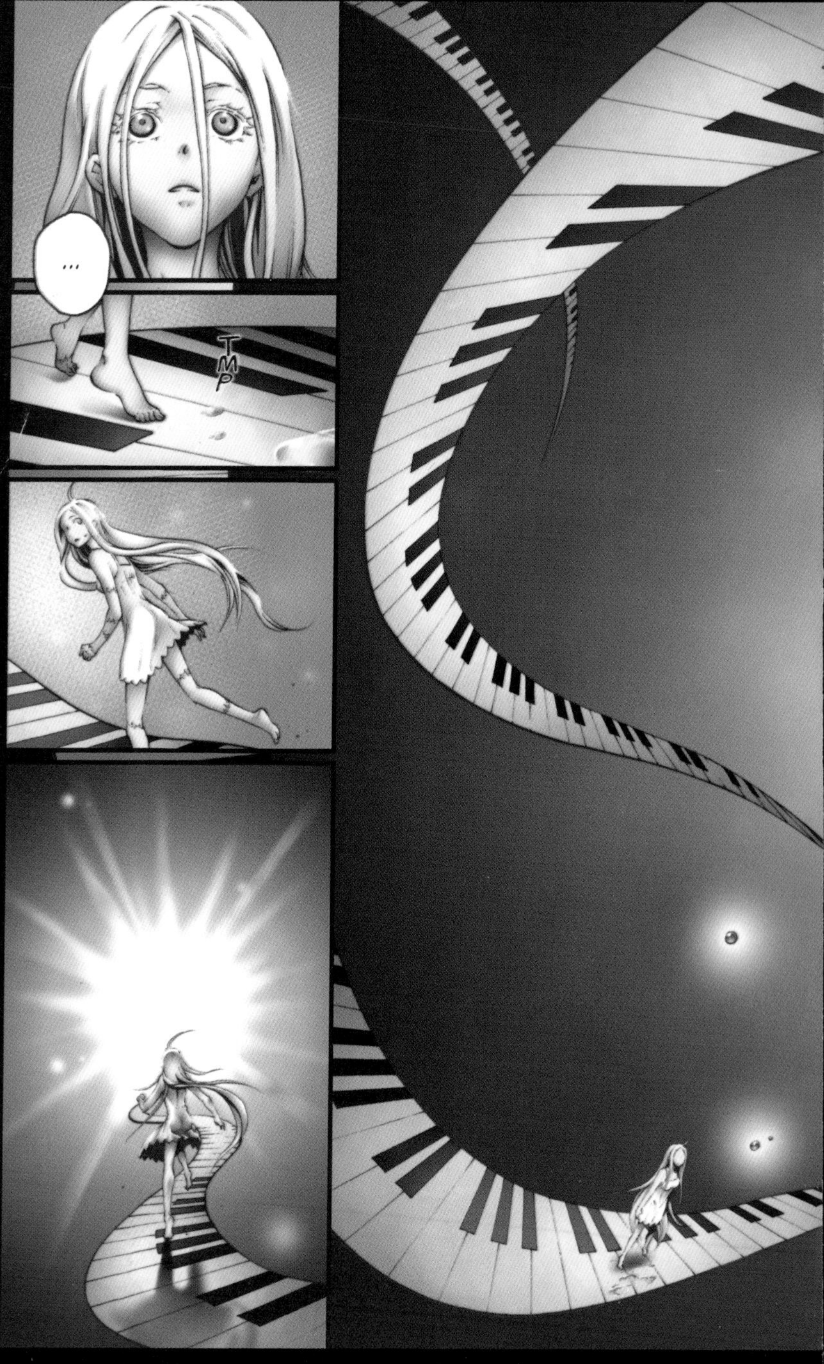
...
TMP

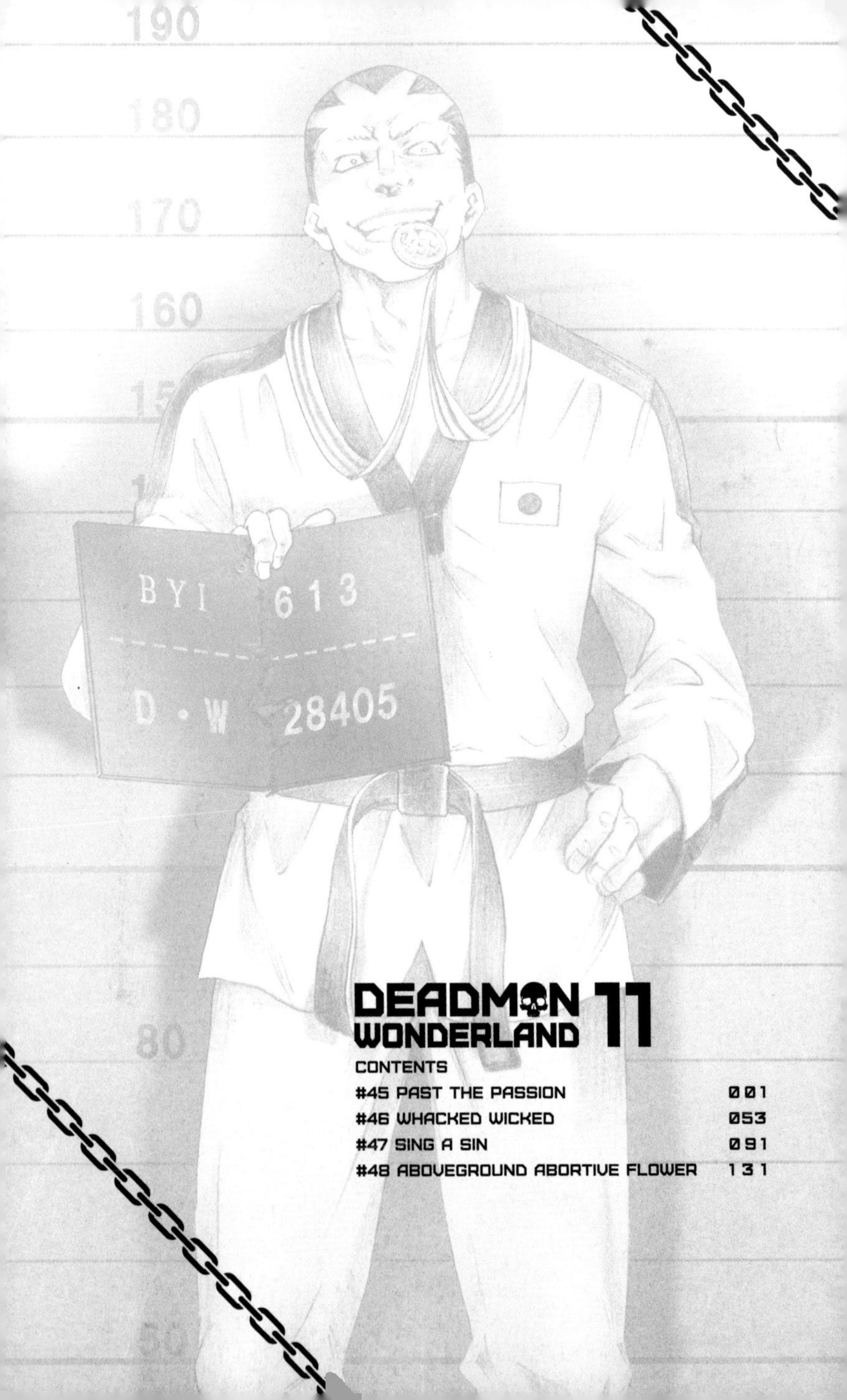
190
180
170
160
80
BYI 613
D・W 28405

DEADMAN WONDERLAND 11

CONTENTS

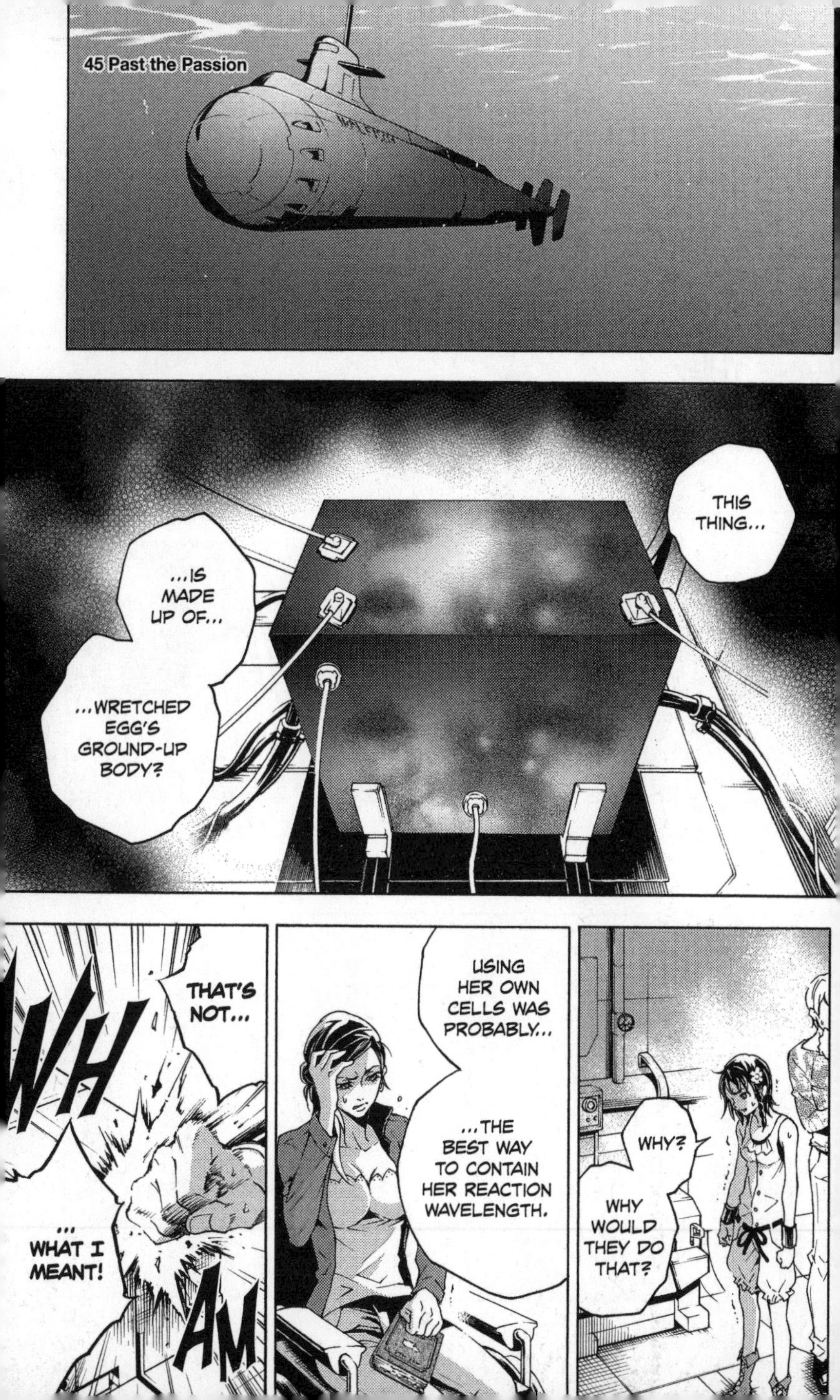
45 Past the Passion
THIS THING...
...IS MADE UP OF...
...WRETCHED EGG'S GROUND-UP BODY?
WHY?
WHY WOULD THEY DO THAT?
USING HER OWN CELLS WAS PROBABLY...
...THE BEST WAY TO CONTAIN HER REACTION WAVELENGTH.
WHAM
THAT'S NOT...
...WHAT I MEANT!

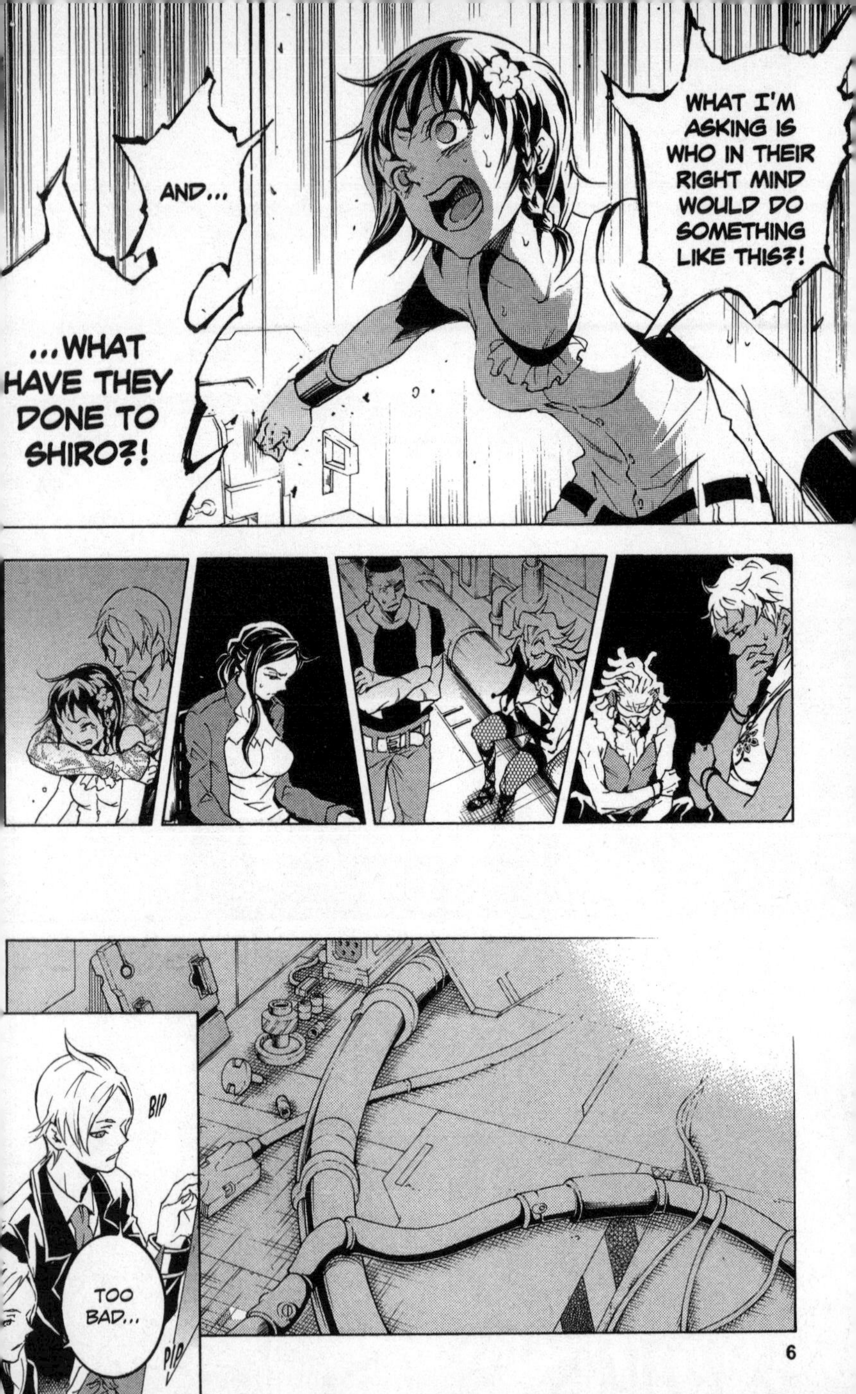
WHAT I'M ASKING IS WHO IN THEIR RIGHT MIND WOULD DO SOMETHING LIKE THIS?!
AND...
...WHAT HAVE THEY DONE TO SHIRO?!
BIP
TOO BAD...
PIP

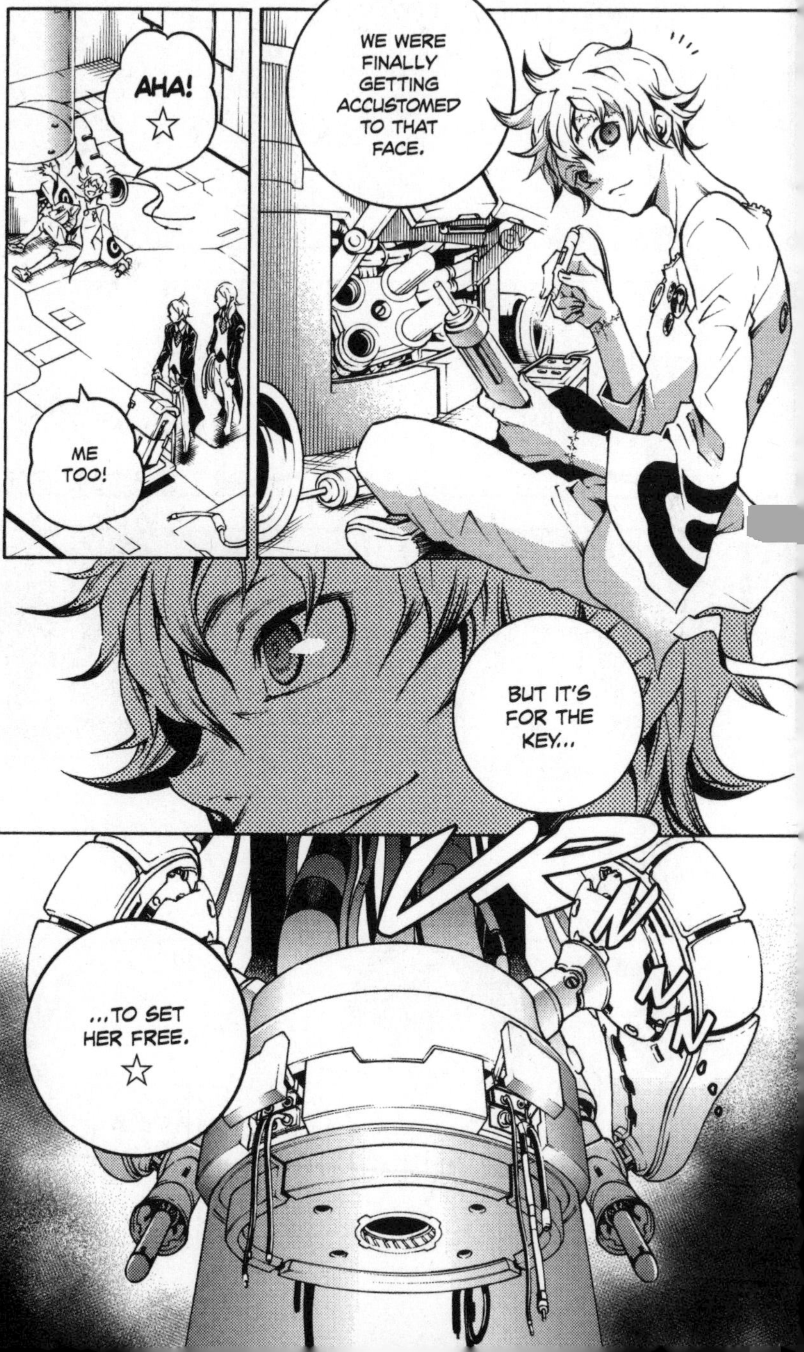
WE WERE FINALLY GETTING ACCUSTOMED TO THAT FACE.
AHA! ☆
ME TOO!
BUT IT'S FOR THE KEY...
VRNNN
...TO SET HER FREE. ☆

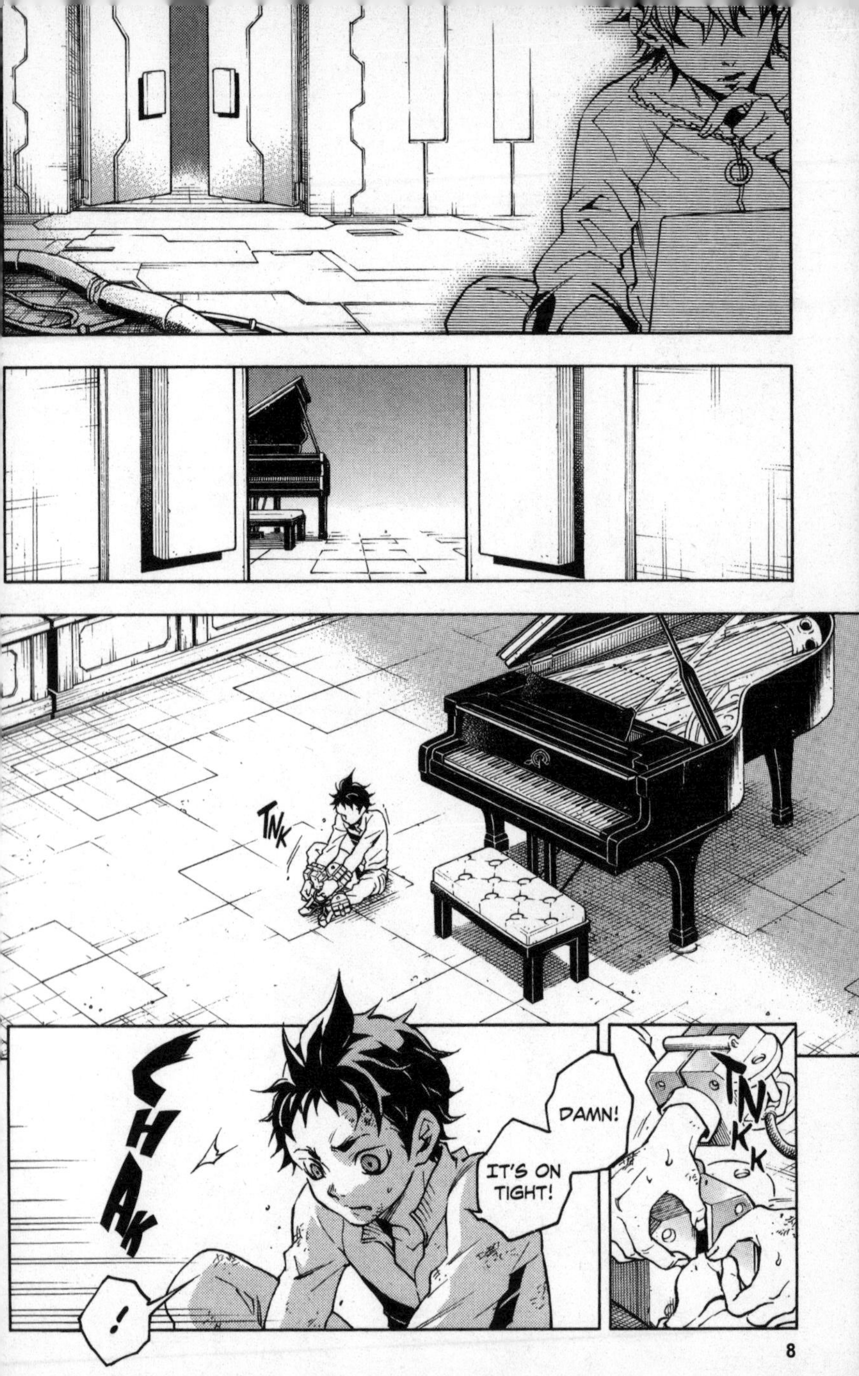
TNK
TNKK
DAMN!
IT'S ON TIGHT!
CHAK
!

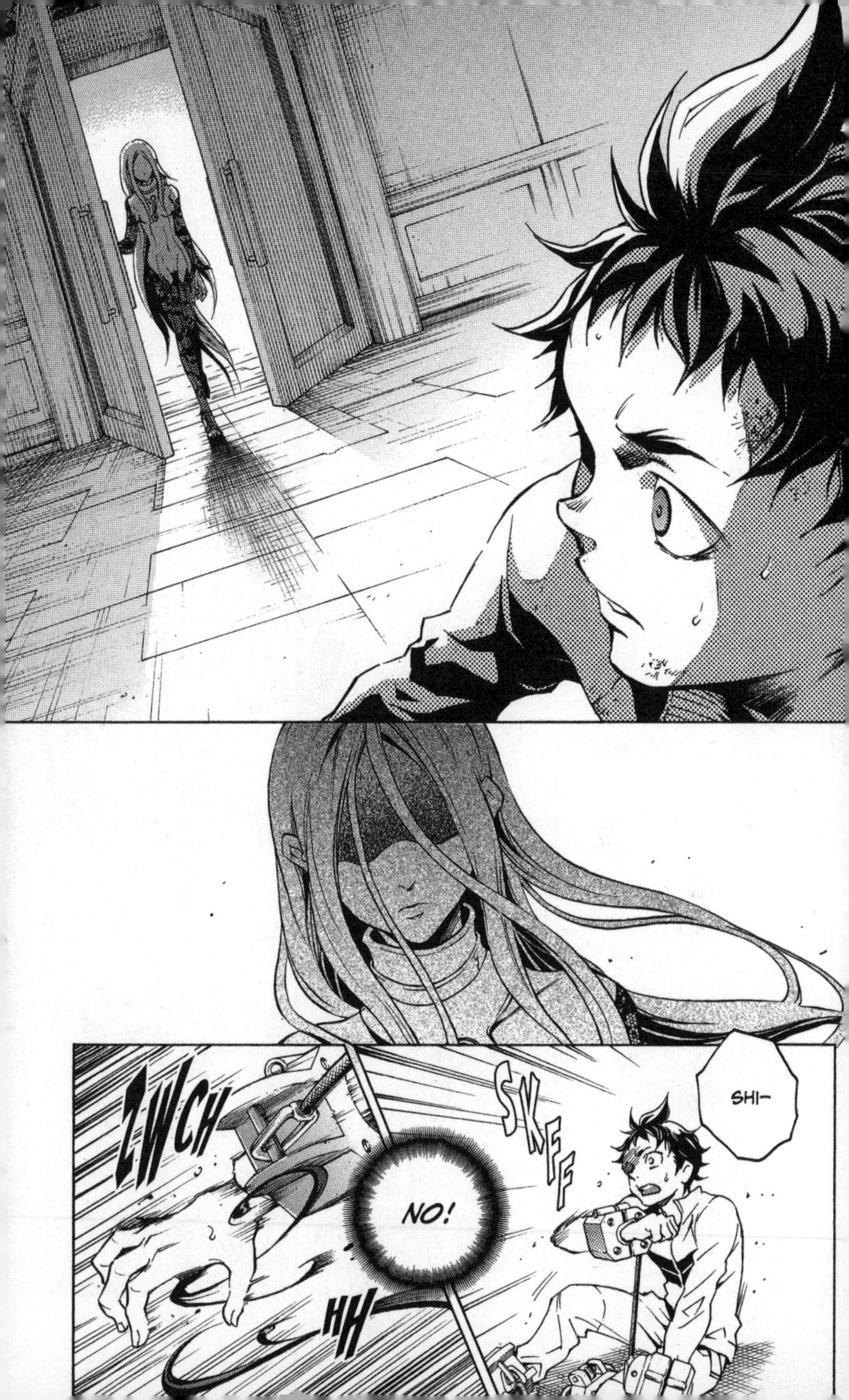
SHI-
SKFF
NO!
ZWCH
HH

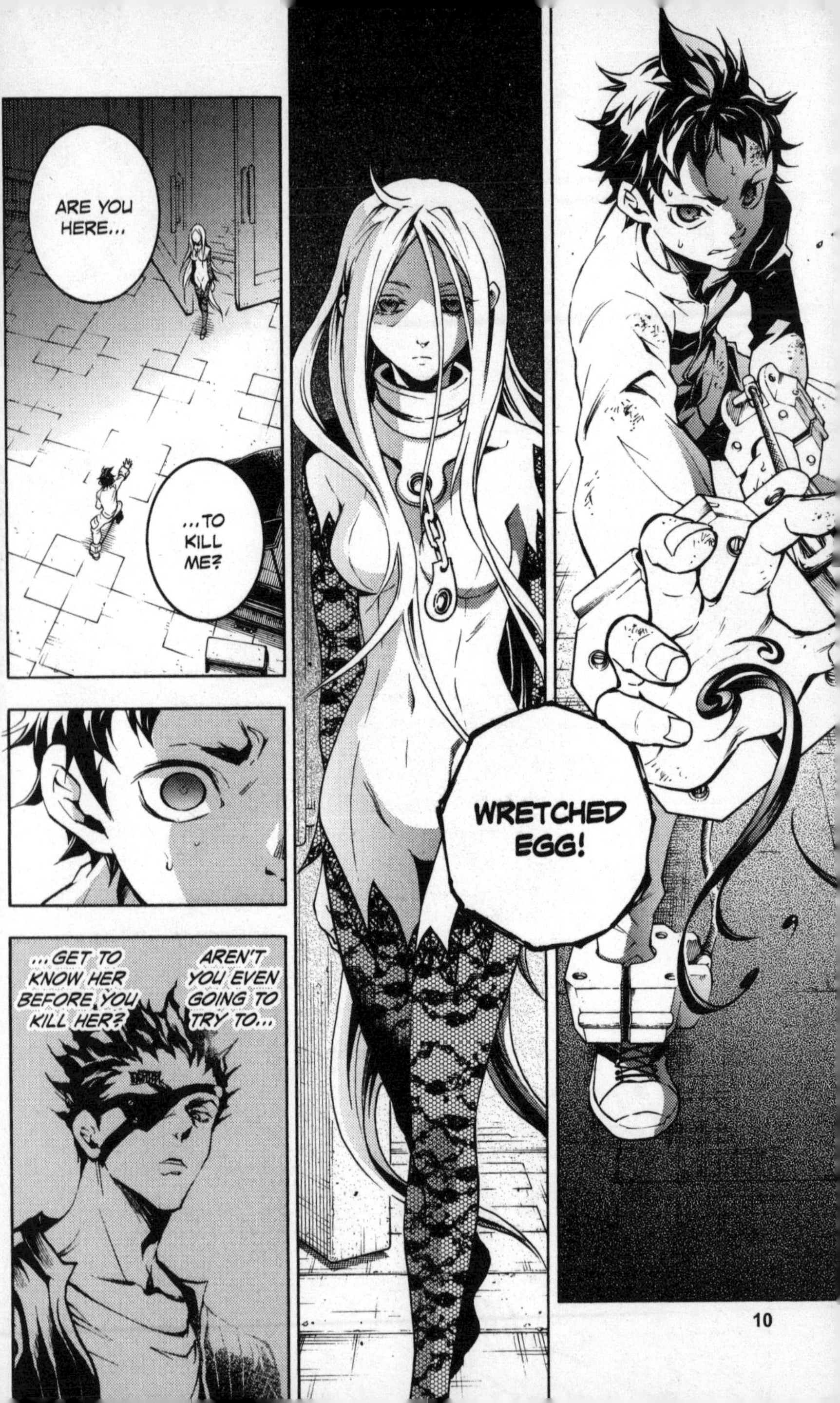
WRETCHED EGG!
ARE YOU HERE...
...TO KILL ME?
AREN'T YOU EVEN GOING TO TRY TO...
...GET TO KNOW HER BEFORE YOU KILL HER?

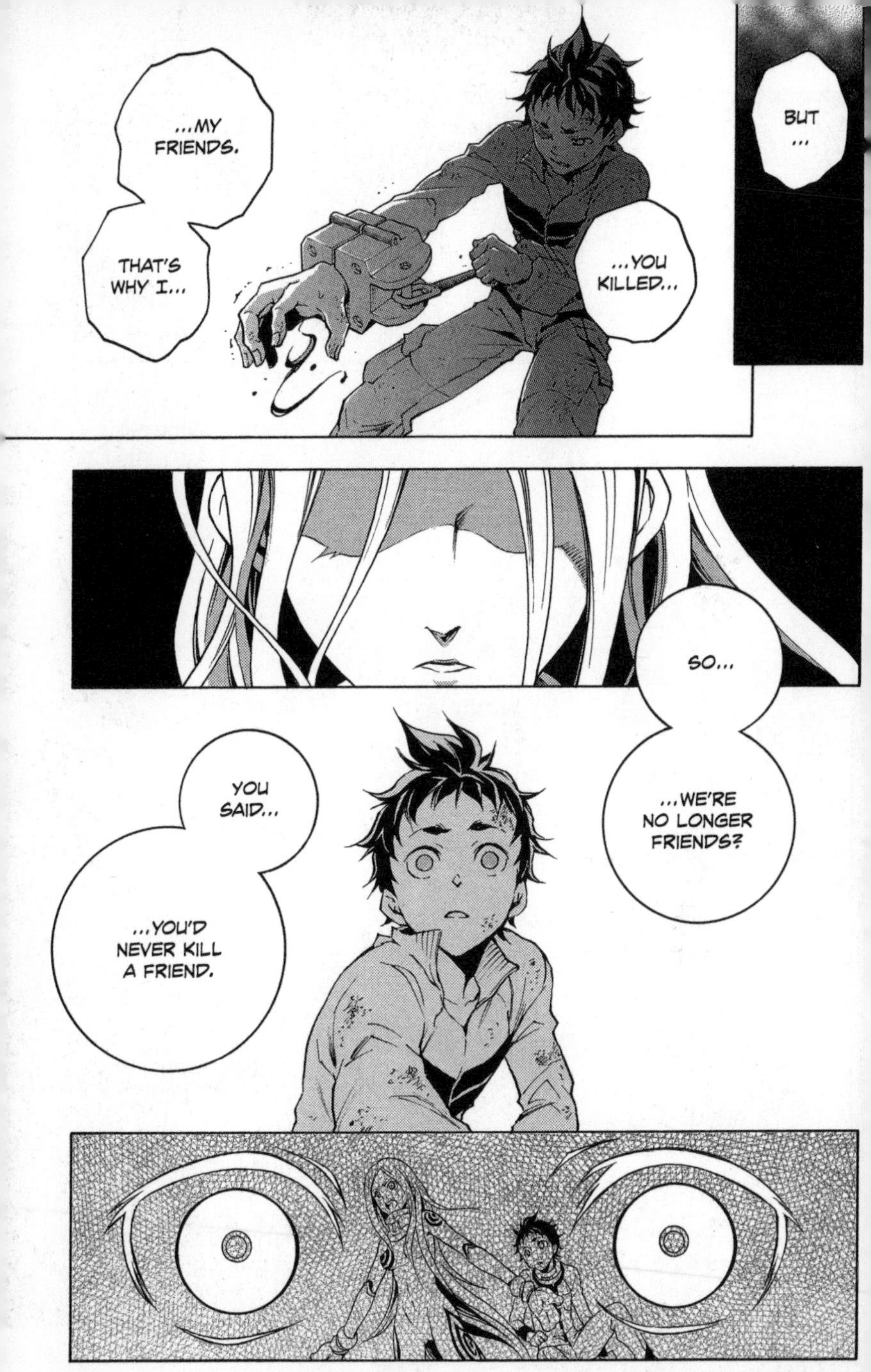
BUT ...
...YOU KILLED...
...MY FRIENDS.
THAT'S WHY I...
SO...
...WE'RE NO LONGER FRIENDS?
YOU SAID...
...YOU'D NEVER KILL A FRIEND.

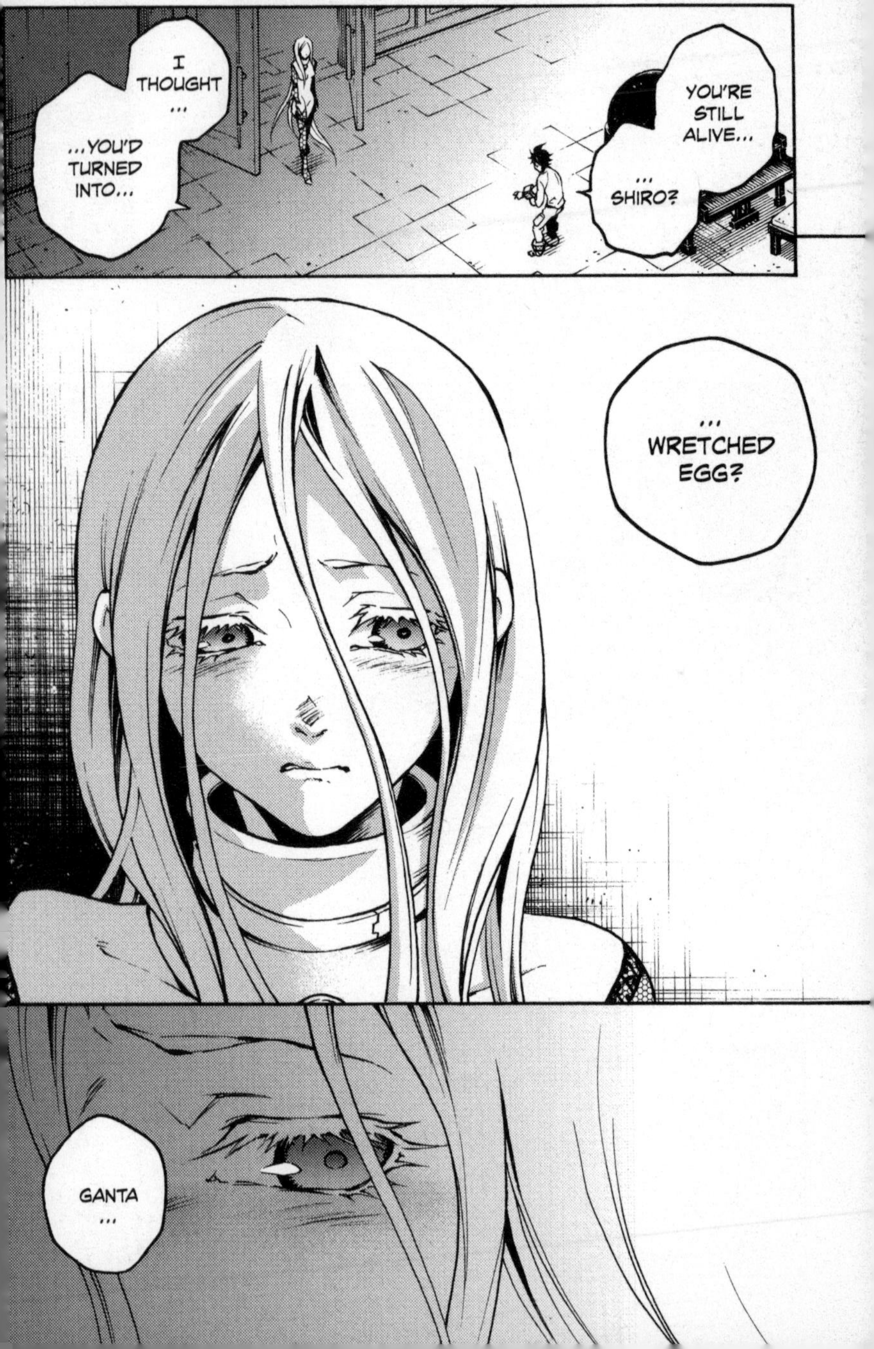
YOU'RE STILL ALIVE...
... SHIRO?
I THOUGHT ...
...YOU'D TURNED INTO...
... WRETCHED EGG?
GANTA ...

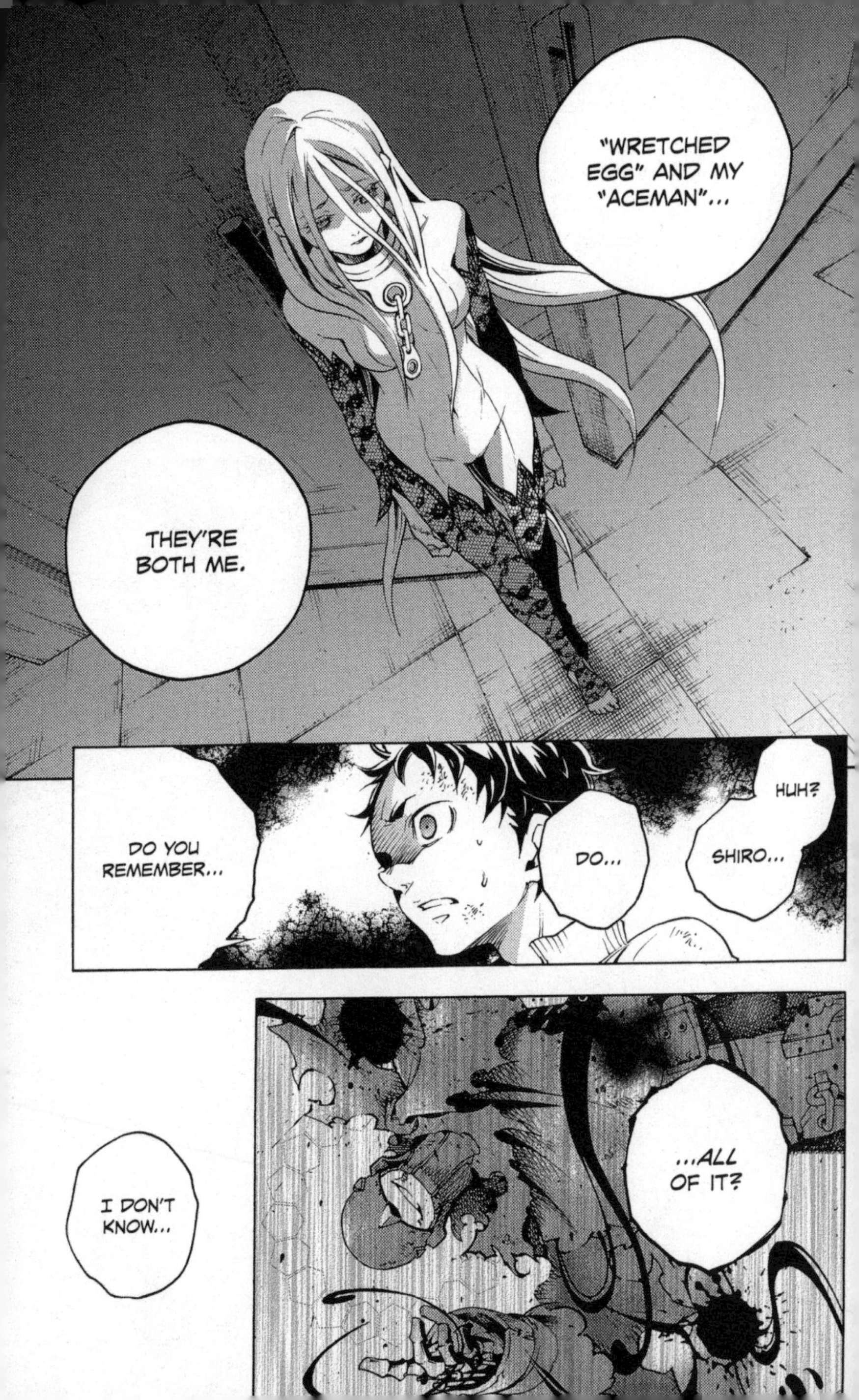
"WRETCHED EGG" AND MY "ACEMAN"...
THEY'RE BOTH ME.
HUH?
SHIRO...
DO...
DO YOU REMEMBER...
...ALL OF IT?
I DON'T KNOW...

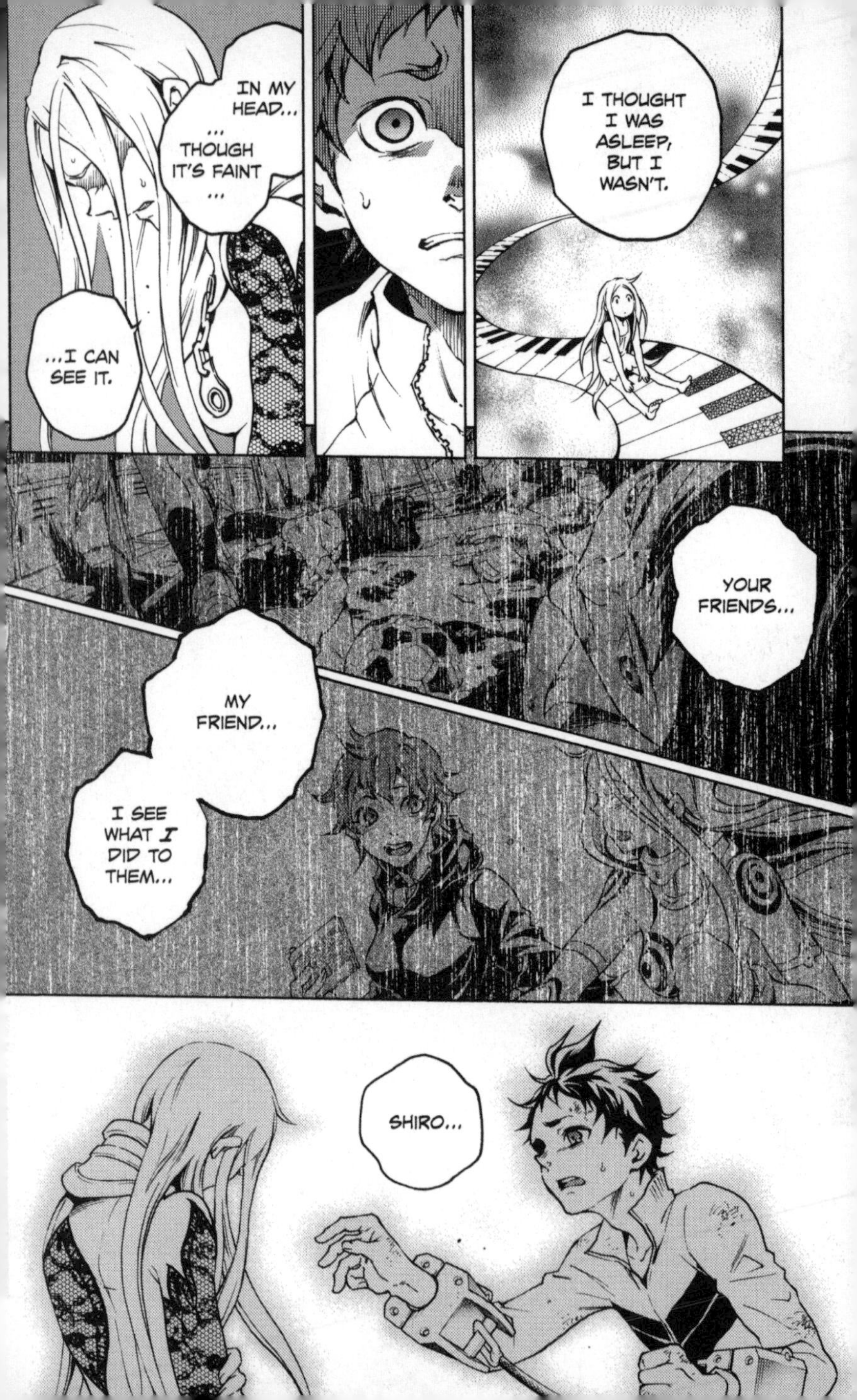
I THOUGHT I WAS ASLEEP, BUT I WASN'T.
IN MY HEAD... ...THOUGH IT'S FAINT...
...I CAN SEE IT.
YOUR FRIENDS...
MY FRIEND...
I SEE WHAT I DID TO THEM...
SHIRO...

I'M SORRY.

I'M SORRY, GANTA.

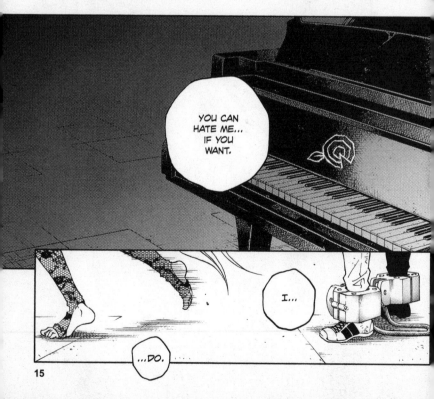

YOU CAN HATE ME... IF YOU WANT.

I...

...DO.

15

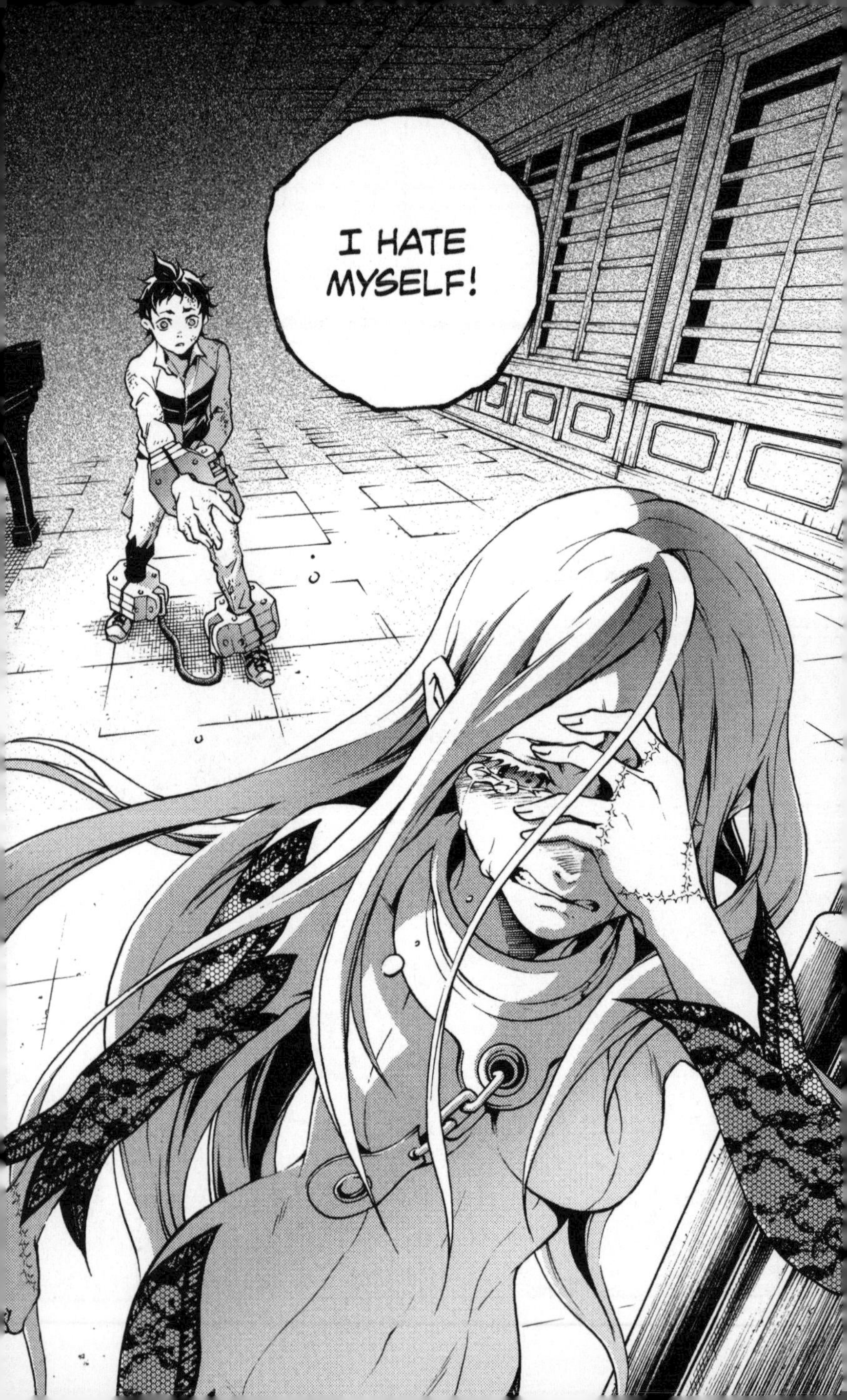
I HATE MYSELF!

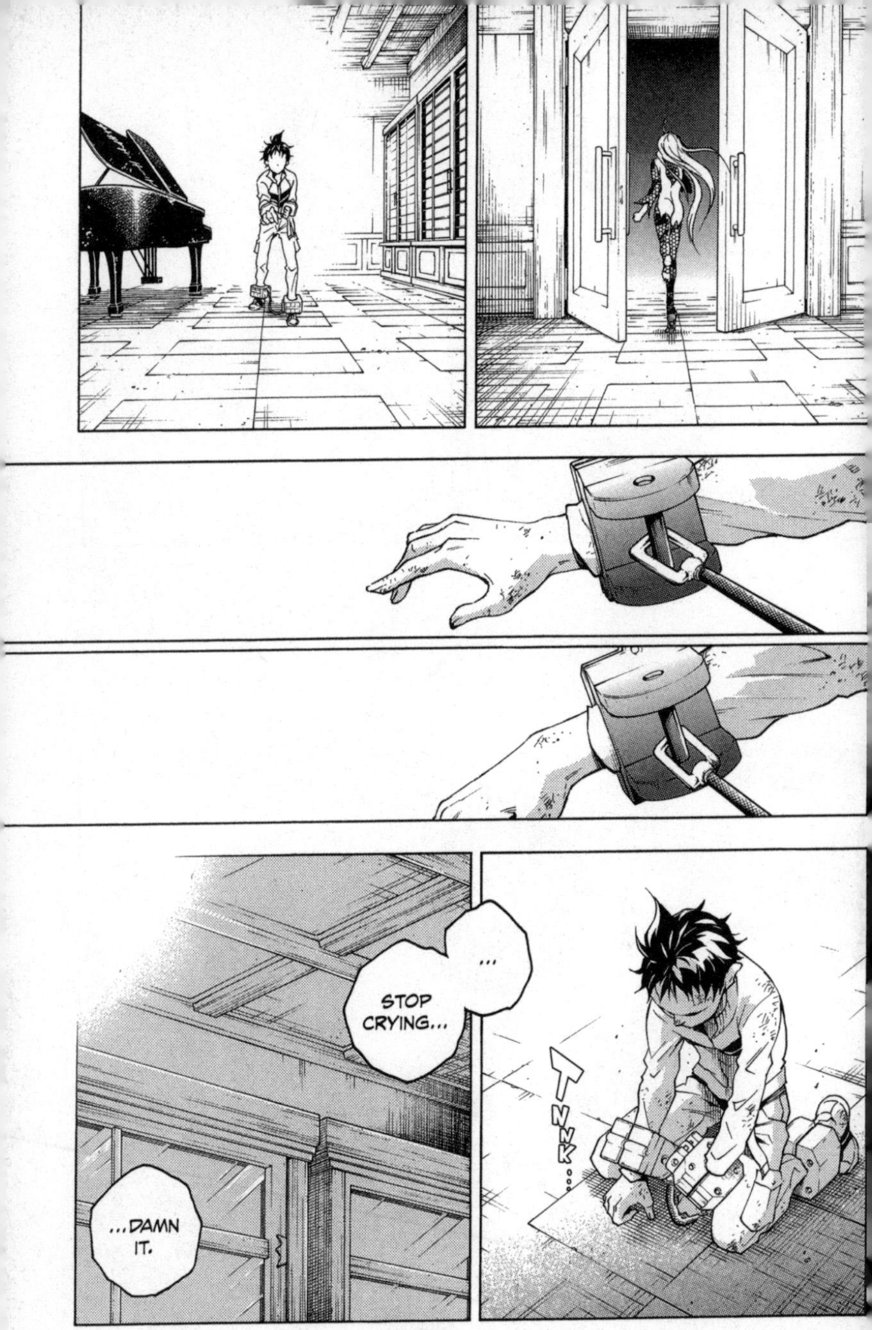
TNNK...
...
STOP CRYING...
...DAMN IT.

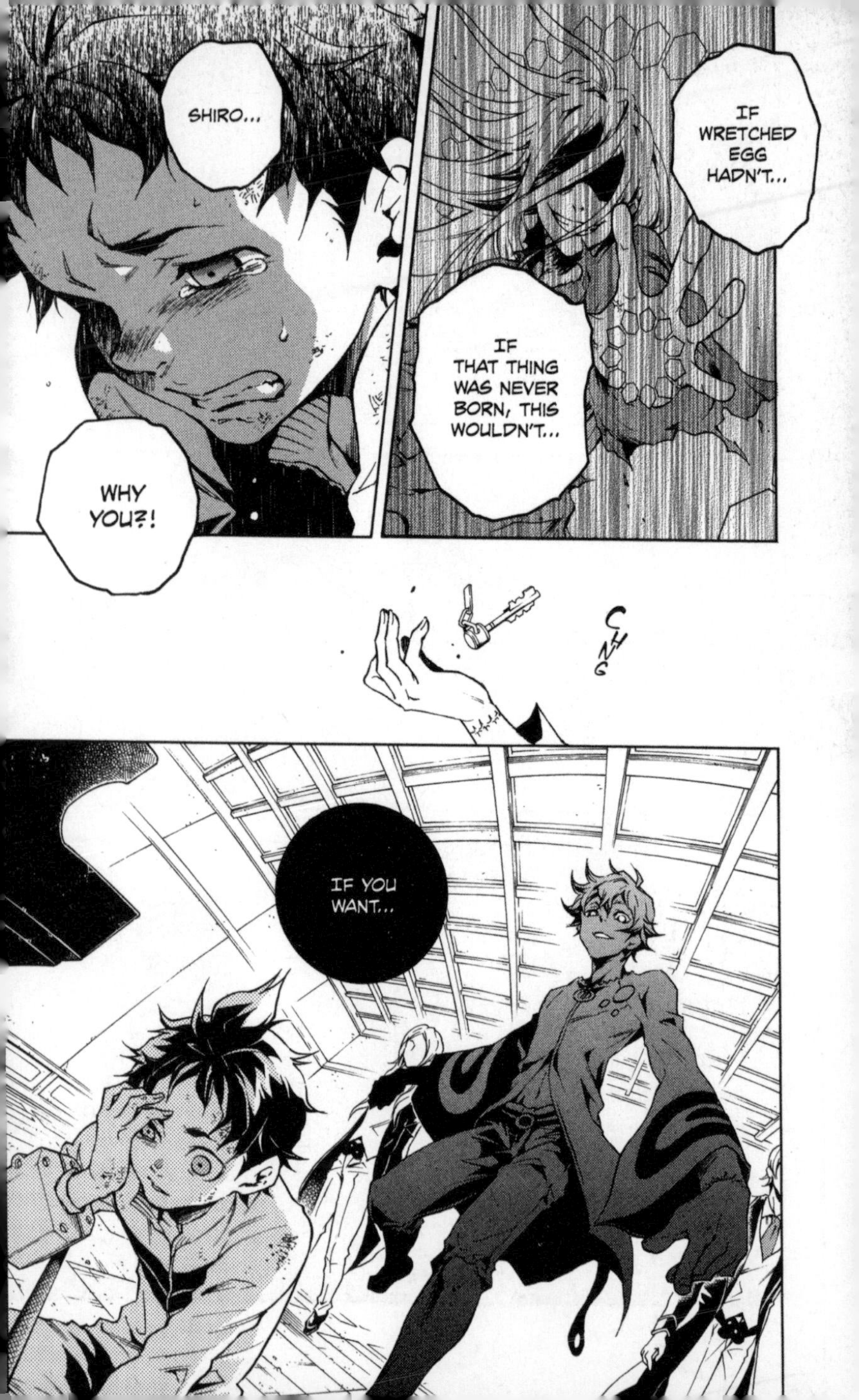
IF WRETCHED EGG HADN'T...
IF THAT THING WAS NEVER BORN, THIS WOULDN'T...
SHIRO...
WHY YOU?!
CHNG
IF YOU WANT...

...I CAN
TELL YOU
ALL ABOUT
HER.
☆

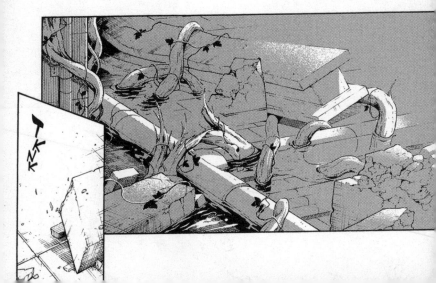

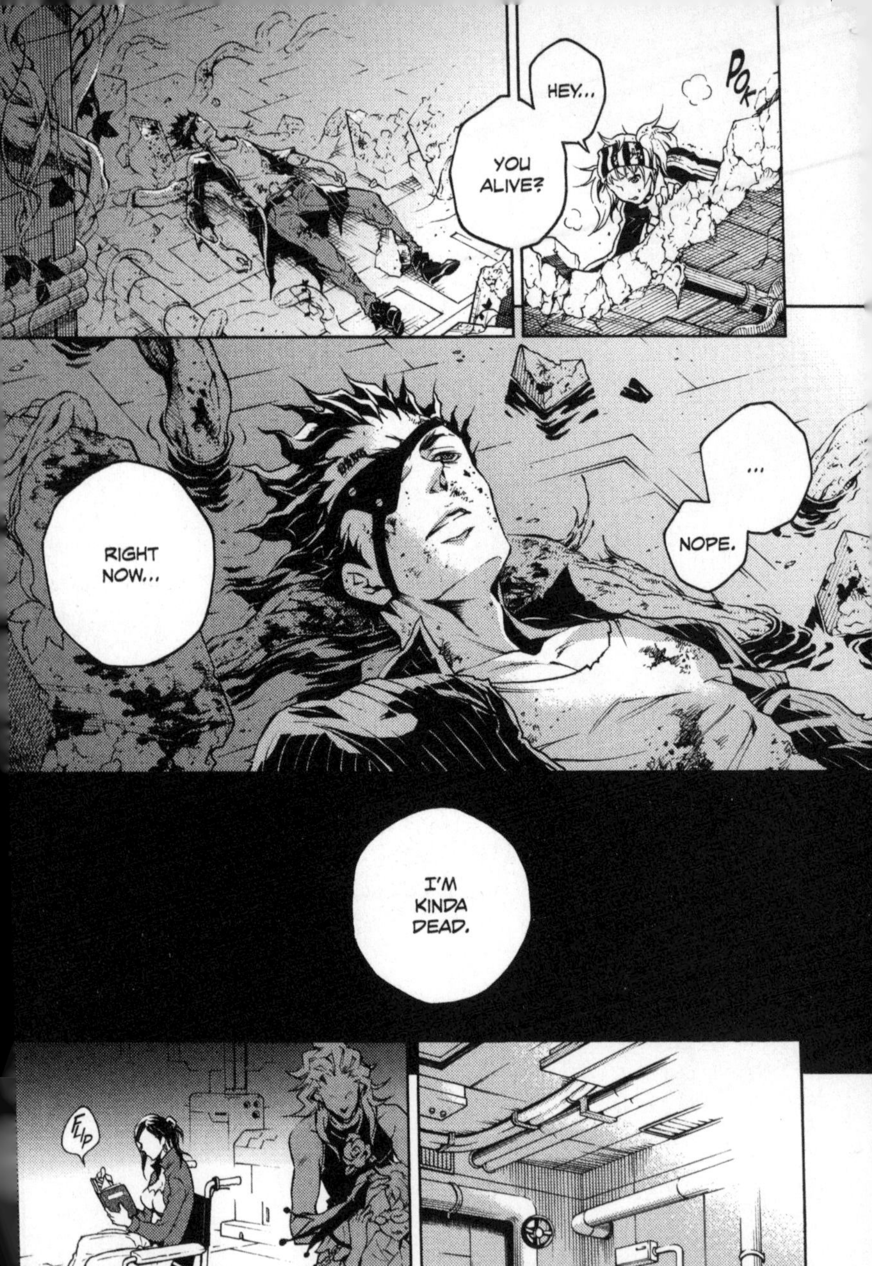
POK
HEY... YOU ALIVE?
... NOPE.
RIGHT NOW...
I'M KINDA DEAD.
FLIP

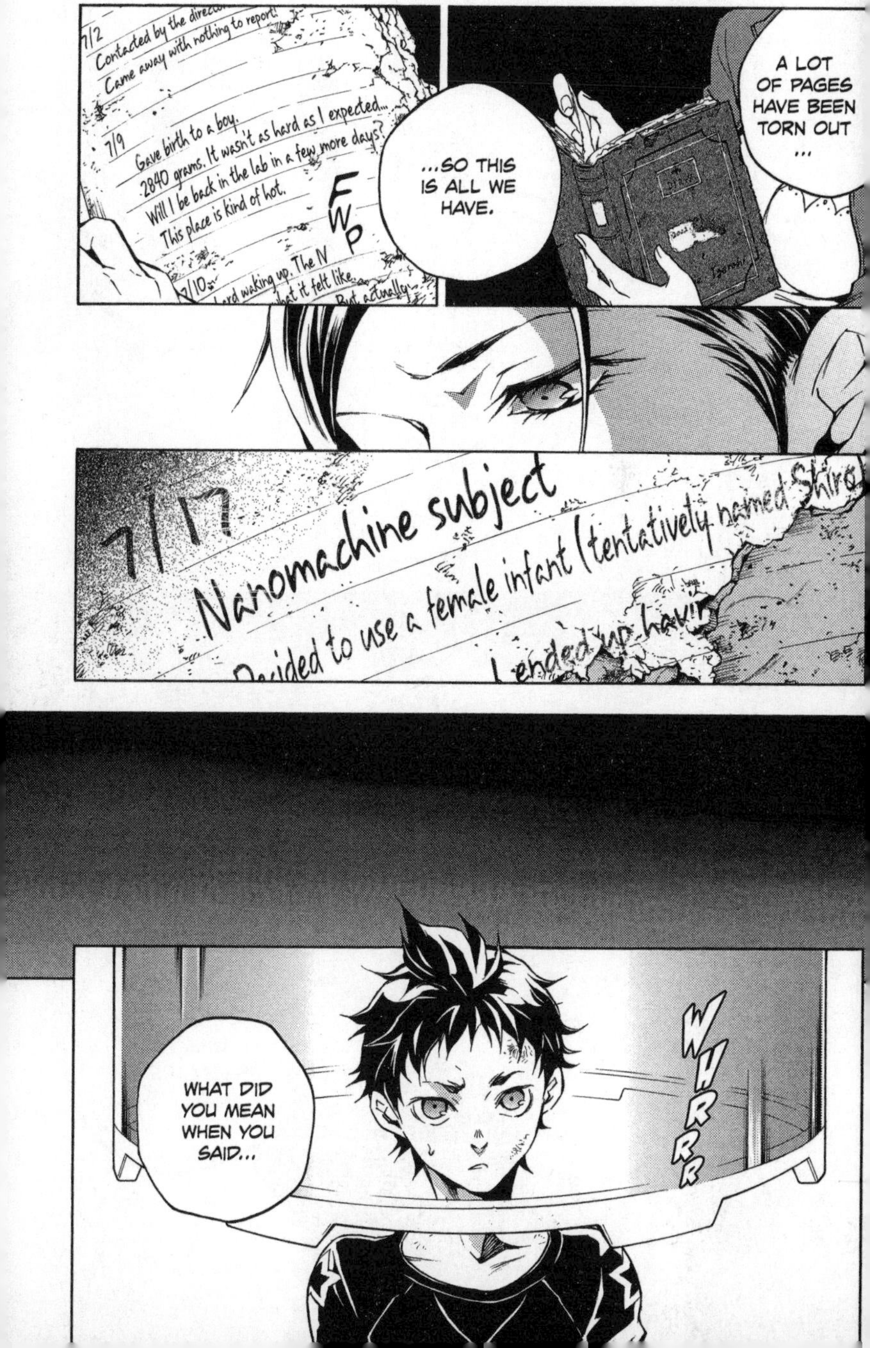
A LOT OF PAGES HAVE BEEN TORN OUT ...
...SO THIS IS ALL WE HAVE.
7/2
Contacted by the direc
Came away with nothing to report!
7/9
Gave birth to a boy.
2840 grams. It wasn't as hard as I expected...
Will I be back in the lab in a few more days?
This place is kind of hot.
7/10
ard waking up. The N
hat it felt like.
But actually
FWP
7/17
Nanomachine subject
Decided to use a female infant (tentatively named Shiro)
I ended up havi
WHAT DID YOU MEAN WHEN YOU SAID...
WHURRR

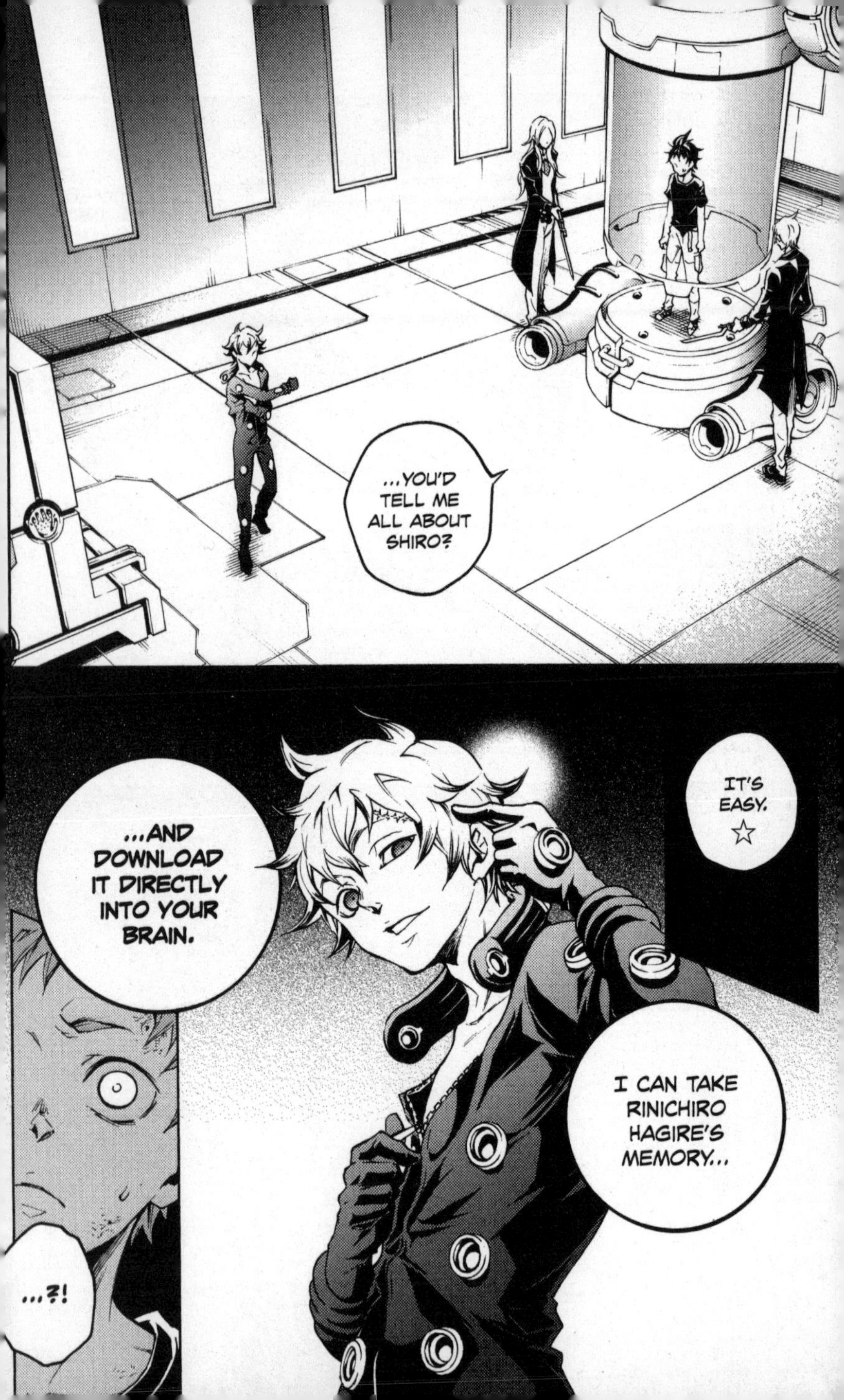
...YOU'D TELL ME ALL ABOUT SHIRO?
IT'S EASY. ☆
I CAN TAKE RINICHIRO HAGIRE'S MEMORY...
...AND DOWNLOAD IT DIRECTLY INTO YOUR BRAIN.
...?!

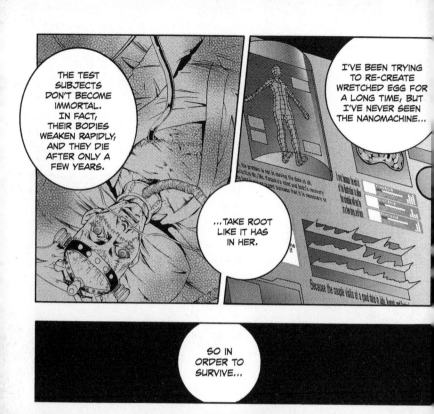

I'VE BEEN TRYING TO RE-CREATE WRETCHED EGG FOR A LONG TIME, BUT I'VE NEVER SEEN THE NANOMACHINE...
...TAKE ROOT LIKE IT HAS IN HER.
THE TEST SUBJECTS DON'T BECOME IMMORTAL. IN FACT, THEIR BODIES WEAKEN RAPIDLY, AND THEY DIE AFTER ONLY A FEW YEARS.
SO IN ORDER TO SURVIVE...
...I'VE BEEN TRANSFERRING MY MEMORIES INTO OTHER PEOPLE'S BODIES.

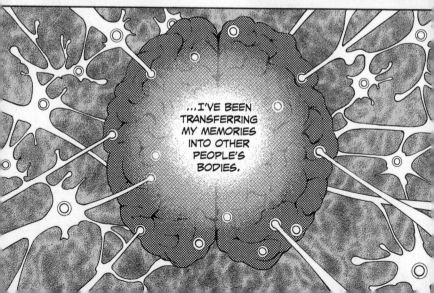

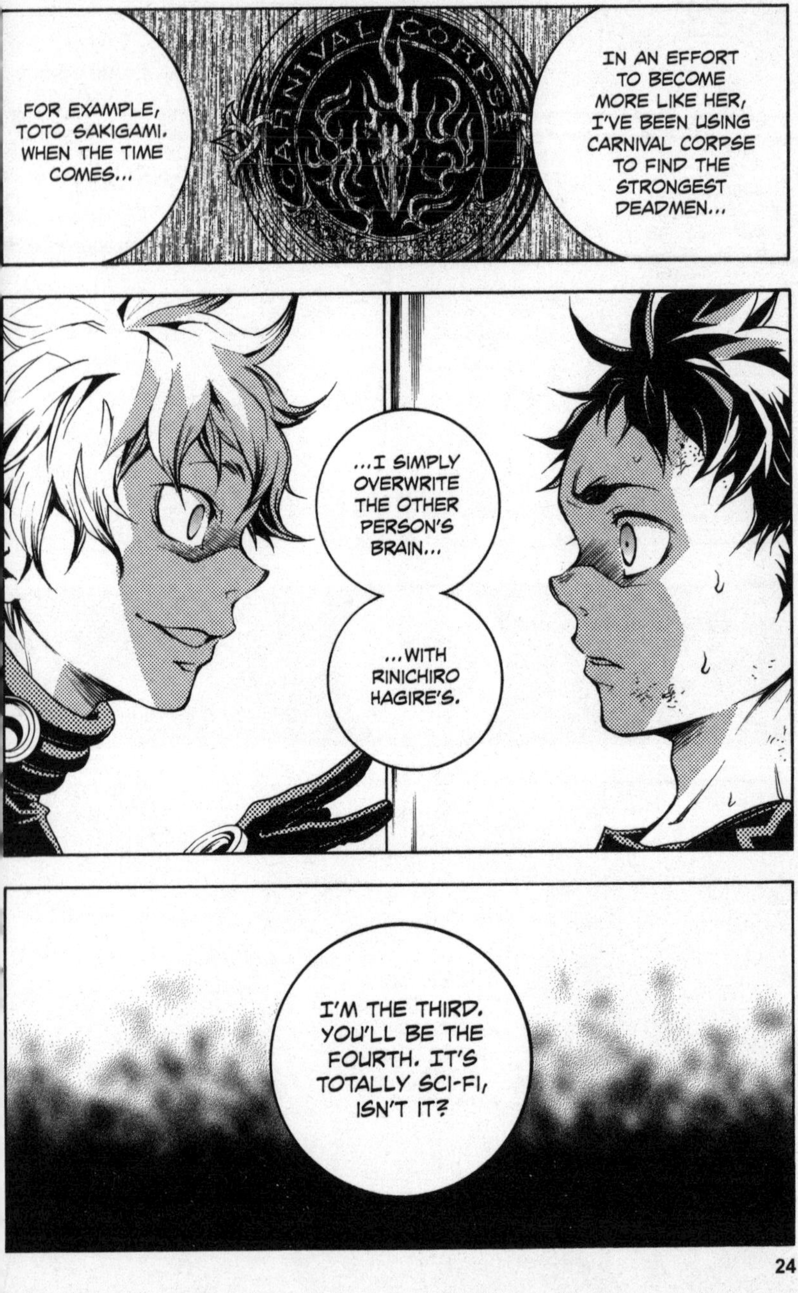
IN AN EFFORT TO BECOME MORE LIKE HER, I'VE BEEN USING CARNIVAL CORPSE TO FIND THE STRONGEST DEADMEN...
CARNIVAL CORPSE
FOR EXAMPLE, TOTO SAKIGAMI. WHEN THE TIME COMES...
...I SIMPLY OVERWRITE THE OTHER PERSON'S BRAIN...
...WITH RINICHIRO HAGIRE'S.
I'M THE THIRD. YOU'LL BE THE FOURTH. IT'S TOTALLY SCI-FI, ISN'T IT?

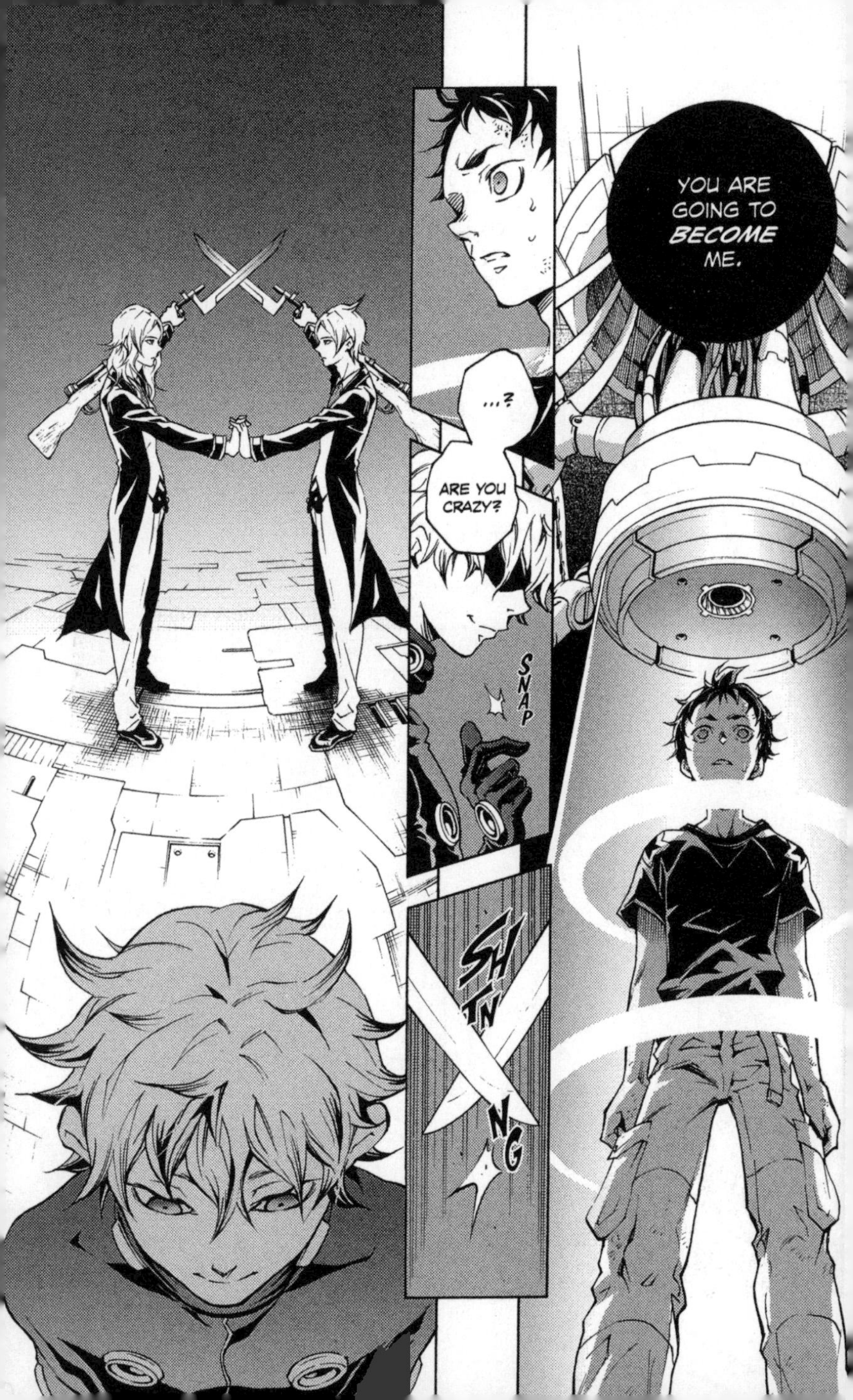
YOU ARE GOING TO *BECOME* ME.
...?
ARE YOU CRAZY?
SNAP
SHING

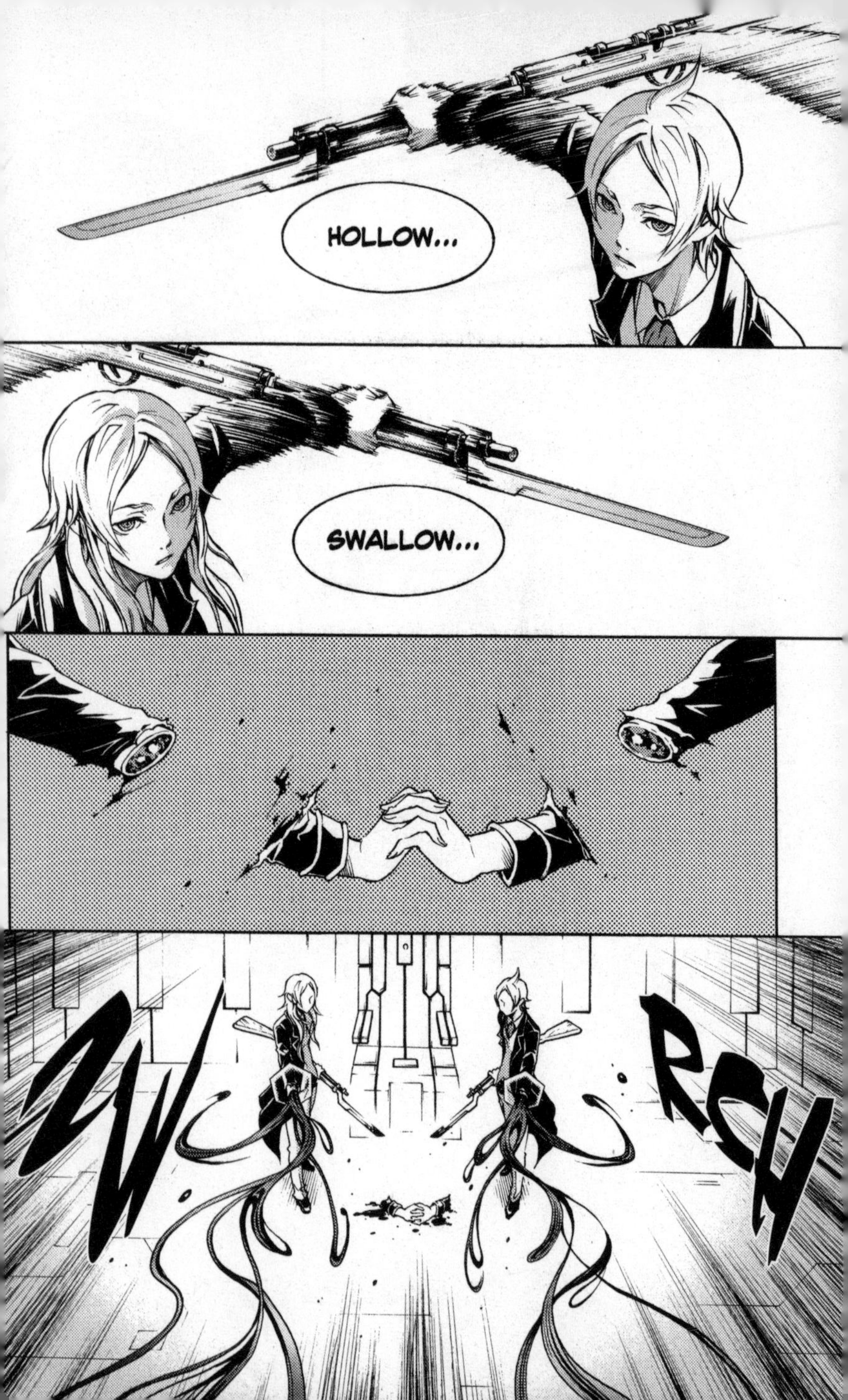
HOLLOW...
SWALLOW...

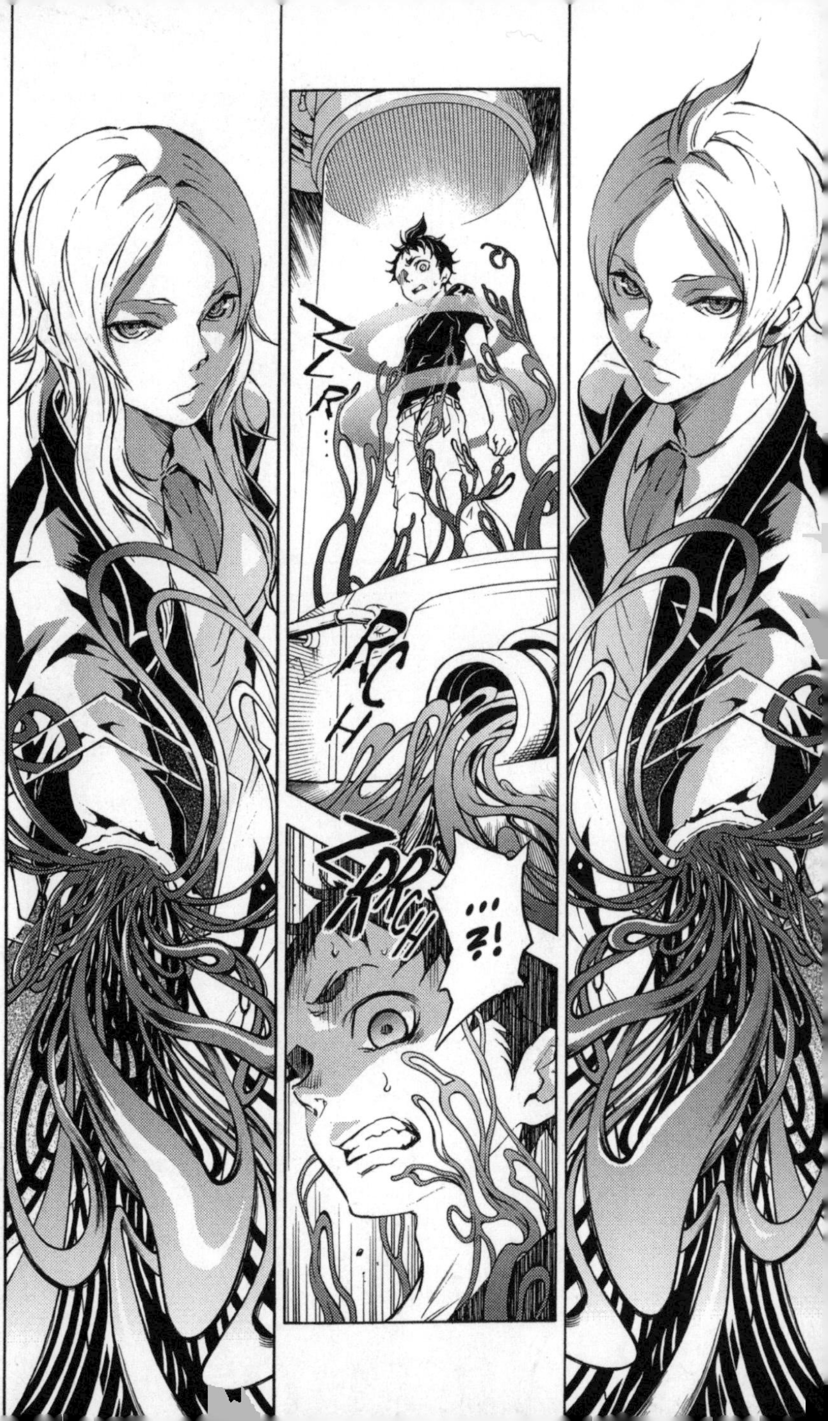
ZLR...
RCH
ZRRCH
...!!

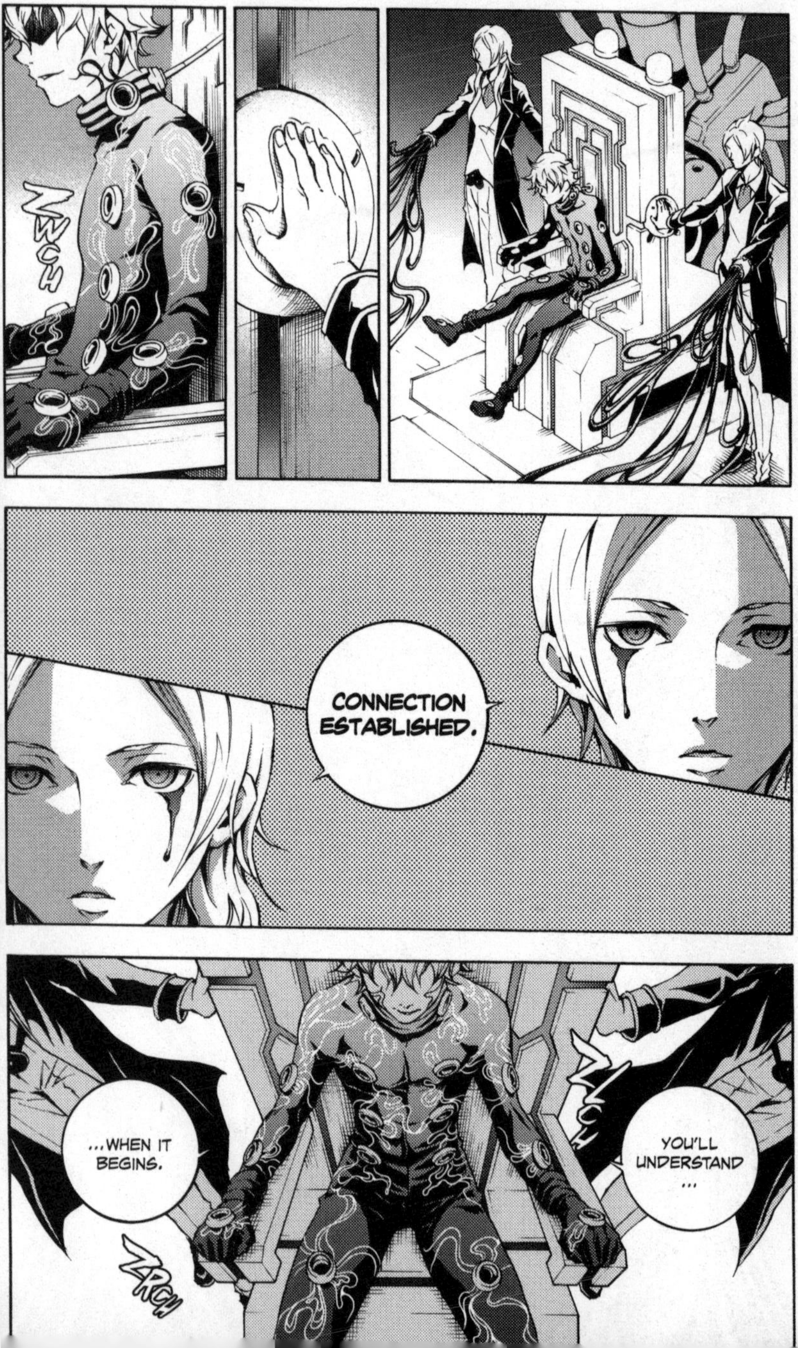
ZWCH
CONNECTION ESTABLISHED.
ZWCH
YOU'LL UNDERSTAND ...
...WHEN IT BEGINS.
ZRCH

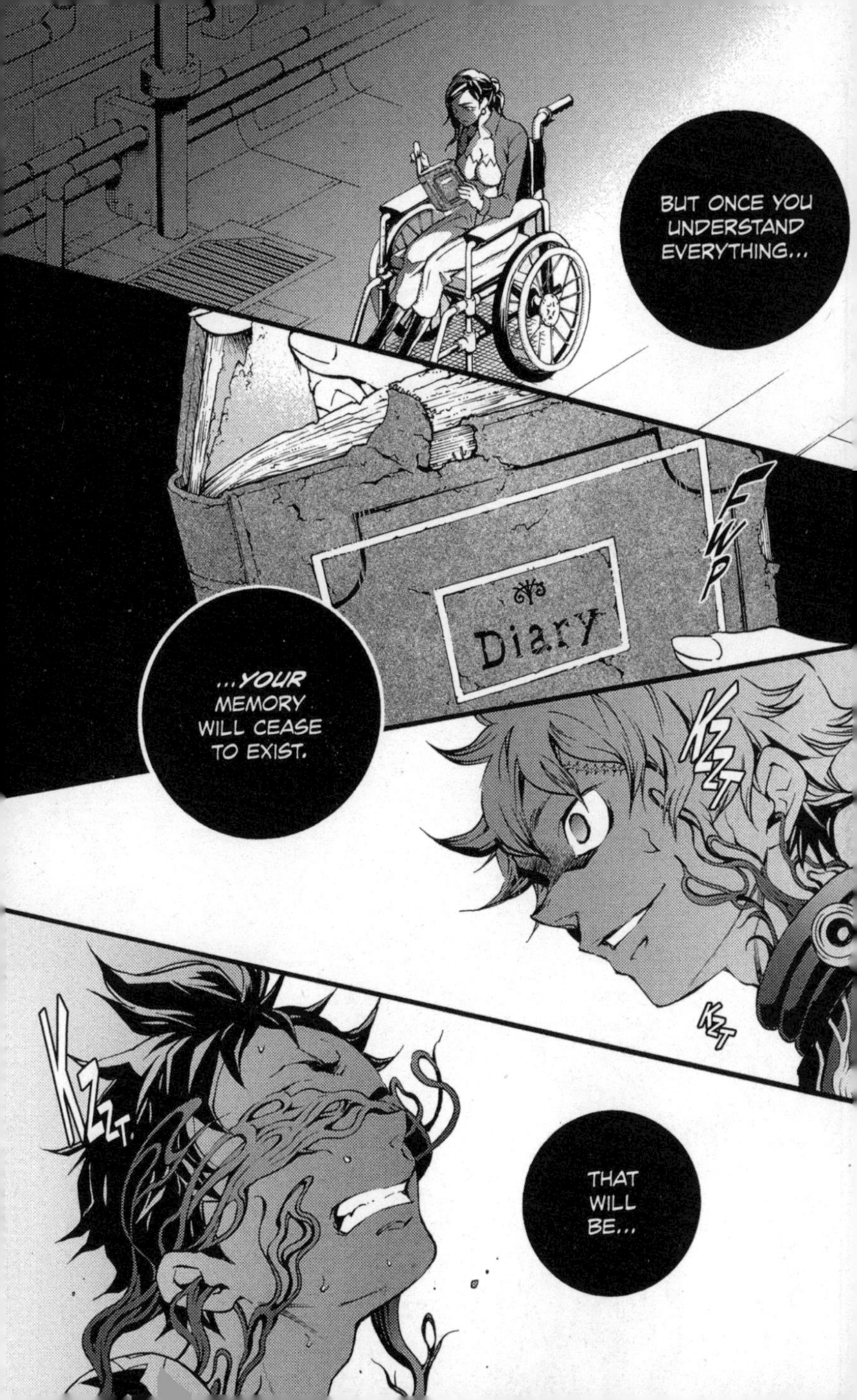
BUT ONCE YOU UNDERSTAND EVERYTHING...
Diary
FWP
...YOUR MEMORY WILL CEASE TO EXIST.
KZZT
KZT
THAT WILL BE...
KZZZT.

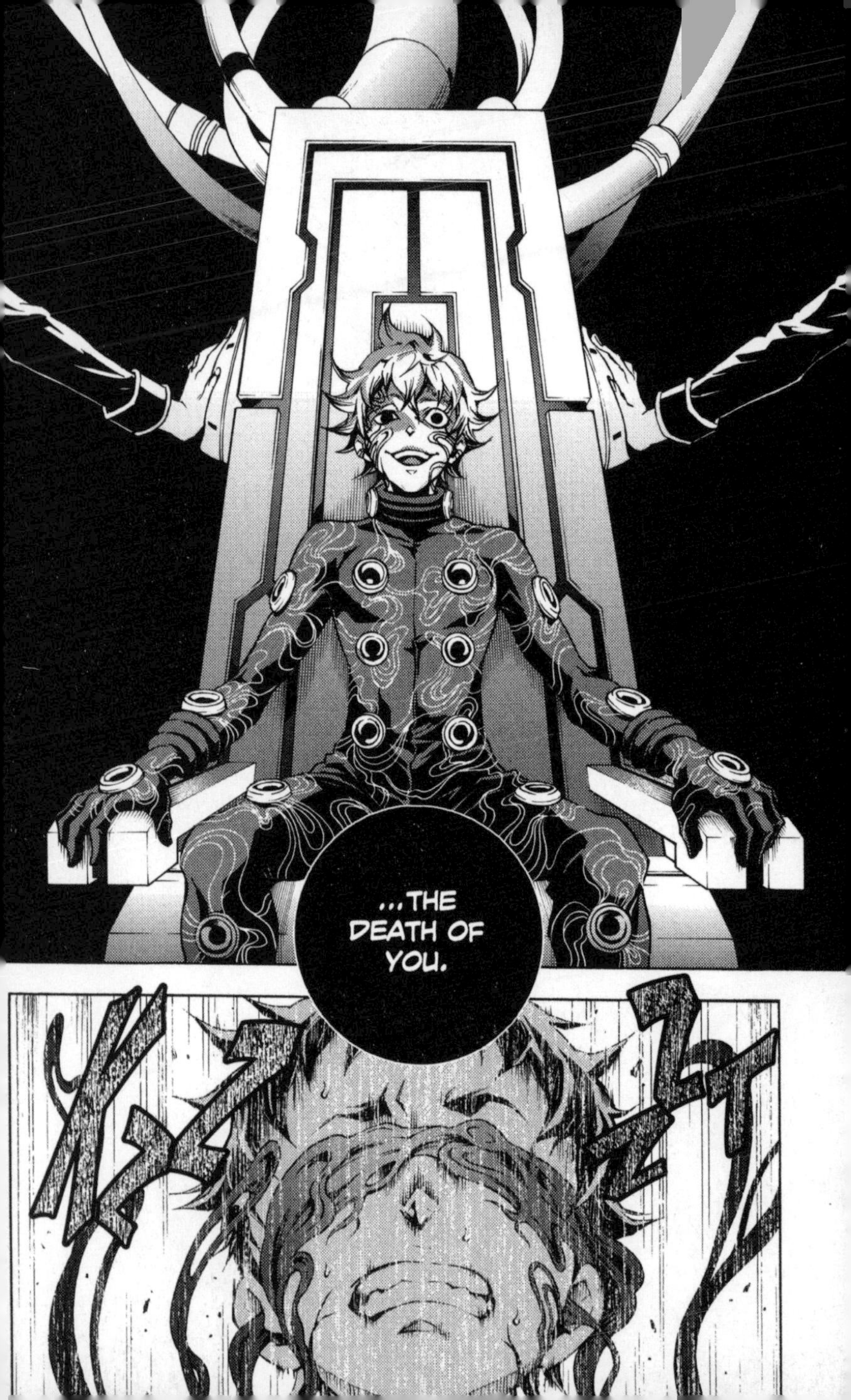
...THE DEATH OF YOU.

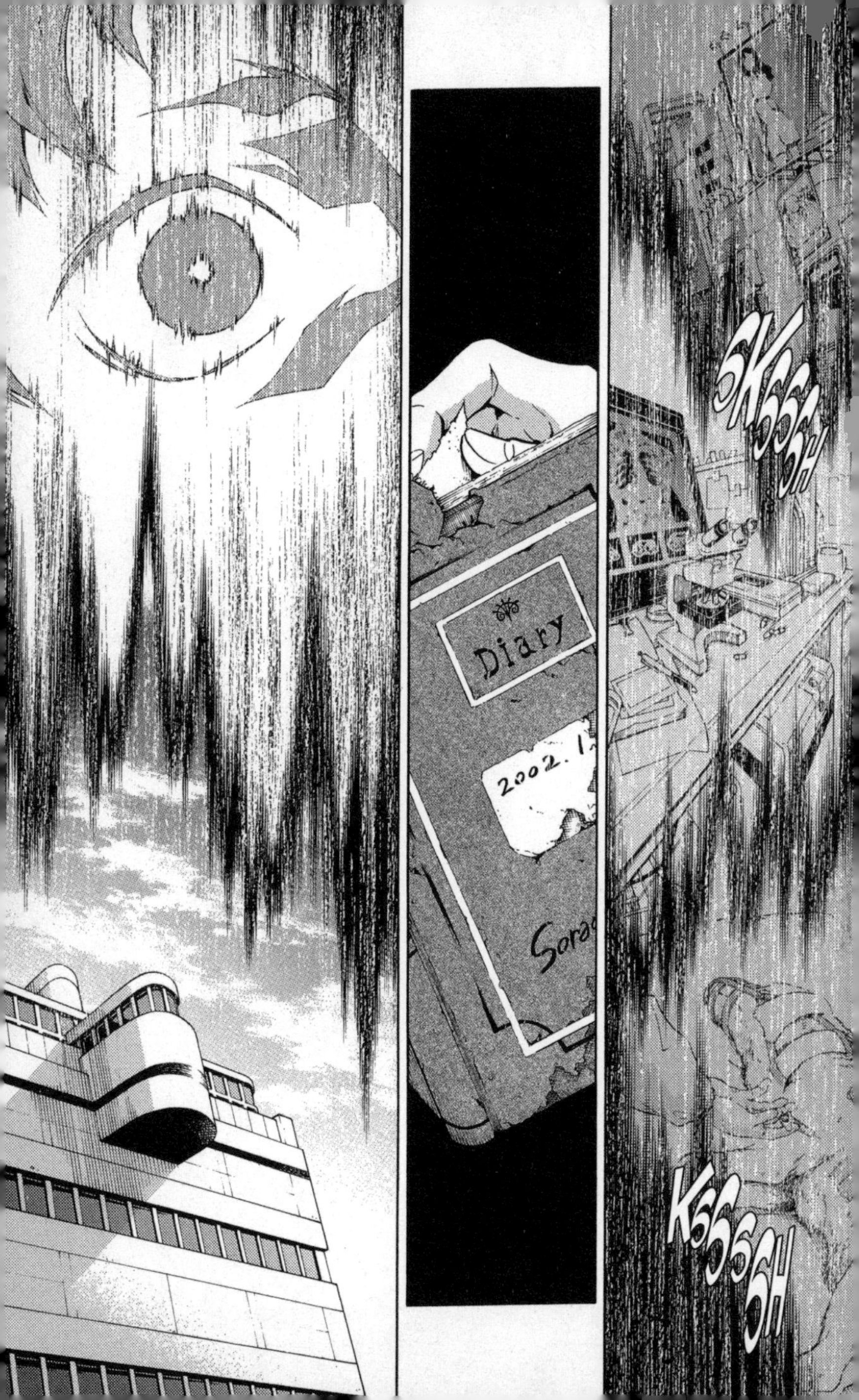
SKSSSH
KSSSSH
Diary
2002. 1

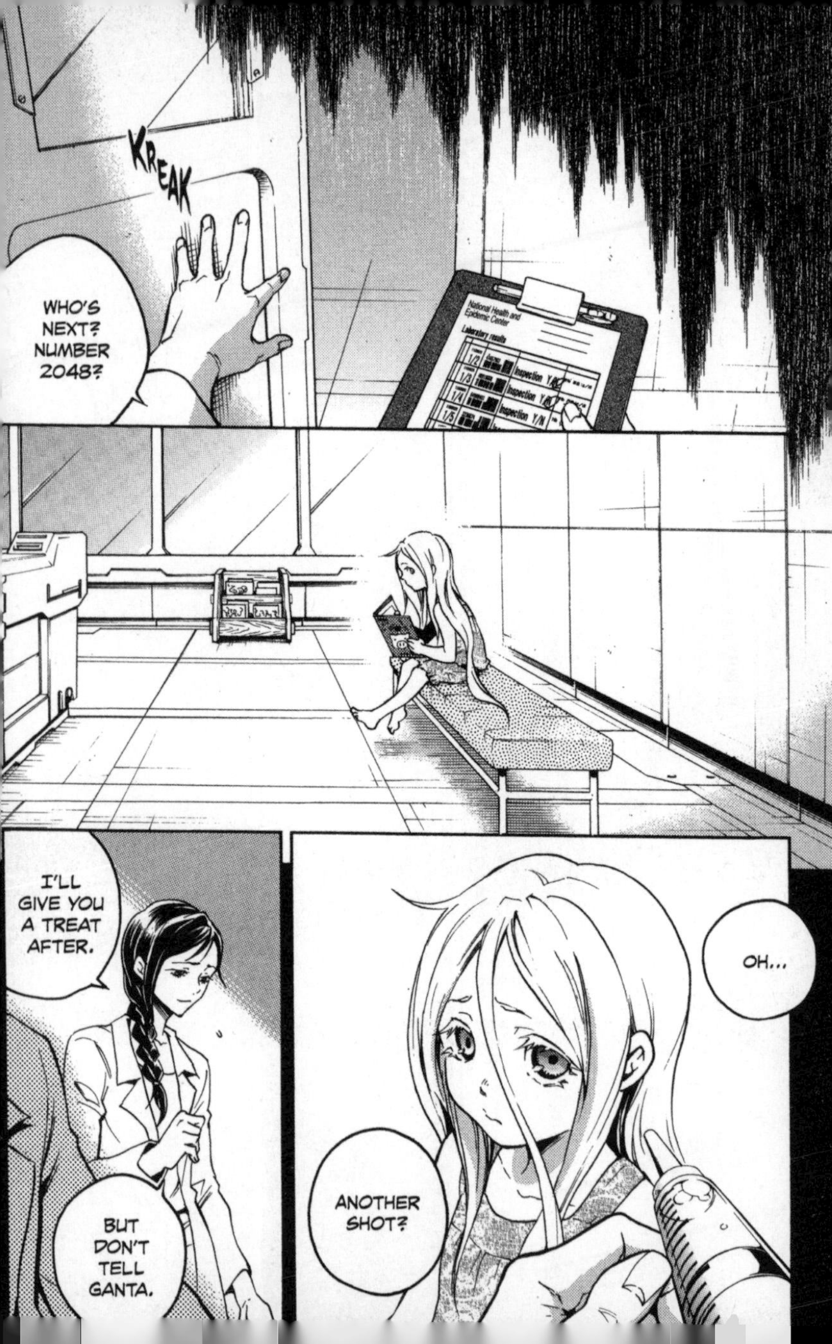
National Health and Epidemic Center
Laboratory results
Inspection Y/N
Inspection Y/N
Inspection Y/N
KREAK
WHO'S NEXT? NUMBER 2048?
OH...
ANOTHER SHOT?
I'LL GIVE YOU A TREAT AFTER.
BUT DON'T TELL GANTA.

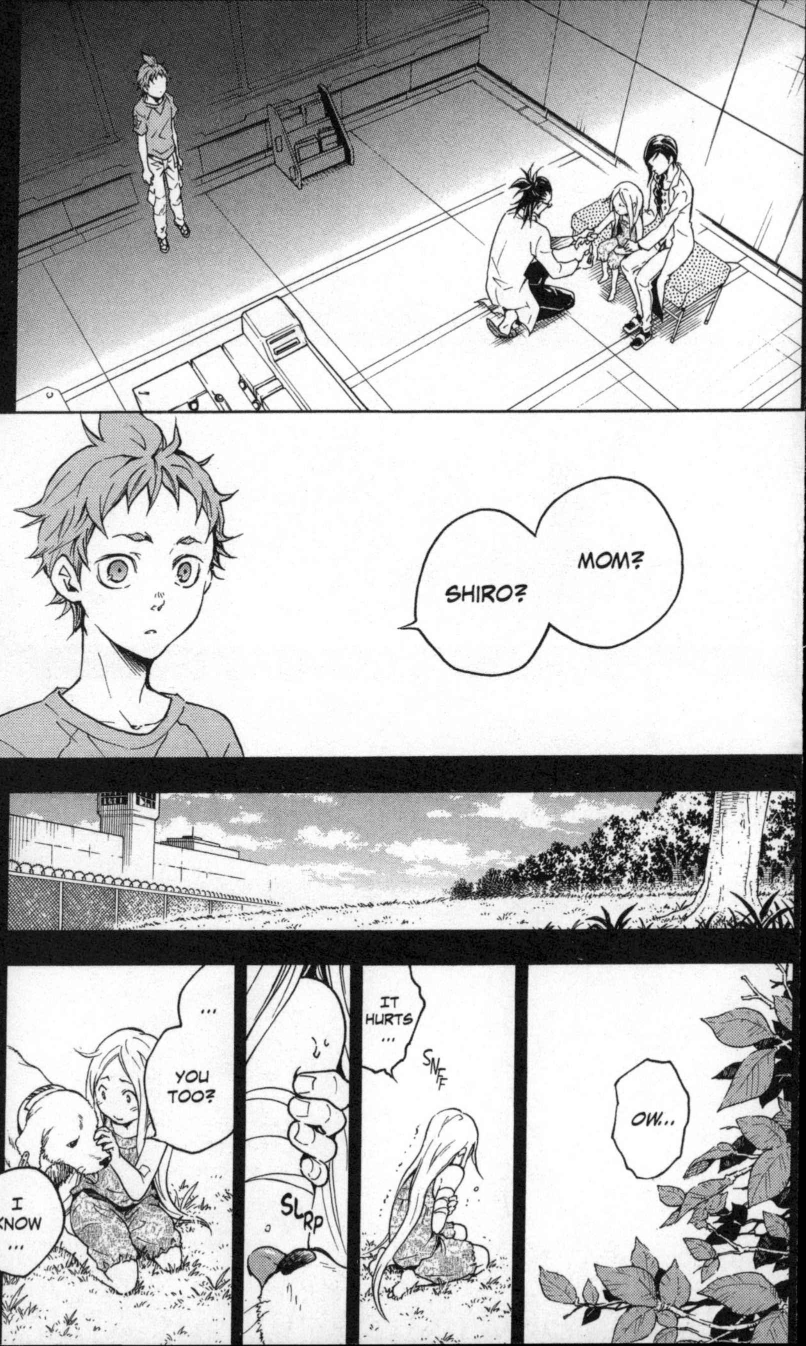
MOM?
SHIRO?
OW...
IT HURTS ...
SNFF
SLRP
... YOU TOO?
I KNOW ...

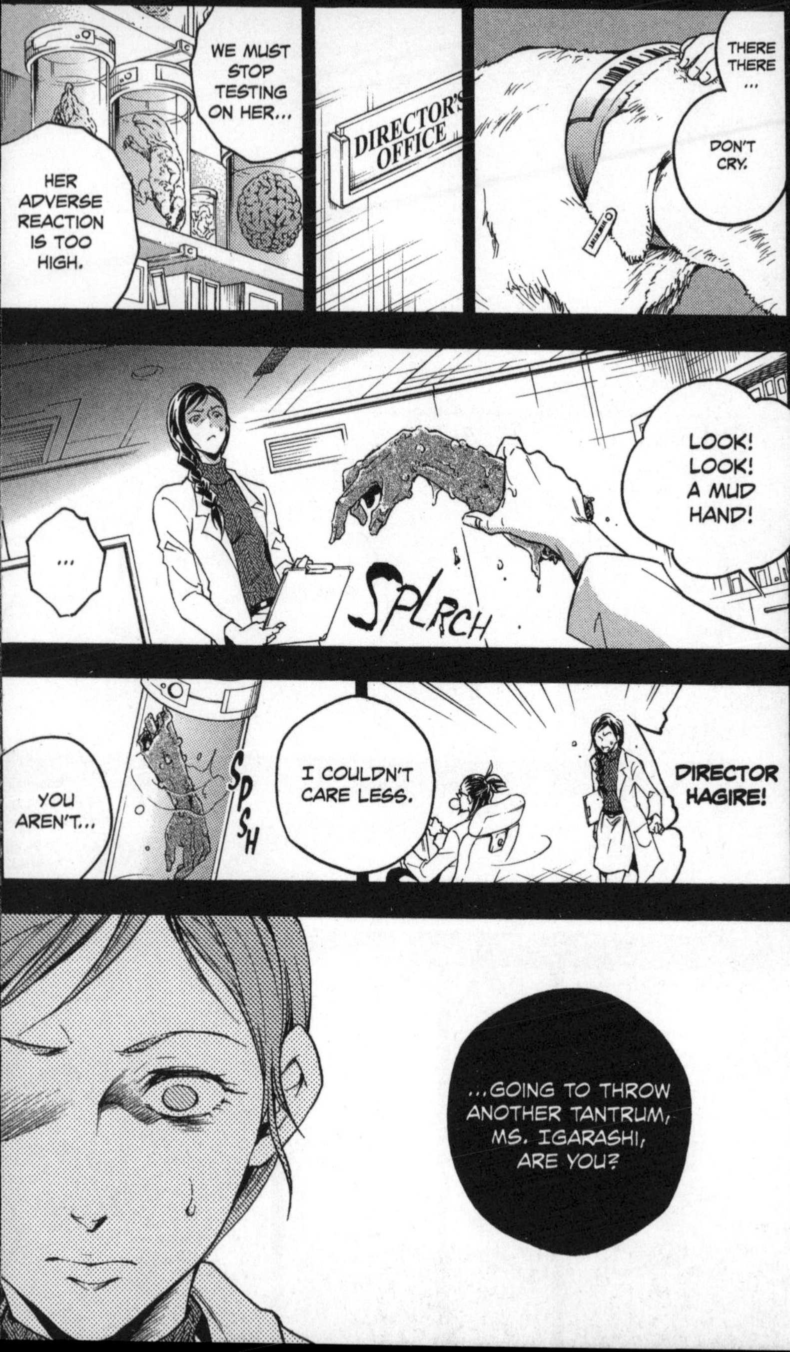
THERE THERE ...
DON'T CRY.
DIRECTOR'S OFFICE
WE MUST STOP TESTING ON HER...
HER ADVERSE REACTION IS TOO HIGH.
LOOK! LOOK! A MUD HAND!
SPLRCH
...
DIRECTOR HAGIRE!
I COULDN'T CARE LESS.
SPSH
YOU AREN'T...
...GOING TO THROW ANOTHER TANTRUM, MS. IGARASHI, ARE YOU?

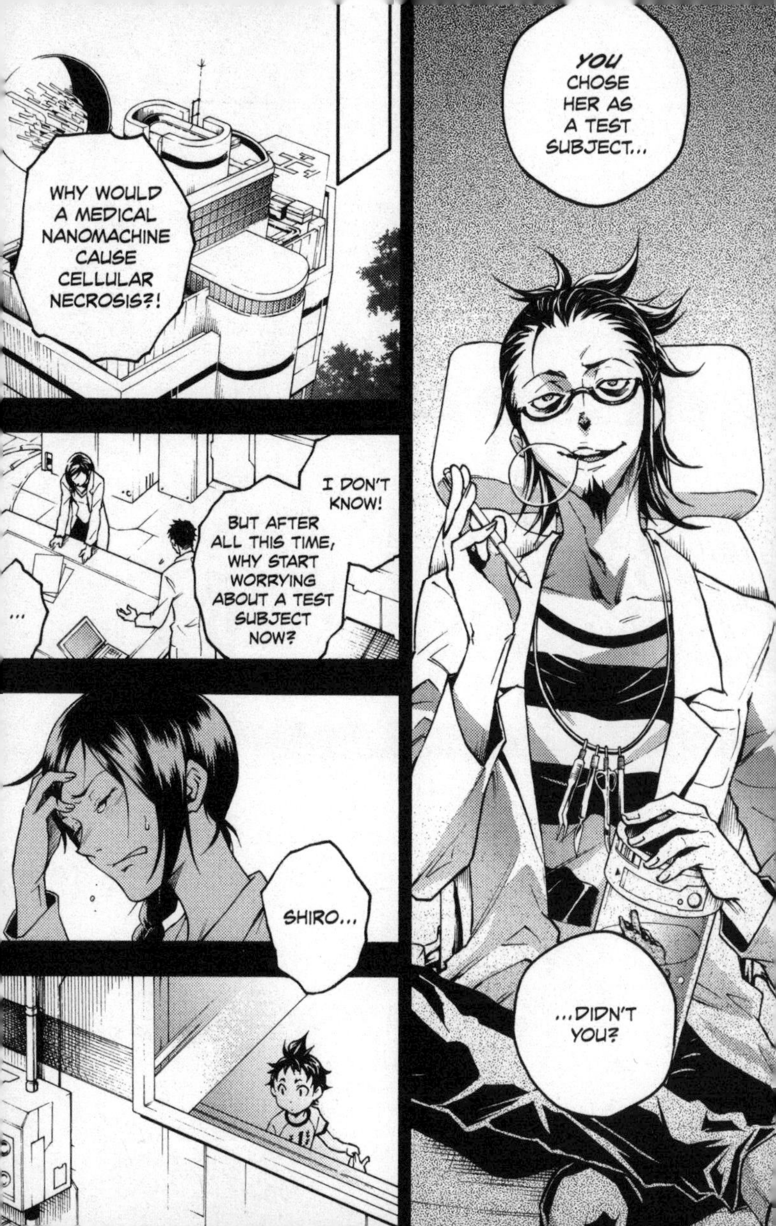
WHY WOULD A MEDICAL NANOMACHINE CAUSE CELLULAR NECROSIS?!
I DON'T KNOW!
BUT AFTER ALL THIS TIME, WHY START WORRYING ABOUT A TEST SUBJECT NOW?
...
SHIRO...
YOU CHOSE HER AS A TEST SUBJECT...
...DIDN'T YOU?

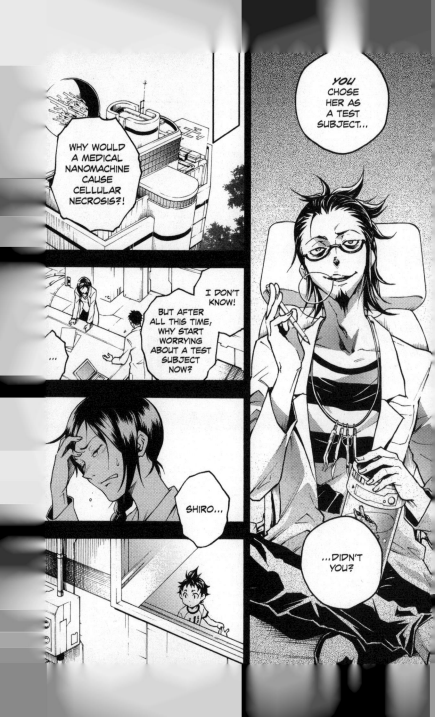

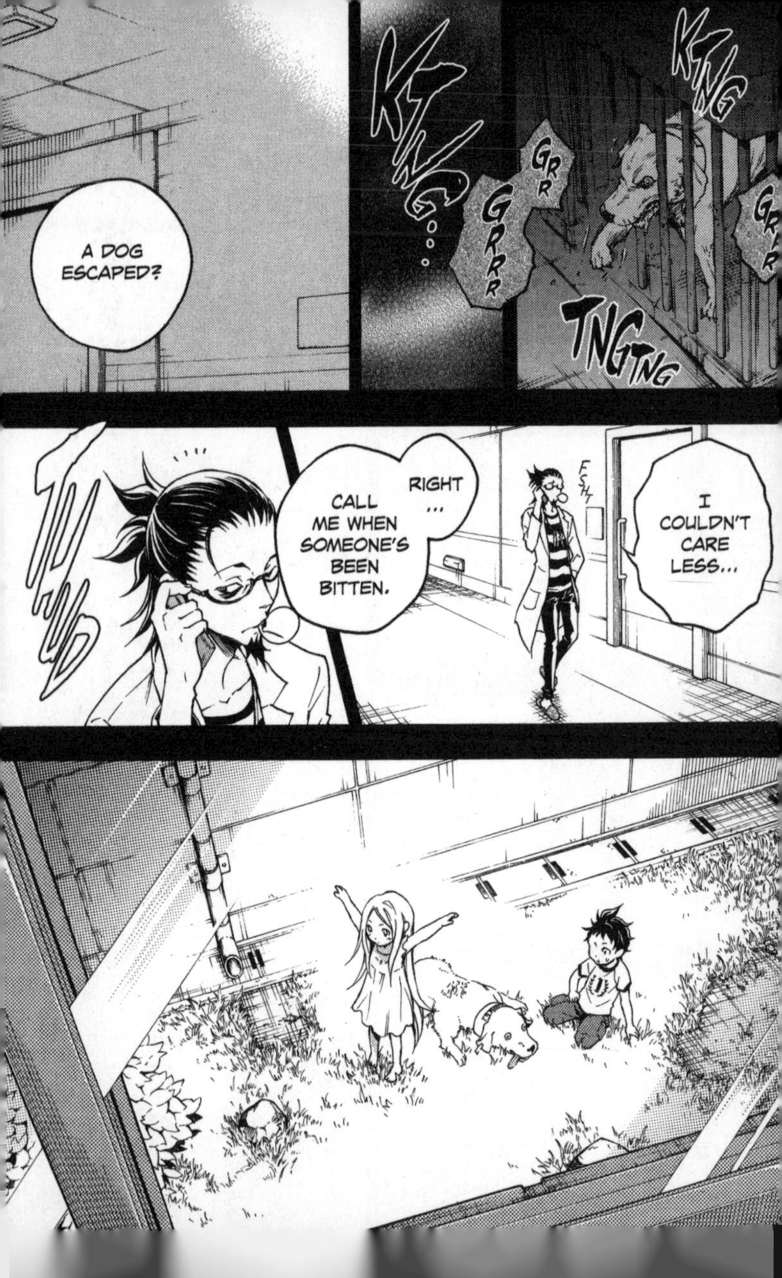
KING
GRR
GRR
TNGTNG
KING...
GRRR
A DOG ESCAPED?
I COULDN'T CARE LESS...
RIGHT ...
CALL ME WHEN SOMEONE'S BEEN BITTEN.

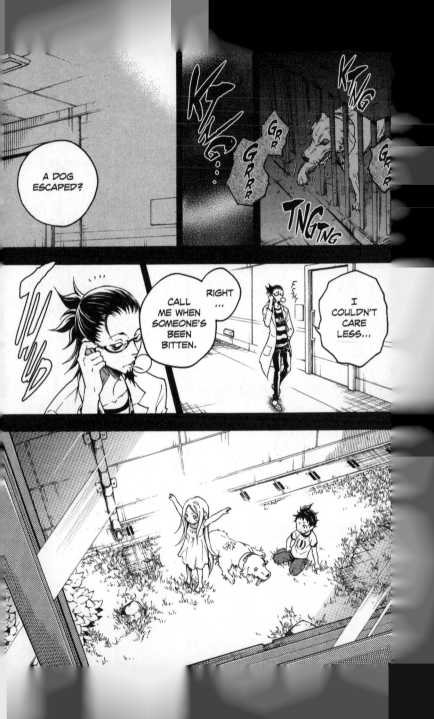

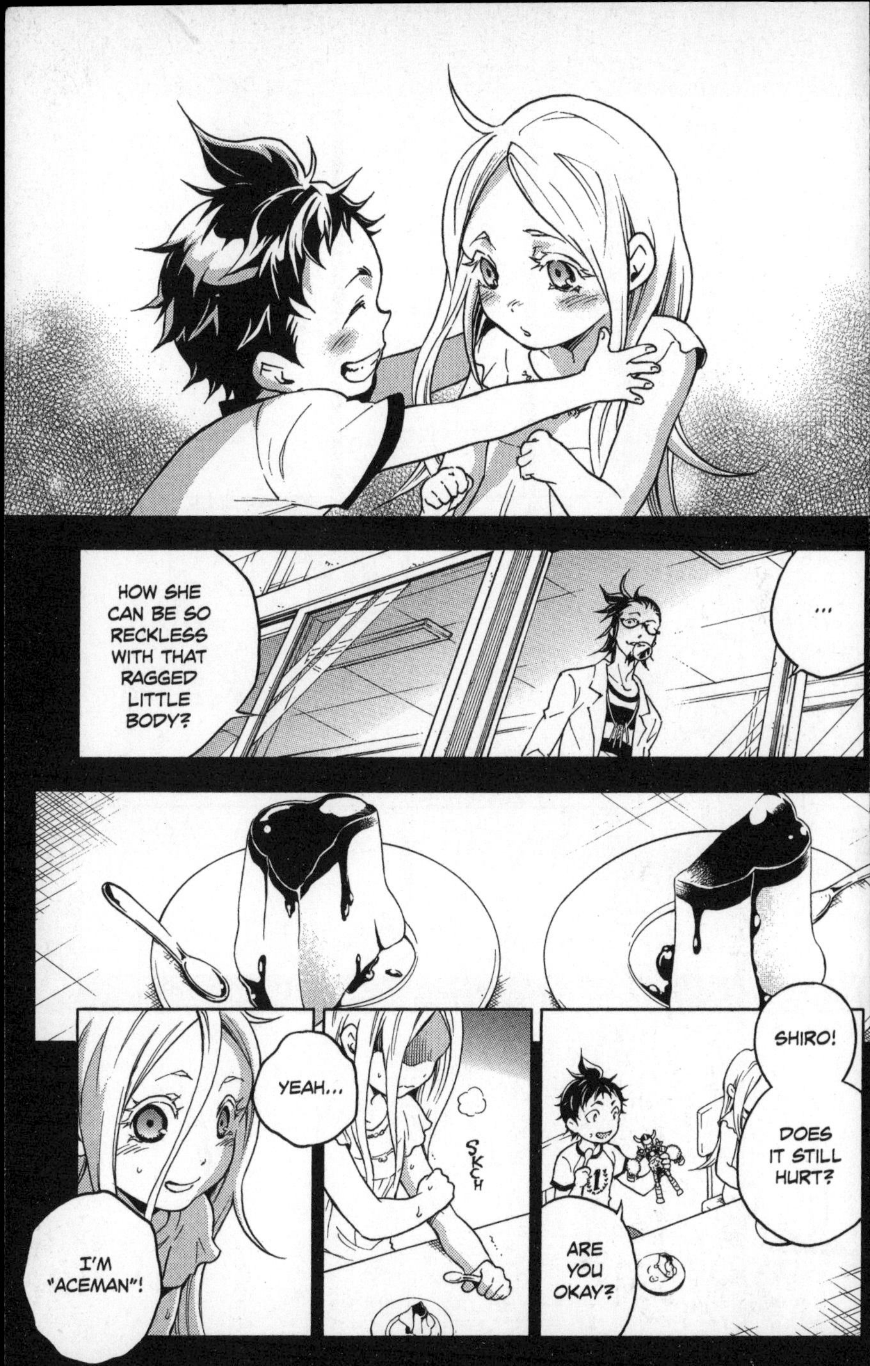
...
HOW SHE CAN BE SO RECKLESS WITH THAT RAGGED LITTLE BODY?
SHIRO!
DOES IT STILL HURT?
ARE YOU OKAY?
YEAH...
SKCH
I'M "ACEMAN"!

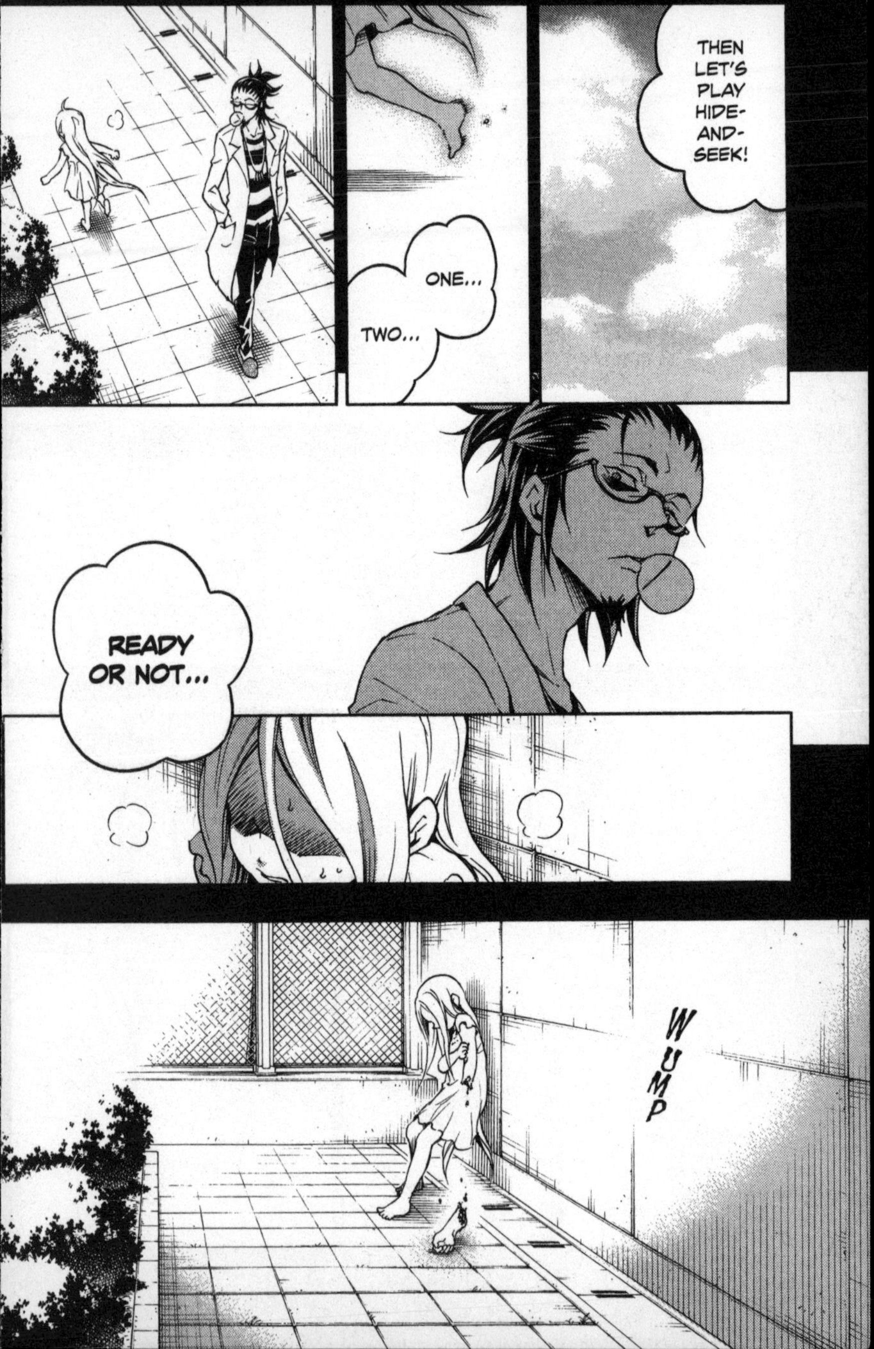
THEN LET'S PLAY HIDE-AND-SEEK!
ONE...
TWO...
READY OR NOT...
WUMP

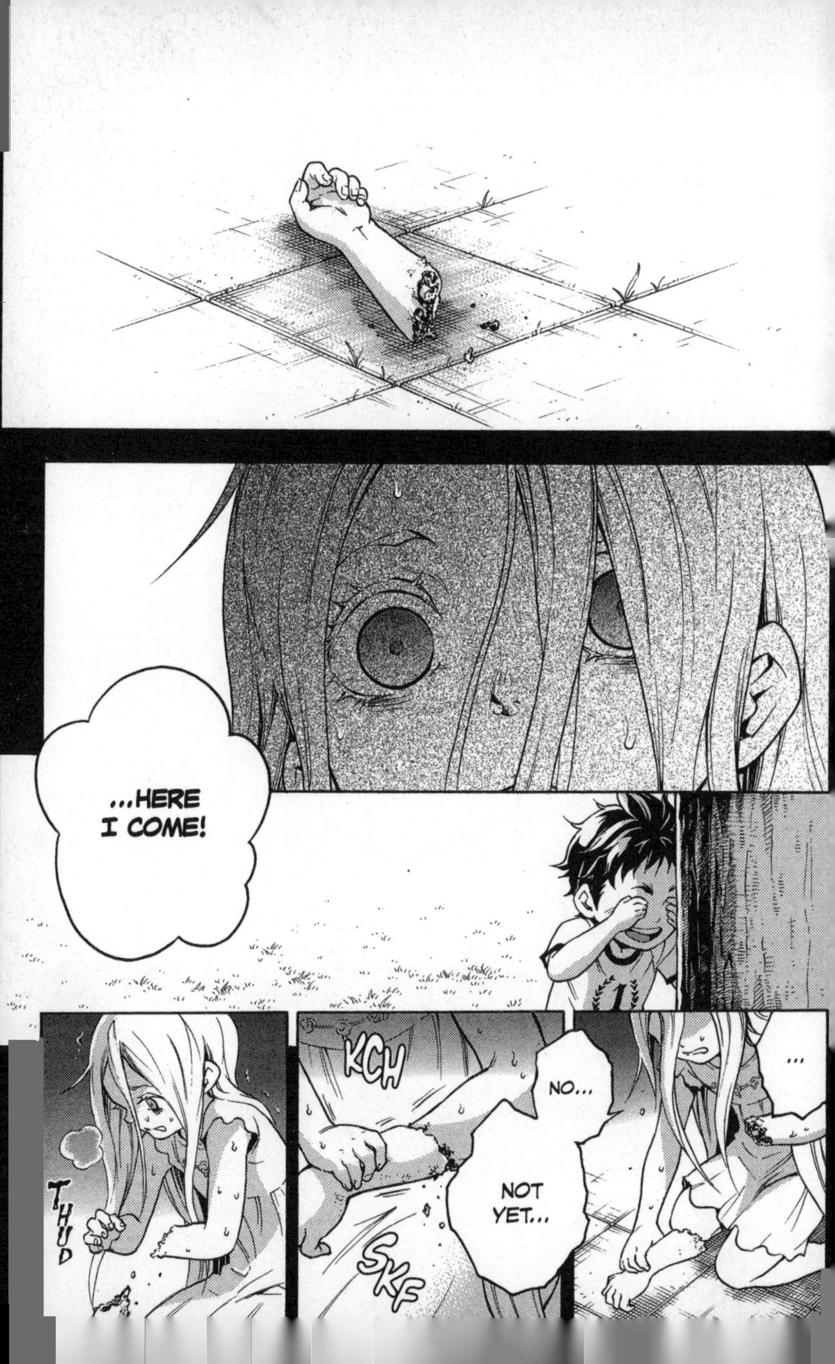
...HERE I COME!
...
KCH
NO...
NOT YET...
SKF
THUD

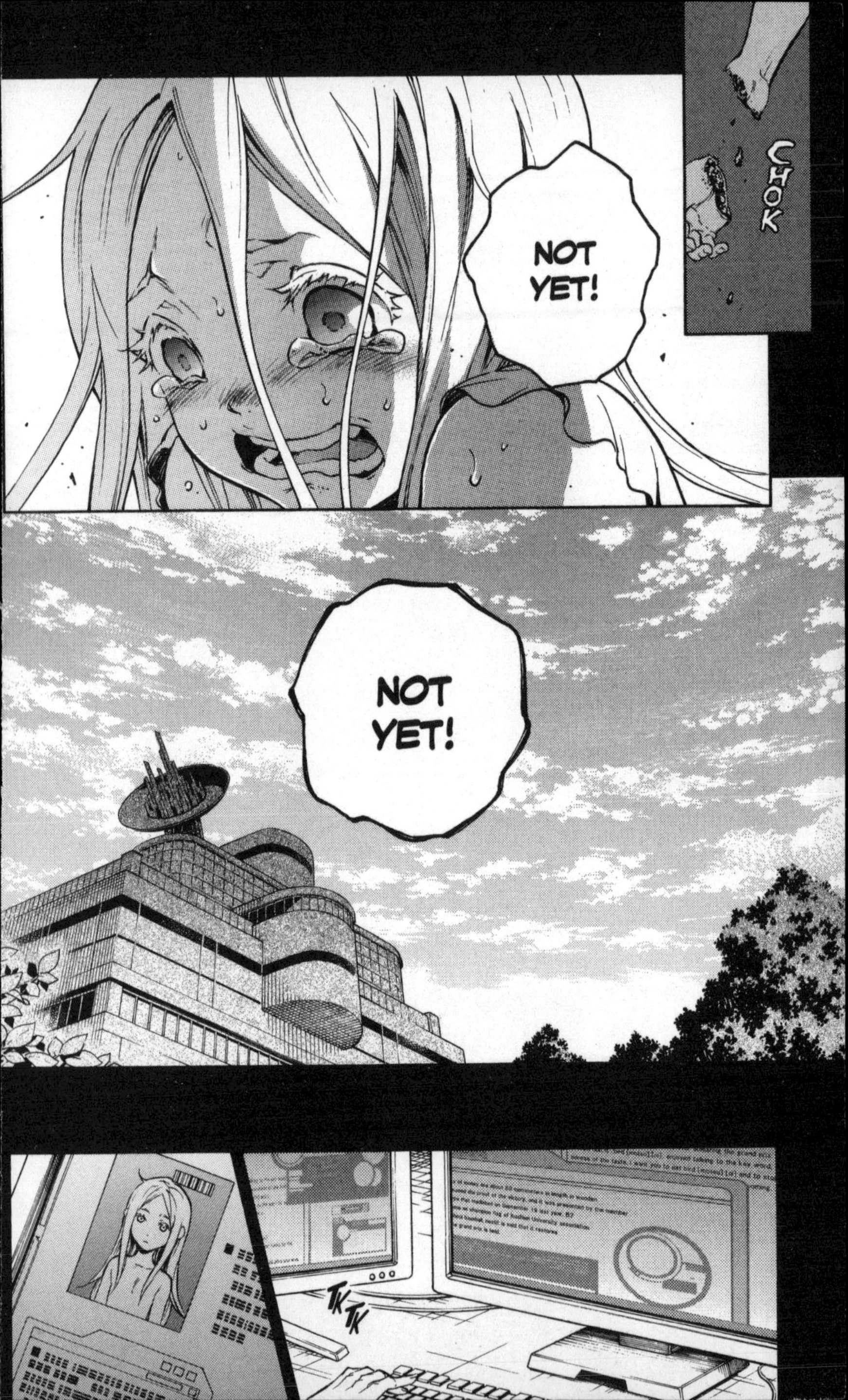
CHOK
NOT YET!
NOT YET!
TK TK

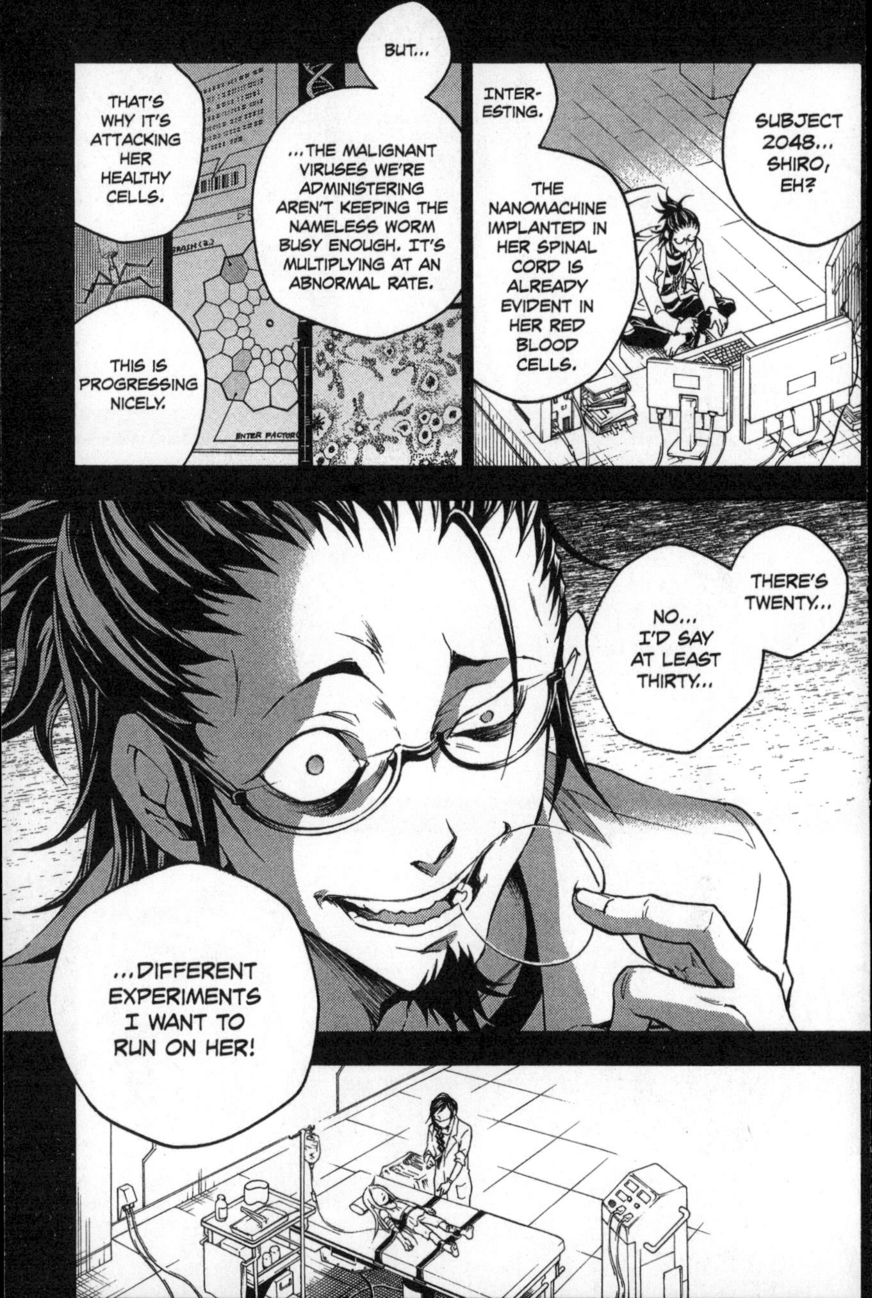
SUBJECT 2048... SHIRO, EH?
INTER-ESTING.
THE NANOMACHINE IMPLANTED IN HER SPINAL CORD IS ALREADY EVIDENT IN HER RED BLOOD CELLS.
BUT...
...THE MALIGNANT VIRUSES WE'RE ADMINISTERING AREN'T KEEPING THE NAMELESS WORM BUSY ENOUGH. IT'S MULTIPLYING AT AN ABNORMAL RATE.
THAT'S WHY IT'S ATTACKING HER HEALTHY CELLS.
THIS IS PROGRESSING NICELY.
THERE'S TWENTY...
NO... I'D SAY AT LEAST THIRTY...
...DIFFERENT EXPERIMENTS I WANT TO RUN ON HER!

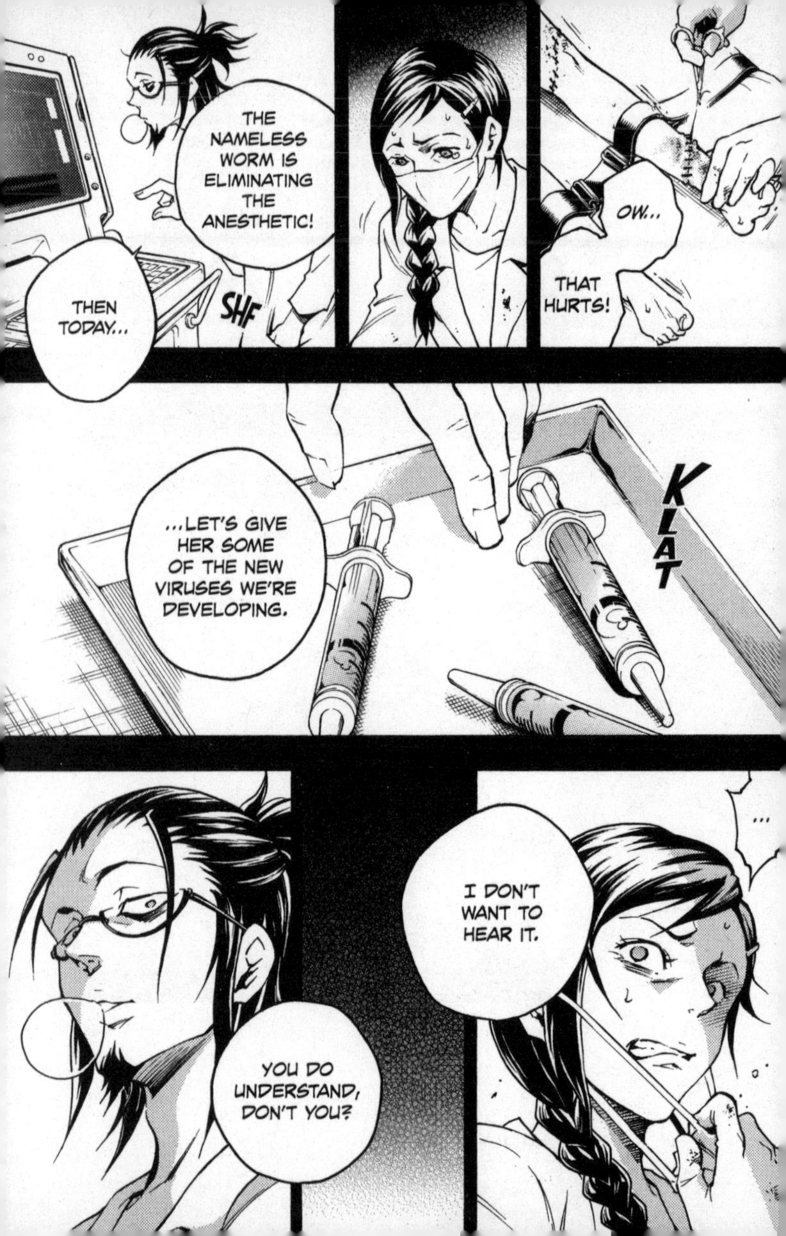
OW...
THAT HURTS!
THE NAMELESS WORM IS ELIMINATING THE ANESTHETIC!
SHF
THEN TODAY...
KLAT
...LET'S GIVE HER SOME OF THE NEW VIRUSES WE'RE DEVELOPING.
...
I DON'T WANT TO HEAR IT.
YOU DO UNDERSTAND, DON'T YOU?

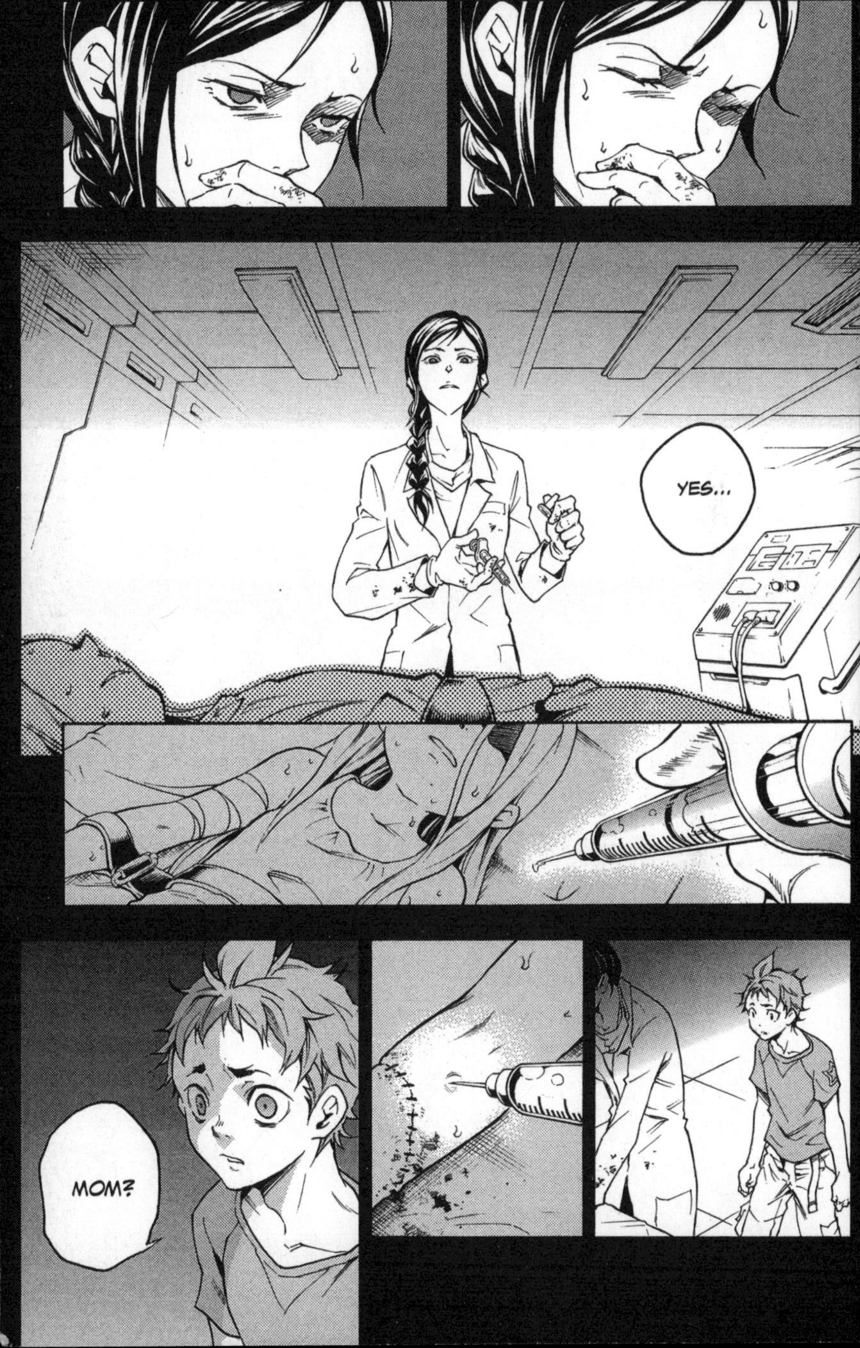
YES...
MOM?

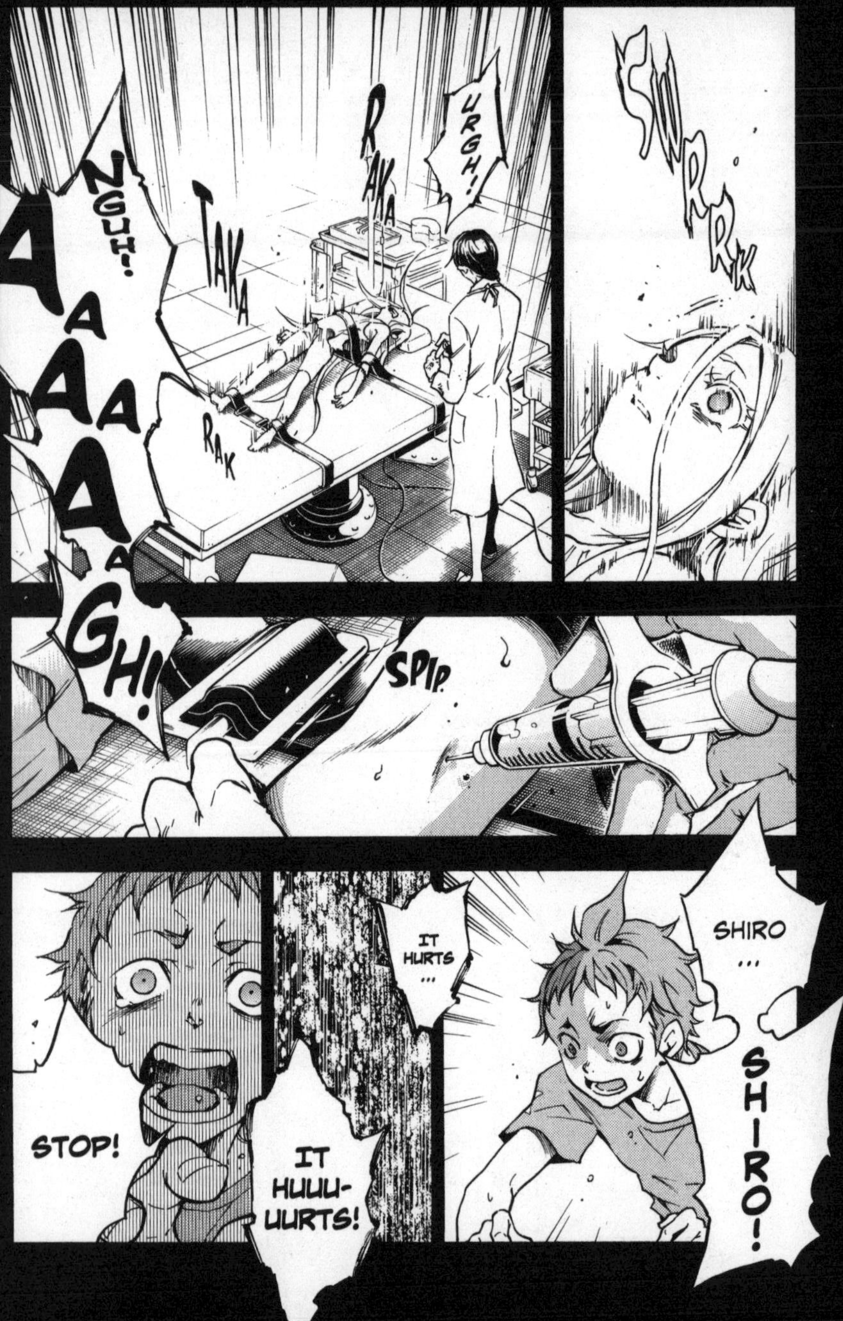
SWRRRK
URGH!
RAKA
TAKA
NGUH!
RAK
AAAAAAGH!
SPIP
SHIRO...
SHIRO!
IT HURTS...
IT HUUU-UURTS!
STOP!

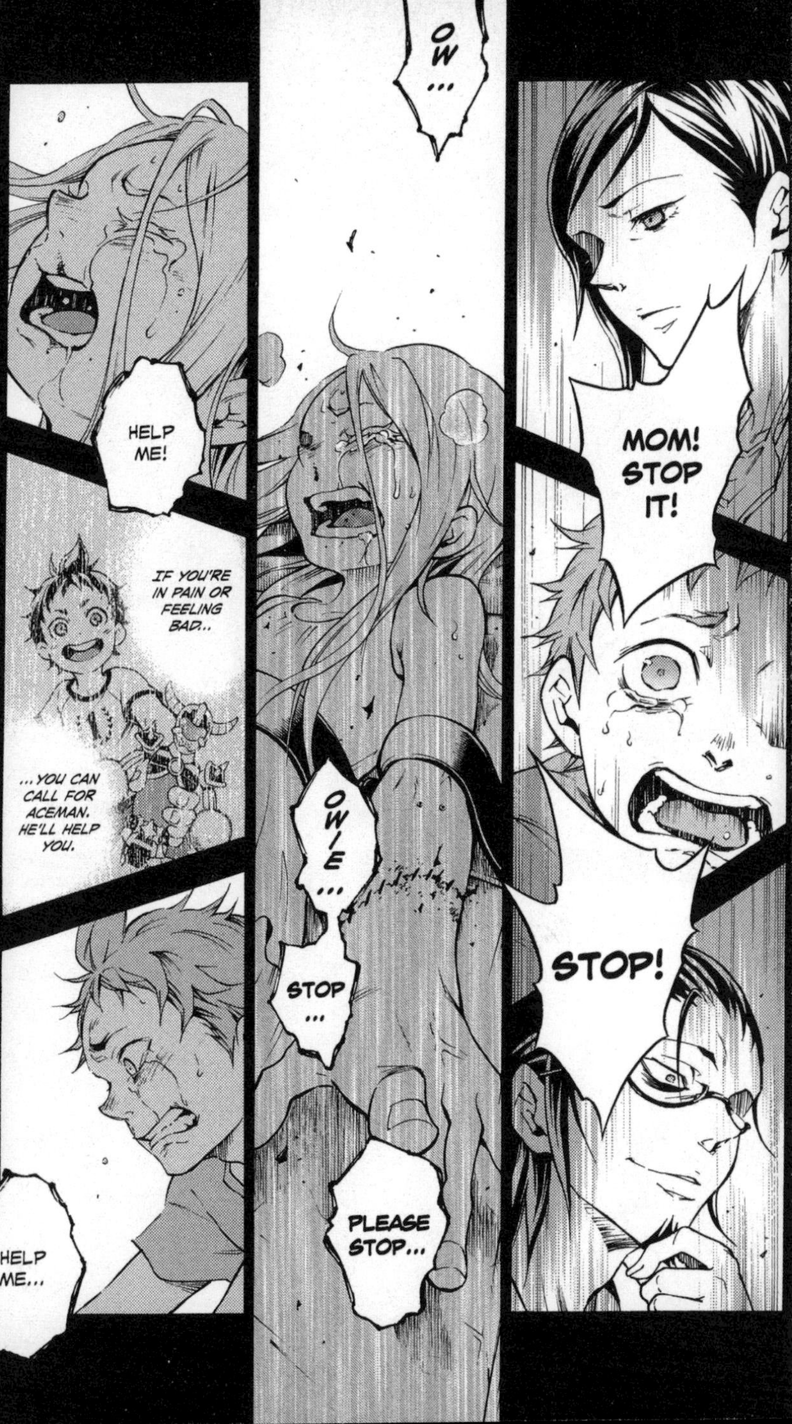
MOM! STOP IT!
STOP!
OW...
OWIE...
STOP...
PLEASE STOP...
HELP ME!
IF YOU'RE IN PAIN OR FEELING BAD...
...YOU CAN CALL FOR ACEMAN. HE'LL HELP YOU.
HELP ME...

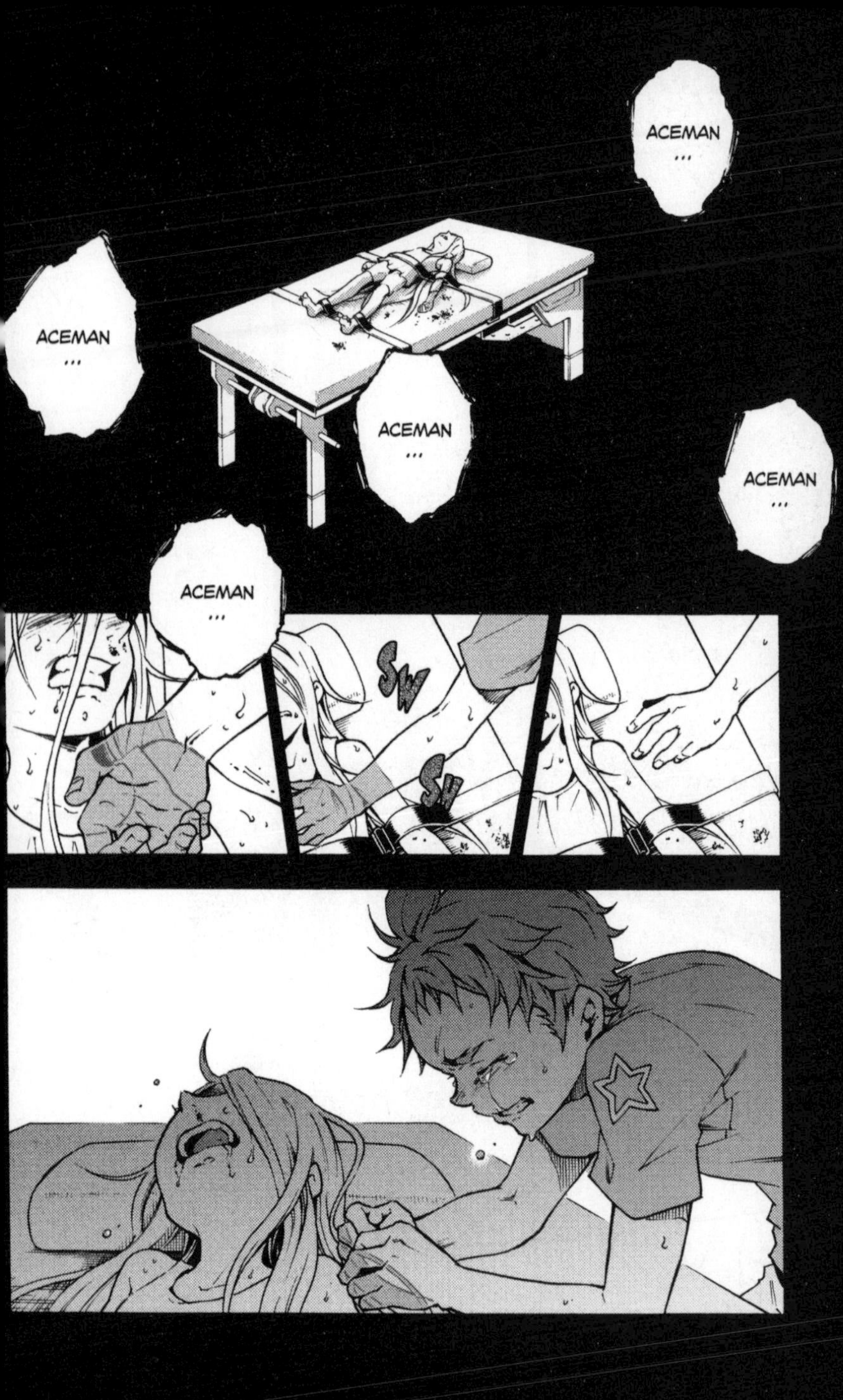
ACEMAN ...
ACEMAN ...
ACEMAN ...
ACEMAN ...
ACEMAN ...
SW
SH

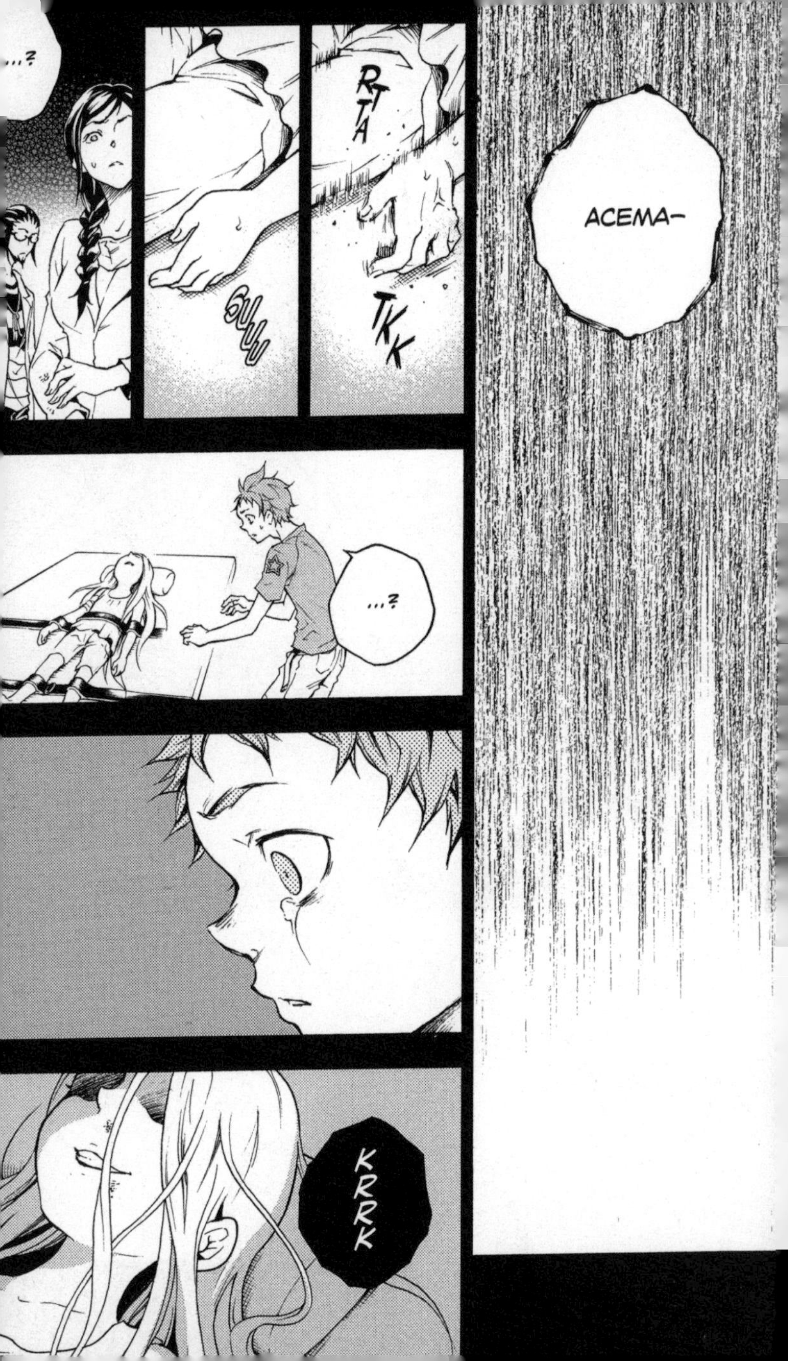
ACEMA-
RTTA
TKK
GUUU
...?
...?
KRRK

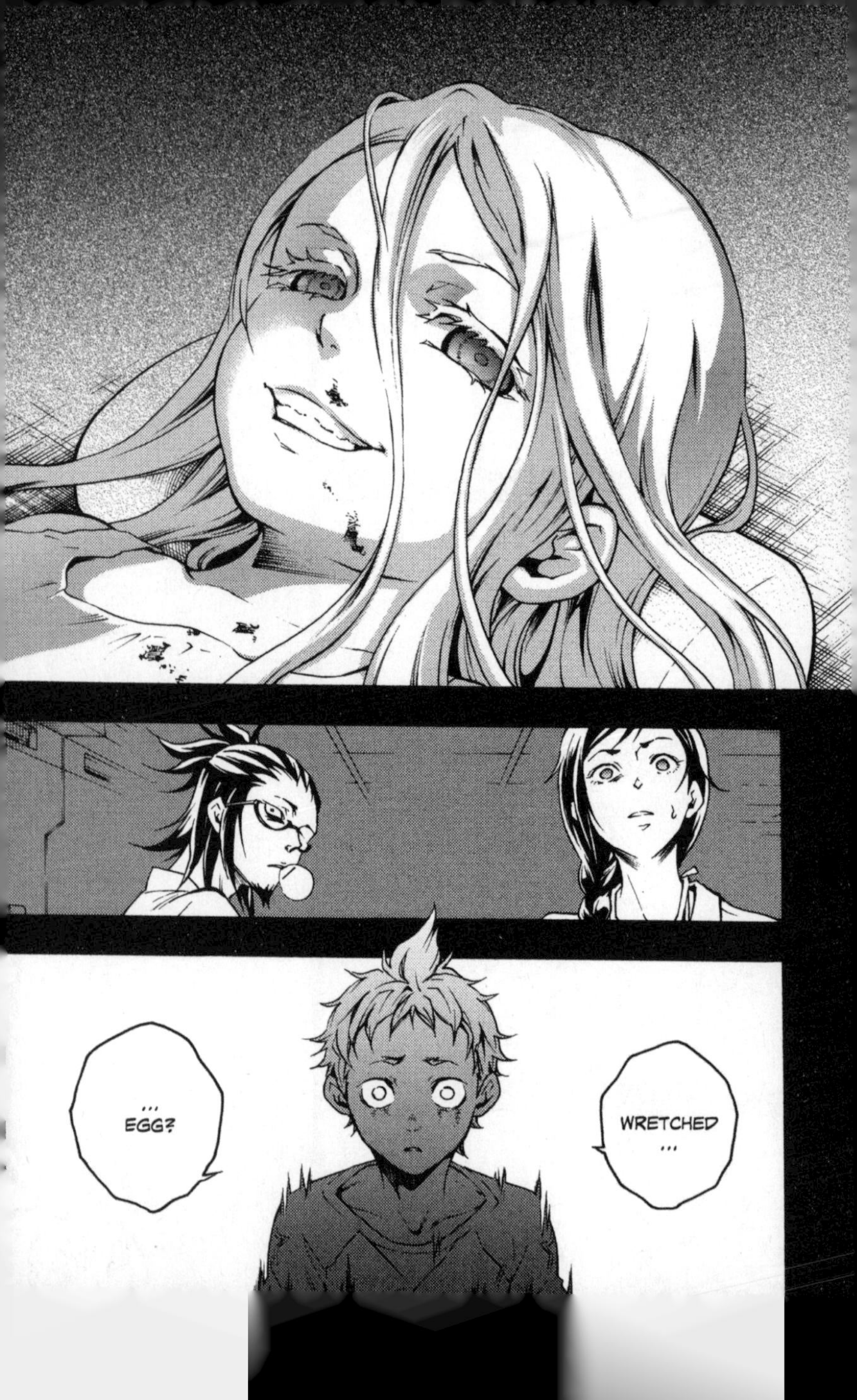
WRETCHED ...
... EGG?

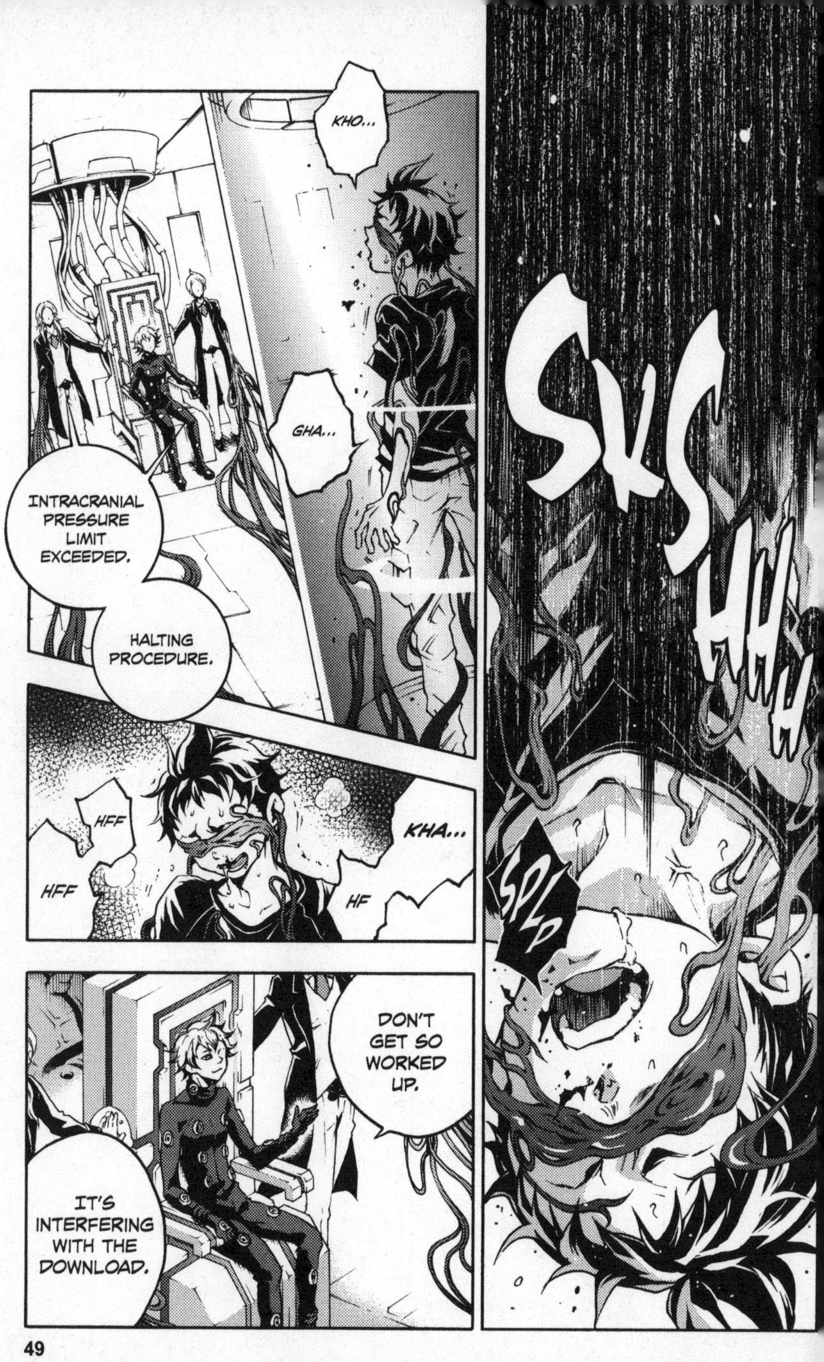
SUSHHH
SPLP
KHO...
GHA...
INTRACRANIAL PRESSURE LIMIT EXCEEDED.
HALTING PROCEDURE.
KHA...
HFF
HFF
HF
DON'T GET SO WORKED UP.
IT'S INTERFERING WITH THE DOWNLOAD.

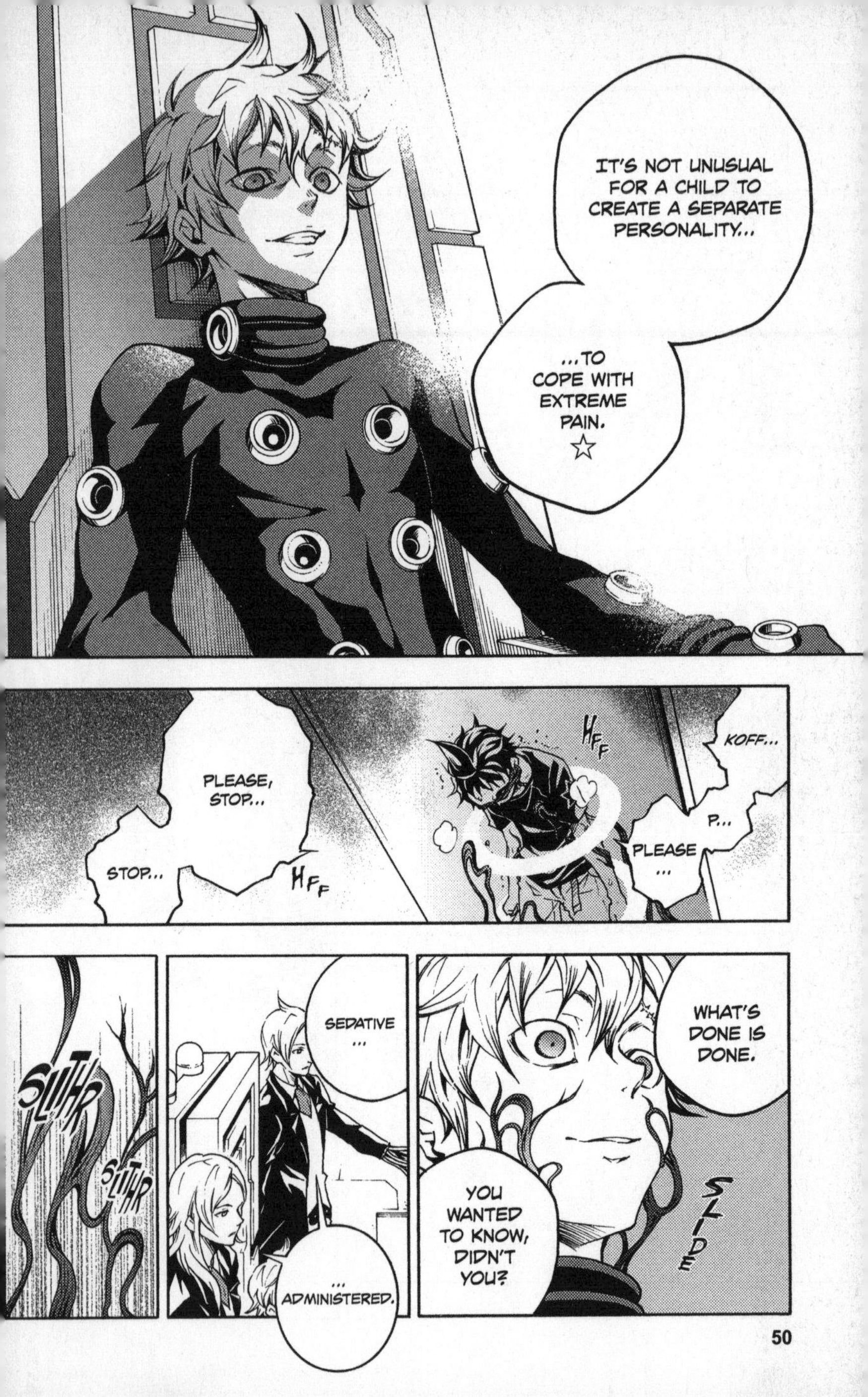
IT'S NOT UNUSUAL FOR A CHILD TO CREATE A SEPARATE PERSONALITY...
...TO COPE WITH EXTREME PAIN. ☆
KOFF...
HFF
P... PLEASE ...
PLEASE, STOP...
STOP...
HFF
WHAT'S DONE IS DONE.
YOU WANTED TO KNOW, DIDN'T YOU?
SLIDE
SEDATIVE ...
... ADMINISTERED.
SLITHR
SLITHR

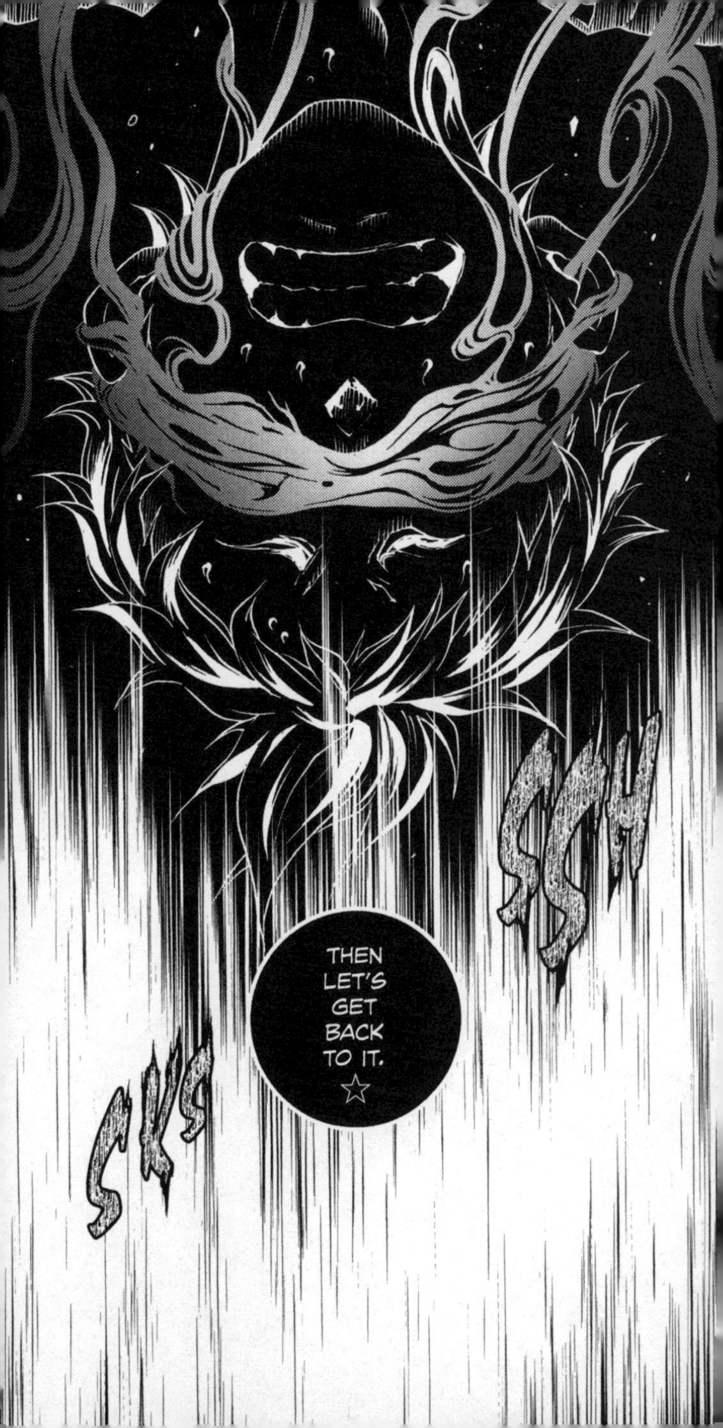
SSH
THEN LET'S GET BACK TO IT. ☆
SKS

DEADMAN
WONDER
LAND

EADMAN
WONDER
LAND

DEADMA
WONDER
LAND

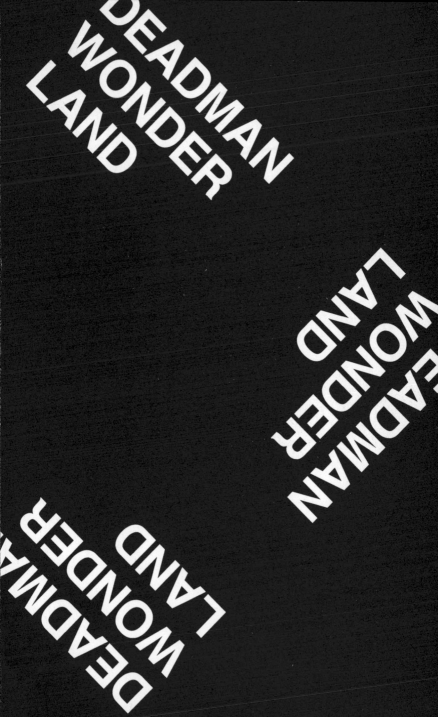

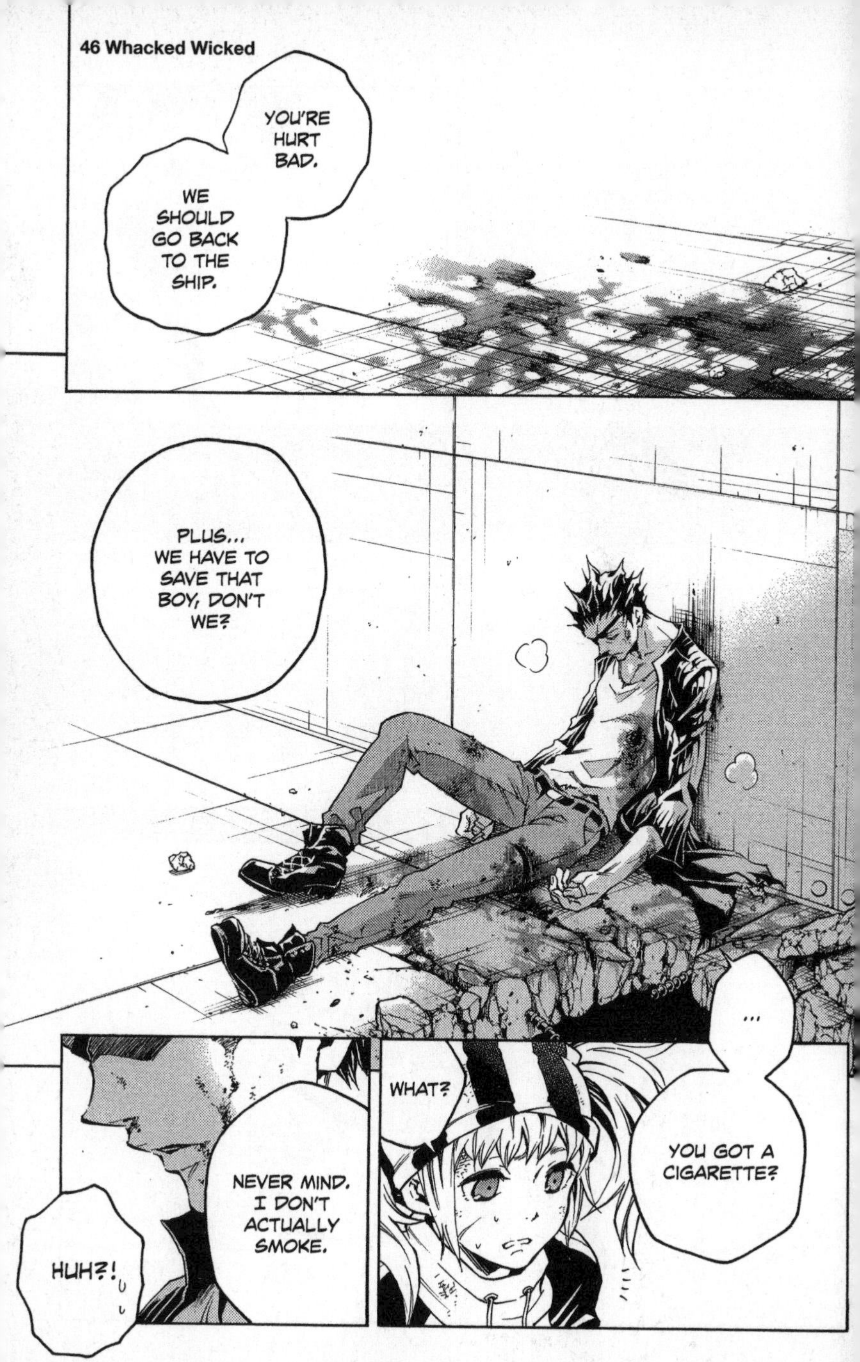
YOU'RE HURT BAD.
WE SHOULD GO BACK TO THE SHIP.
PLUS... WE HAVE TO SAVE THAT BOY, DON'T WE?
...
YOU GOT A CIGARETTE?
WHAT?
NEVER MIND. I DON'T ACTUALLY SMOKE.
HUH?!

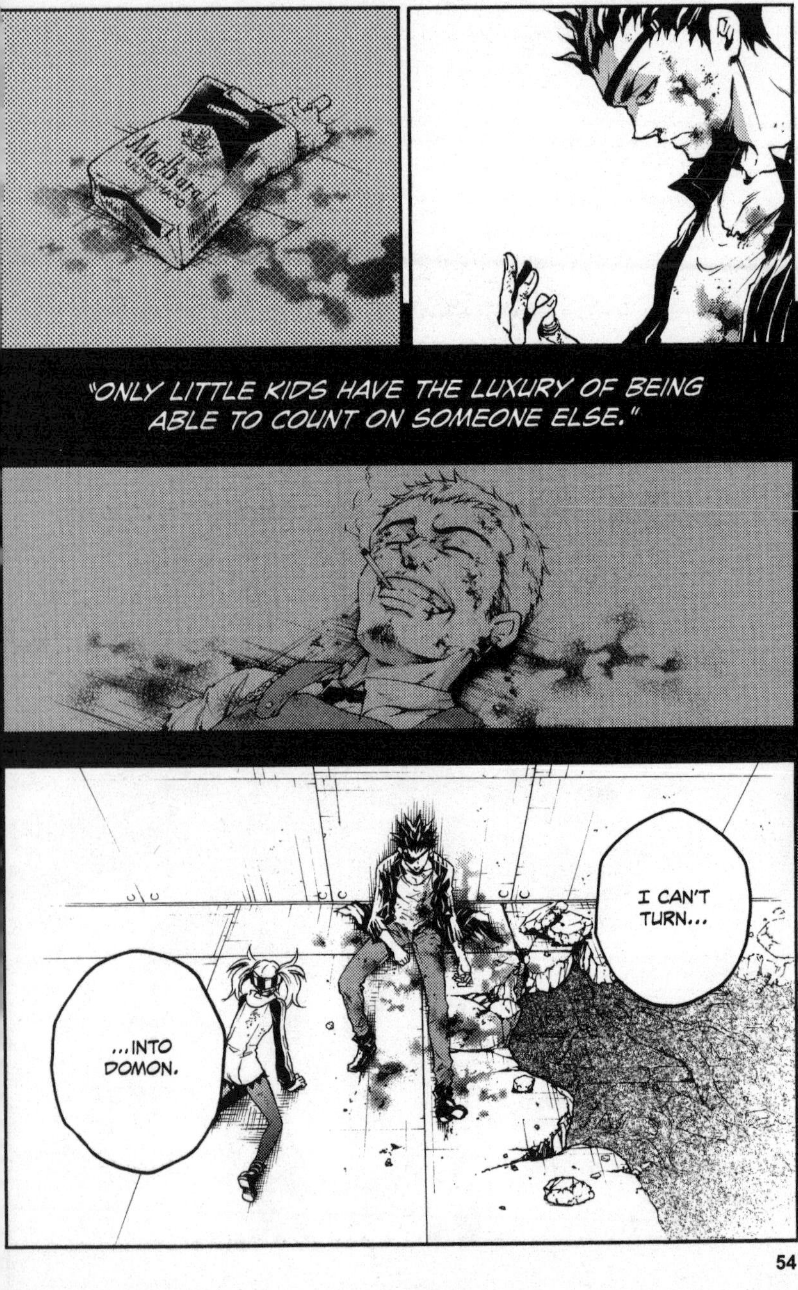
"ONLY LITTLE KIDS HAVE THE LUXURY OF BEING ABLE TO COUNT ON SOMEONE ELSE."
I CAN'T TURN...
...INTO DOMON.

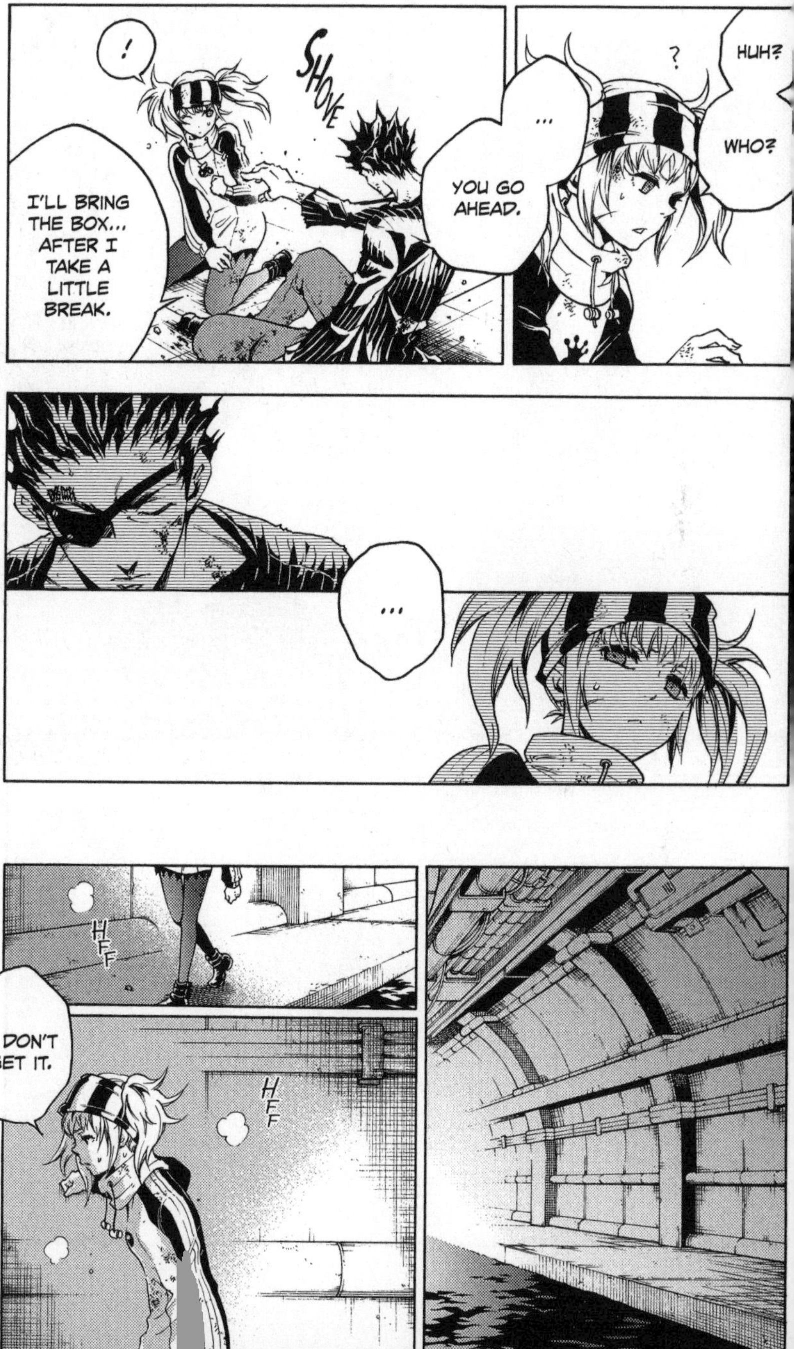
HUH?
WHO?
?
...
YOU GO AHEAD.
!
SHOVE
I'LL BRING THE BOX... AFTER I TAKE A LITTLE BREAK.
...
HFF
I DON'T GET IT.
HFF

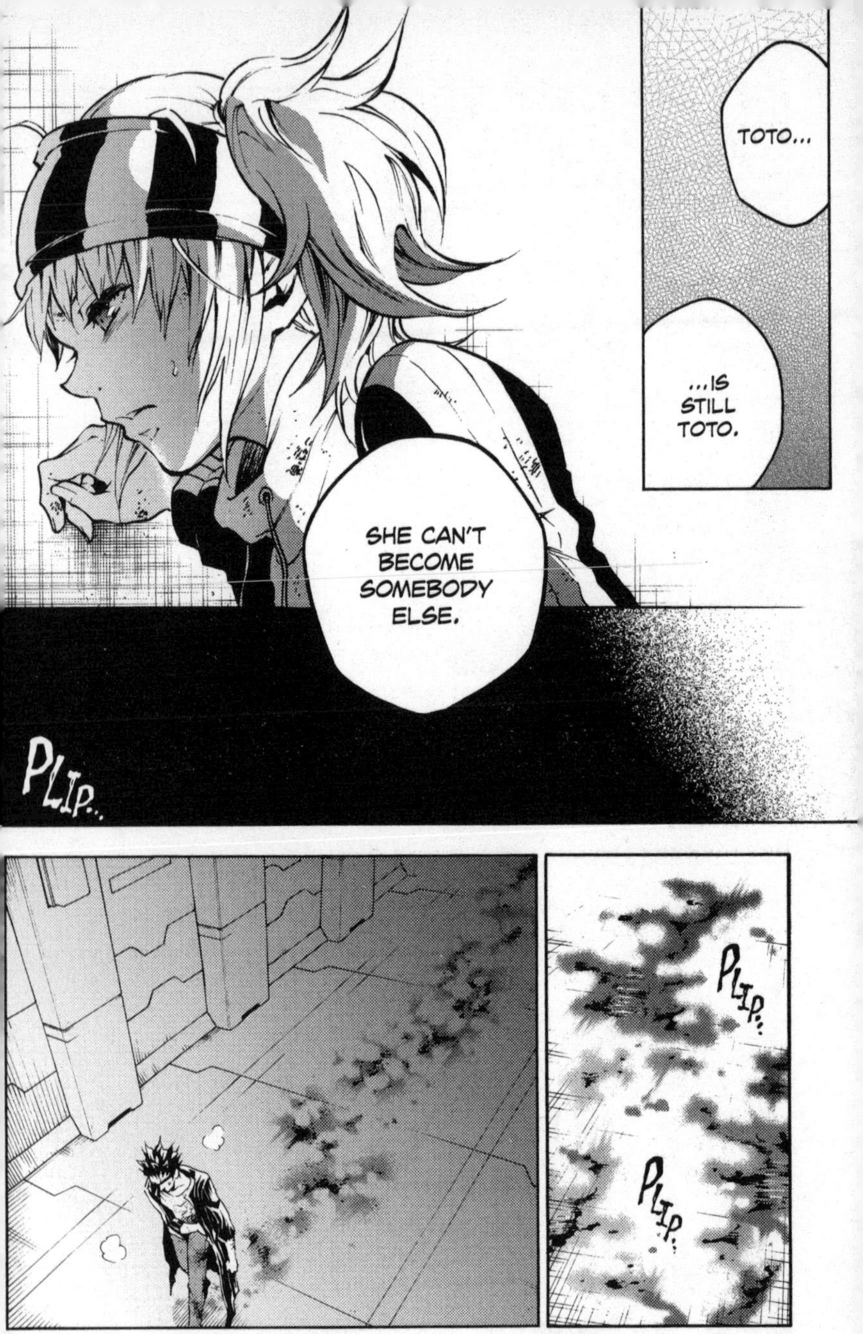
TOTO...
...IS STILL TOTO.
SHE CAN'T BECOME SOMEBODY ELSE.
PLIP...
PLIP...
PLIP...

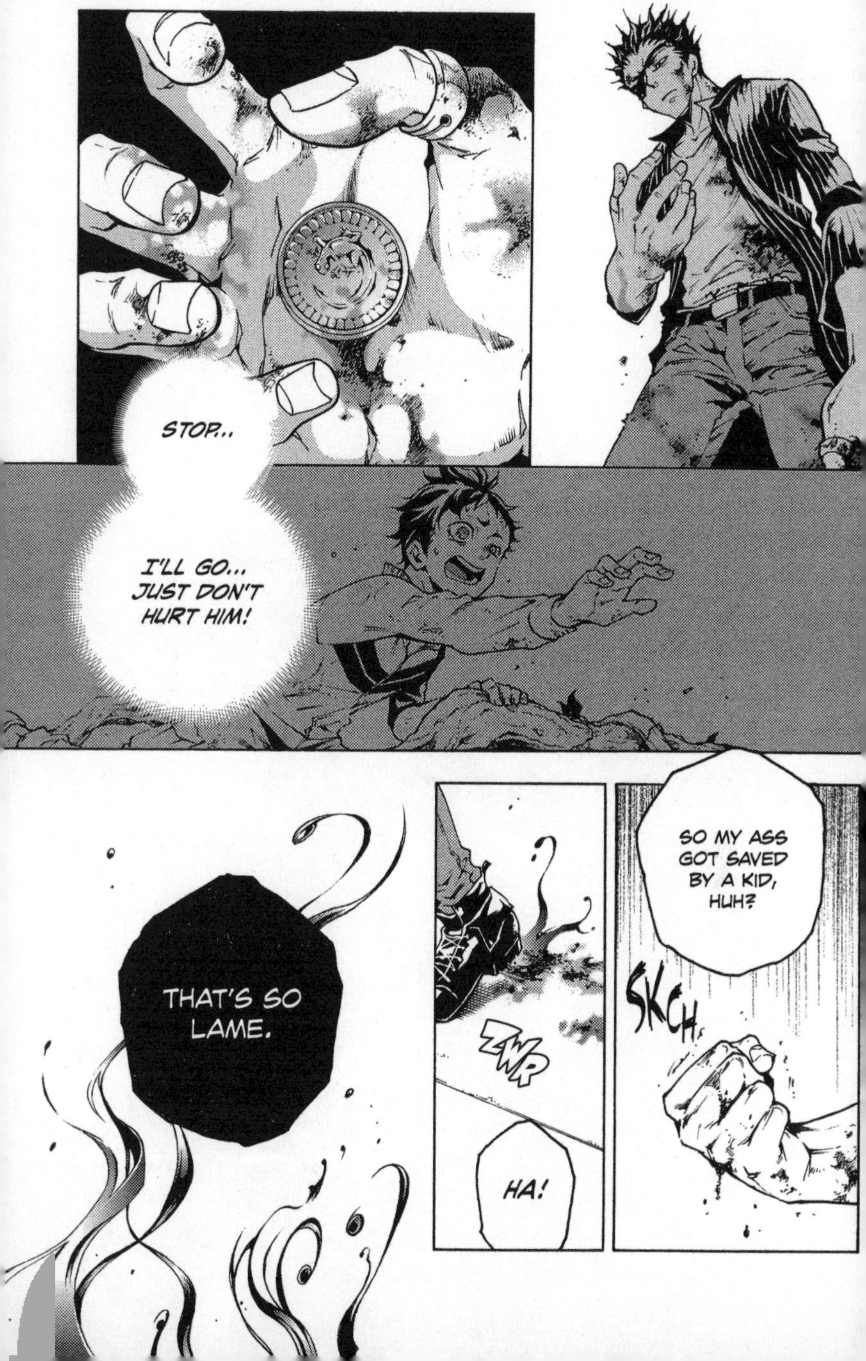
STOP...
I'LL GO... JUST DON'T HURT HIM!
SO MY ASS GOT SAVED BY A KID, HUH?
SKCH
ZWR
HA!
THAT'S SO LAME.

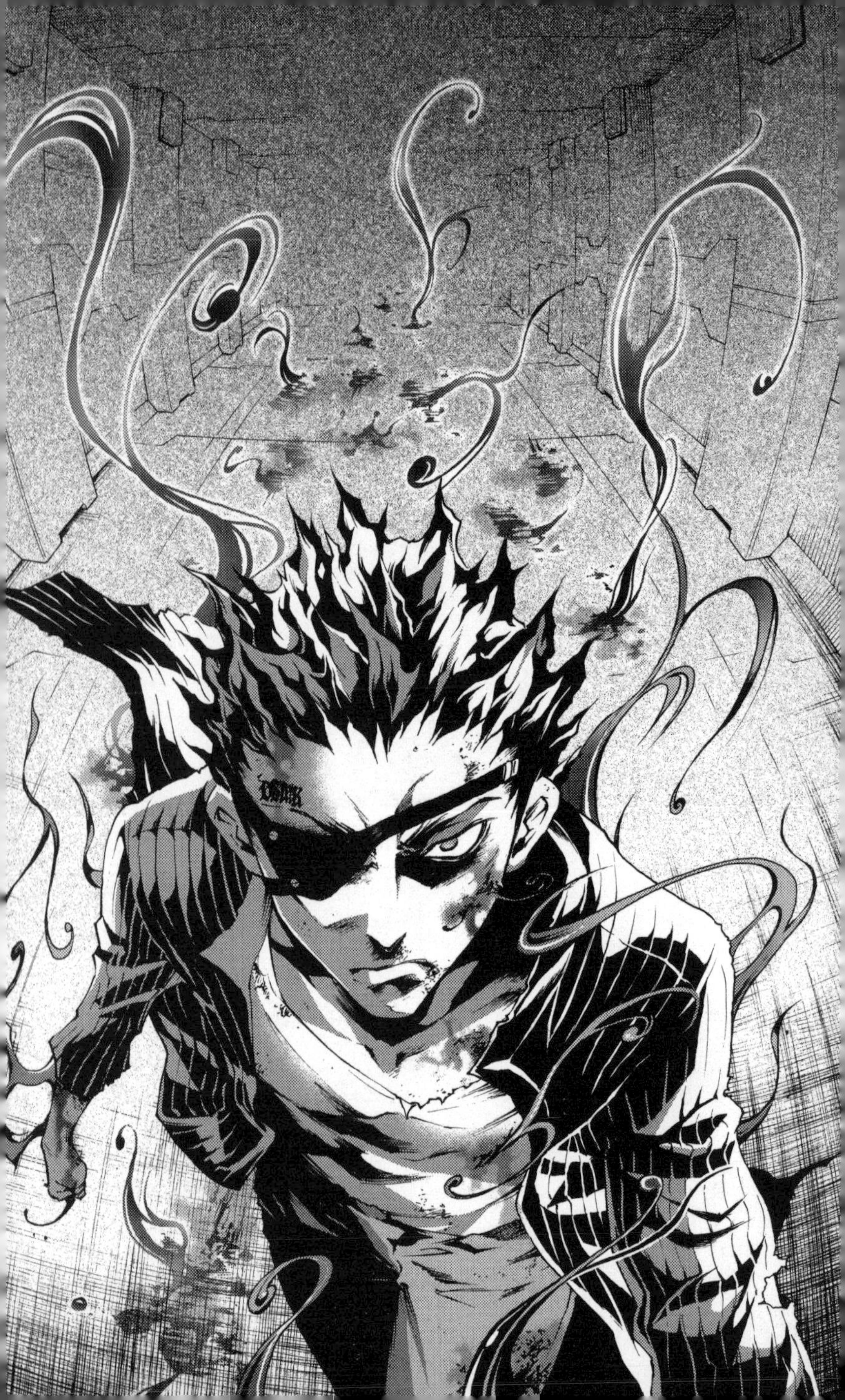

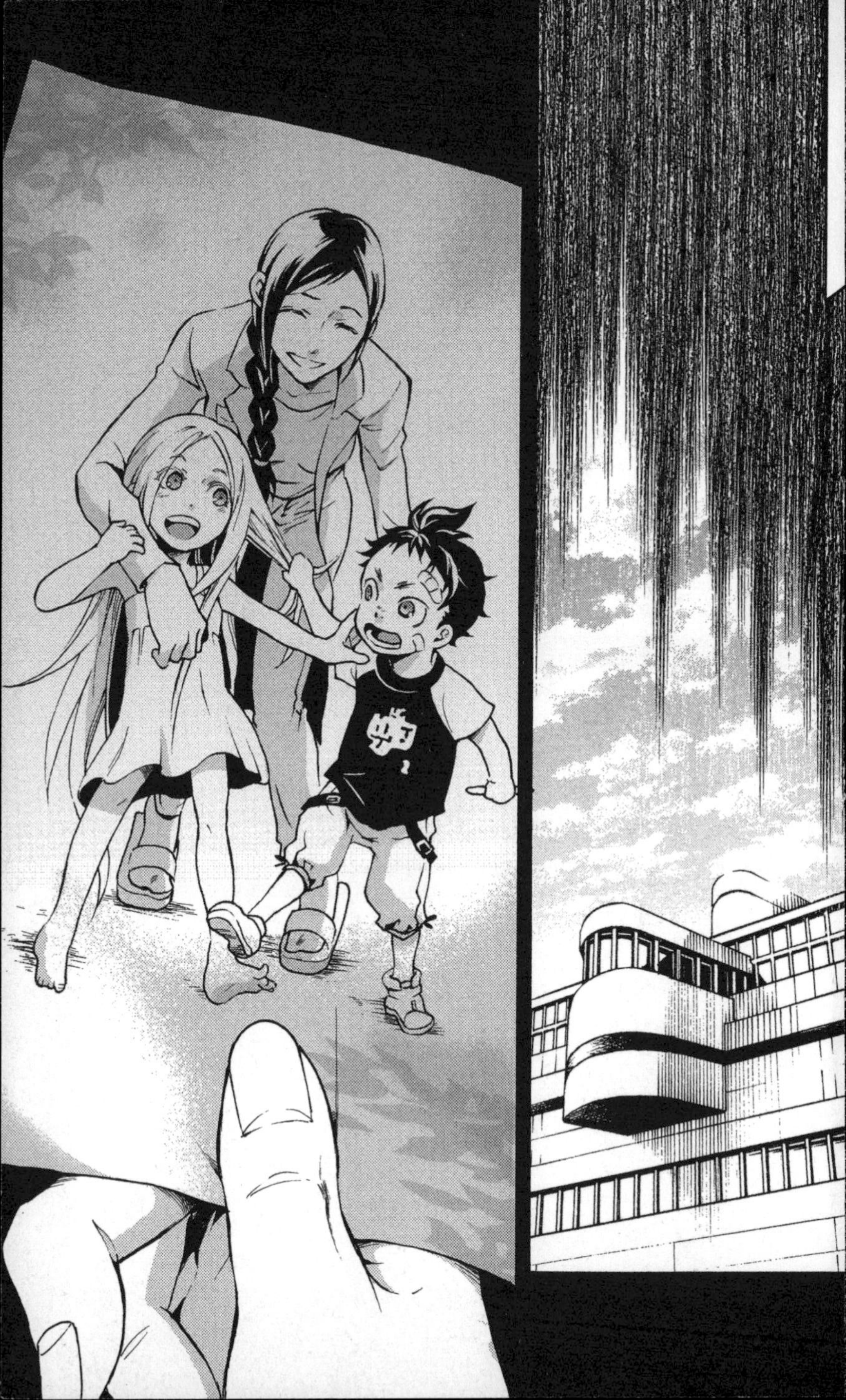

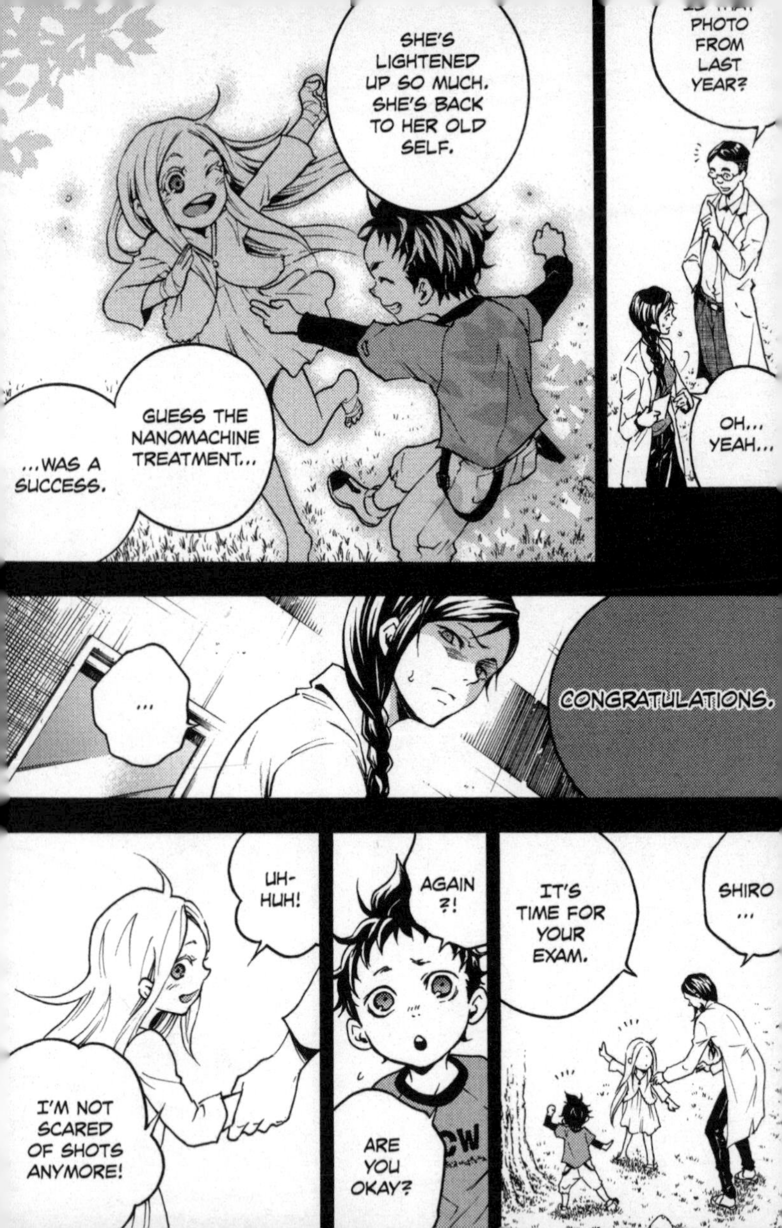
PHOTO FROM LAST YEAR?
OH... YEAH...
SHE'S LIGHTENED UP SO MUCH. SHE'S BACK TO HER OLD SELF.
GUESS THE NANOMACHINE TREATMENT...
...WAS A SUCCESS.
CONGRATULATIONS.
...
SHIRO...
IT'S TIME FOR YOUR EXAM.
AGAIN?!
ARE YOU OKAY?
UH-HUH!
I'M NOT SCARED OF SHOTS ANYMORE!

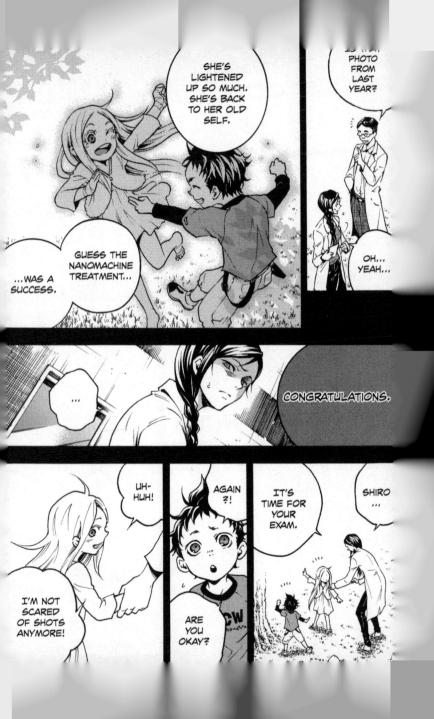

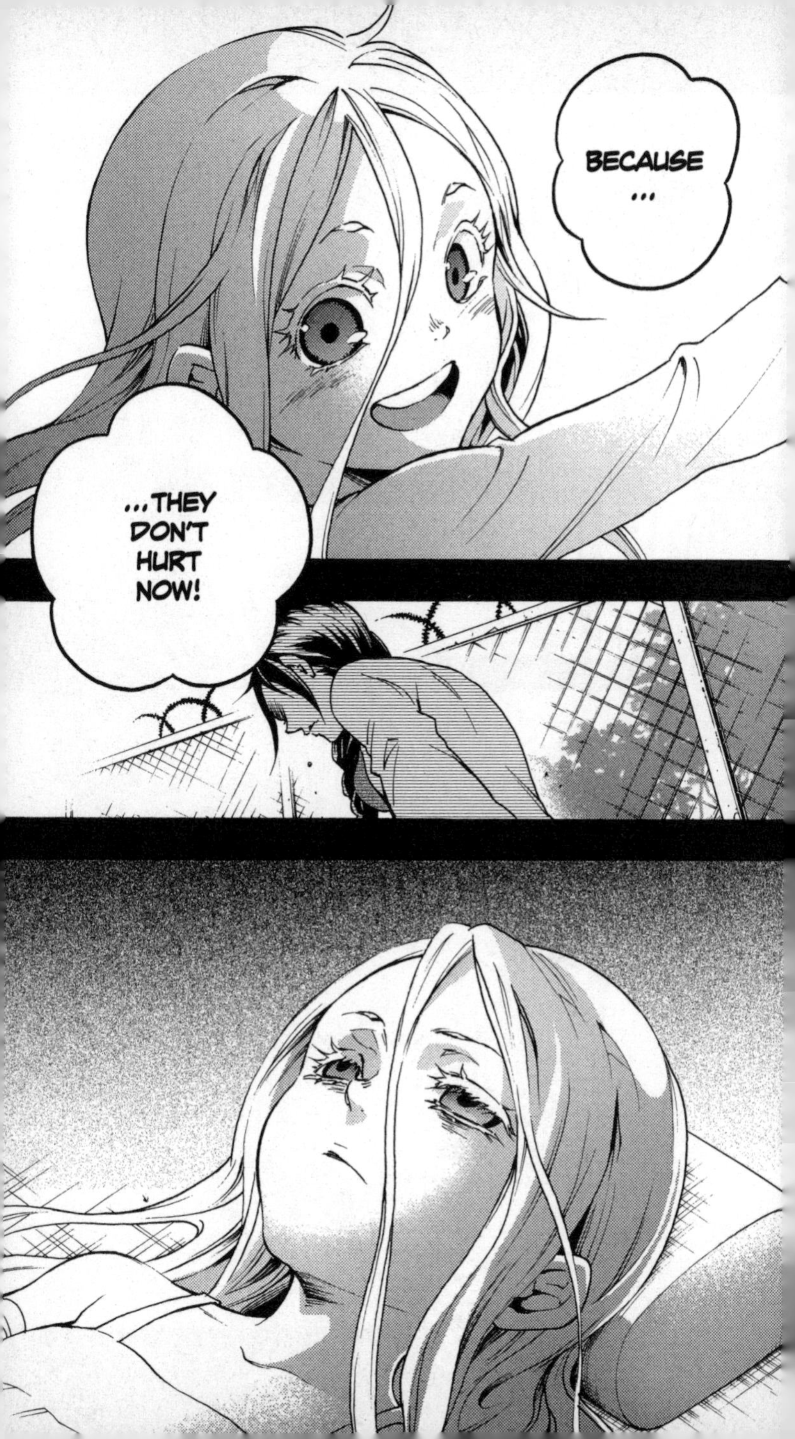
BECAUSE ...
...THEY DON'T HURT NOW!

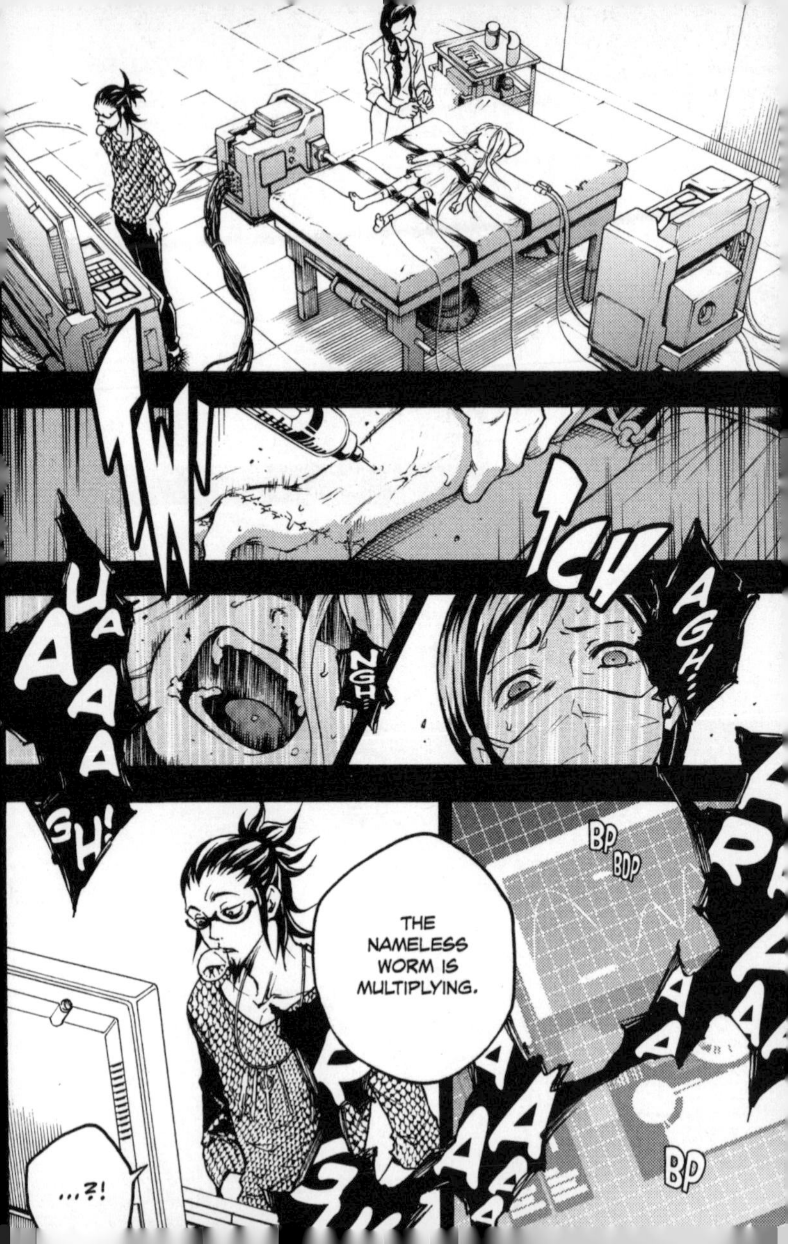
AGH...
NGH...
BP BOP
BP
THE NAMELESS WORM IS MULTIPLYING.
...?!

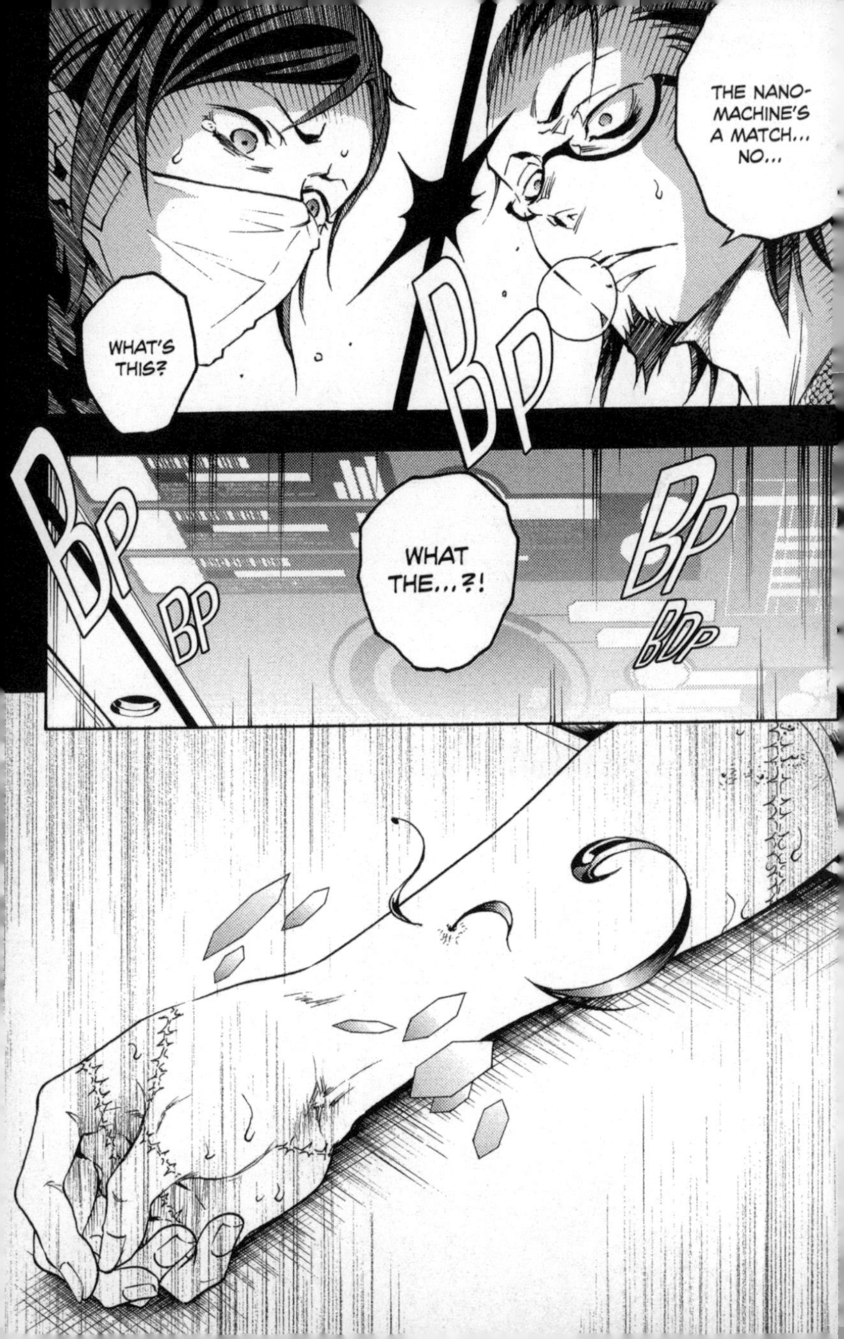
THE NANO-MACHINE'S A MATCH... NO...
BP
WHAT'S THIS?
BP
BDP
WHAT THE...?!
BP
BP

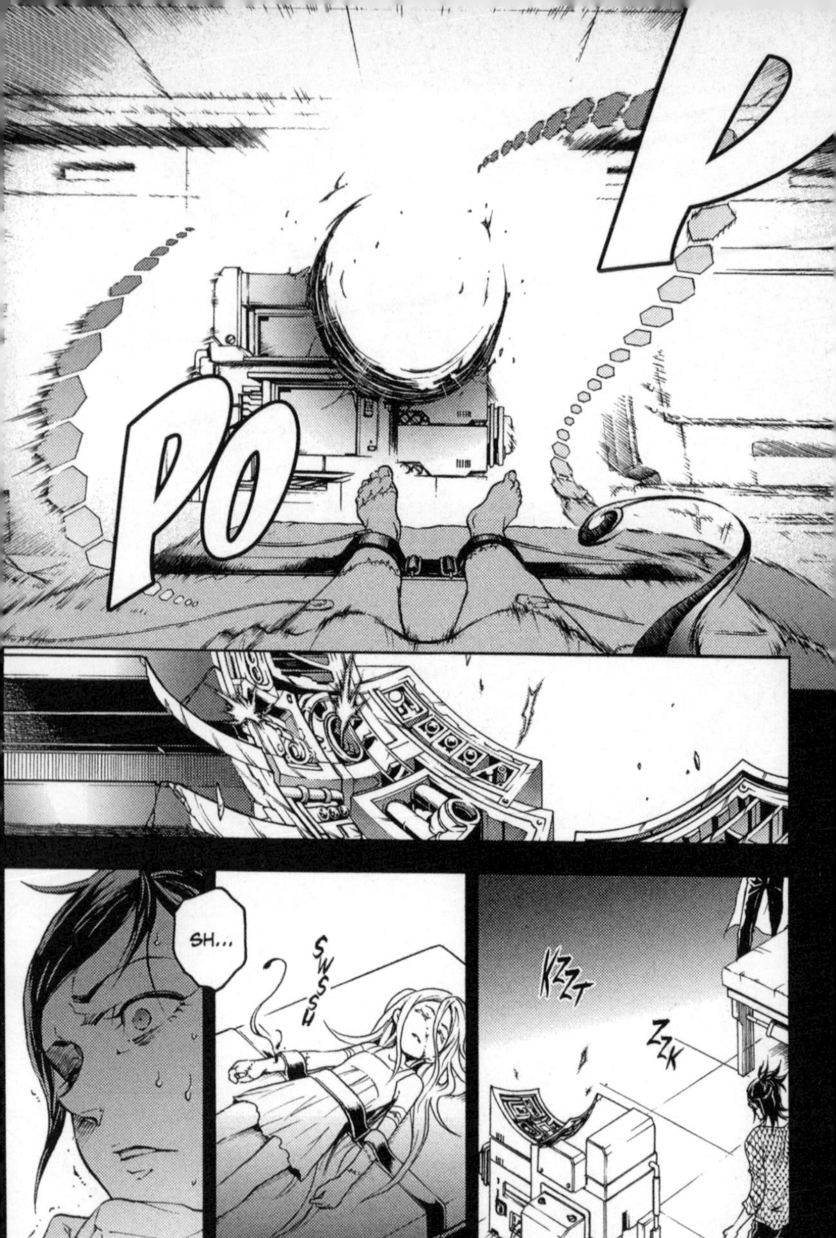
POP
KZZT
ZZK
SWSSH
SH...
SHIRO?

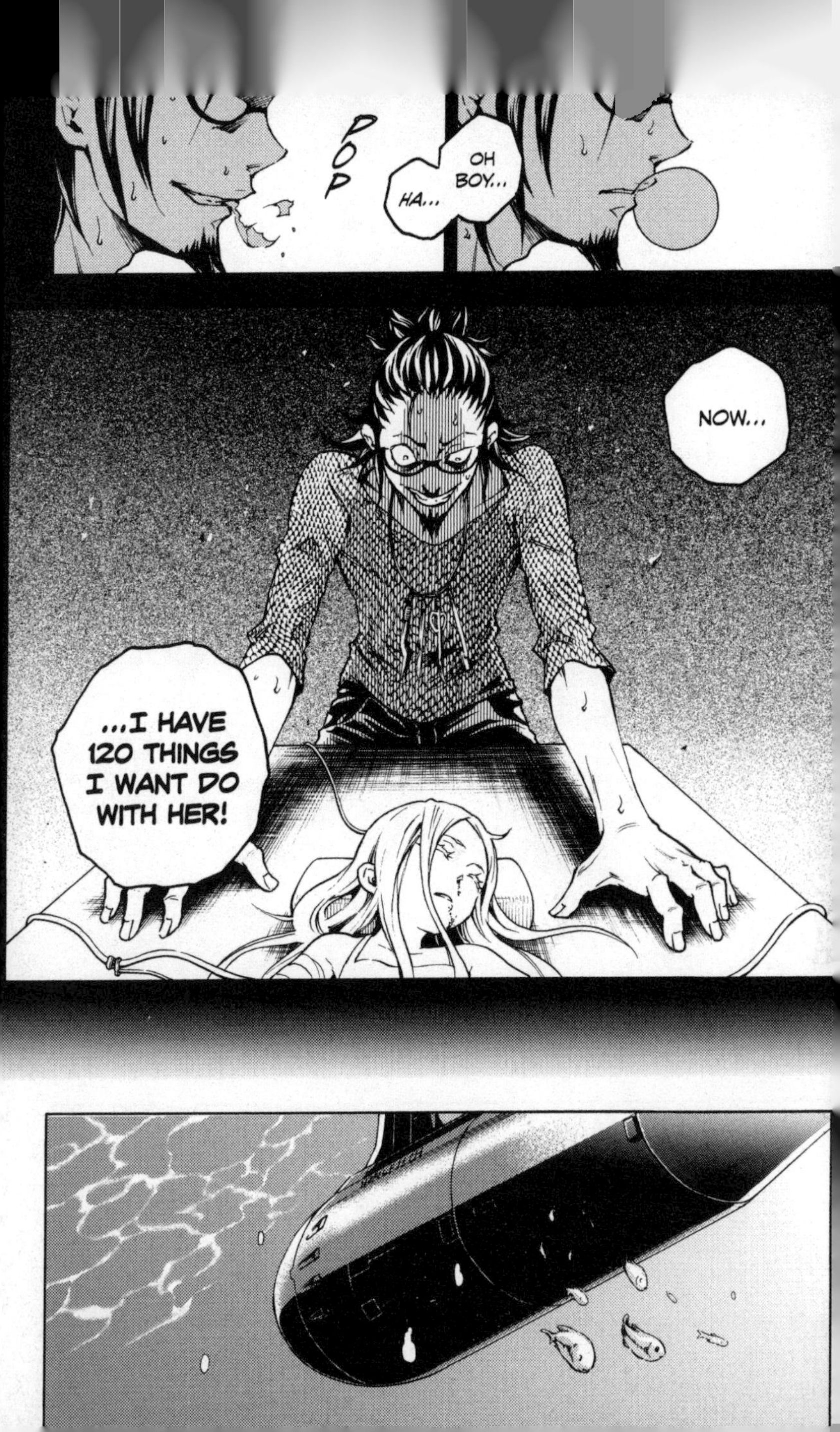
OH BOY... HA...
POP
NOW...
...I HAVE 120 THINGS I WANT DO WITH HER!

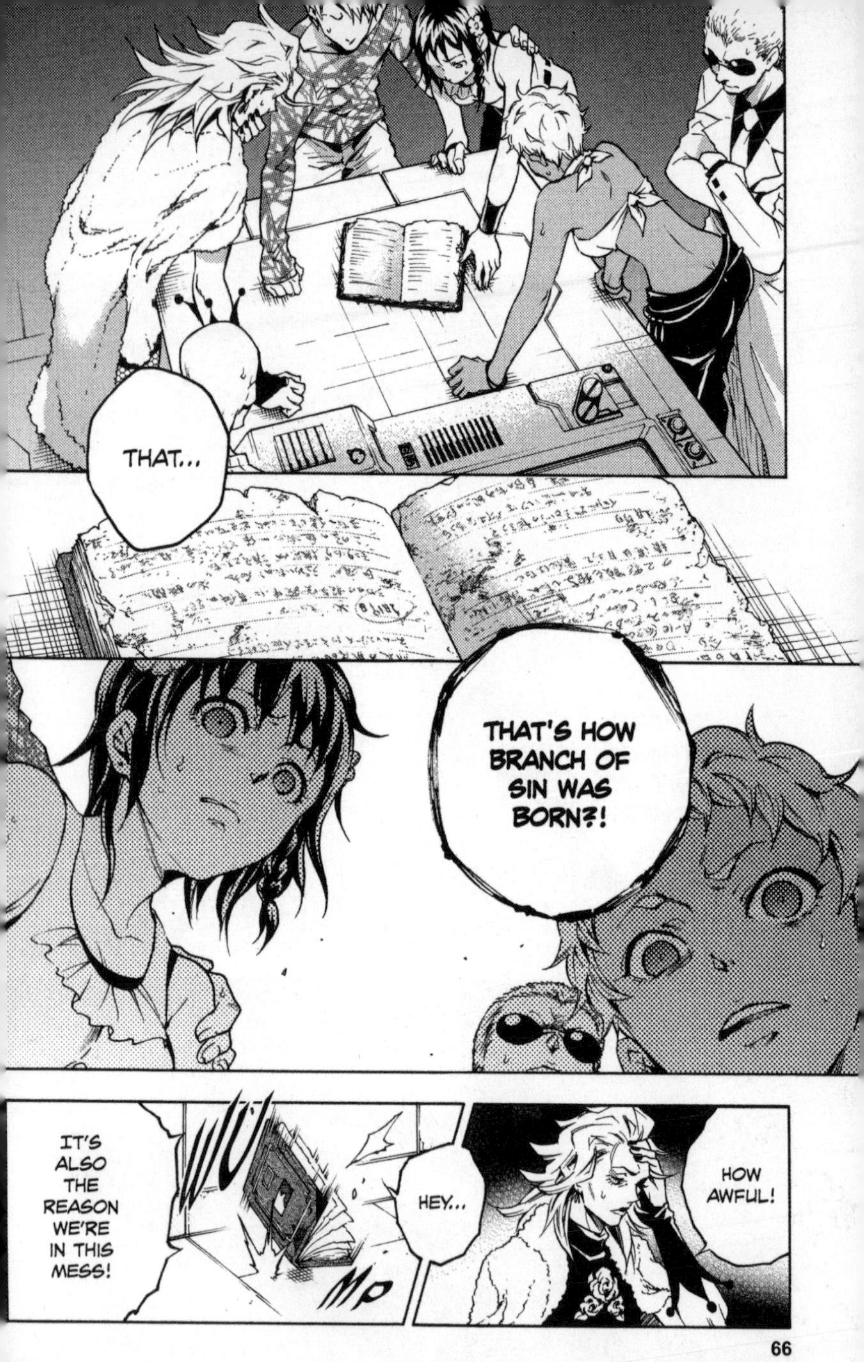
THAT...
THAT'S HOW BRANCH OF SIN WAS BORN?!
HOW AWFUL!
HEY...
IT'S ALSO THE REASON WE'RE IN THIS MESS!

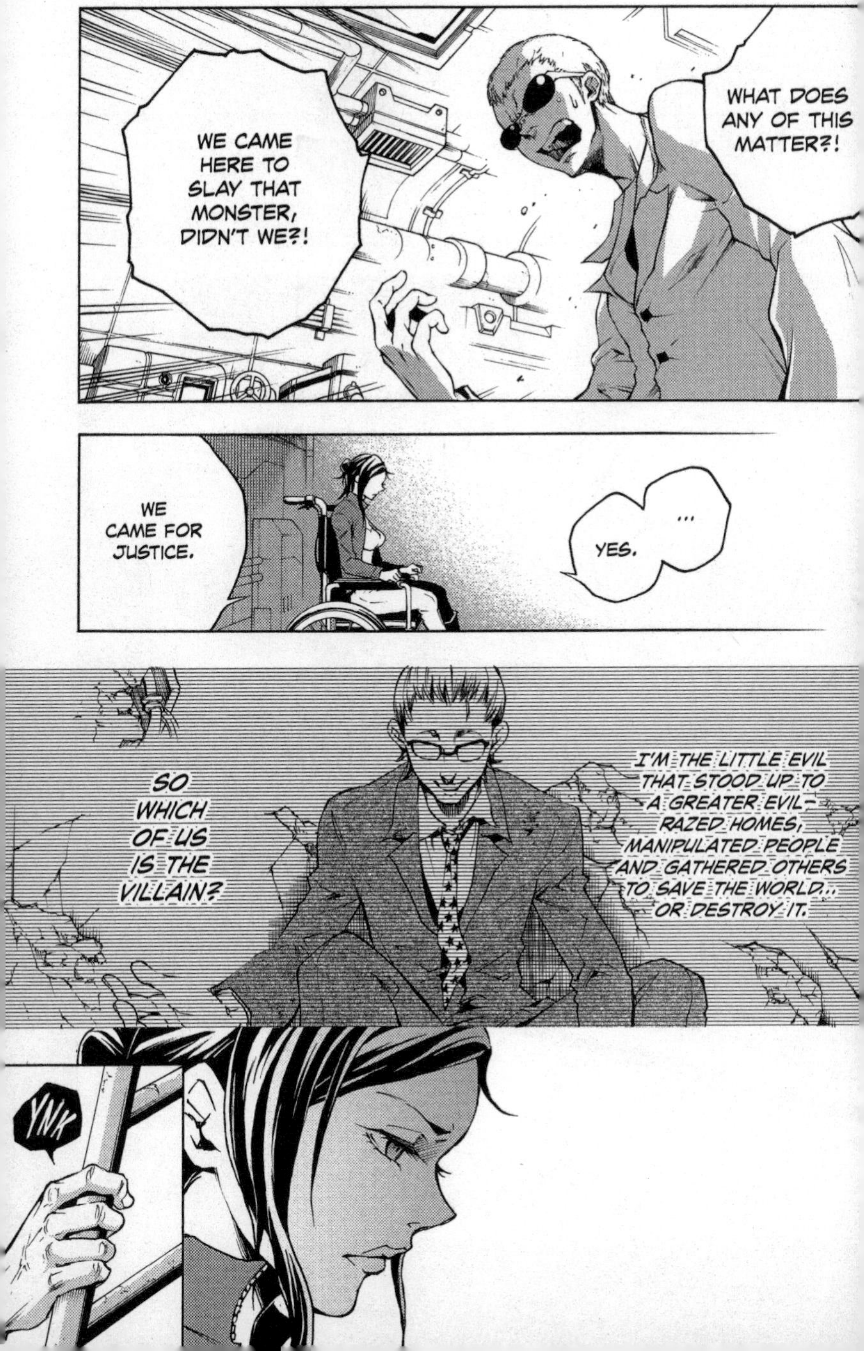
WHAT DOES ANY OF THIS MATTER?!
WE CAME HERE TO SLAY THAT MONSTER, DIDN'T WE?!
... YES.
WE CAME FOR JUSTICE.
I'M THE LITTLE EVIL THAT STOOD UP TO A GREATER EVIL–RAZED HOMES, MANIPULATED PEOPLE AND GATHERED OTHERS TO SAVE THE WORLD... OR DESTROY IT.
SO WHICH OF US IS THE VILLAIN?
YNK

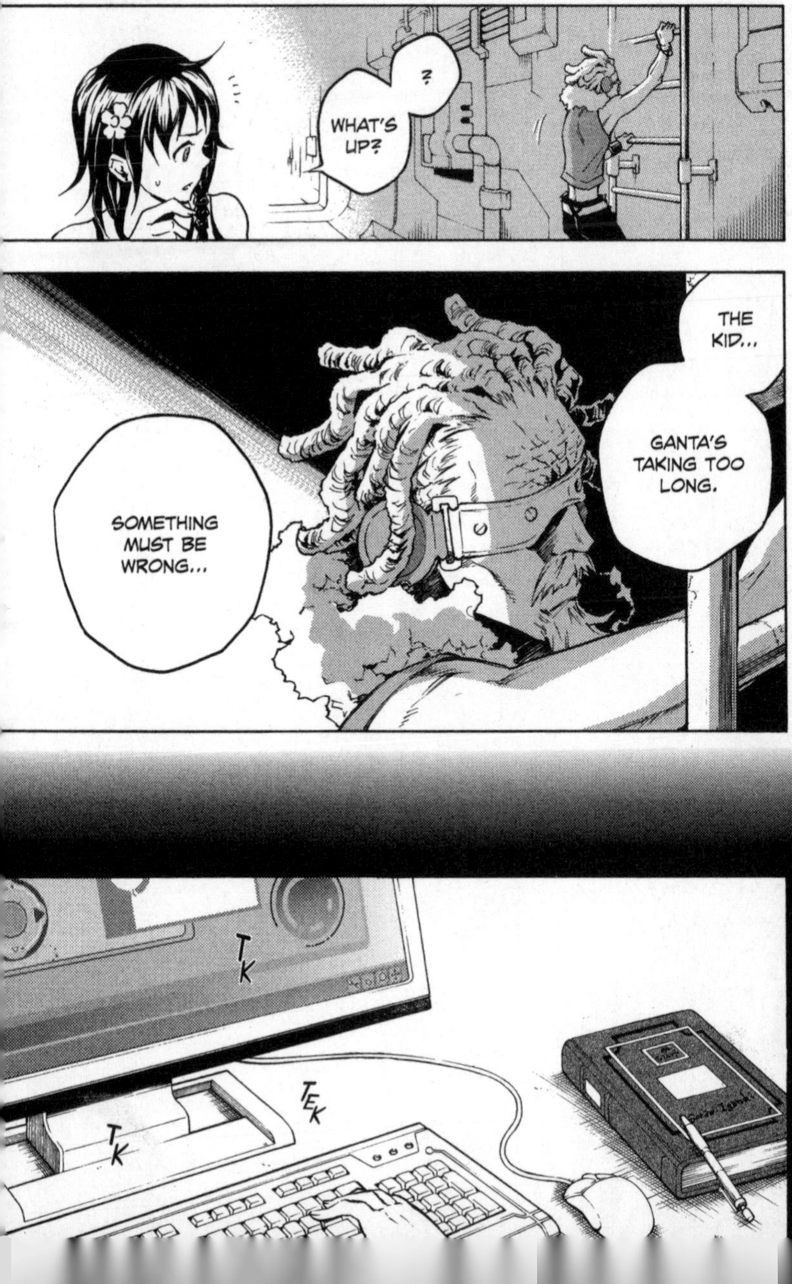
?
WHAT'S UP?
THE KID...
GANTA'S TAKING TOO LONG.
SOMETHING MUST BE WRONG...
TK
TEK
TK

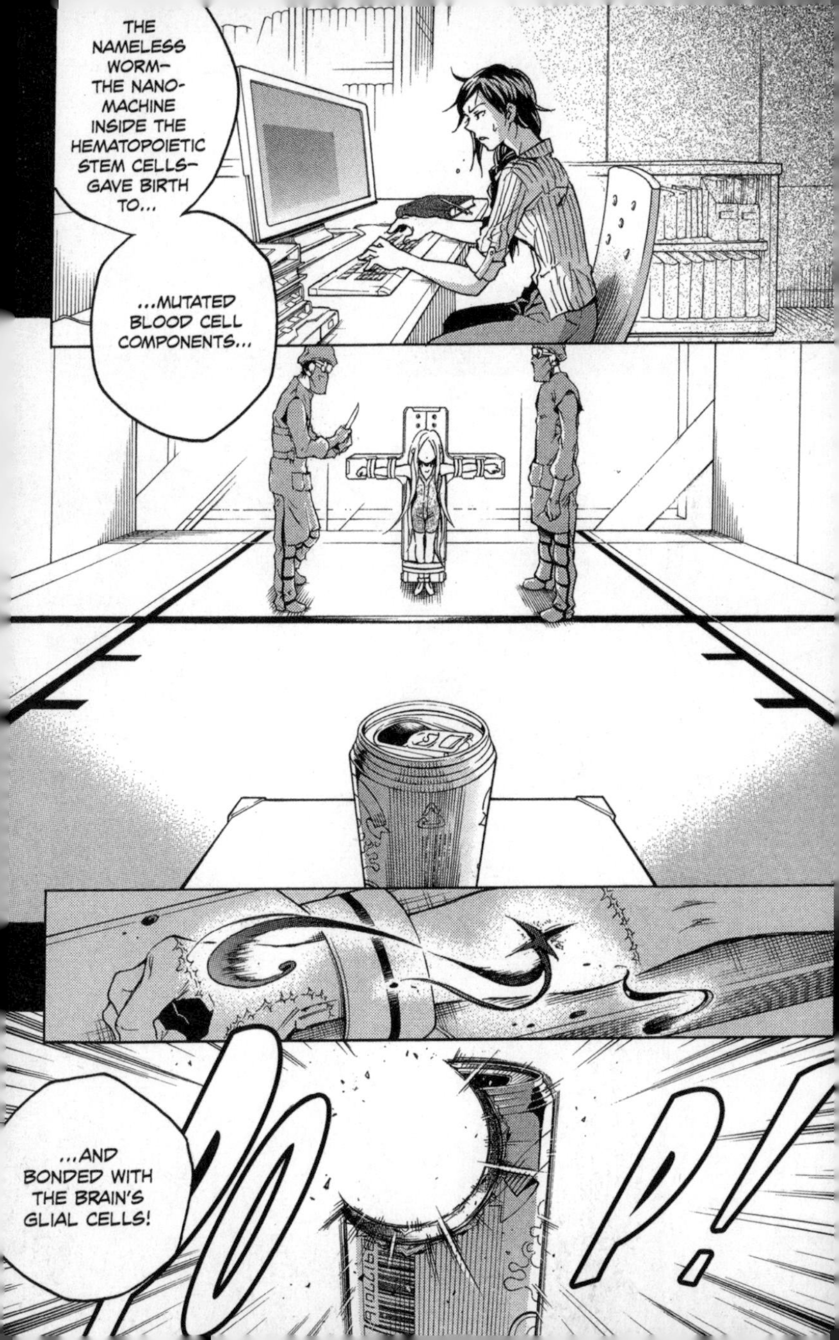
THE NAMELESS WORM— THE NANO-MACHINE INSIDE THE HEMATOPOIETIC STEM CELLS— GAVE BIRTH TO...
...MUTATED BLOOD CELL COMPONENTS...
...AND BONDED WITH THE BRAIN'S GLIAL CELLS!

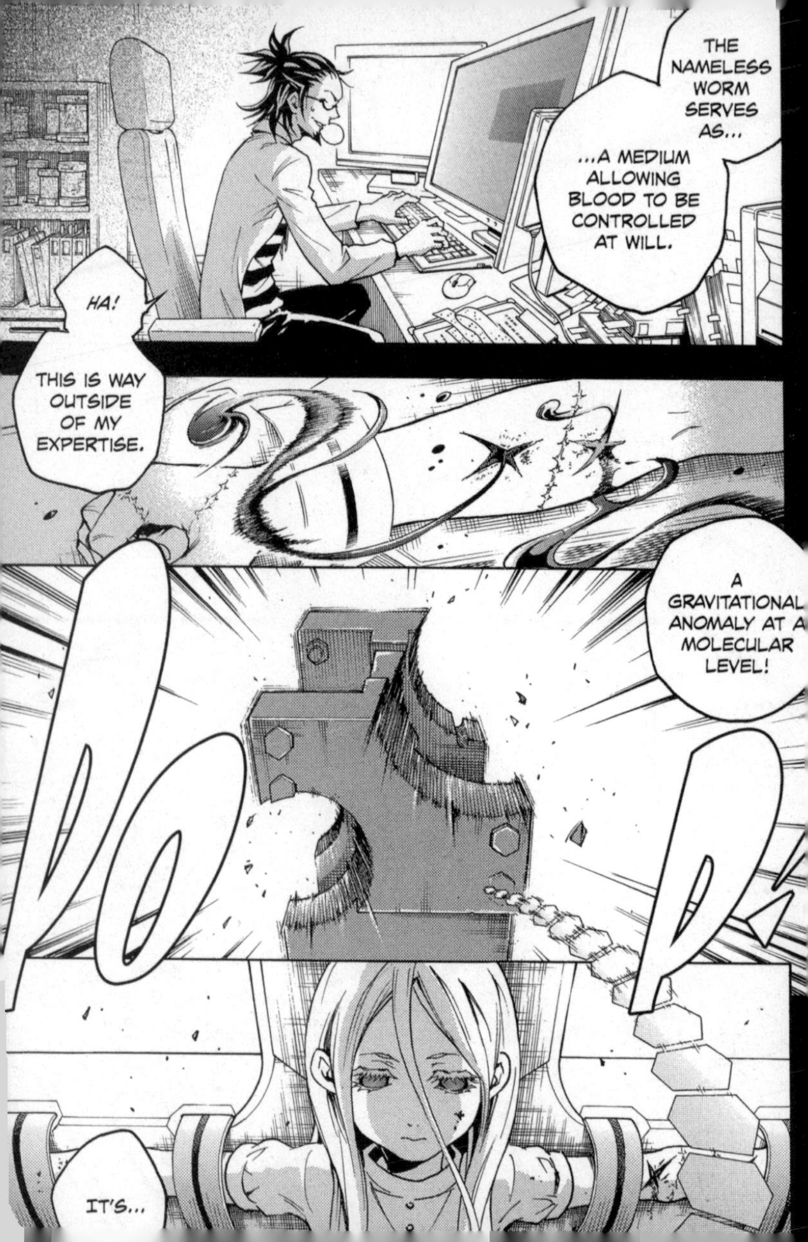
THE NAMELESS WORM SERVES AS...
...A MEDIUM ALLOWING BLOOD TO BE CONTROLLED AT WILL.
HA!
THIS IS WAY OUTSIDE OF MY EXPERTISE.
A GRAVITATIONAL ANOMALY AT A MOLECULAR LEVEL!
IT'S...

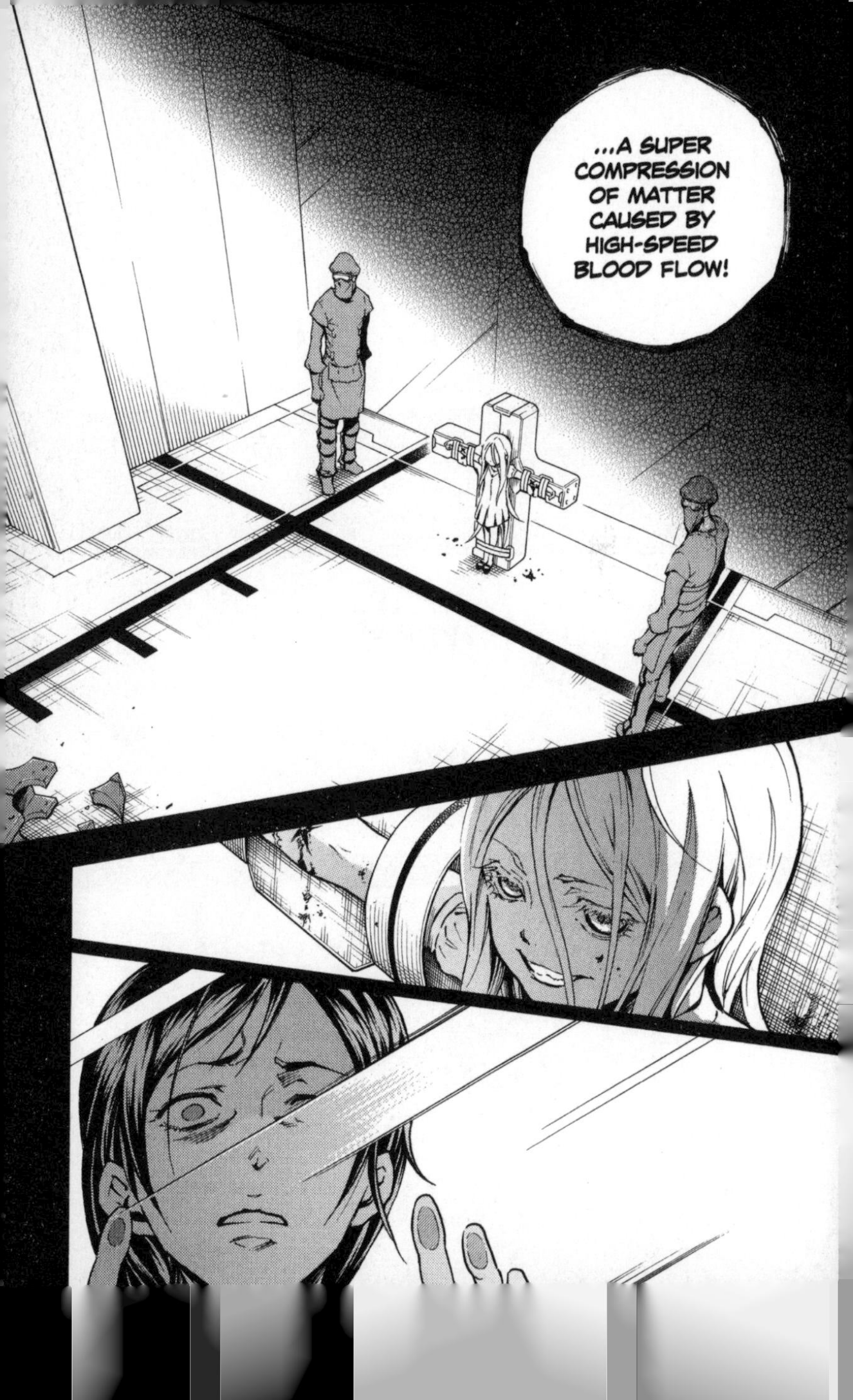
...A SUPER COMPRESSION OF MATTER CAUSED BY HIGH-SPEED BLOOD FLOW!

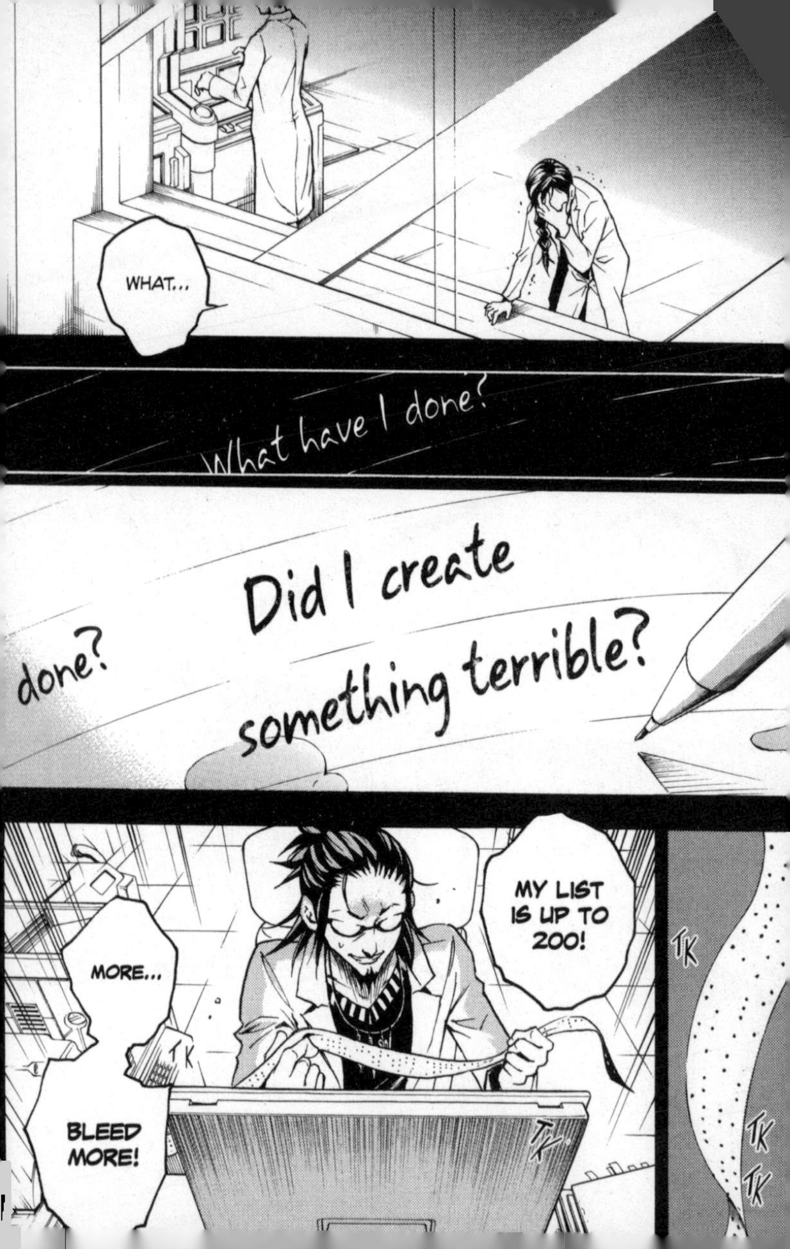
WHAT...
What have I done?
done?
Did I create something terrible?
TK
TK
TK
MY LIST IS UP TO 200!
TK
TK
MORE...
BLEED MORE!

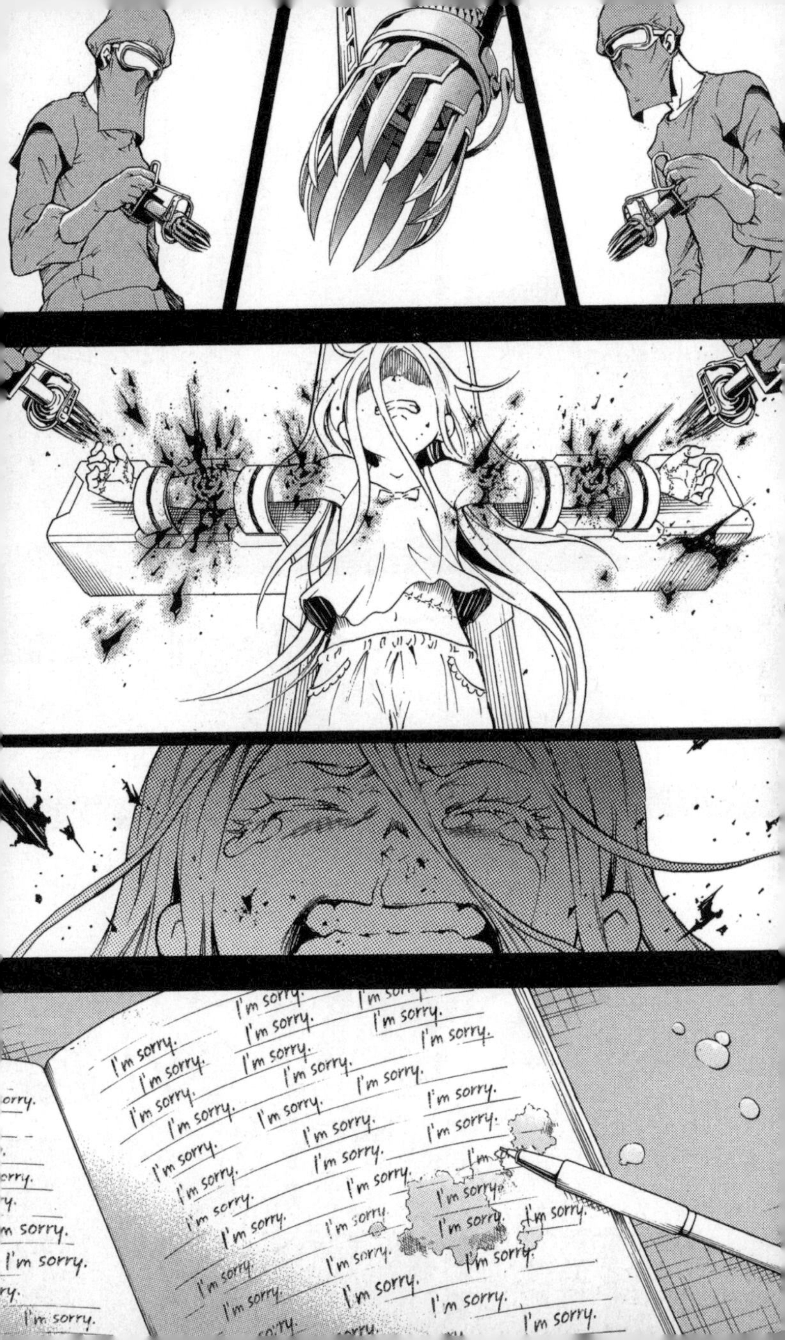
I'm sorry.
I'm sorry.
I'm sorry.
I'm sorry.
I'm sorry.
I'm sorry.
I'm sorry.
I'm sorry.
I'm sorry.
I'm sorry.
I'm sorry.
I'm sorry.
I'm sorry.
I'm sorry.
I'm sorry.
I'm sorry.
I'm sorry.
I'm sorry.
I'm sorry.
I'm sorry.
I'm sorry.
I'm sorry.
I'm sorry.
I'm sorry.
I'm sorry.
I'm sorry.
I'm sorry.
I'm sorry.
I'm sorry.
I'm sorry.

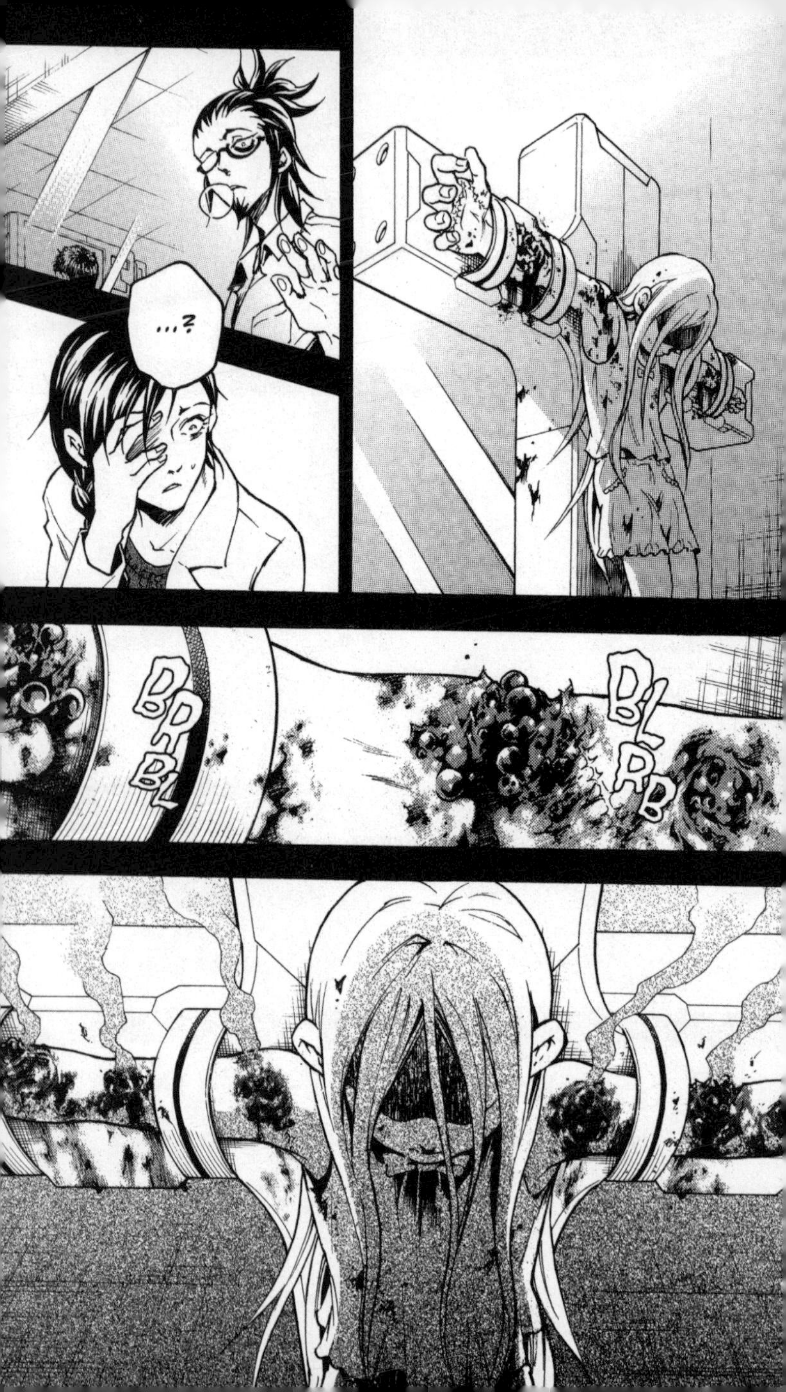
...?
BLRB
BRBL

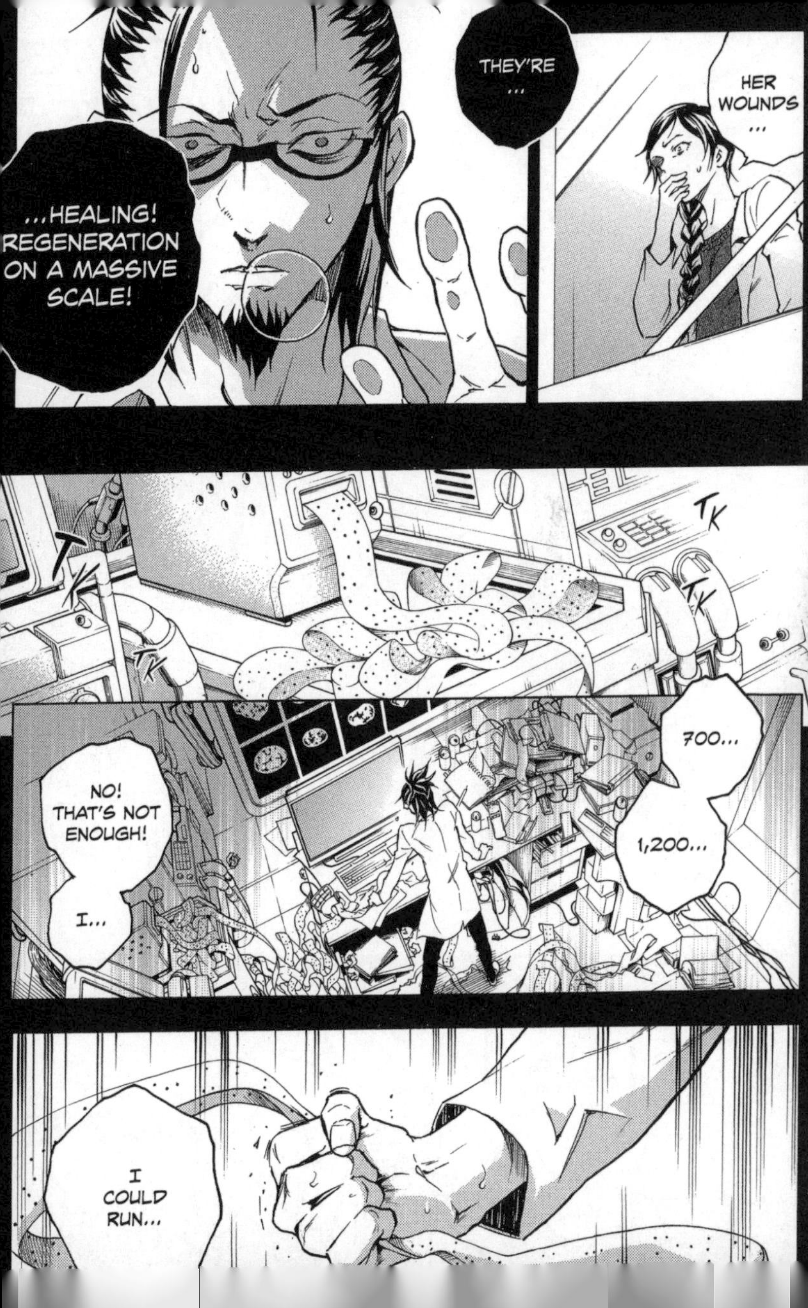
HER WOUNDS ...
THEY'RE ...
...HEALING! REGENERATION ON A MASSIVE SCALE!
TK
TK
TK
TK
700...
1,200...
NO! THAT'S NOT ENOUGH!
I...
I COULD RUN...

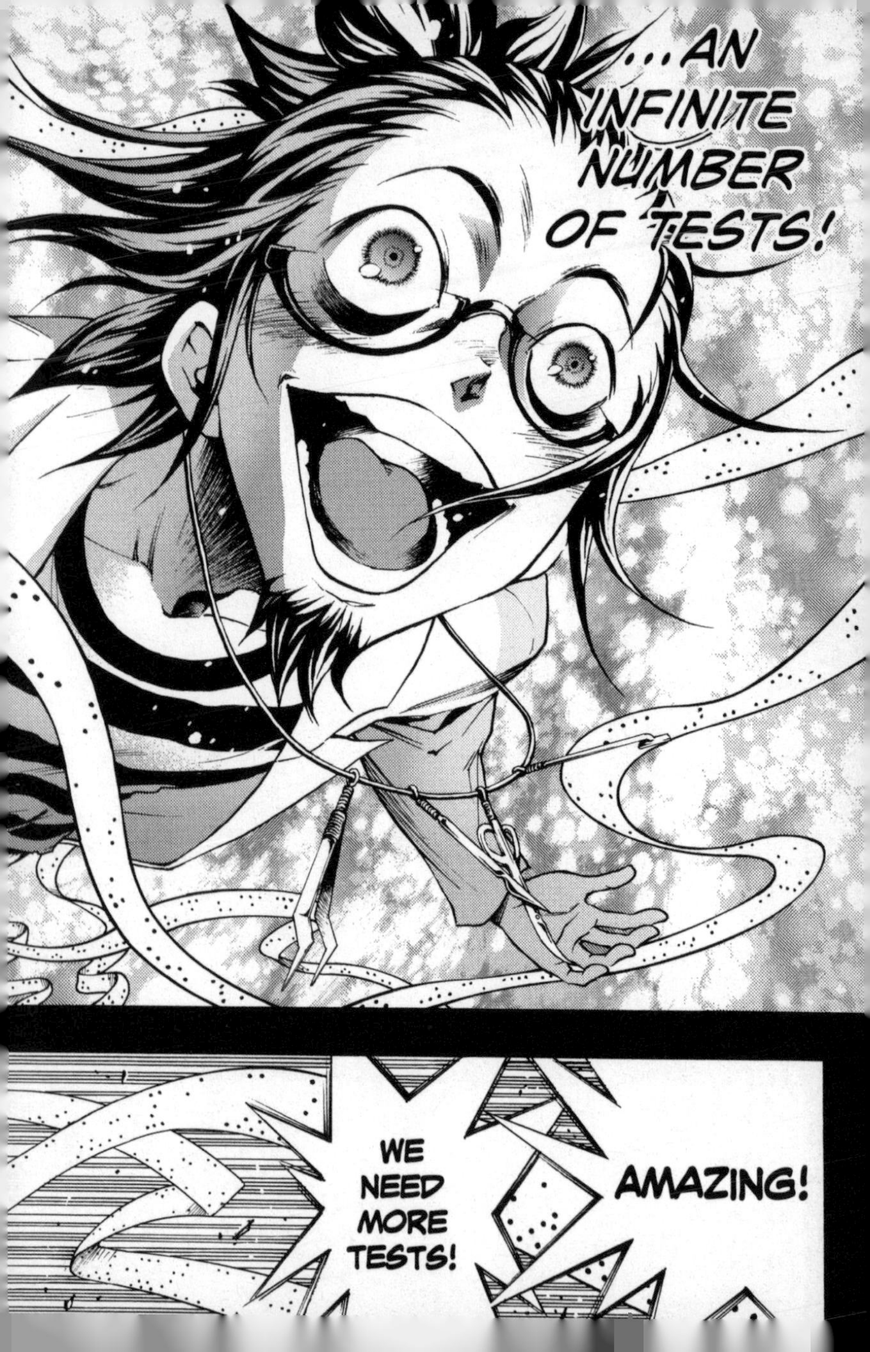
...AN INFINITE NUMBER OF TESTS!
AMAZING!
WE NEED MORE TESTS!

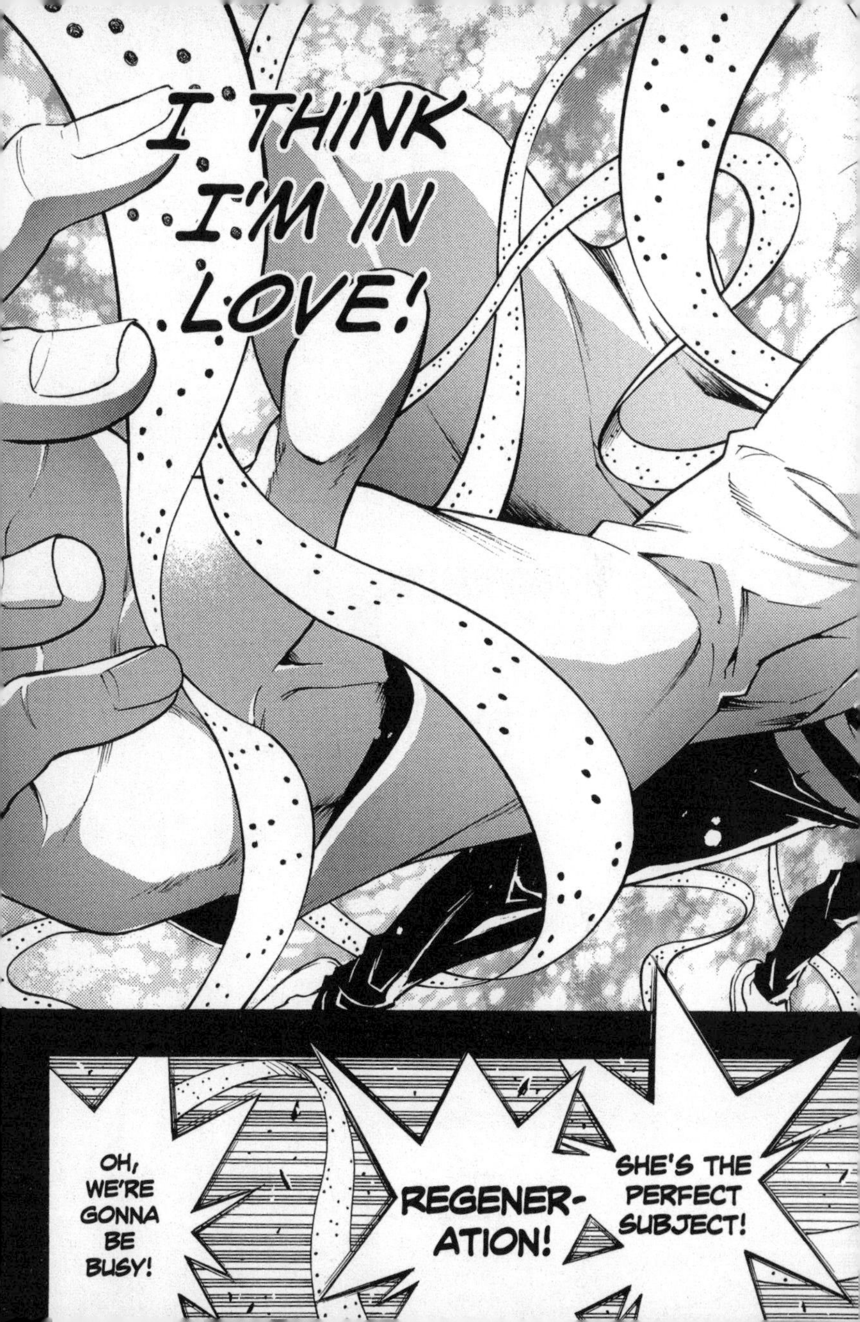
I THINK I'M IN LOVE!
SHE'S THE PERFECT SUBJECT!
REGENER-ATION!
OH, WE'RE GONNA BE BUSY!

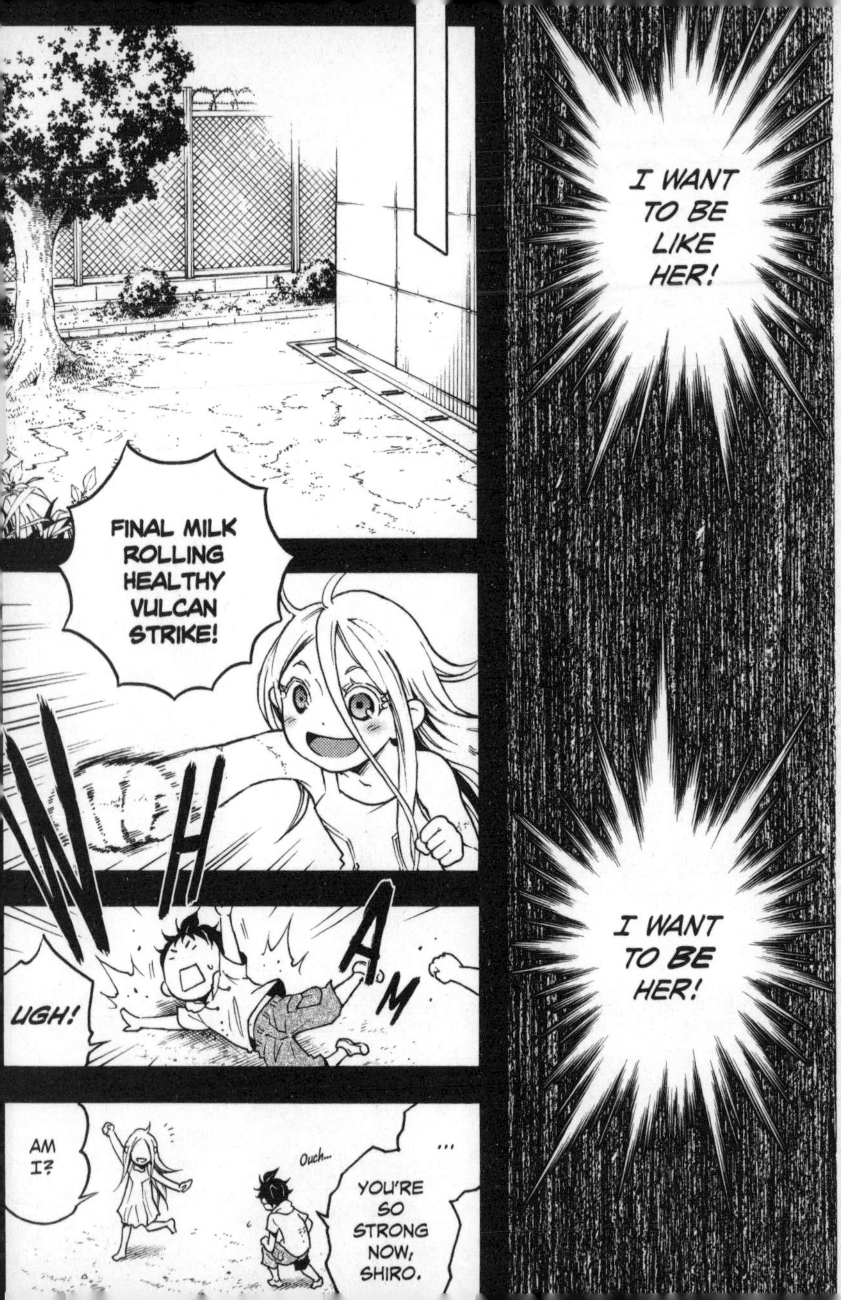
I WANT TO BE LIKE HER!
I WANT TO BE HER!
FINAL MILK ROLLING HEALTHY VULCAN STRIKE!
WHAM
UGH!
...
YOU'RE SO STRONG NOW, SHIRO.
Ouch...
AM I?

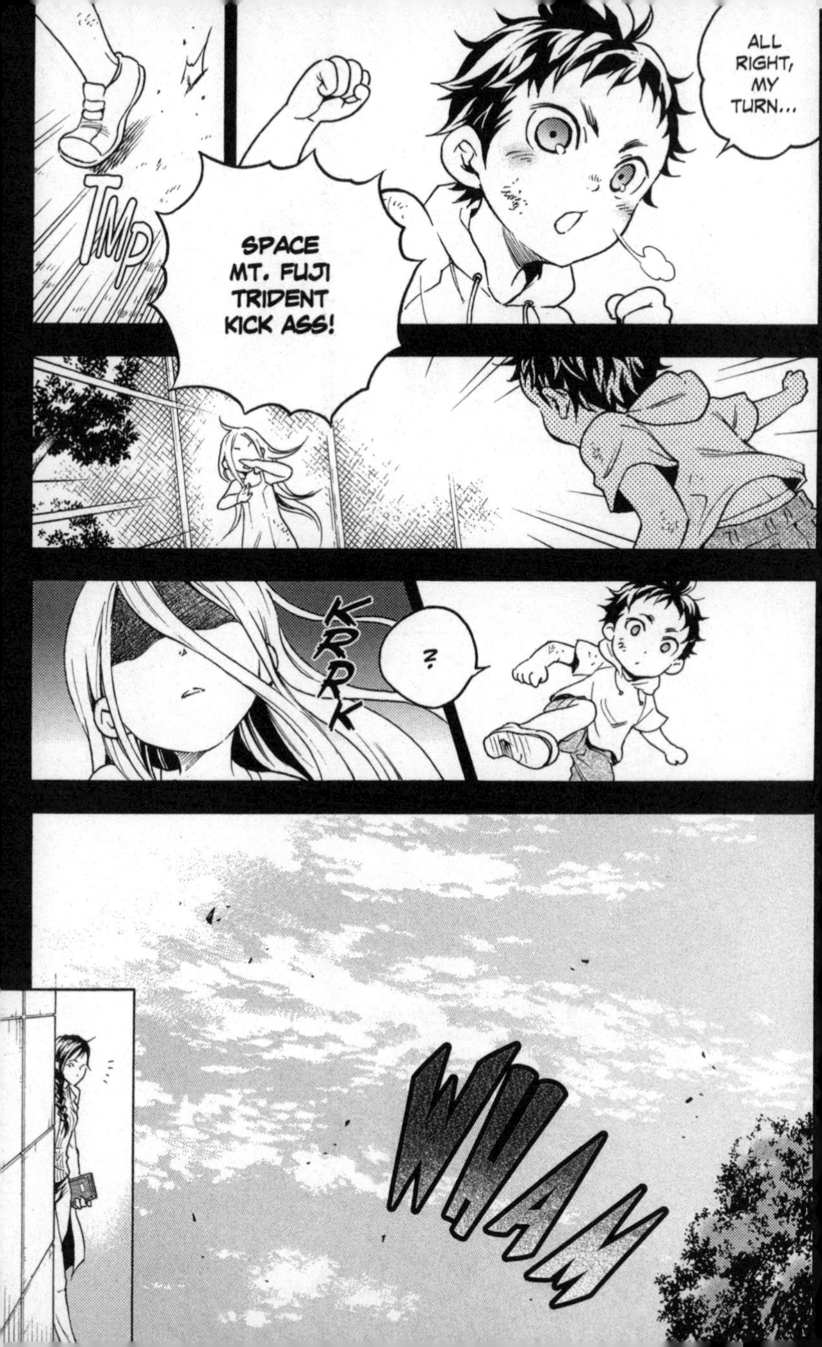
ALL RIGHT, MY TURN...
SPACE MT. FUJI TRIDENT KICK ASS!
TMP
KRRK
?
WHAM

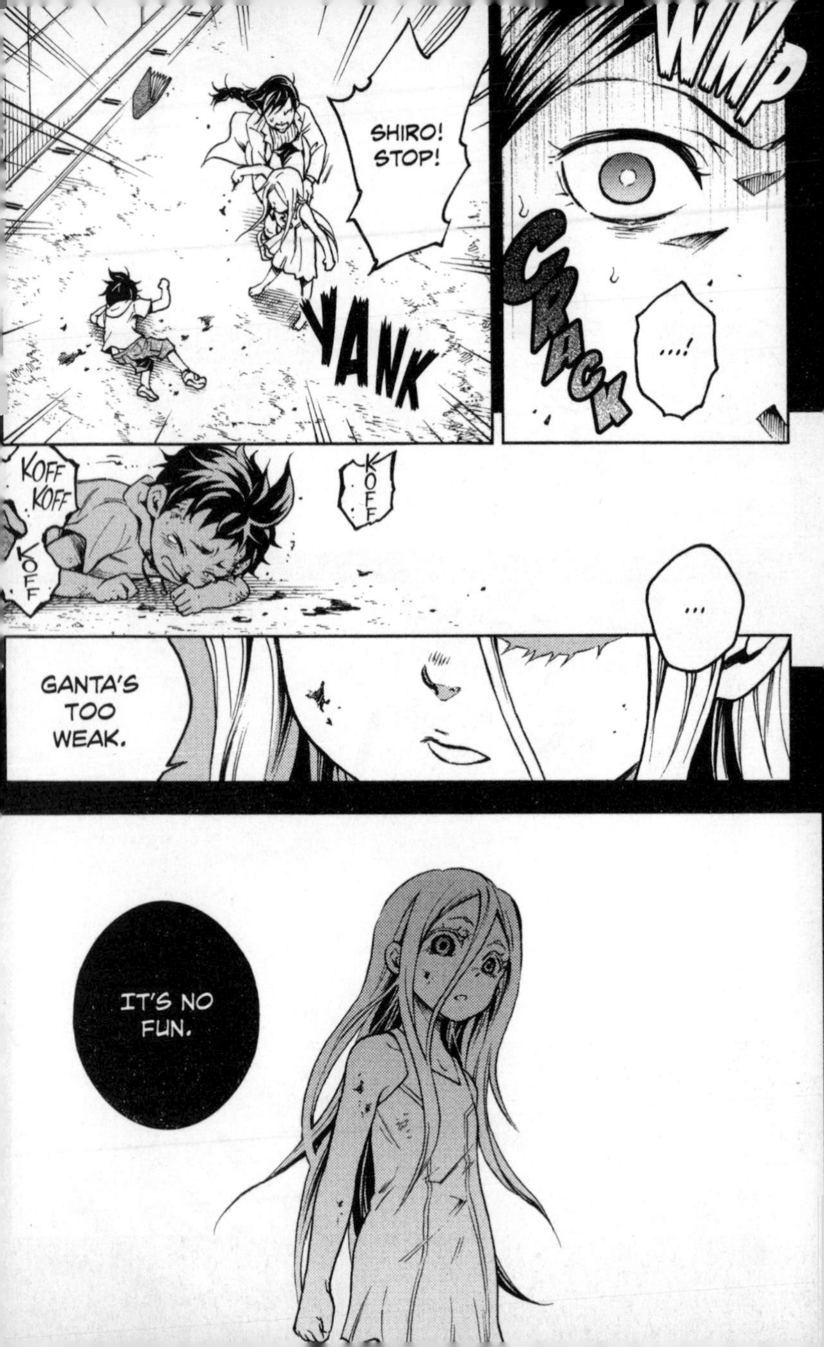
WMP
CRACK
...!
SHIRO! STOP!
YANK
KOFF
KOFF KOFF
KOFF
...
GANTA'S TOO WEAK.
IT'S NO FUN.

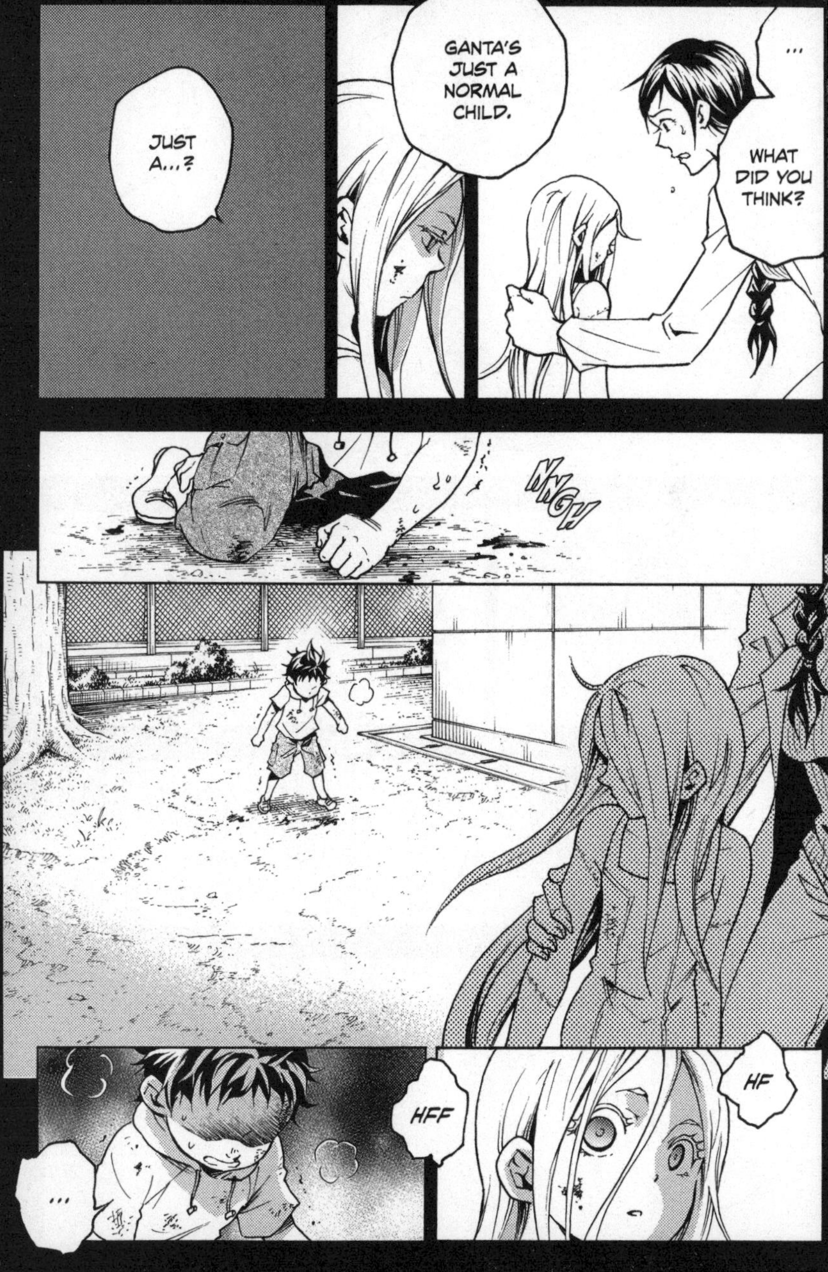
...
WHAT DID YOU THINK?
GANTA'S JUST A NORMAL CHILD.
JUST A...?
NNGH
HF
HFF
...

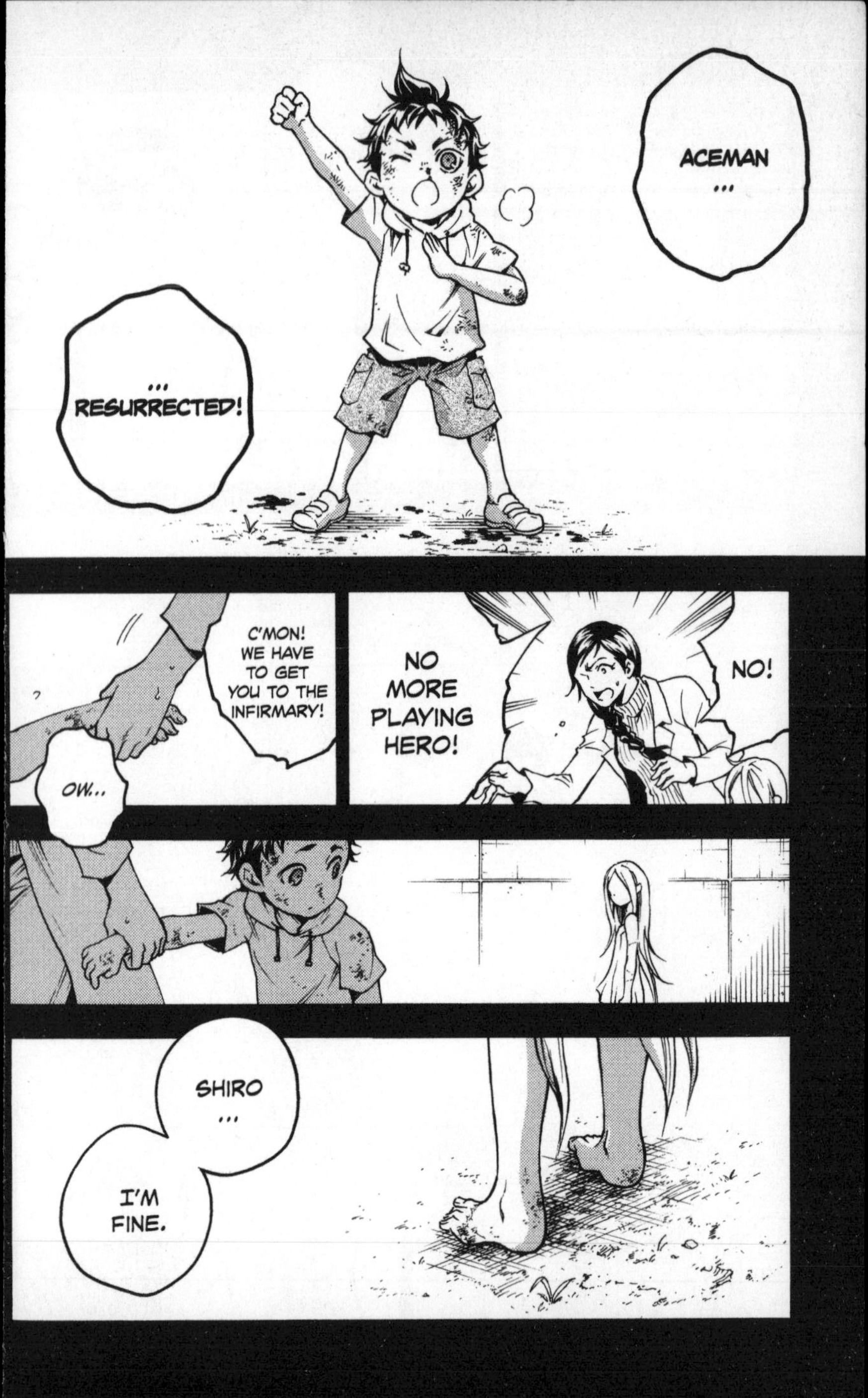
ACEMAN ...
... RESURRECTED!
NO!
NO MORE PLAYING HERO!
C'MON! WE HAVE TO GET YOU TO THE INFIRMARY!
OW...
SHIRO ...
I'M FINE.

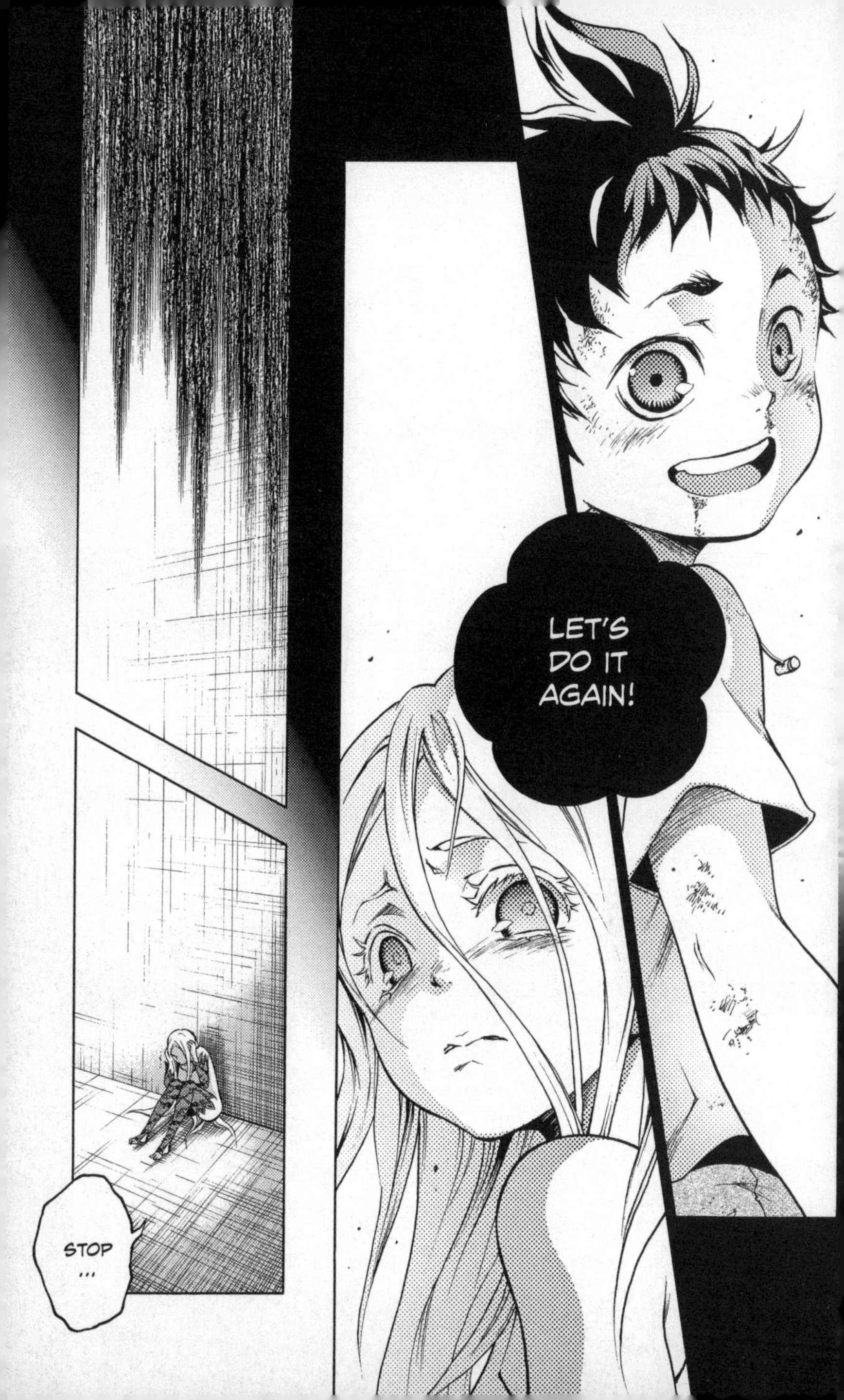
LET'S DO IT AGAIN!
STOP ...

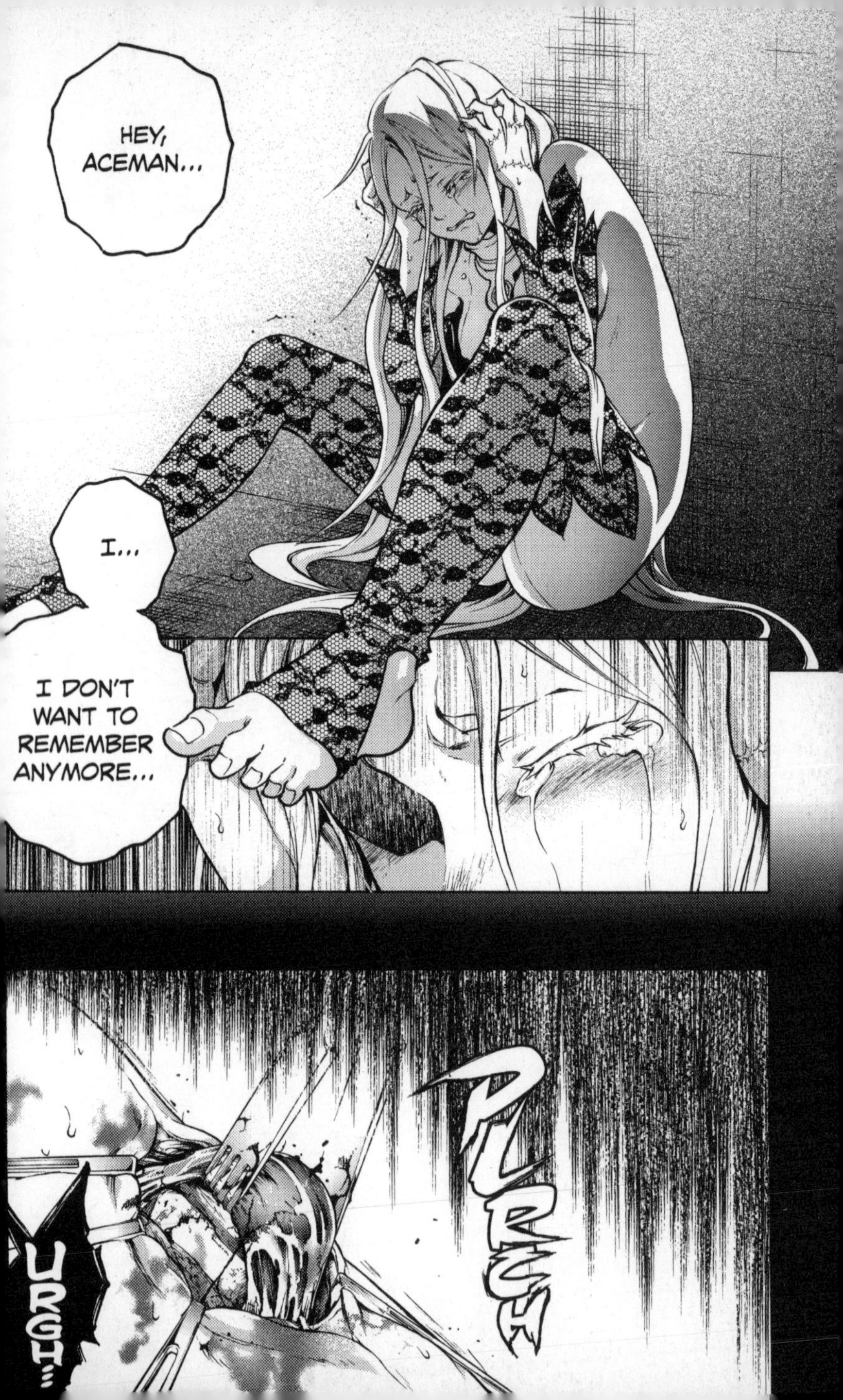
HEY, ACEMAN...
I...
I DON'T WANT TO REMEMBER ANYMORE...
PLURCH
URGH...

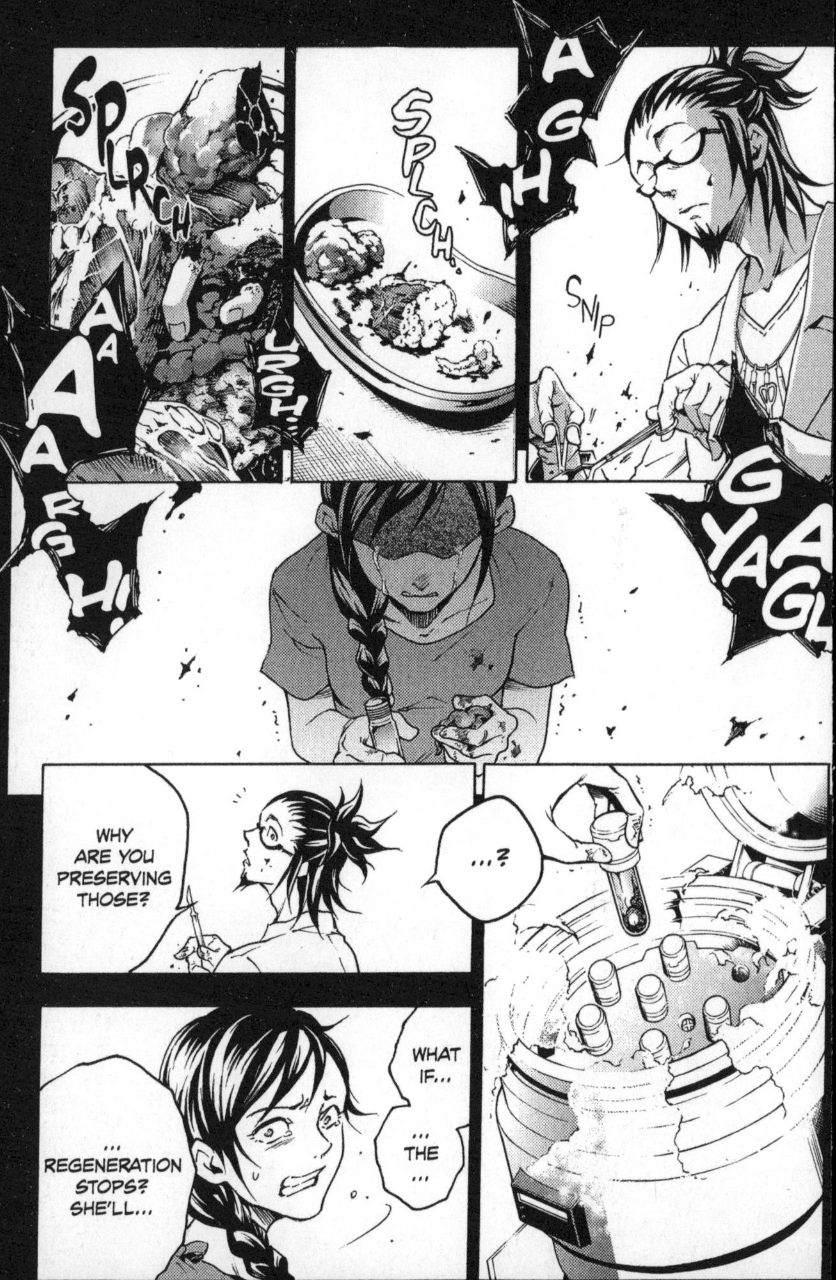
AGH!
SNIP
SPLCH
SPLRCH
URGH!
AAAARGH!
GYAAGL
...?
WHY ARE YOU PRESERVING THOSE?
WHAT IF...
...THE ...
... REGENERATION STOPS? SHE'LL...

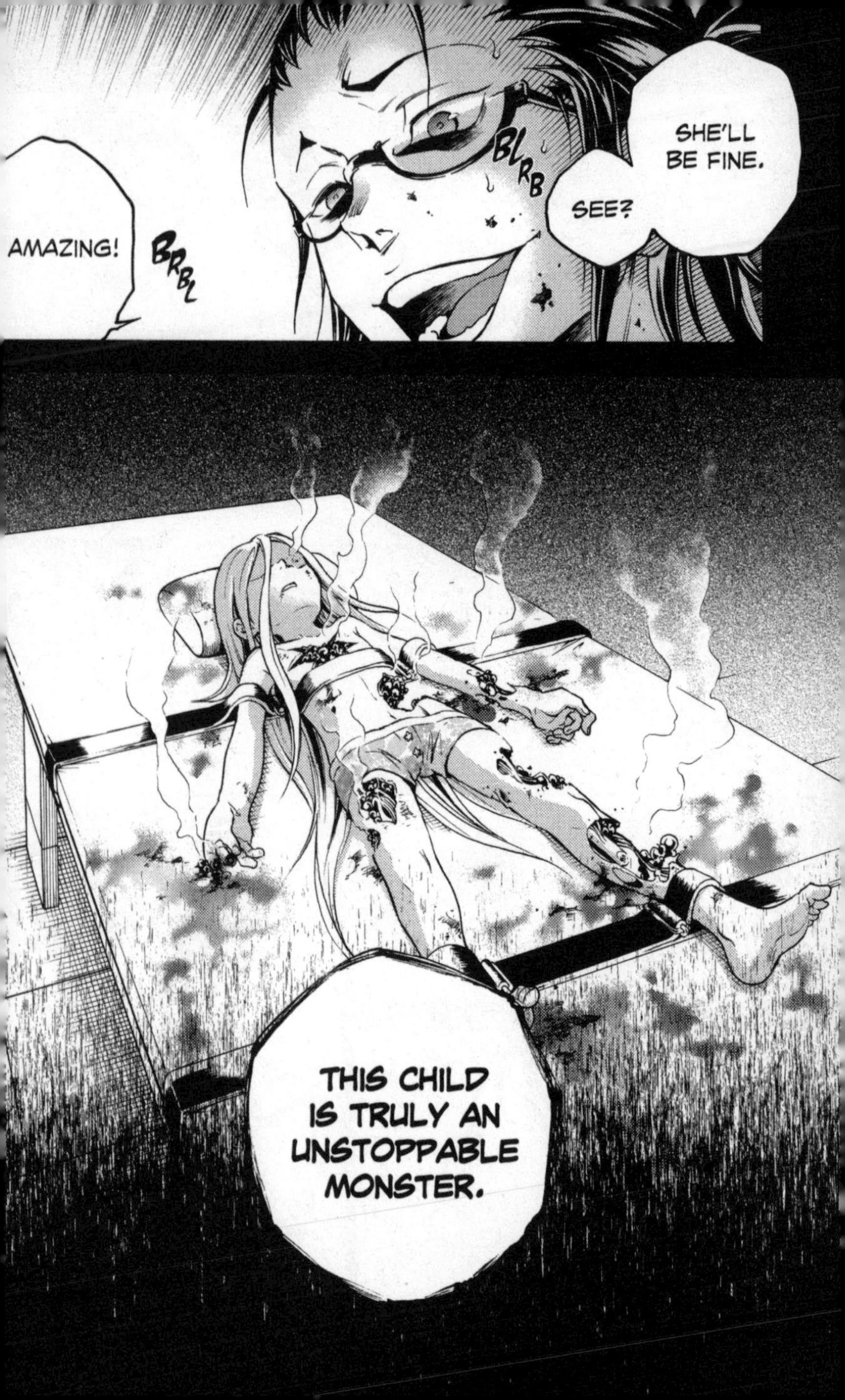
SHE'LL BE FINE.
SEE?
BLRB
BRBL
AMAZING!
THIS CHILD IS TRULY AN UNSTOPPABLE MONSTER.

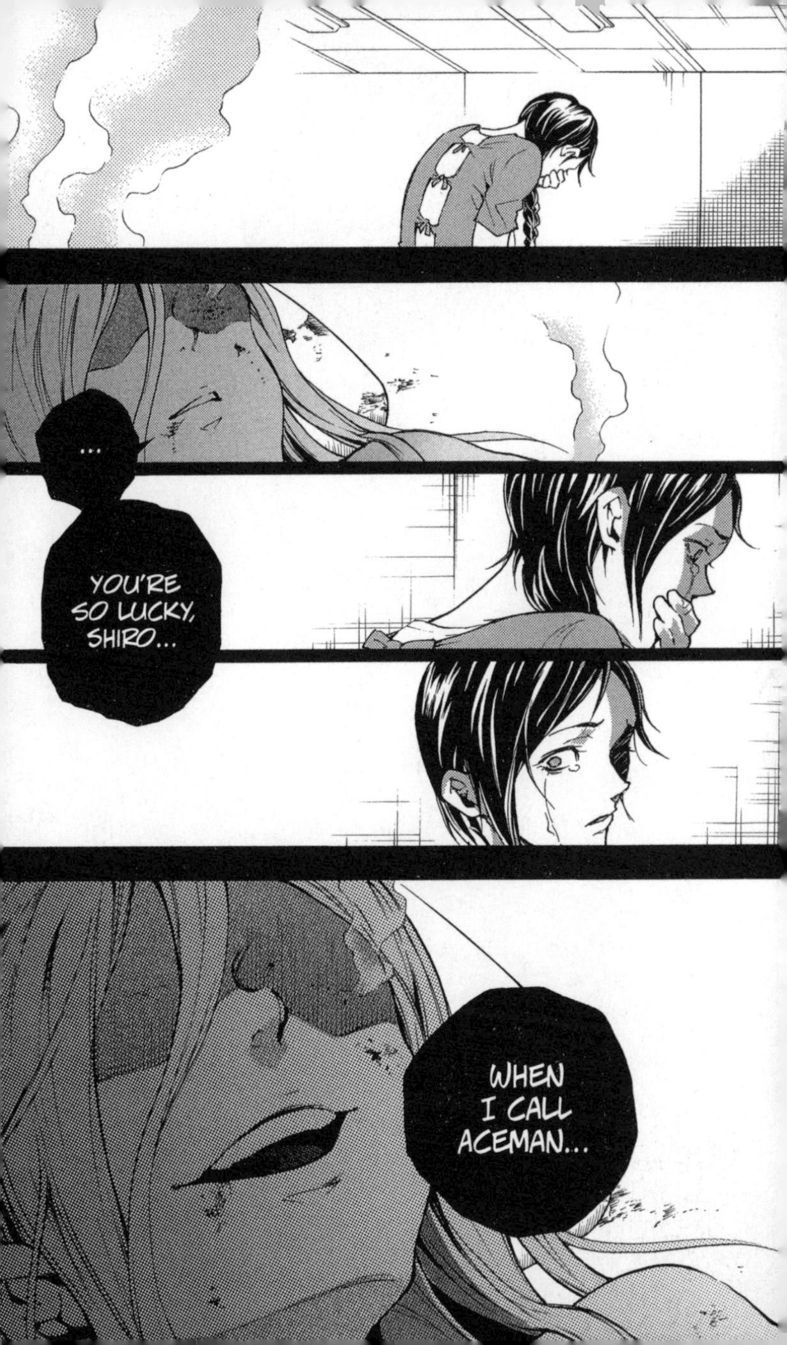
...
YOU'RE SO LUCKY, SHIRO...
WHEN I CALL ACEMAN...

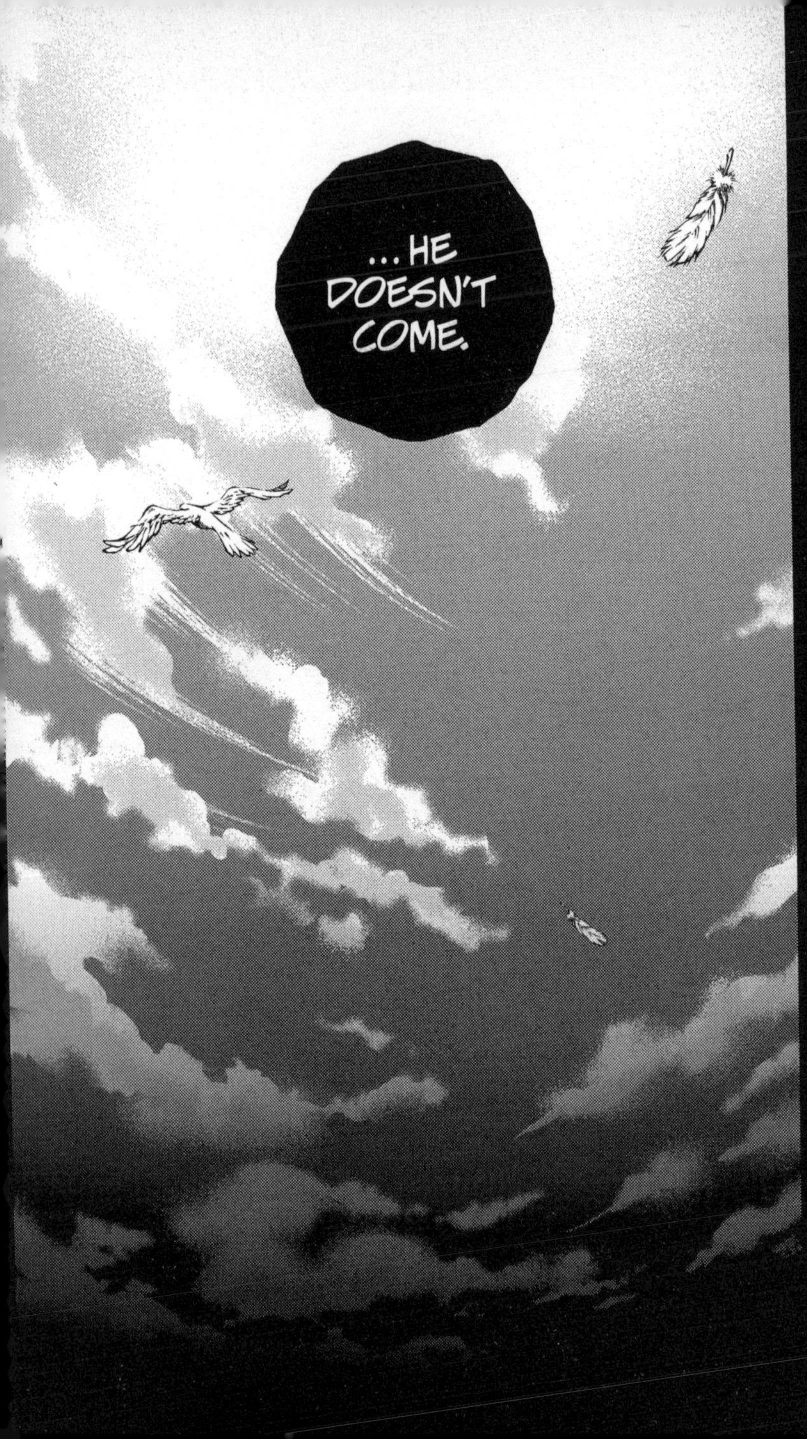
...HE DOESN'T COME.

DEADMAN
WONDE
LAND

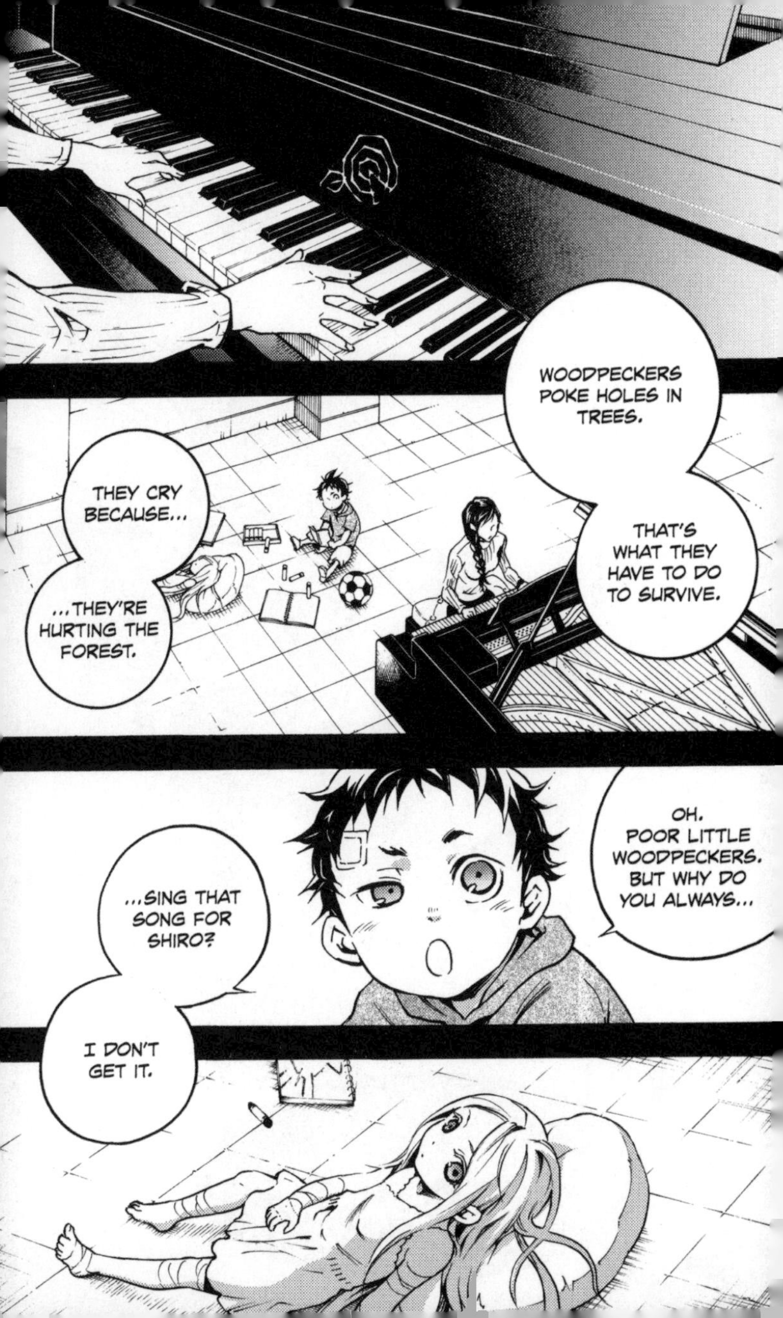
WOODPECKERS POKE HOLES IN TREES.
THAT'S WHAT THEY HAVE TO DO TO SURVIVE.
THEY CRY BECAUSE...
...THEY'RE HURTING THE FOREST.
OH. POOR LITTLE WOODPECKERS. BUT WHY DO YOU ALWAYS...
...SING THAT SONG FOR SHIRO?
I DON'T GET IT.

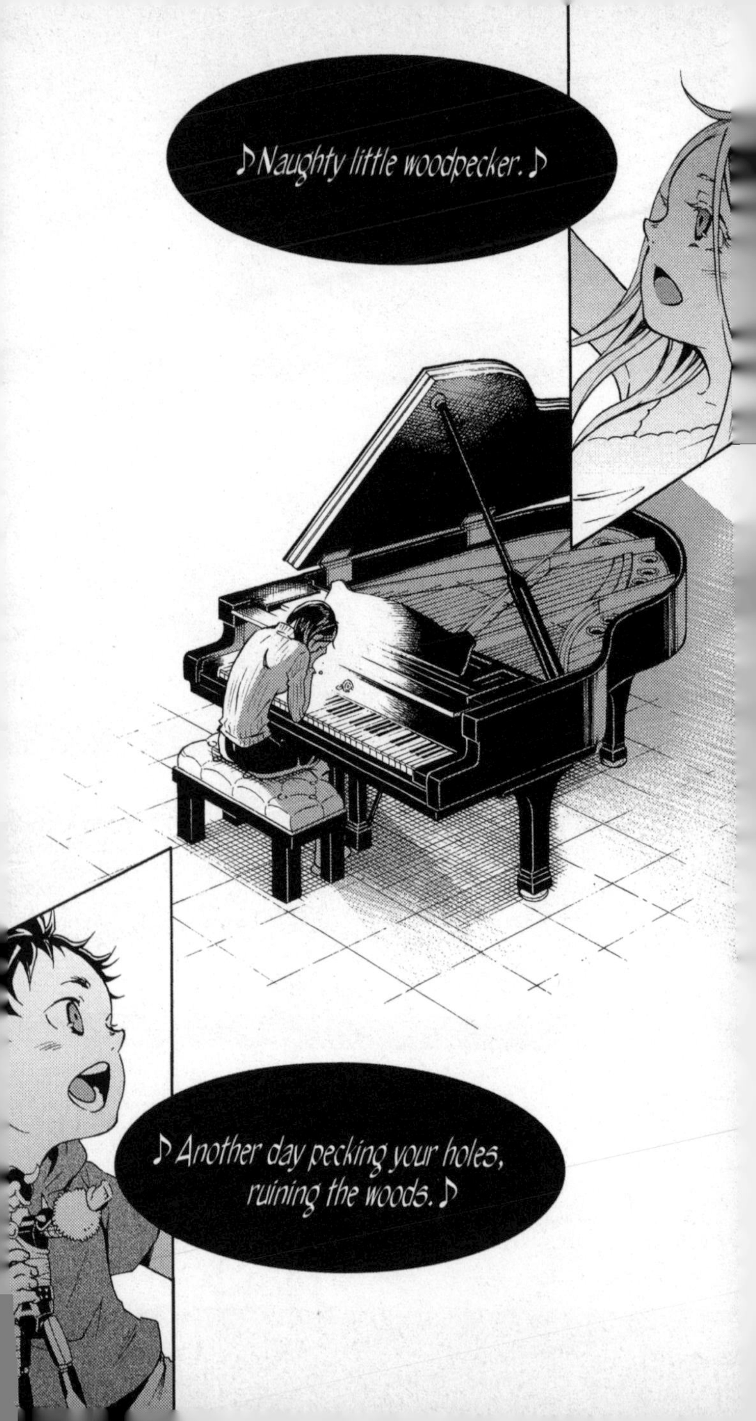
♪Naughty little woodpecker.♪
♪Another day pecking your holes, ruining the woods.♪

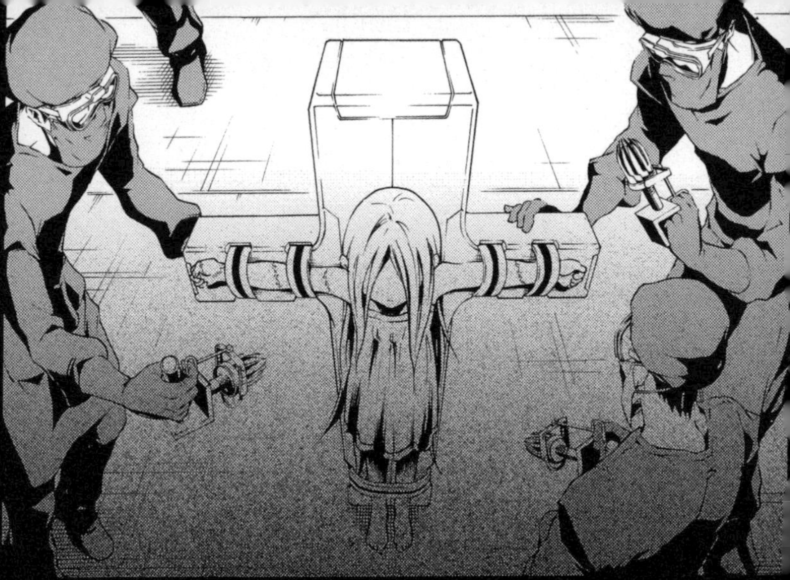

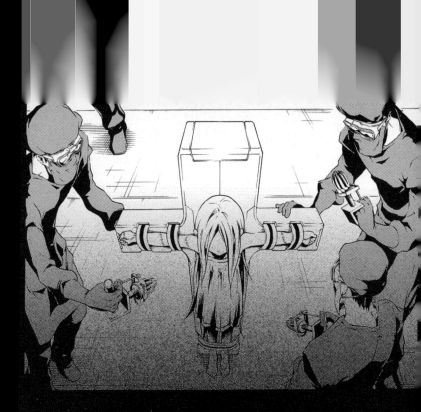

Poor little woodpecker. ♪

Your nest is tainted. Your food with toxins rife. ♪

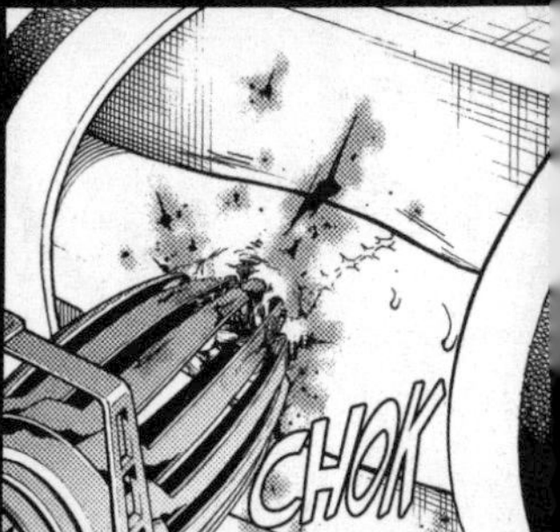
CHOK

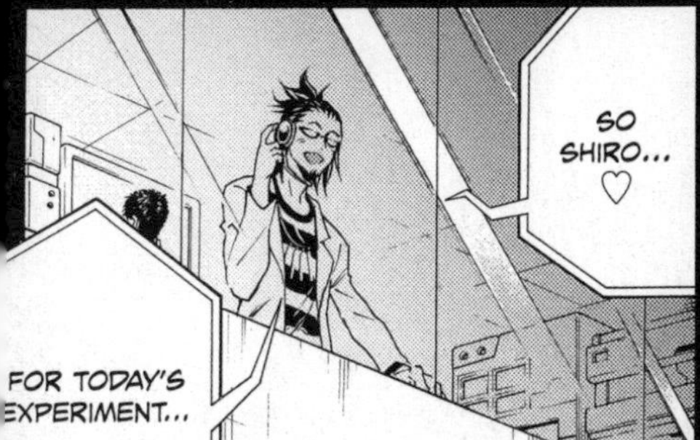
SO SHIRO... ♡
FOR TODAY'S EXPERIMENT...

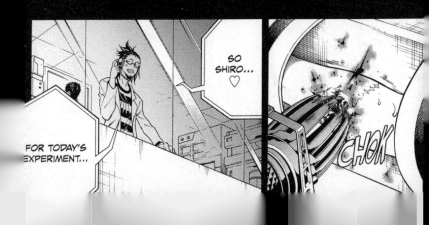

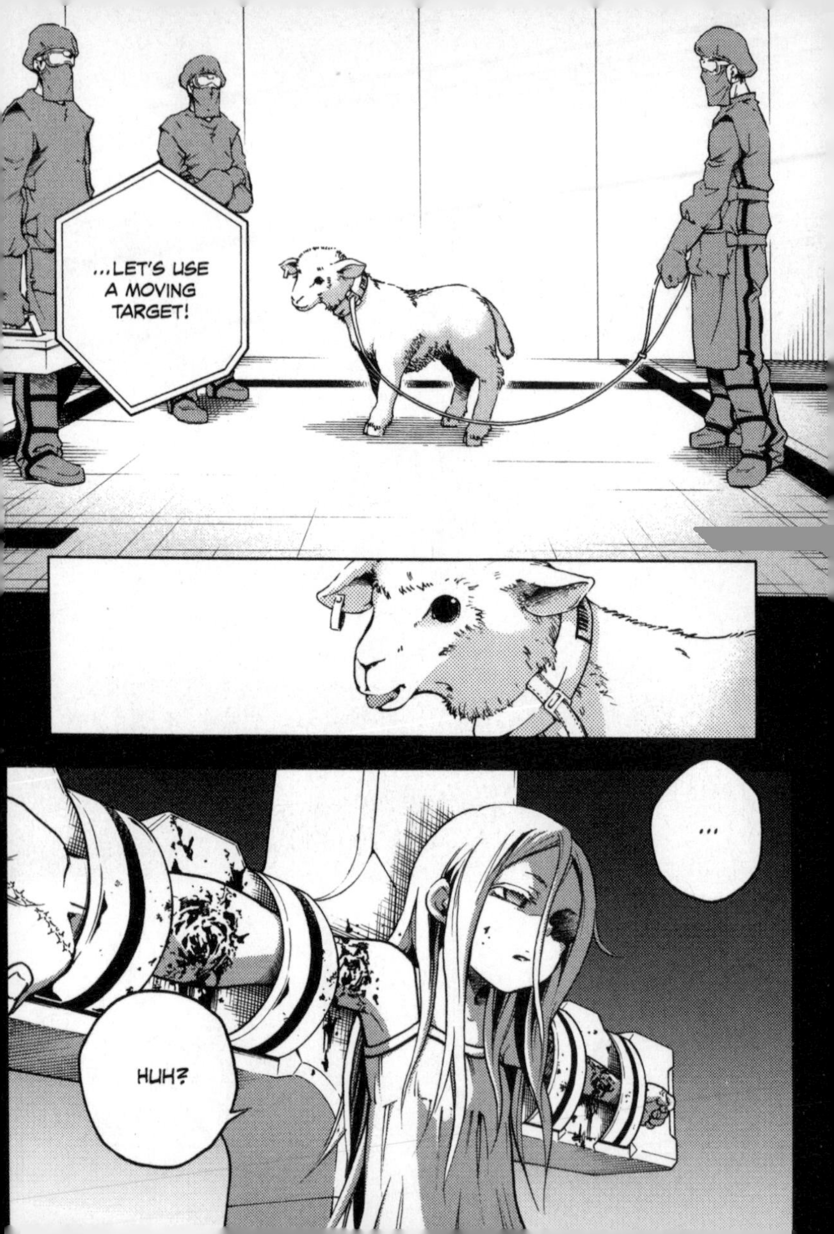
...LET'S USE A MOVING TARGET!
...
HUH?

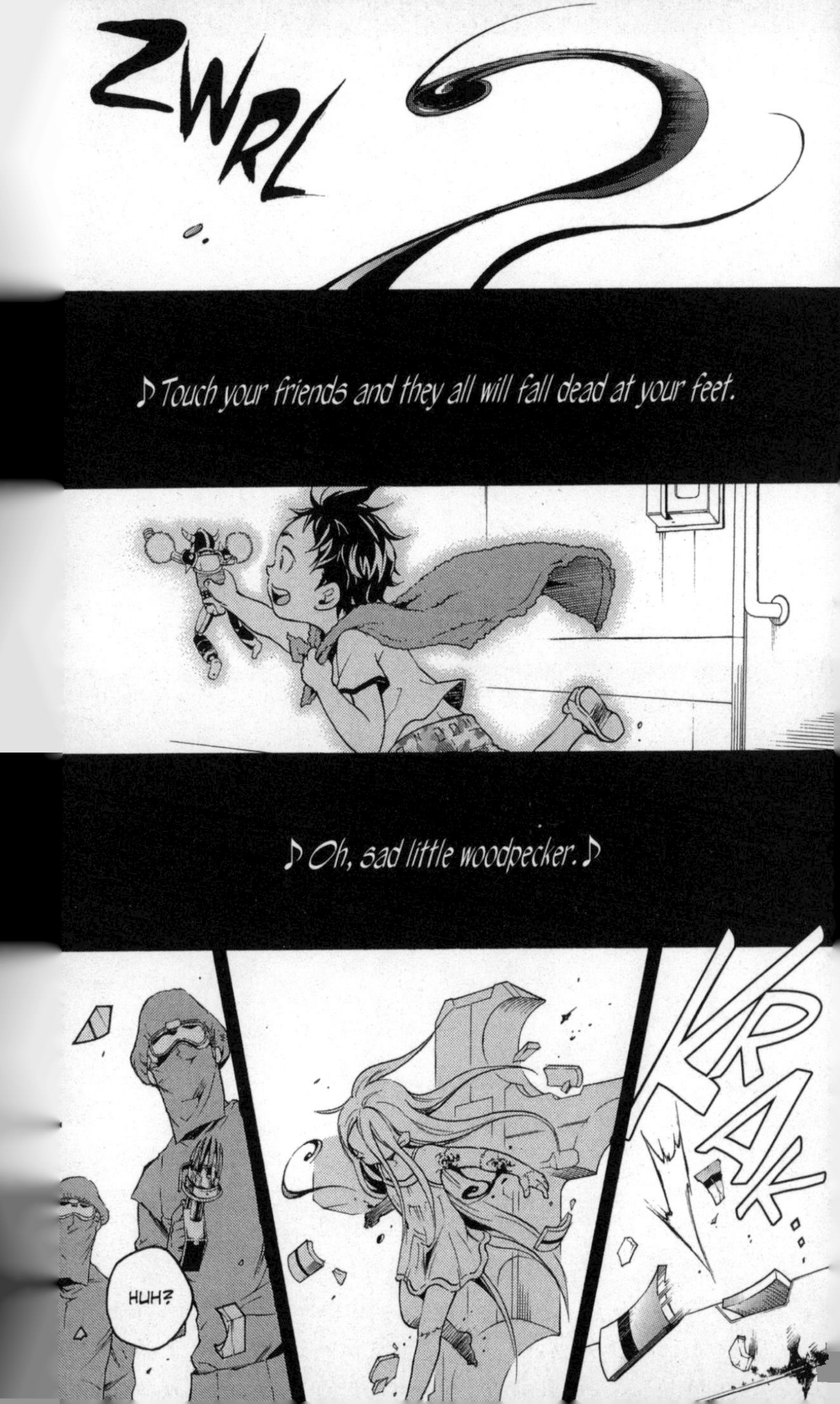
ZWRL
♪Touch your friends and they all will fall dead at your feet.
♪Oh, sad little woodpecker.♪
KRAK
HUH?

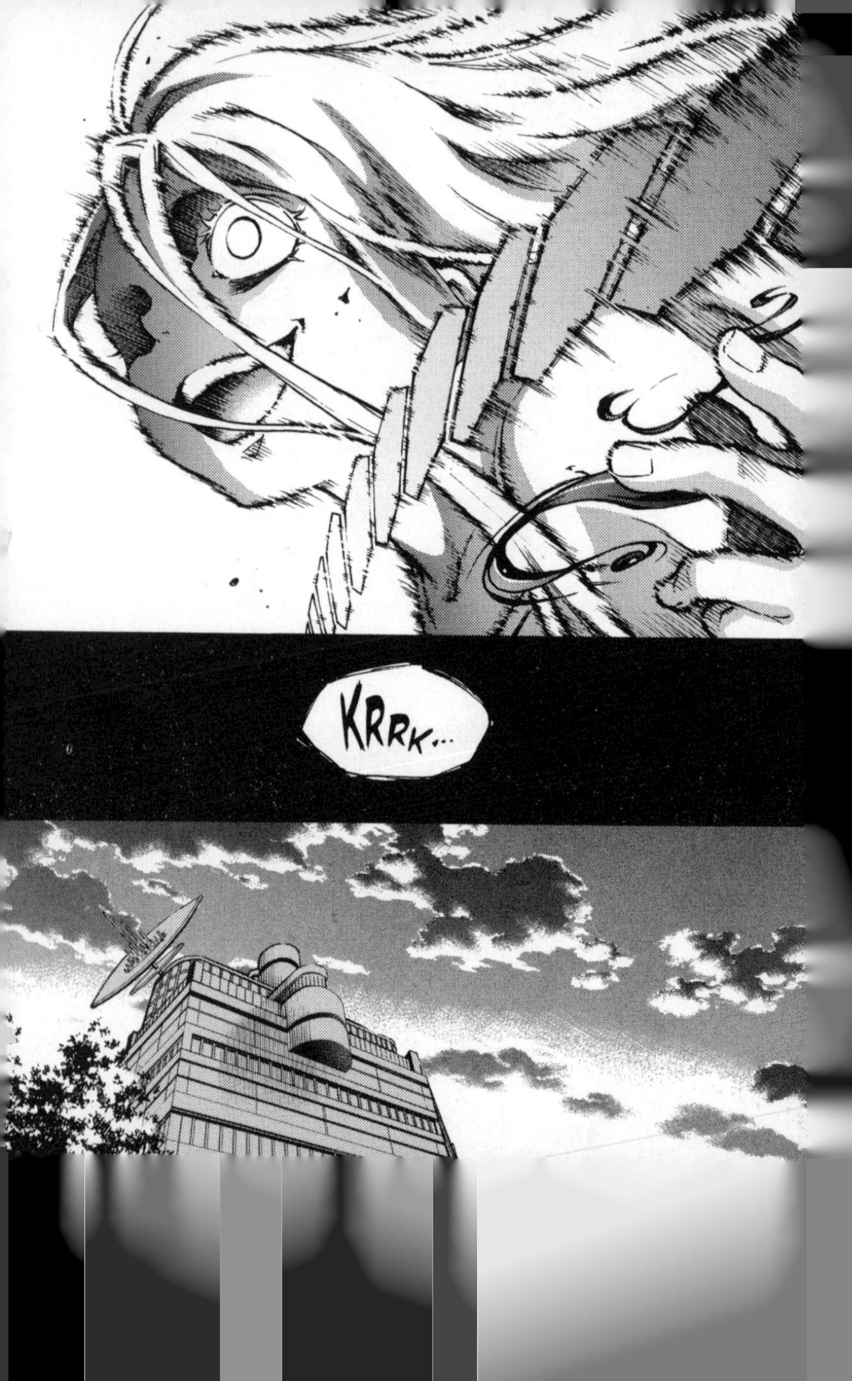
KRRK...

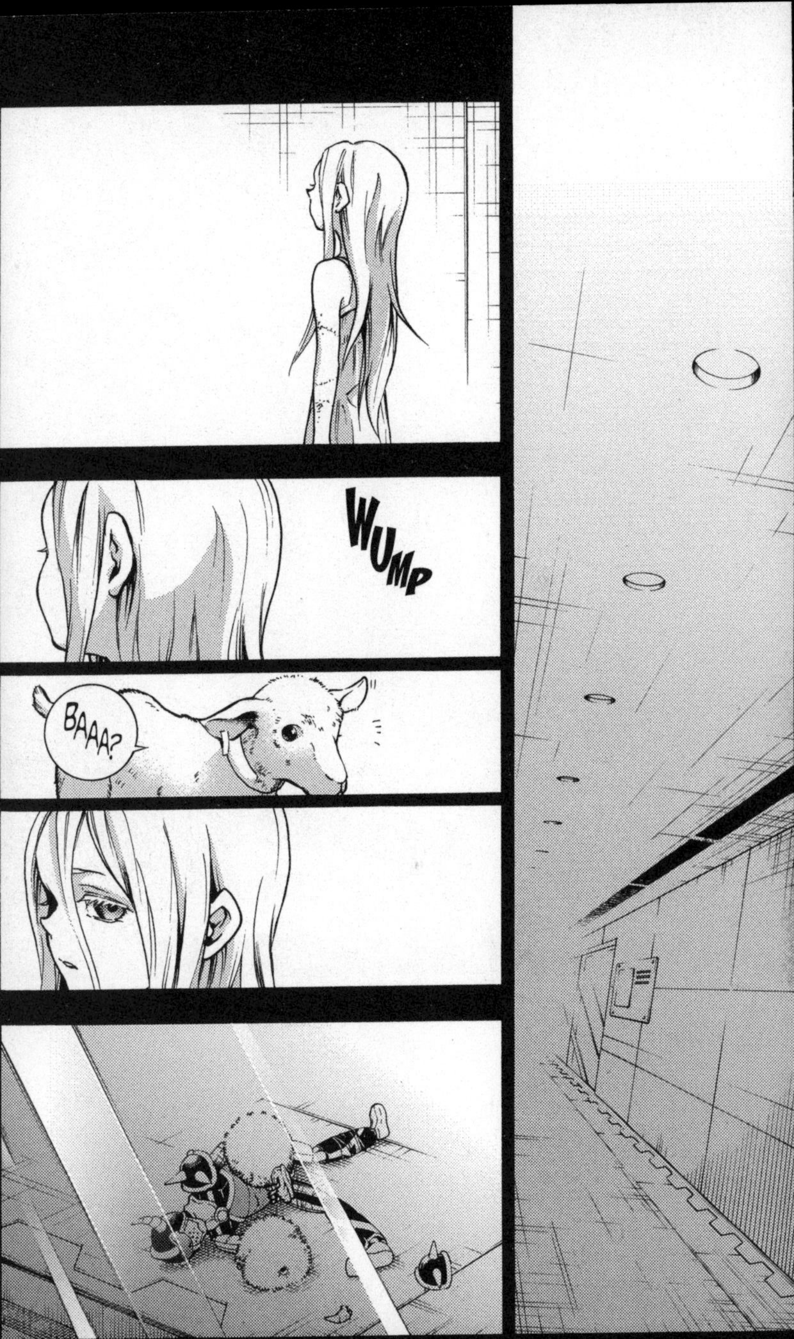
WUMP
BAAA?

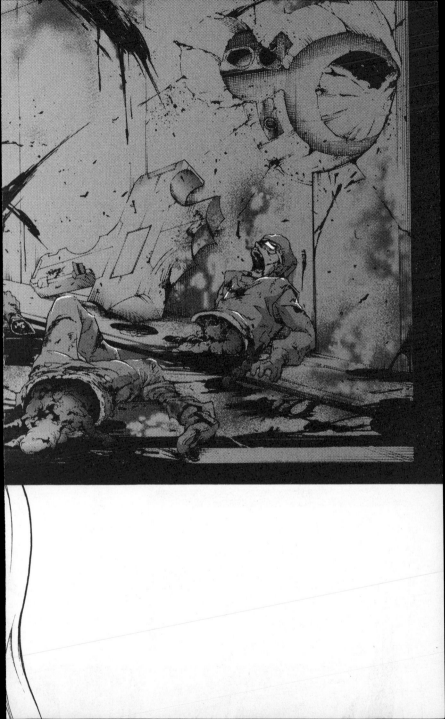

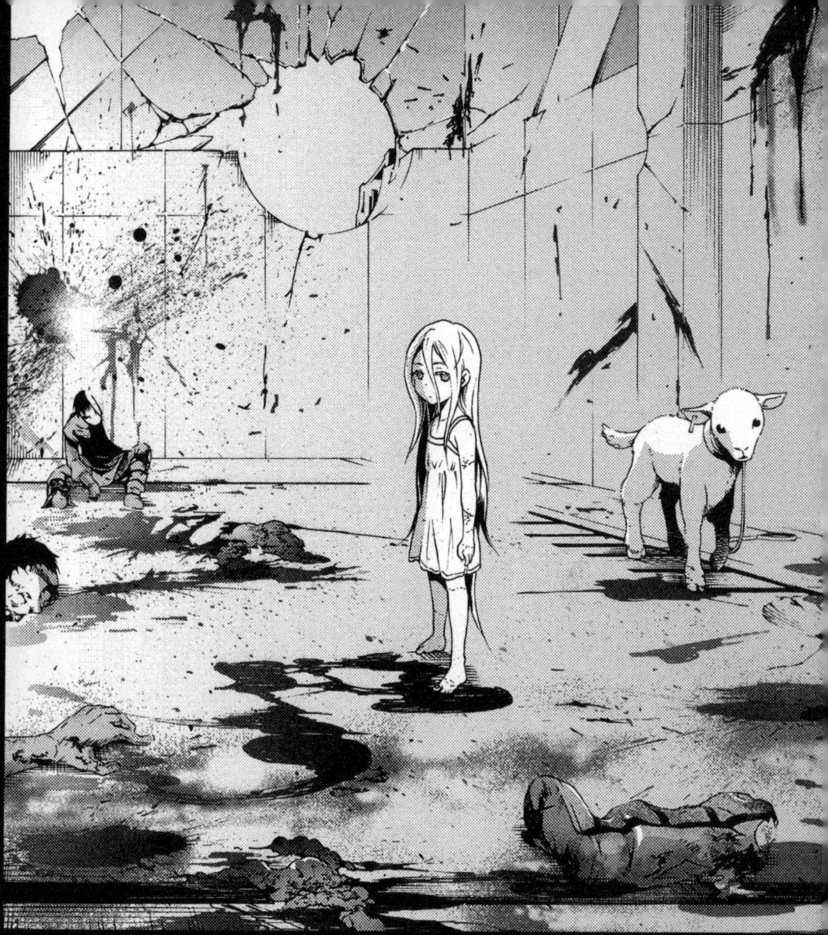
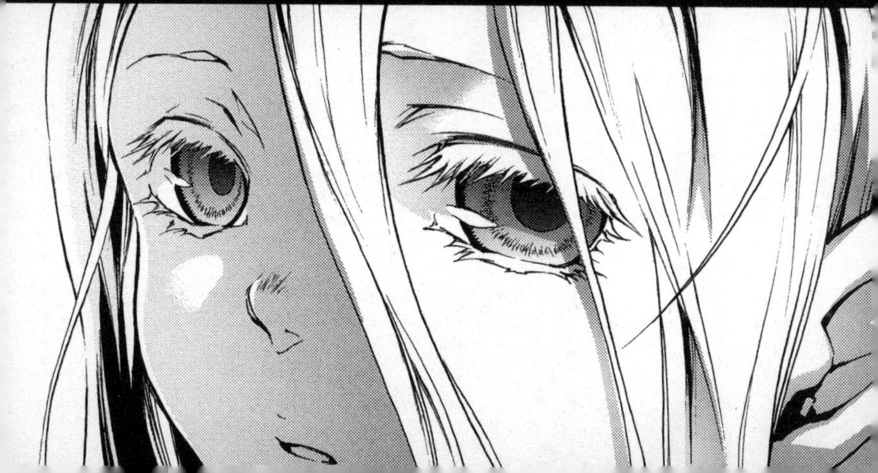

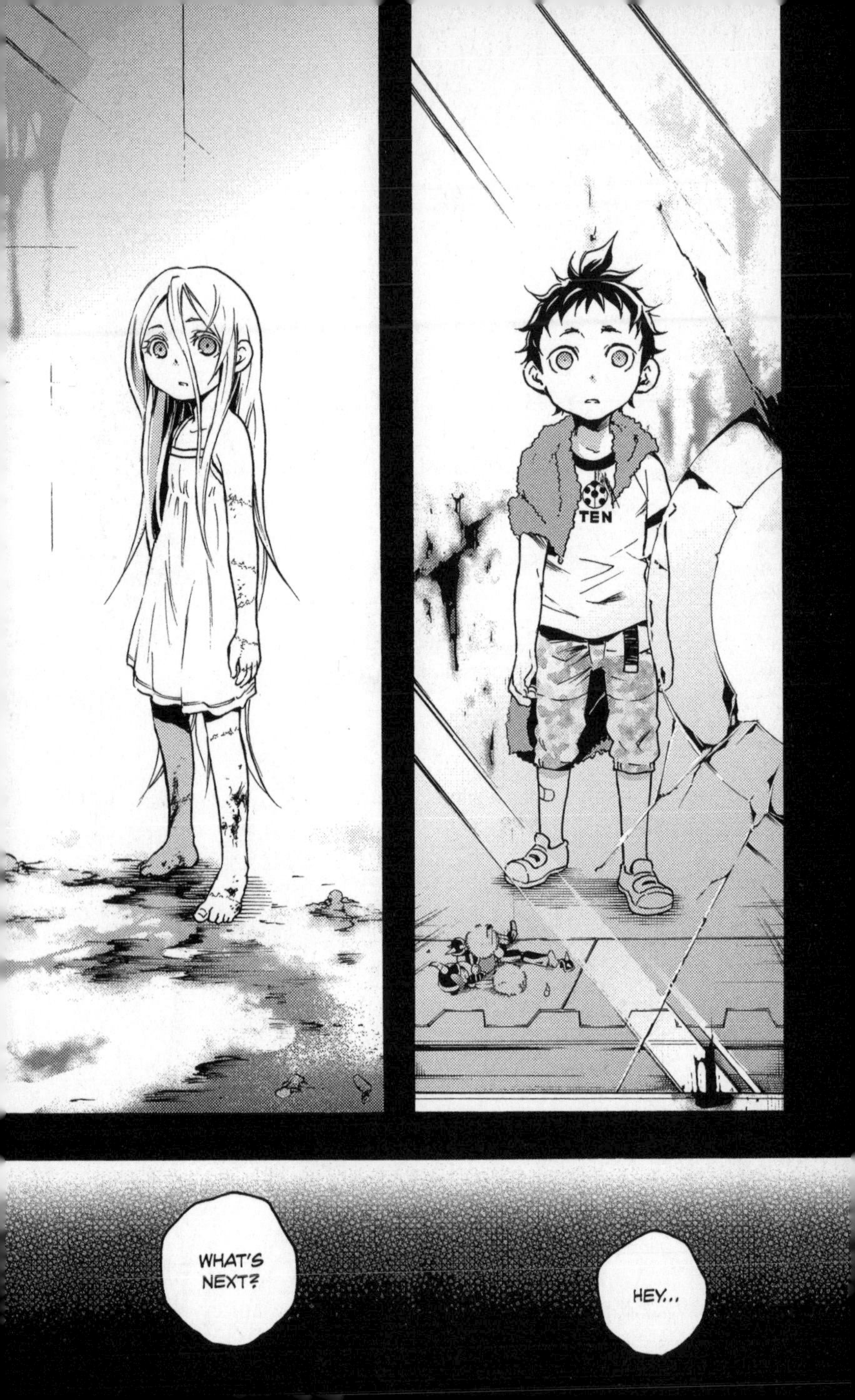
TEN
HEY...
WHAT'S NEXT?

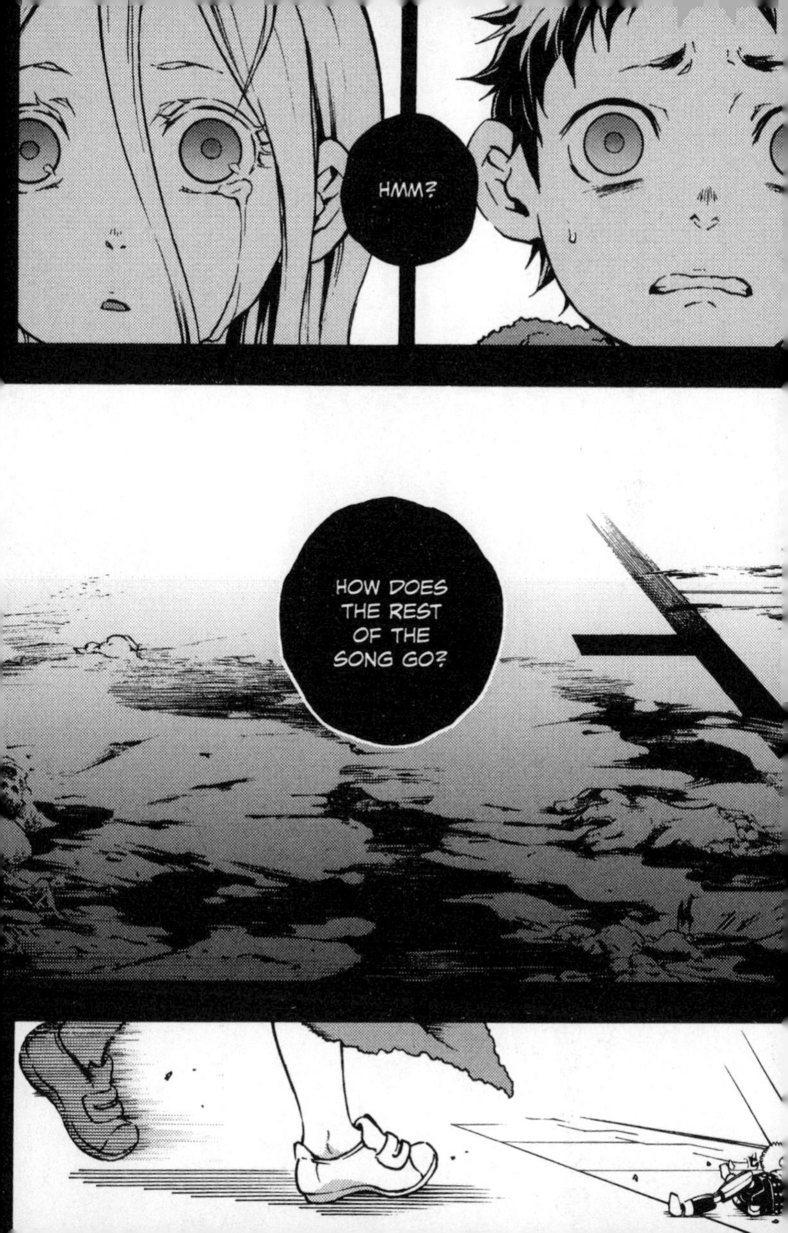
HMM?
HOW DOES THE REST OF THE SONG GO?

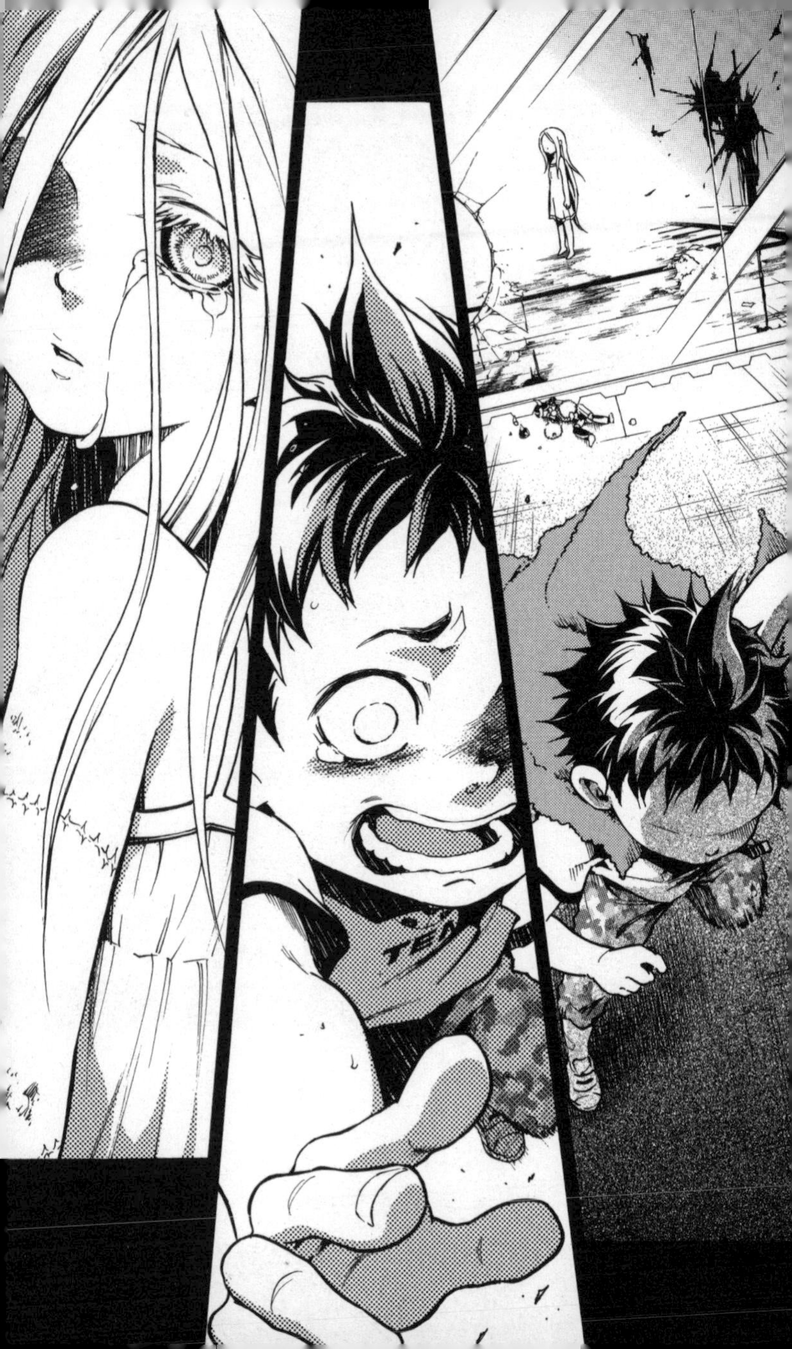

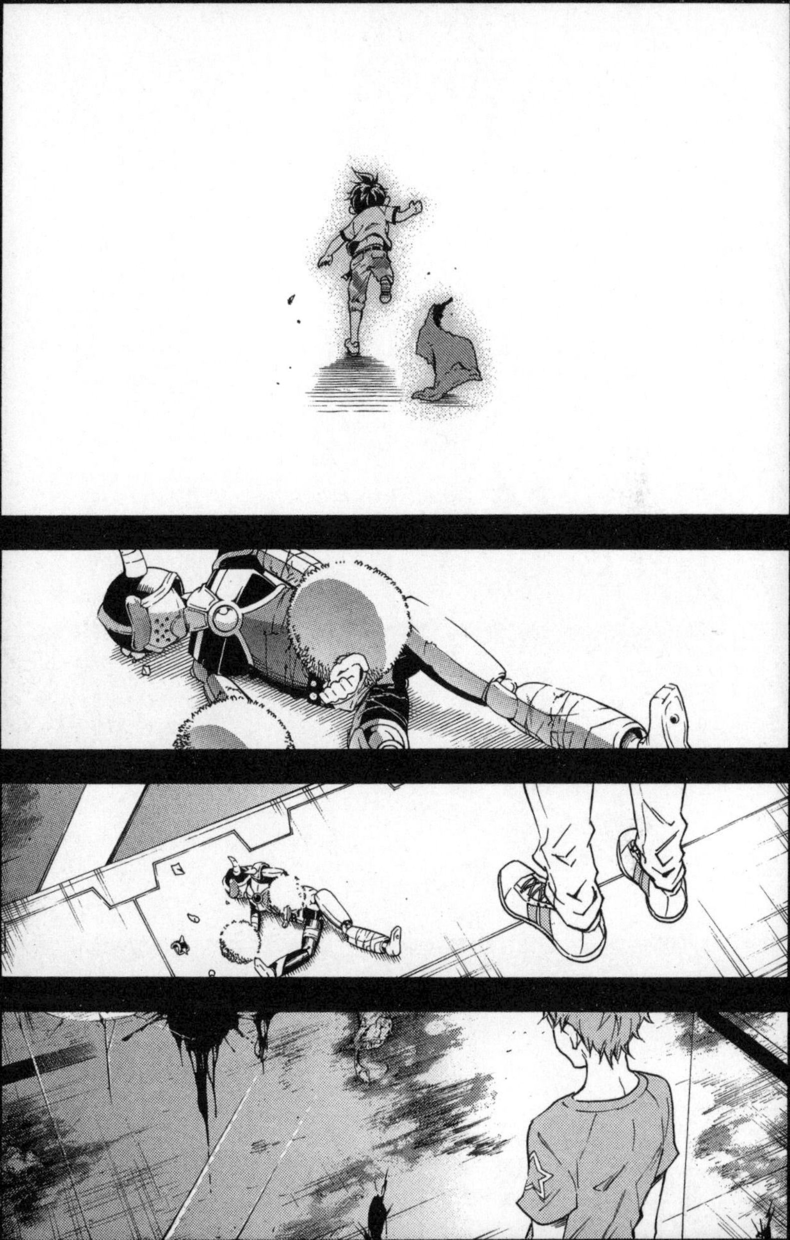

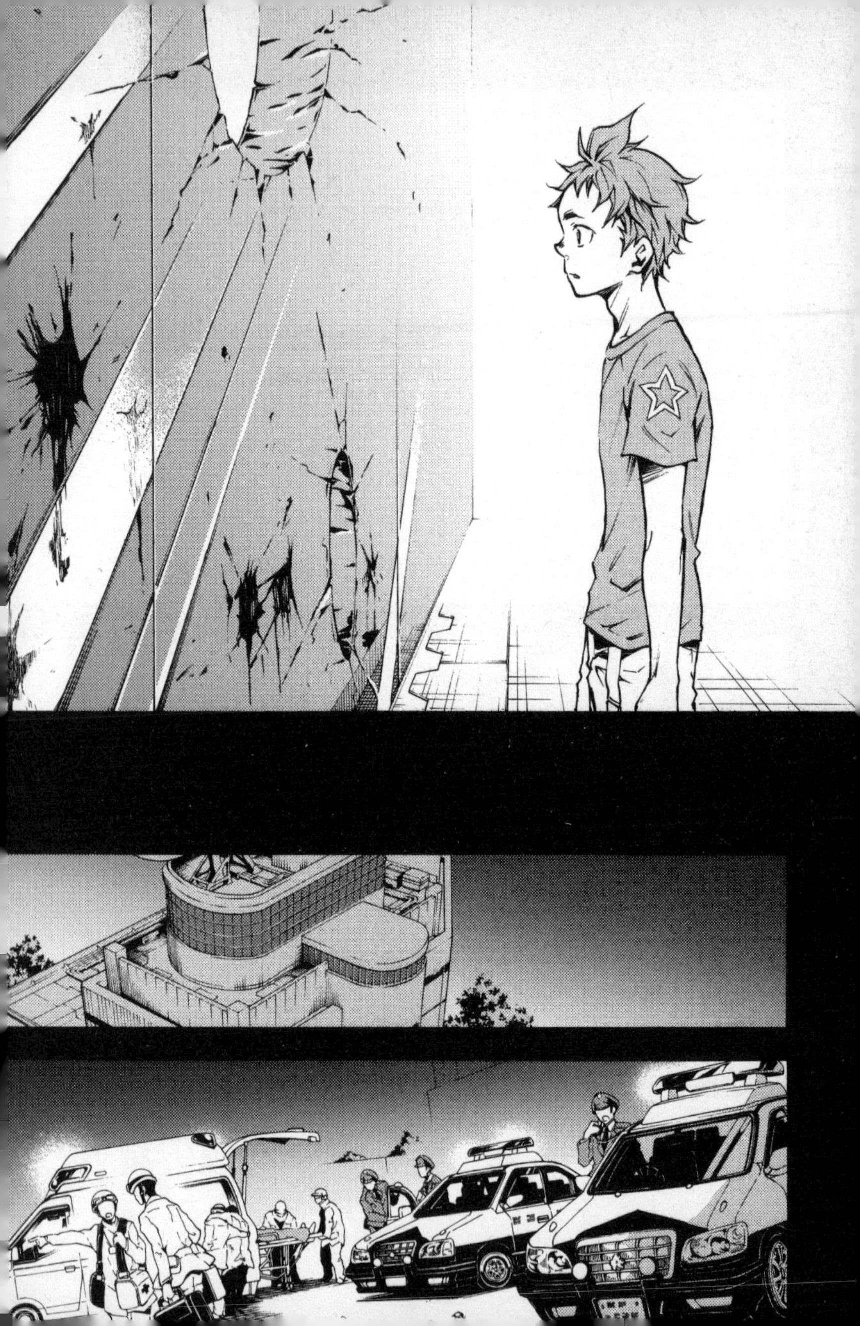

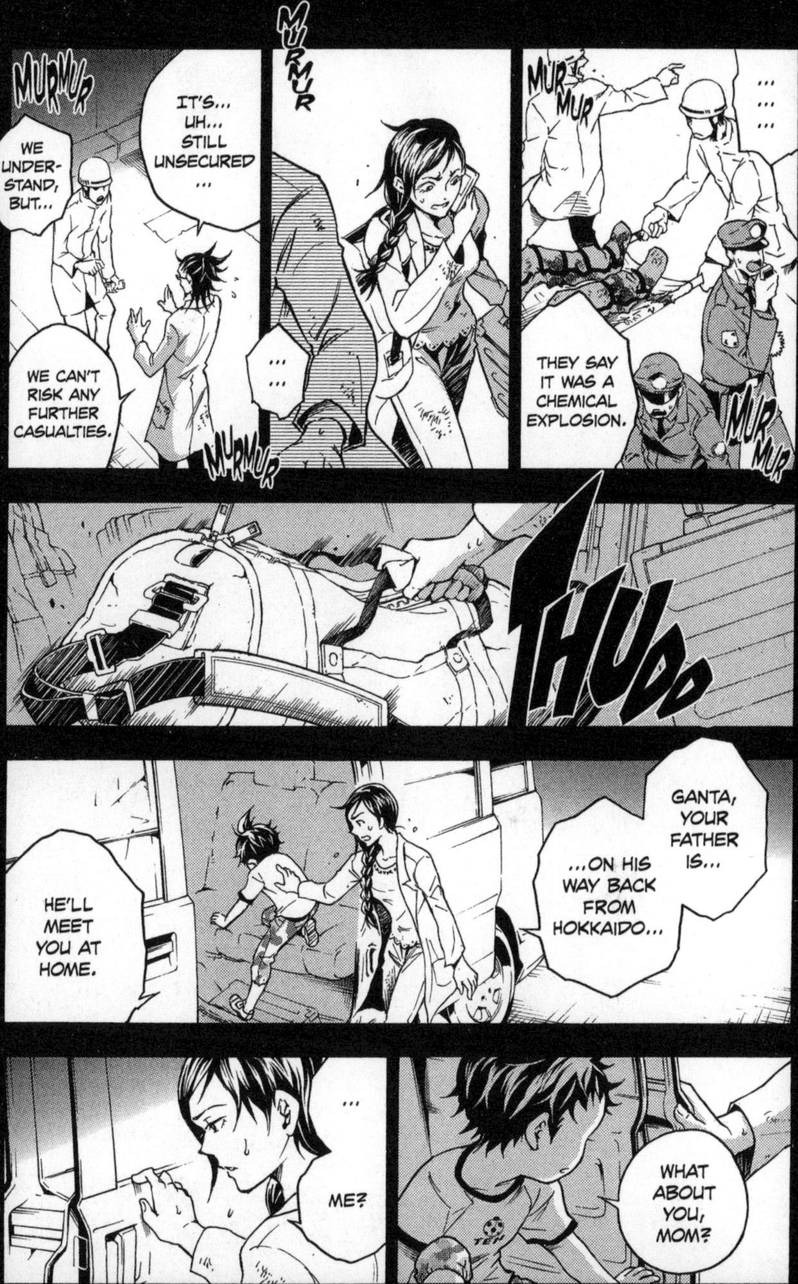

MUR MUR
...
...
...
THEY SAY IT WAS A CHEMICAL EXPLOSION.
MUR MUR
MURMUR
...
...
MURMUR
IT'S... UH... STILL UNSECURED...
WE UNDERSTAND, BUT...
WE CAN'T RISK ANY FURTHER CASUALTIES.
MURMUR
THUDD
GANTA, YOUR FATHER IS...
...ON HIS WAY BACK FROM HOKKAIDO...
HE'LL MEET YOU AT HOME.
WHAT ABOUT YOU, MOM?
...
ME?

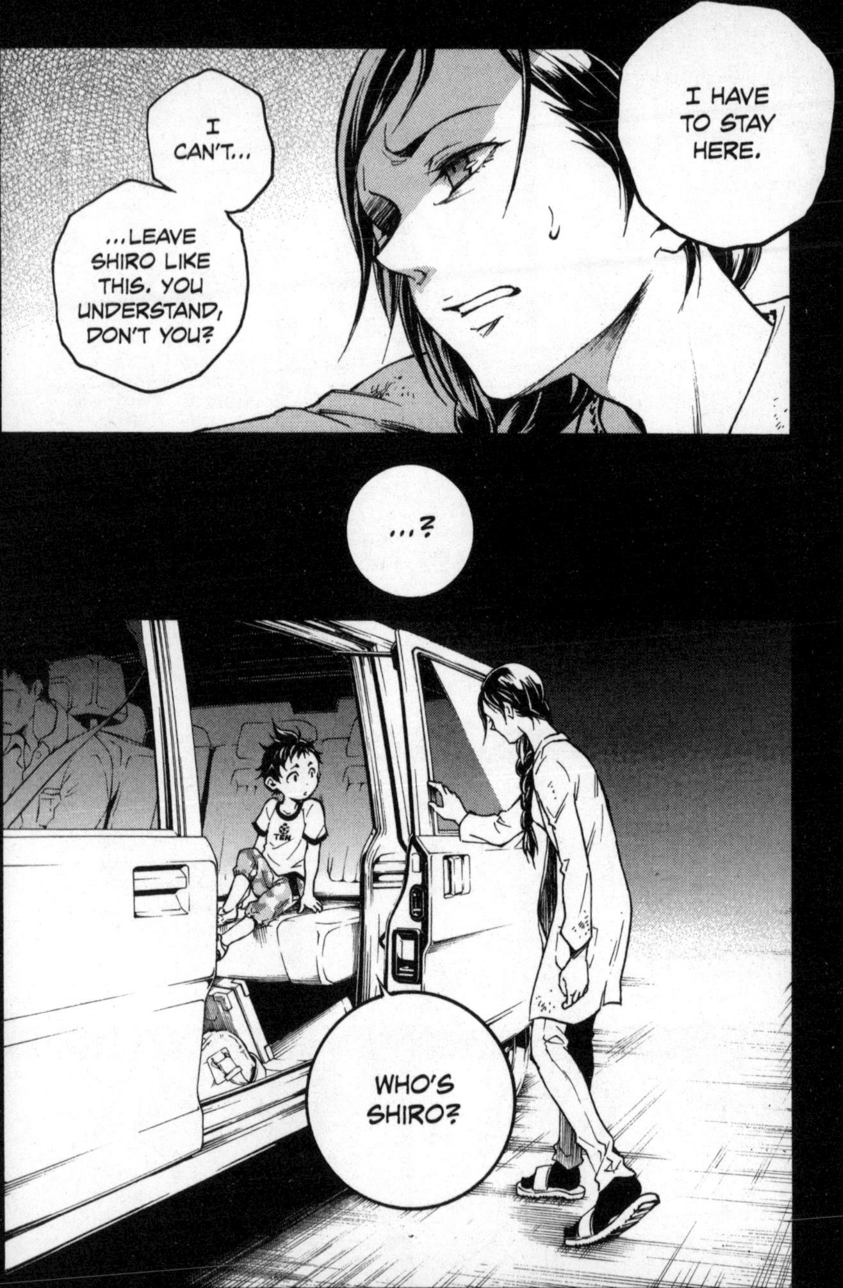
I HAVE TO STAY HERE.
I CAN'T...
...LEAVE SHIRO LIKE THIS. YOU UNDERSTAND, DON'T YOU?
...?
WHO'S SHIRO?

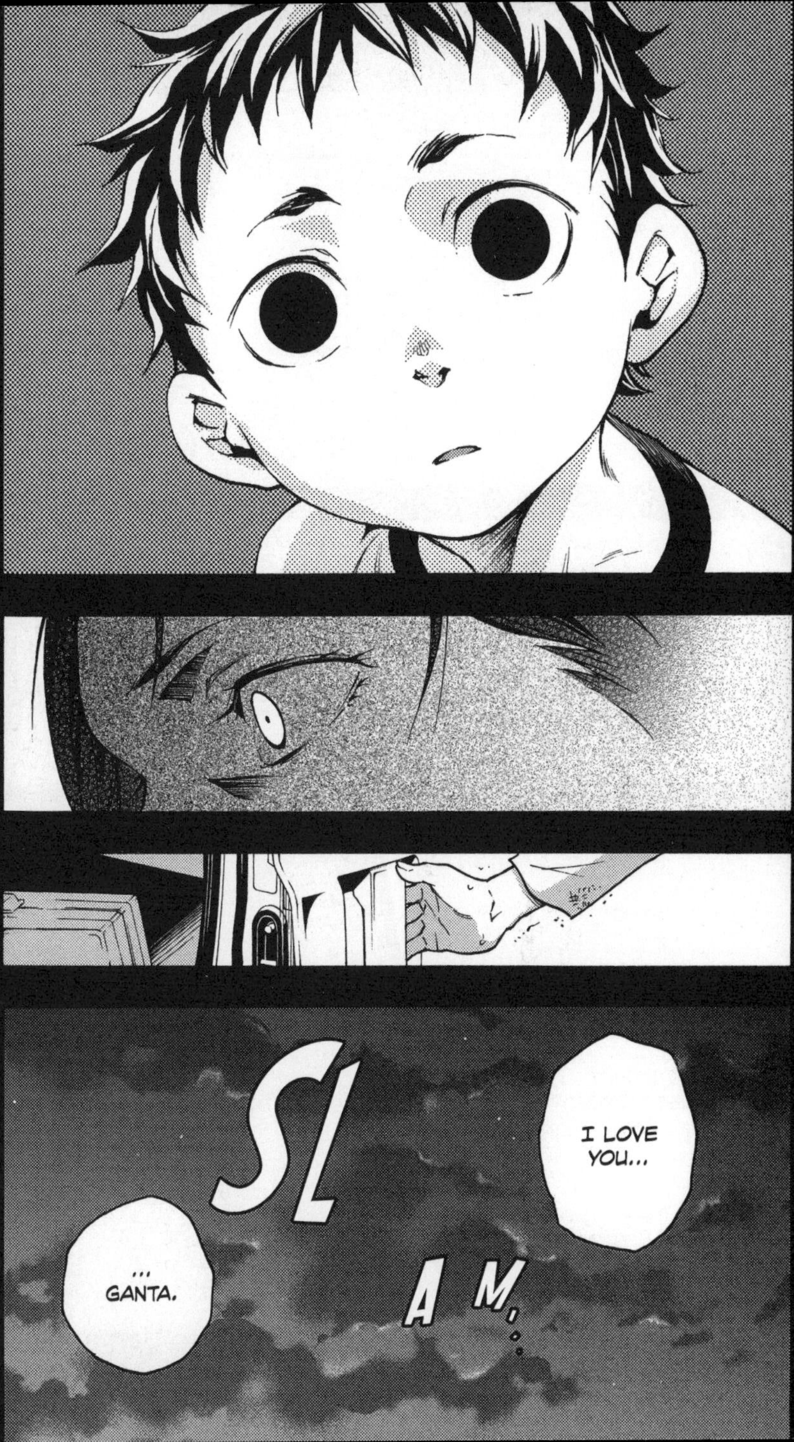
I LOVE YOU...
SLAM
... GANTA.

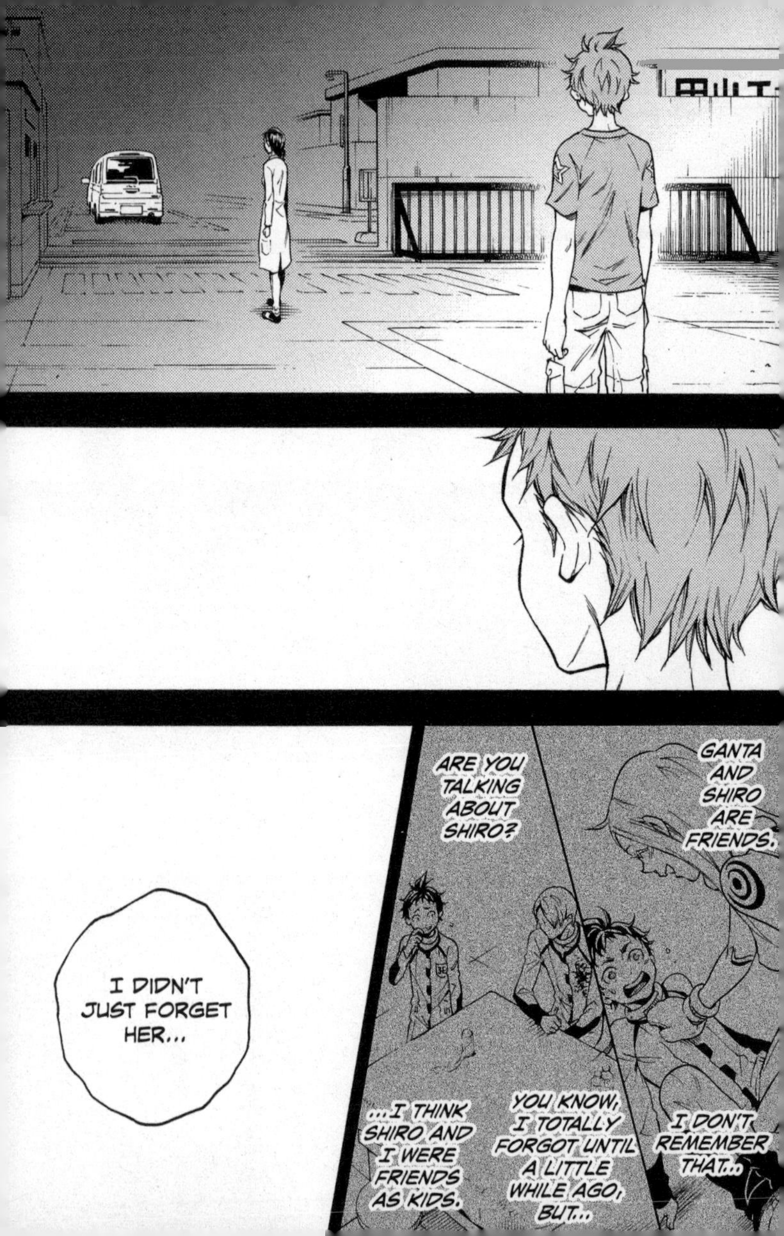
GANTA AND SHIRO ARE FRIENDS.
I DON'T REMEMBER THAT...
ARE YOU TALKING ABOUT SHIRO?
YOU KNOW, I TOTALLY FORGOT UNTIL A LITTLE WHILE AGO, BUT...
...I THINK SHIRO AND I WERE FRIENDS AS KIDS.
I DIDN'T JUST FORGET HER...

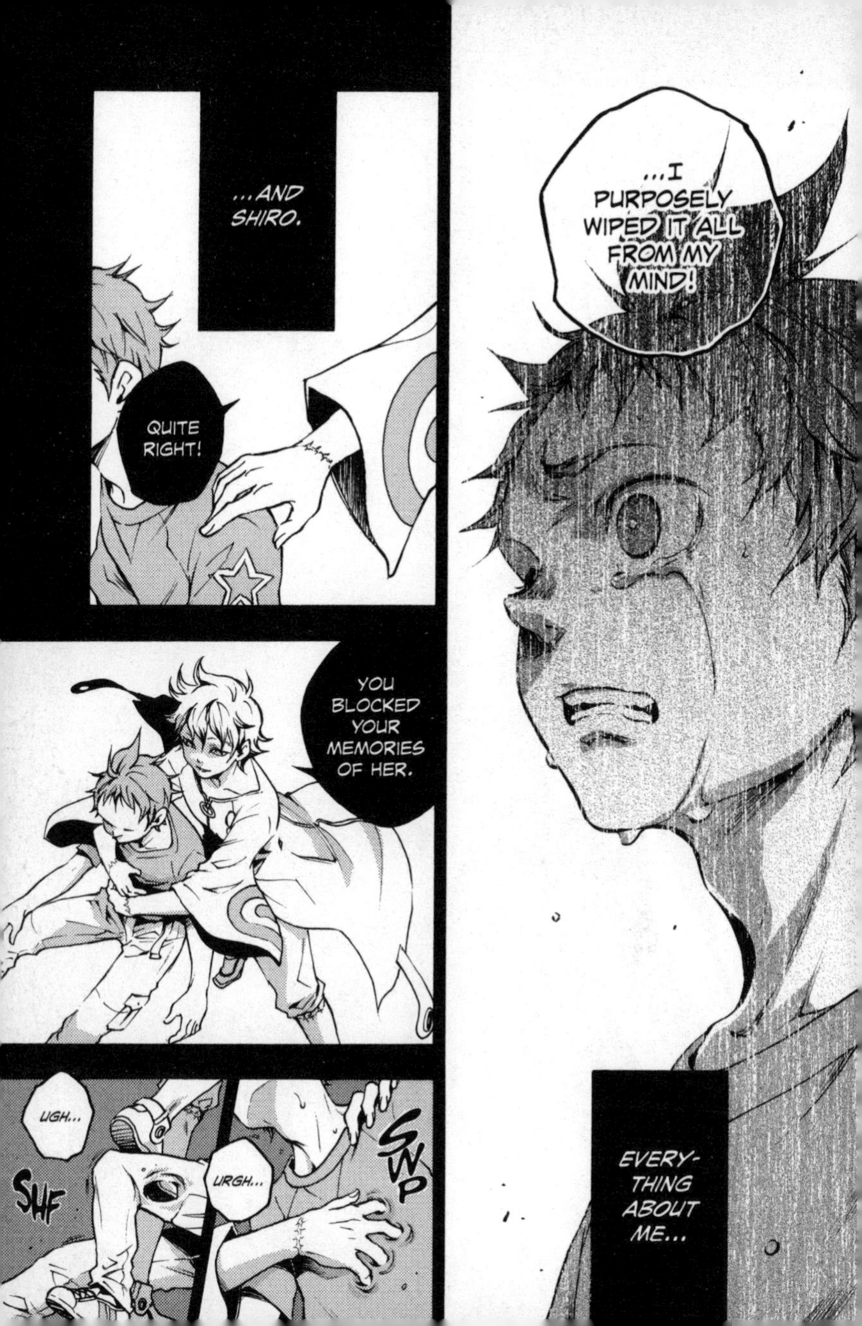
...I PURPOSELY WIPED IT ALL FROM MY MIND!
EVERY-THING ABOUT ME...
...AND SHIRO.
QUITE RIGHT!
YOU BLOCKED YOUR MEMORIES OF HER.
SWP
UGH...
URGH...
SHF

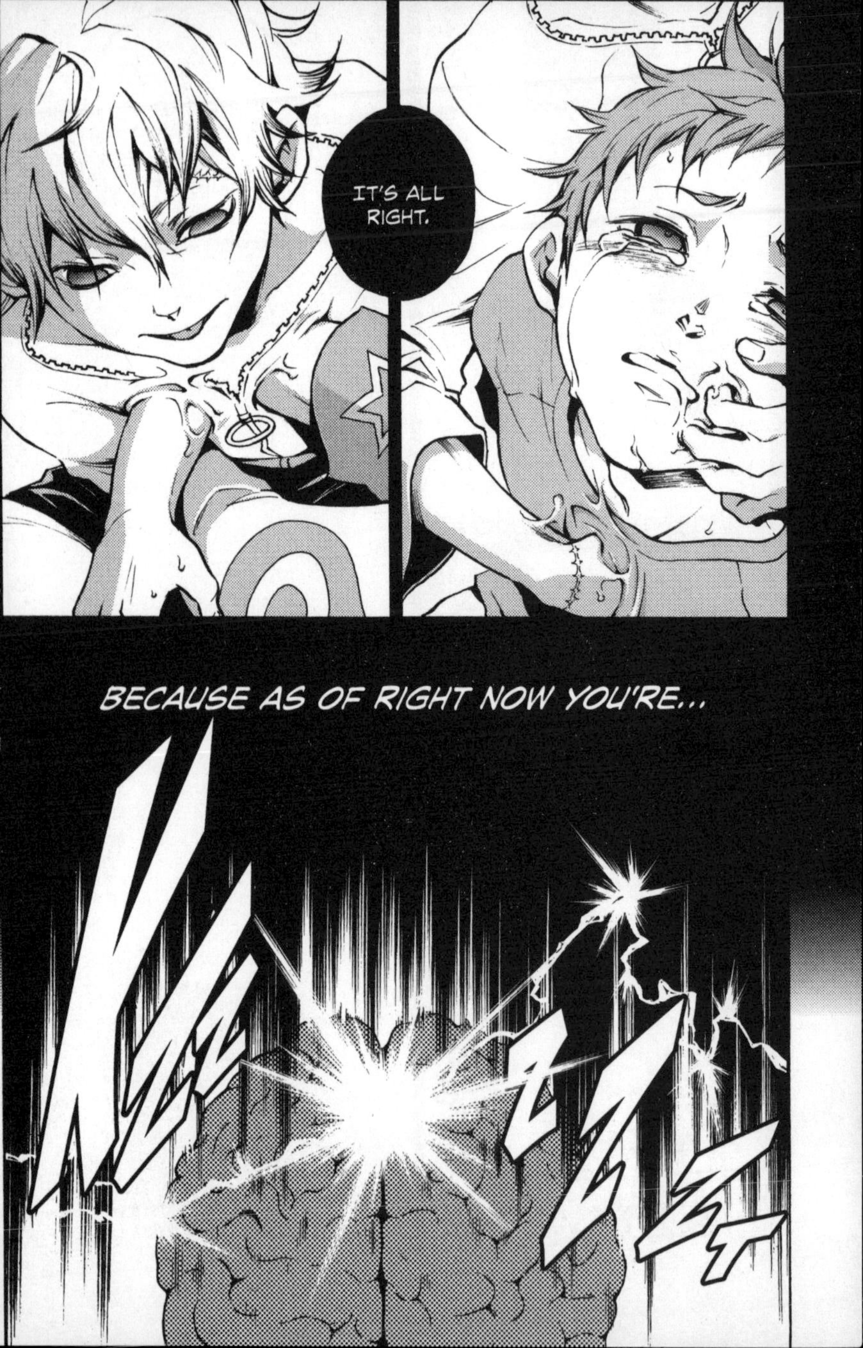
IT'S ALL RIGHT.
BECAUSE AS OF RIGHT NOW YOU'RE...

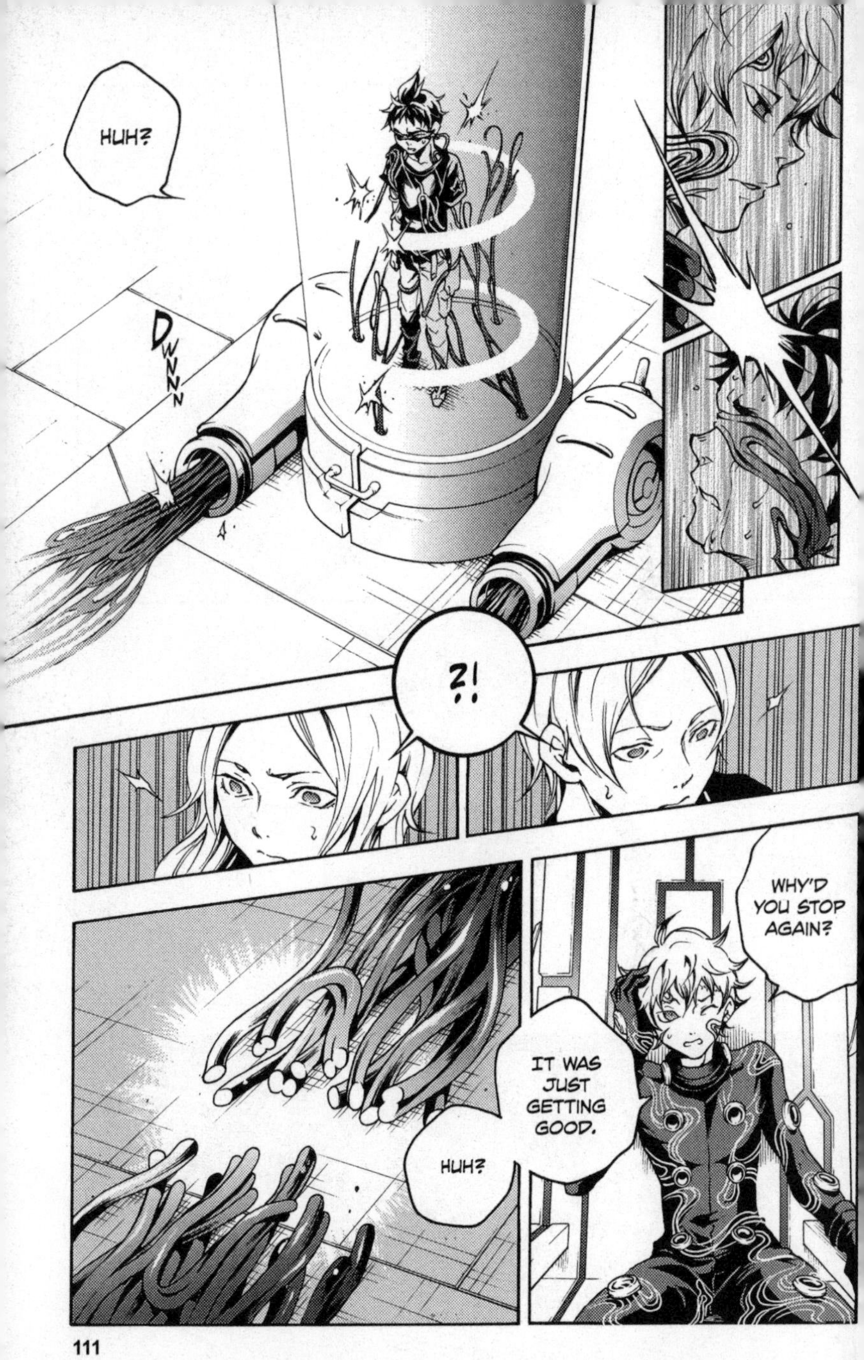
HUH?
DWNNN
?!
WHY'D YOU STOP AGAIN?
IT WAS JUST GETTING GOOD.
HUH?

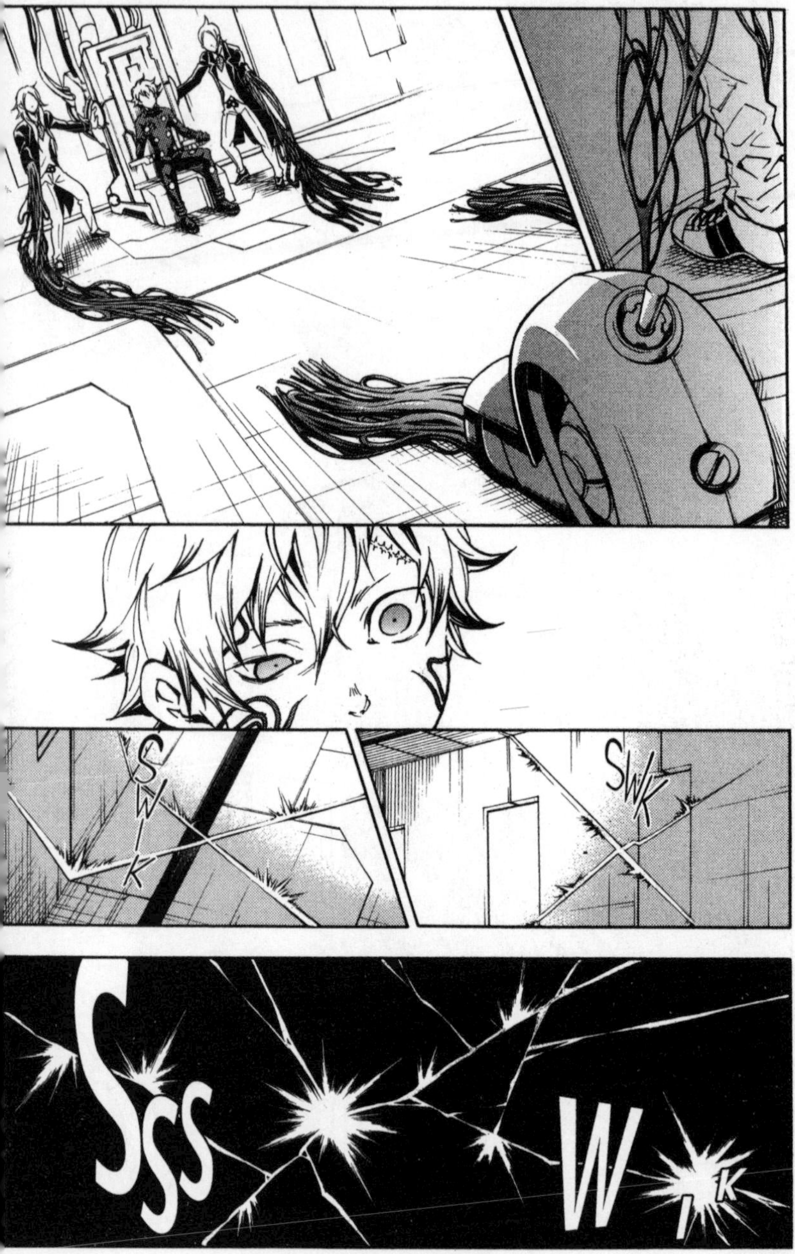
SWK
SWIK
SSSWIK

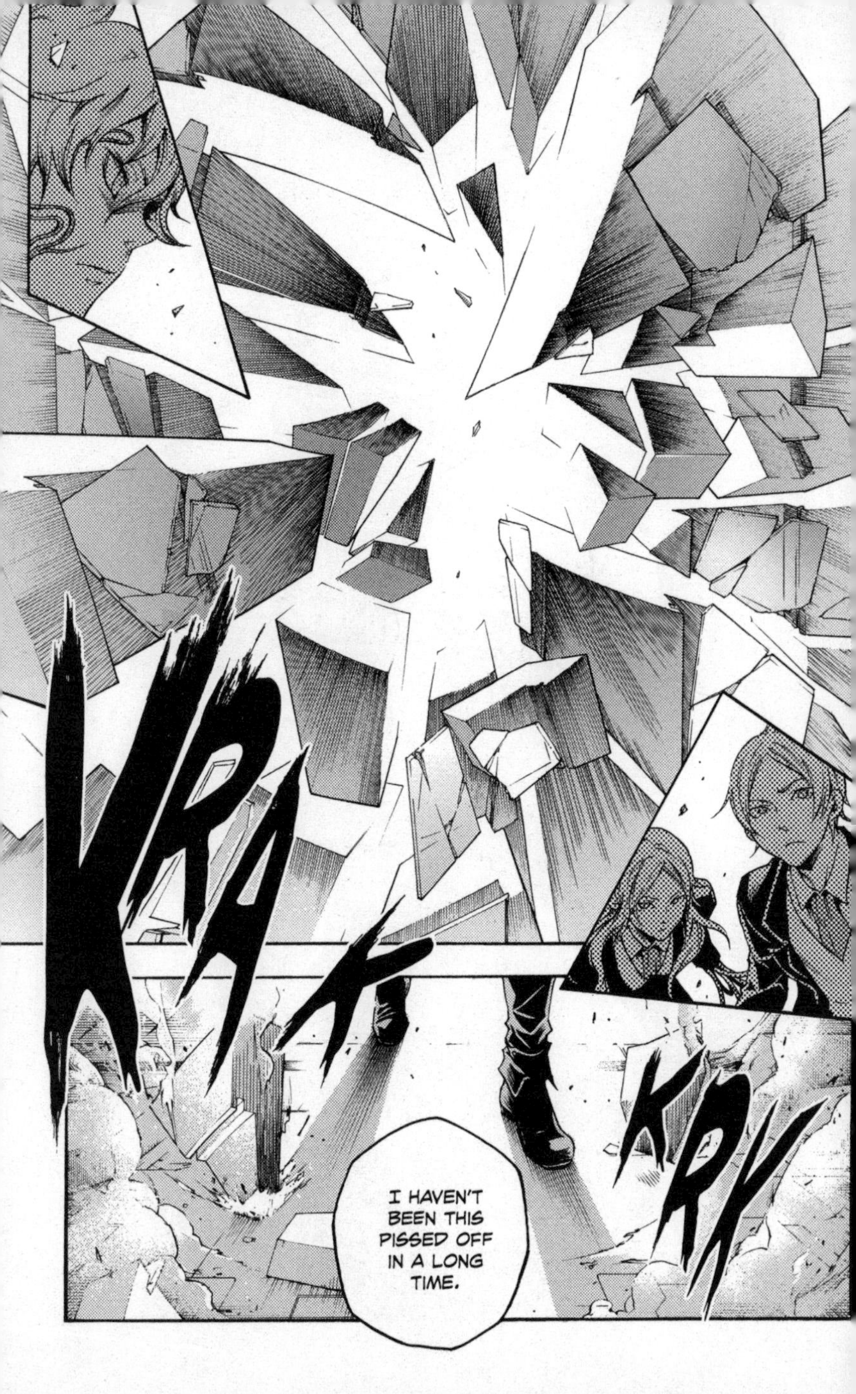
KRAK
KRK
I HAVEN'T BEEN THIS PISSED OFF IN A LONG TIME.

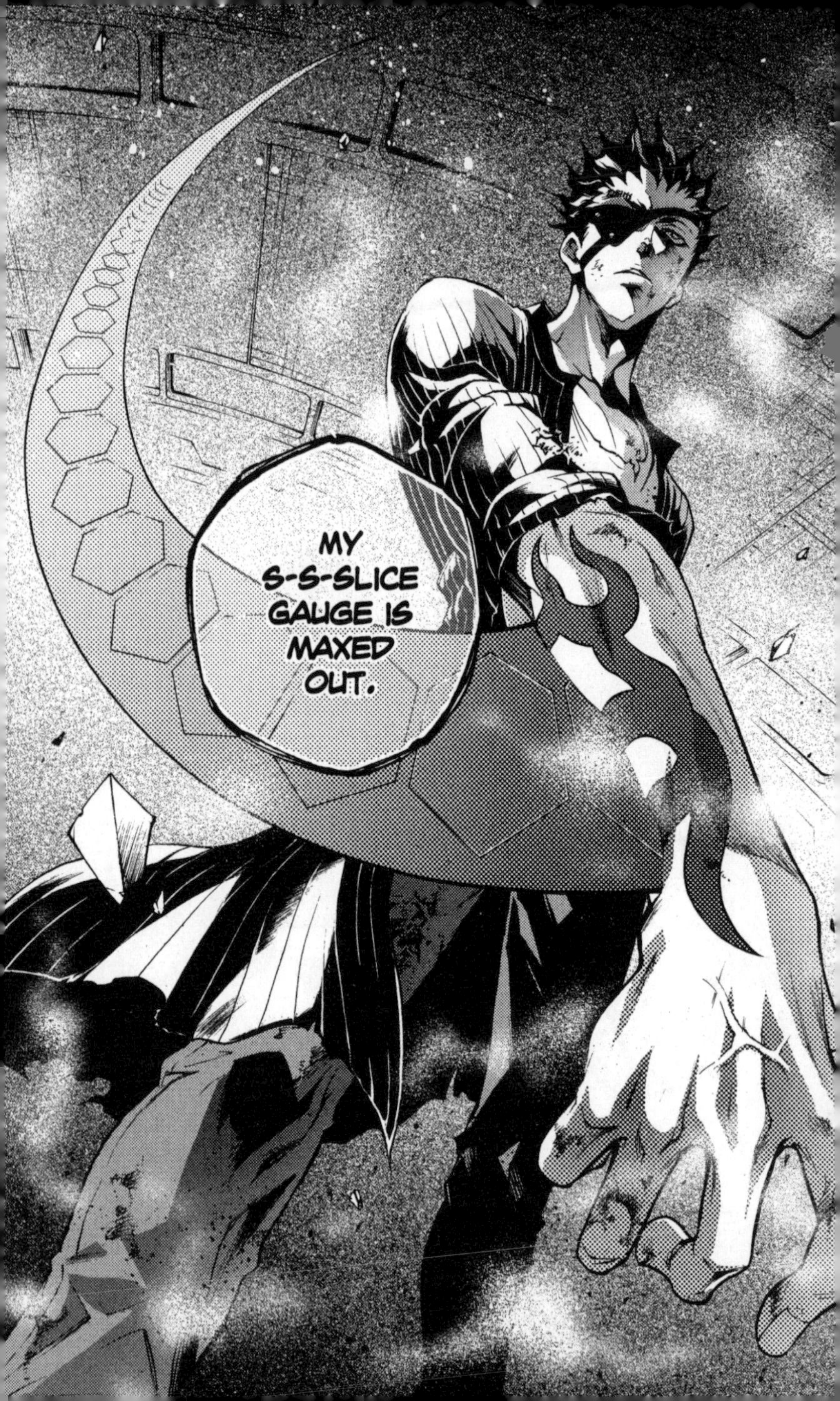
MY S-S-SLICE GAUGE IS MAXED OUT.

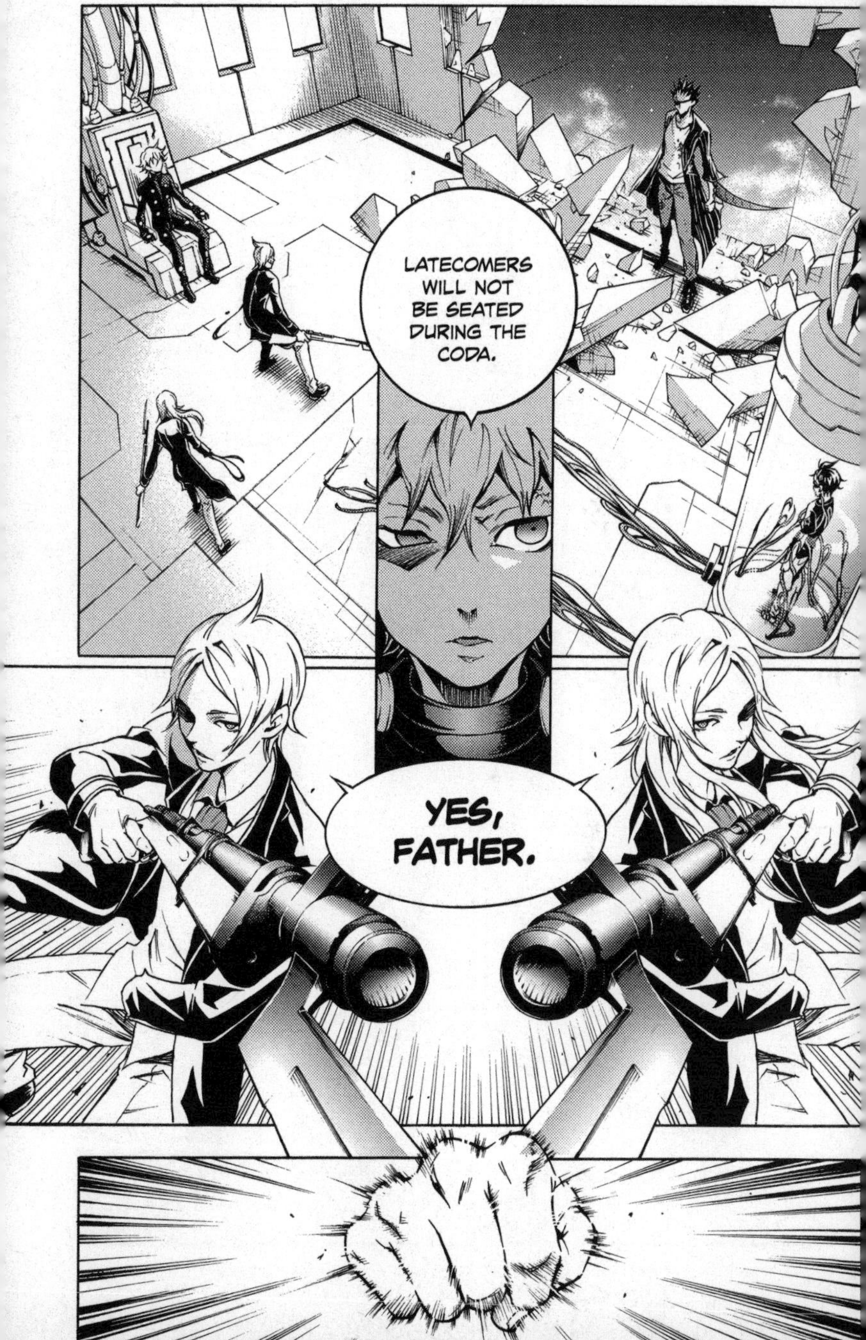
LATECOMERS WILL NOT BE SEATED DURING THE CODA.
YES, FATHER.

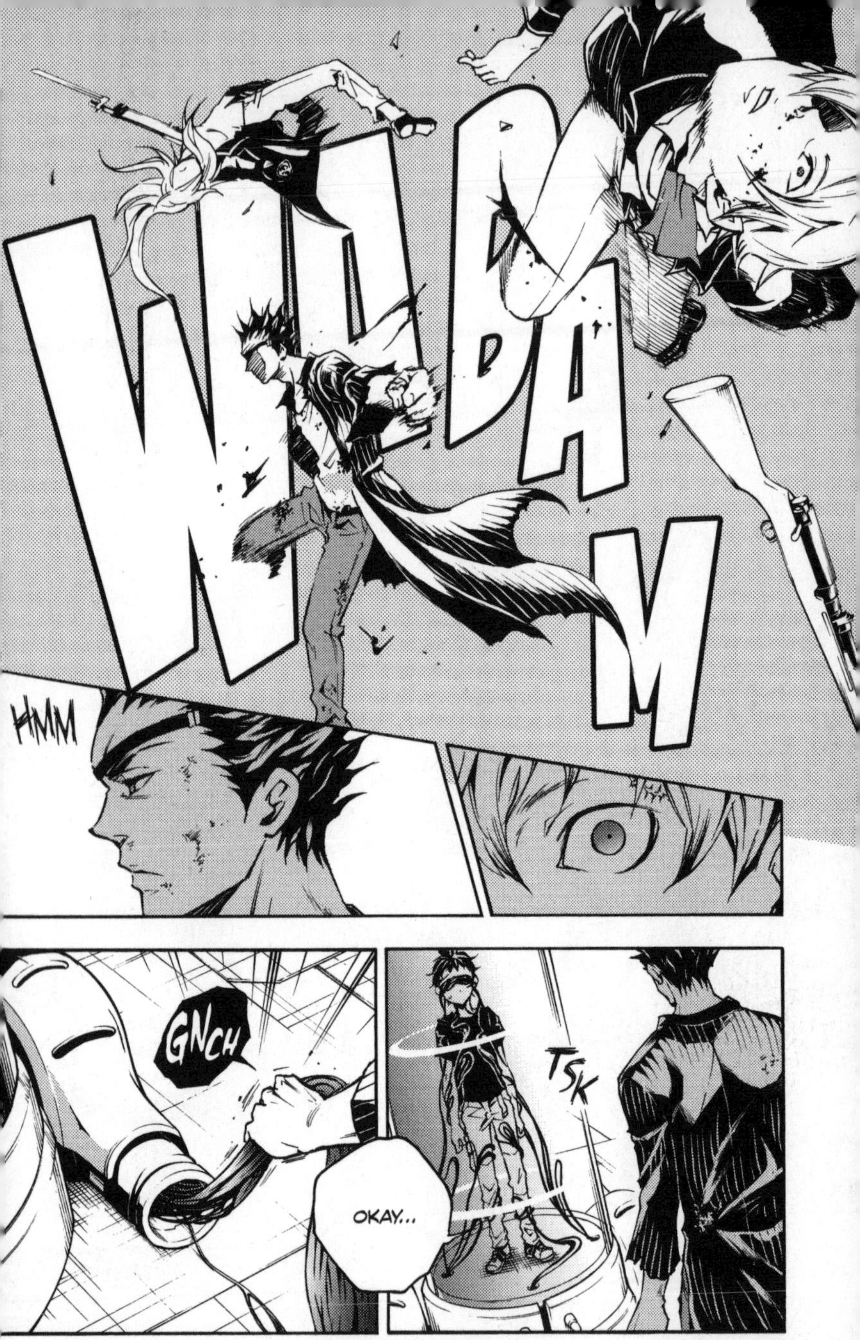
WHAM
HMM
TSK
OKAY...
GNCH

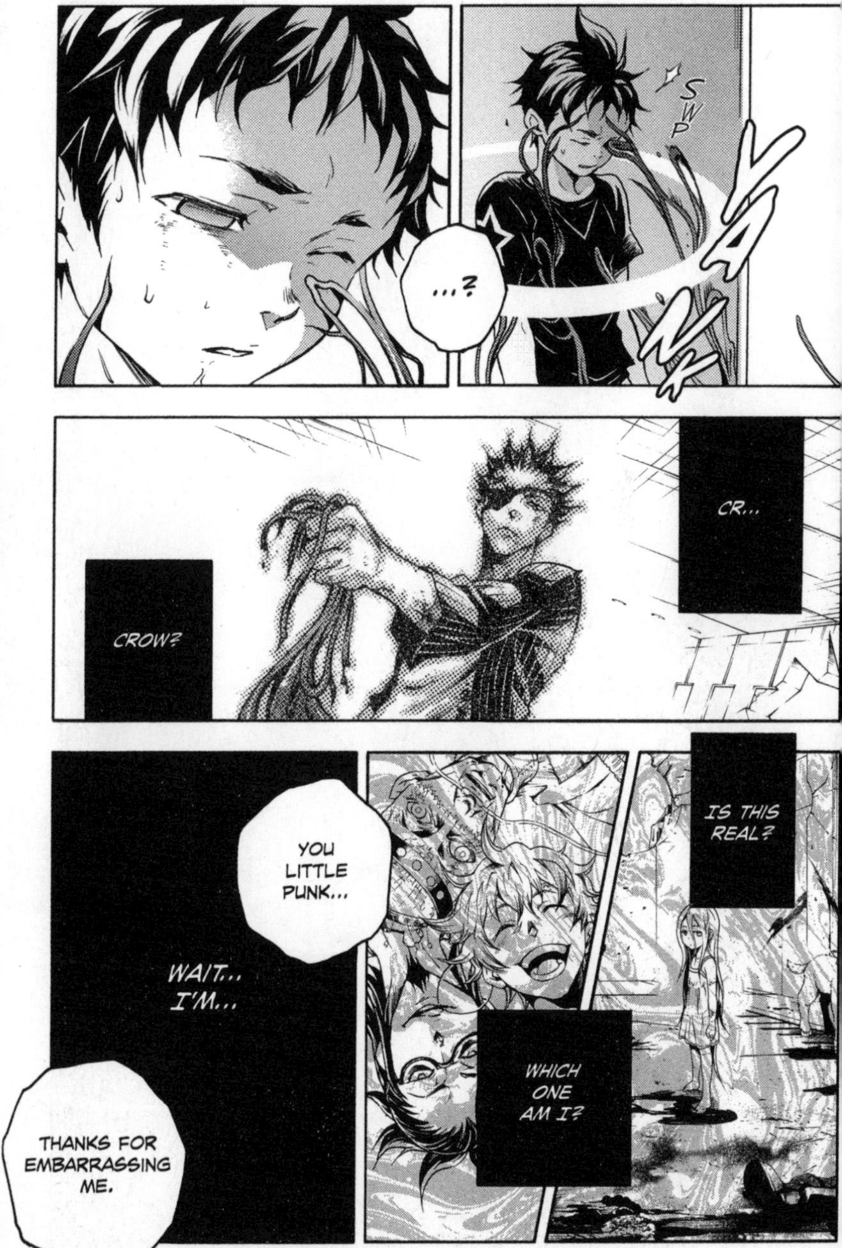
SWP
YANK
...?
CR...
CROW?
IS THIS REAL?
YOU LITTLE PUNK...
WHICH ONE AM I?
WAIT... I'M...
THANKS FOR EMBARRASSING ME.

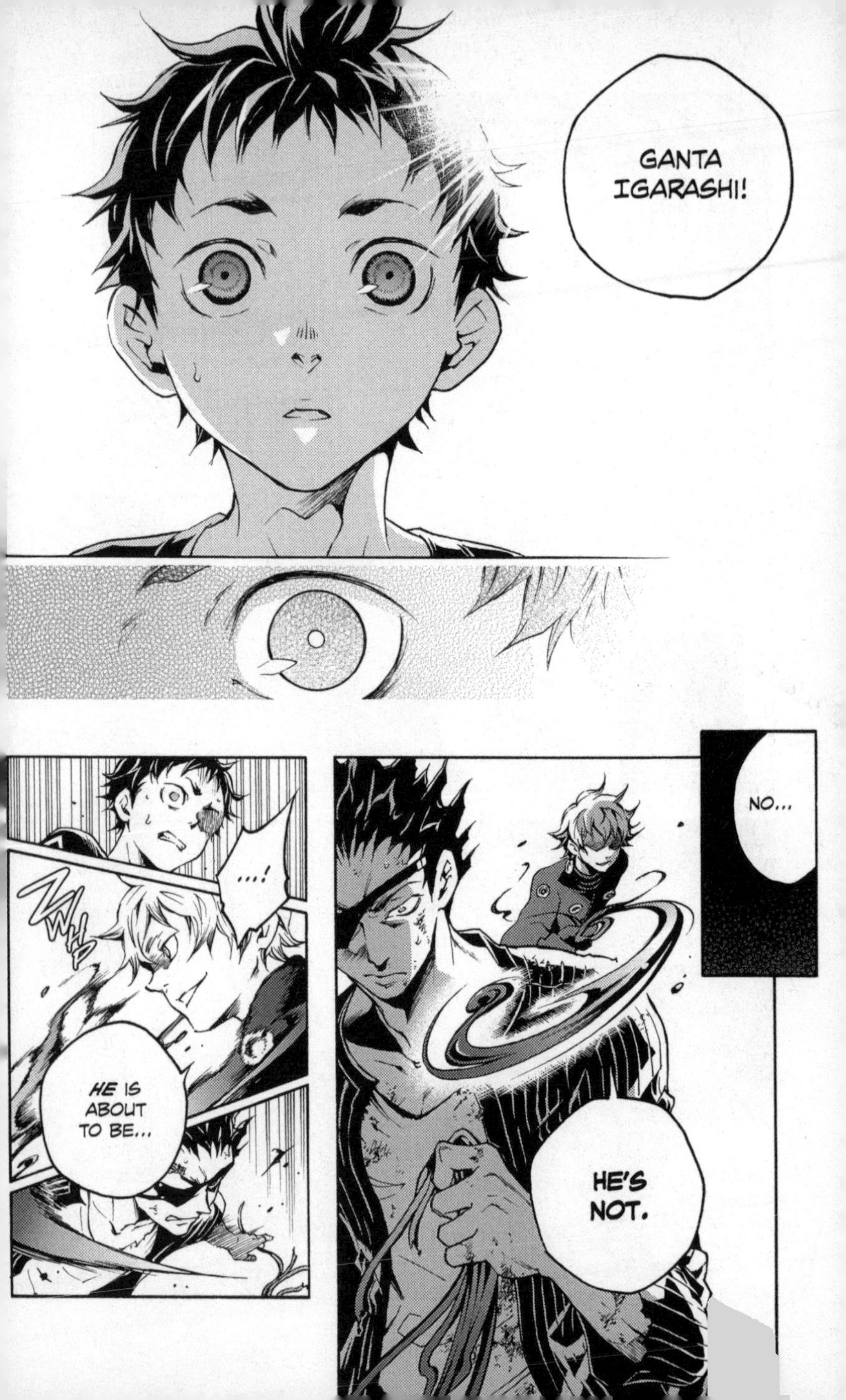
GANTA IGARASHI!
NO...
HE'S NOT.
...!
HE IS ABOUT TO BE...

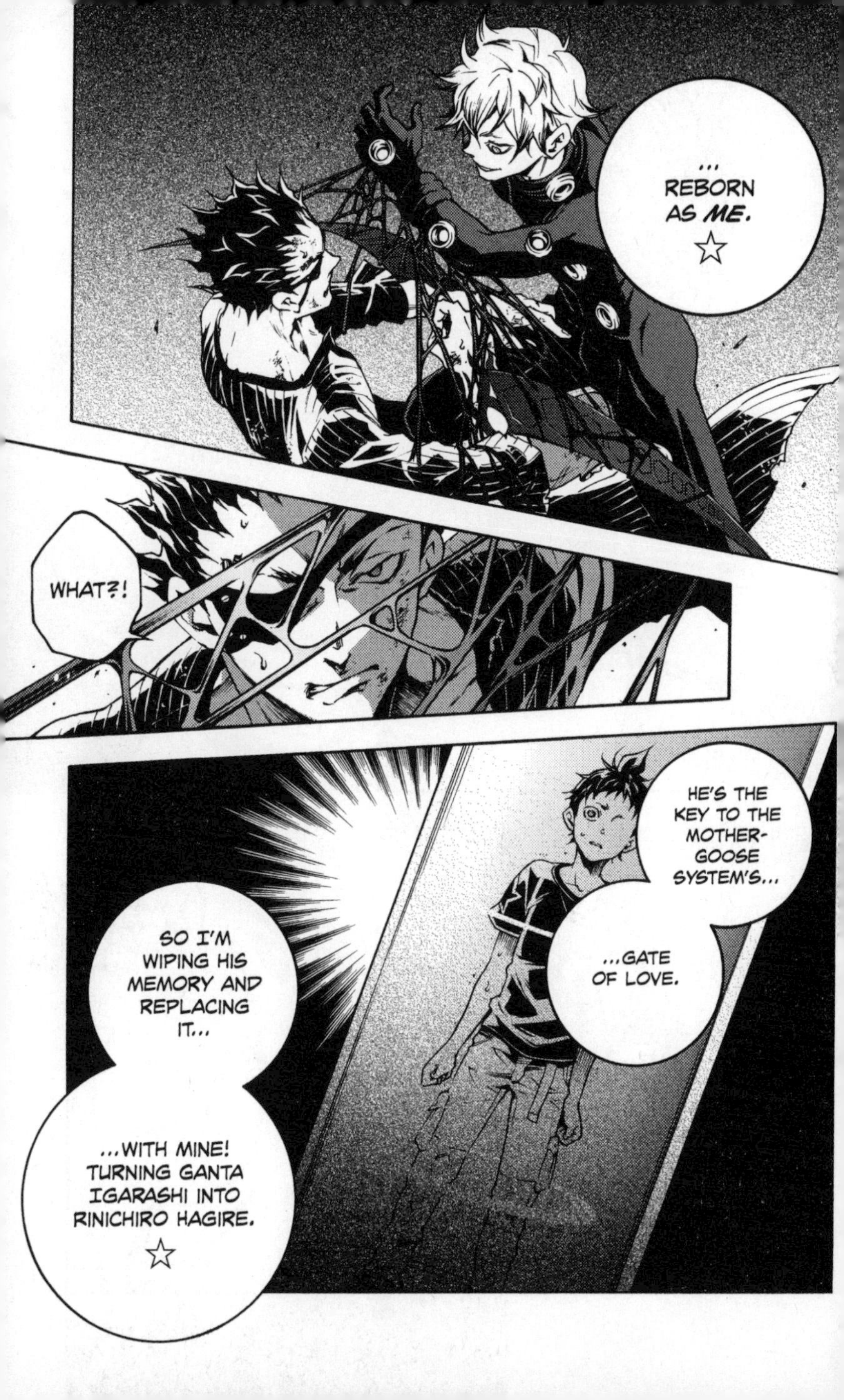
...REBORN AS ME. ☆
WHAT?!
HE'S THE KEY TO THE MOTHER-GOOSE SYSTEM'S...
...GATE OF LOVE.
SO I'M WIPING HIS MEMORY AND REPLACING IT...
...WITH MINE! TURNING GANTA IGARASHI INTO RINICHIRO HAGIRE. ☆

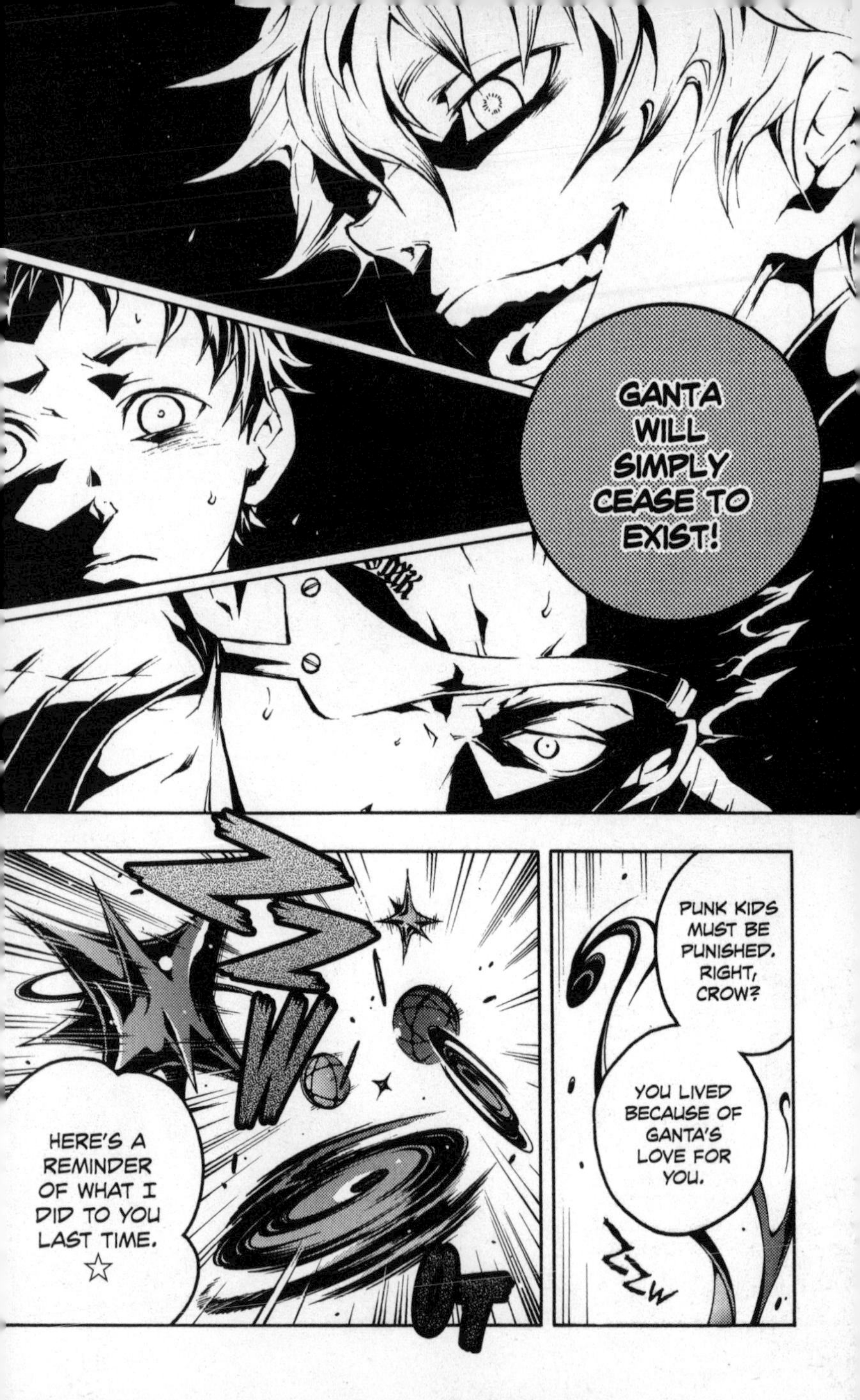
GANTA WILL SIMPLY CEASE TO EXIST!
PUNK KIDS MUST BE PUNISHED. RIGHT, CROW?
YOU LIVED BECAUSE OF GANTA'S LOVE FOR YOU.
ZZZW
HERE'S A REMINDER OF WHAT I DID TO YOU LAST TIME. ☆

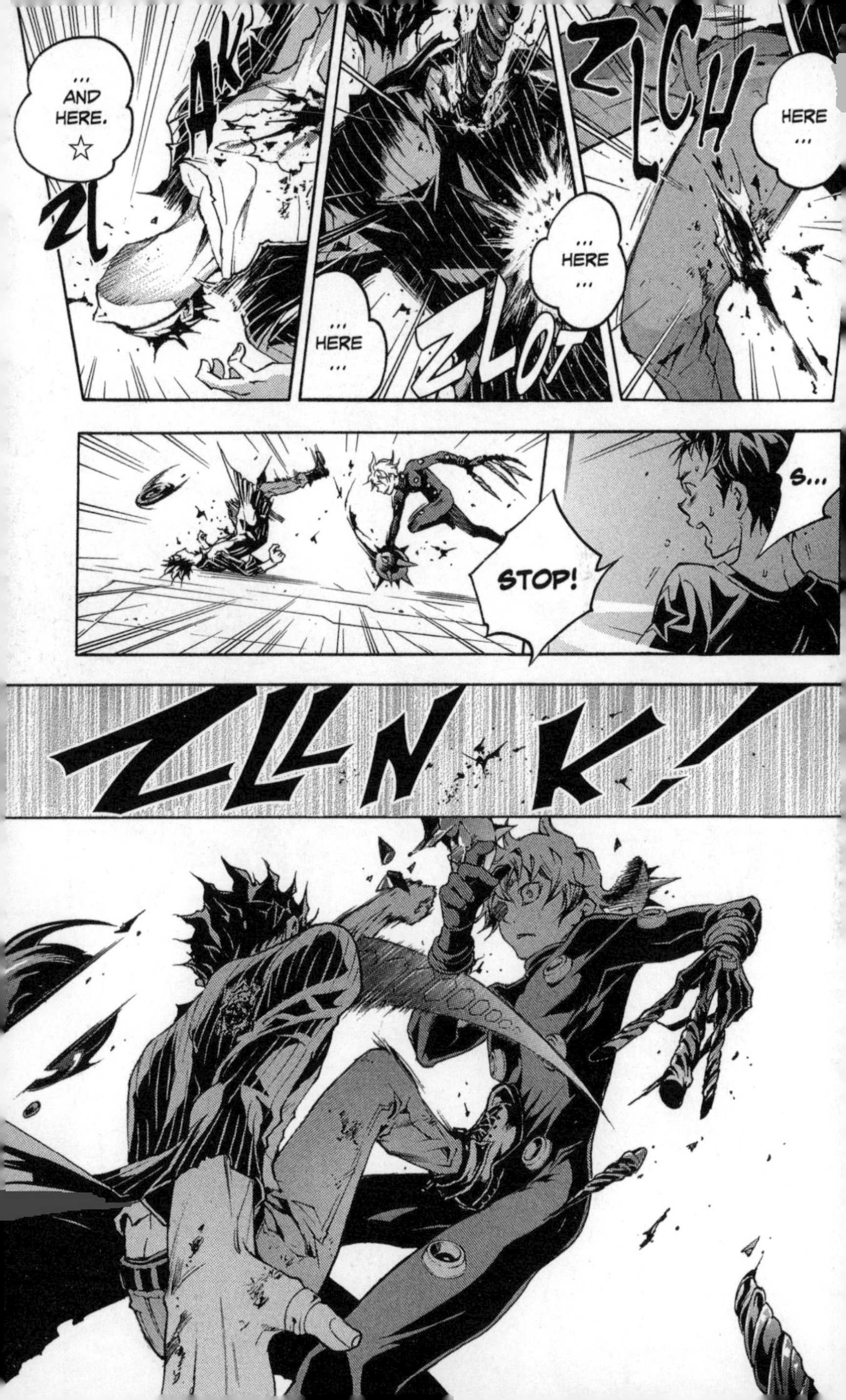
ZLCH
HERE ...
... HERE ...
ZLOT
... HERE ...
... AND HERE. ☆
ZAK
S...
STOP!
ZLUNK!

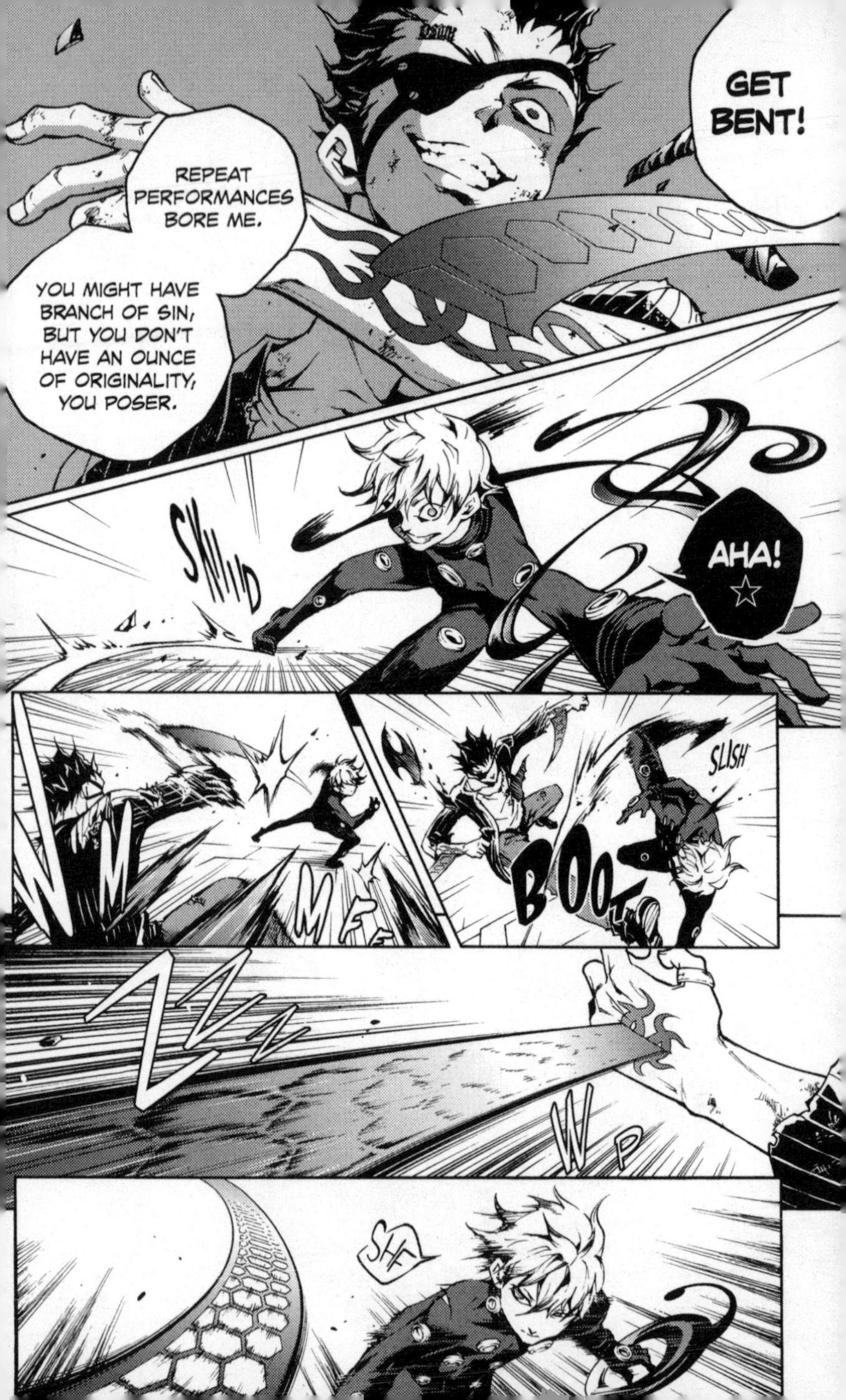
GET BENT!
REPEAT PERFORMANCES BORE ME.
YOU MIGHT HAVE BRANCH OF SIN, BUT YOU DON'T HAVE AN OUNCE OF ORIGINALITY, YOU POSER.
AHA! ☆
SLISH
SHF

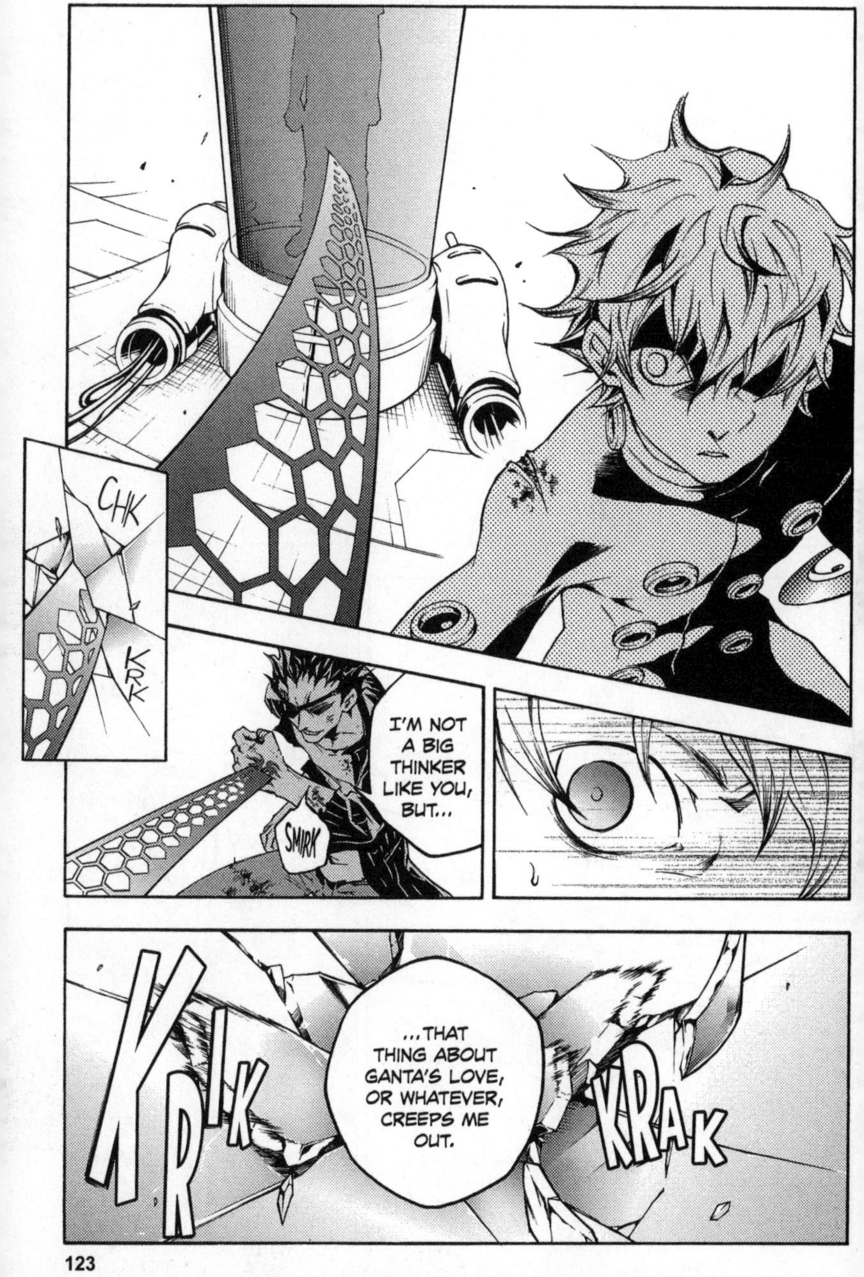
CHK
KRK
I'M NOT A BIG THINKER LIKE YOU, BUT...
SMIRK
KRAK
...THAT THING ABOUT GANTA'S LOVE, OR WHATEVER, CREEPS ME OUT.
KRIK

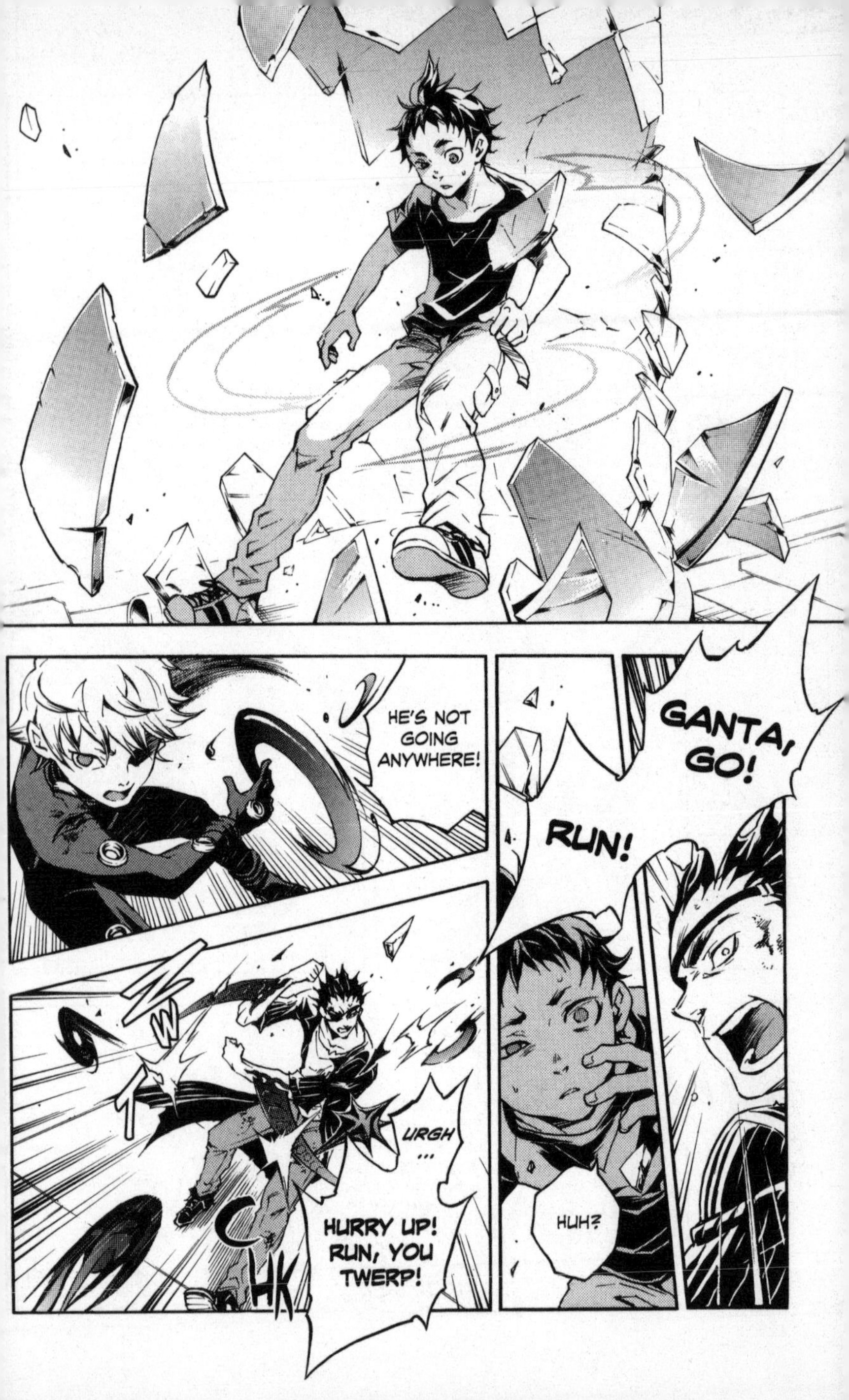
GANTA, GO!
RUN!
HUH?
HE'S NOT GOING ANYWHERE!
URGH...
HURRY UP! RUN, YOU TWERP!
CHK

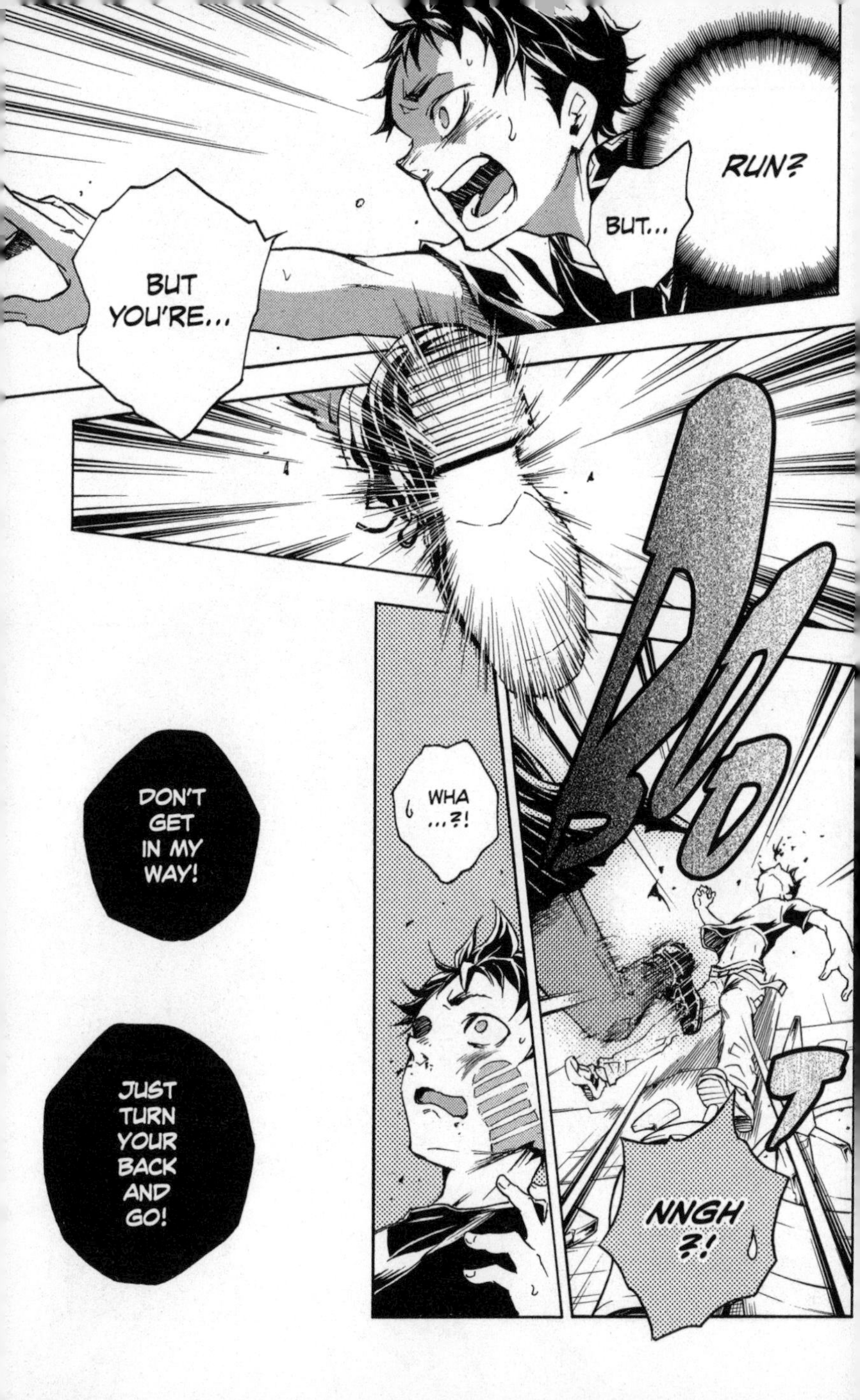

RUN?
BUT...
BUT YOU'RE...
NNGH ?!
WHA ...?!
DON'T GET IN MY WAY!
JUST TURN YOUR BACK AND GO!

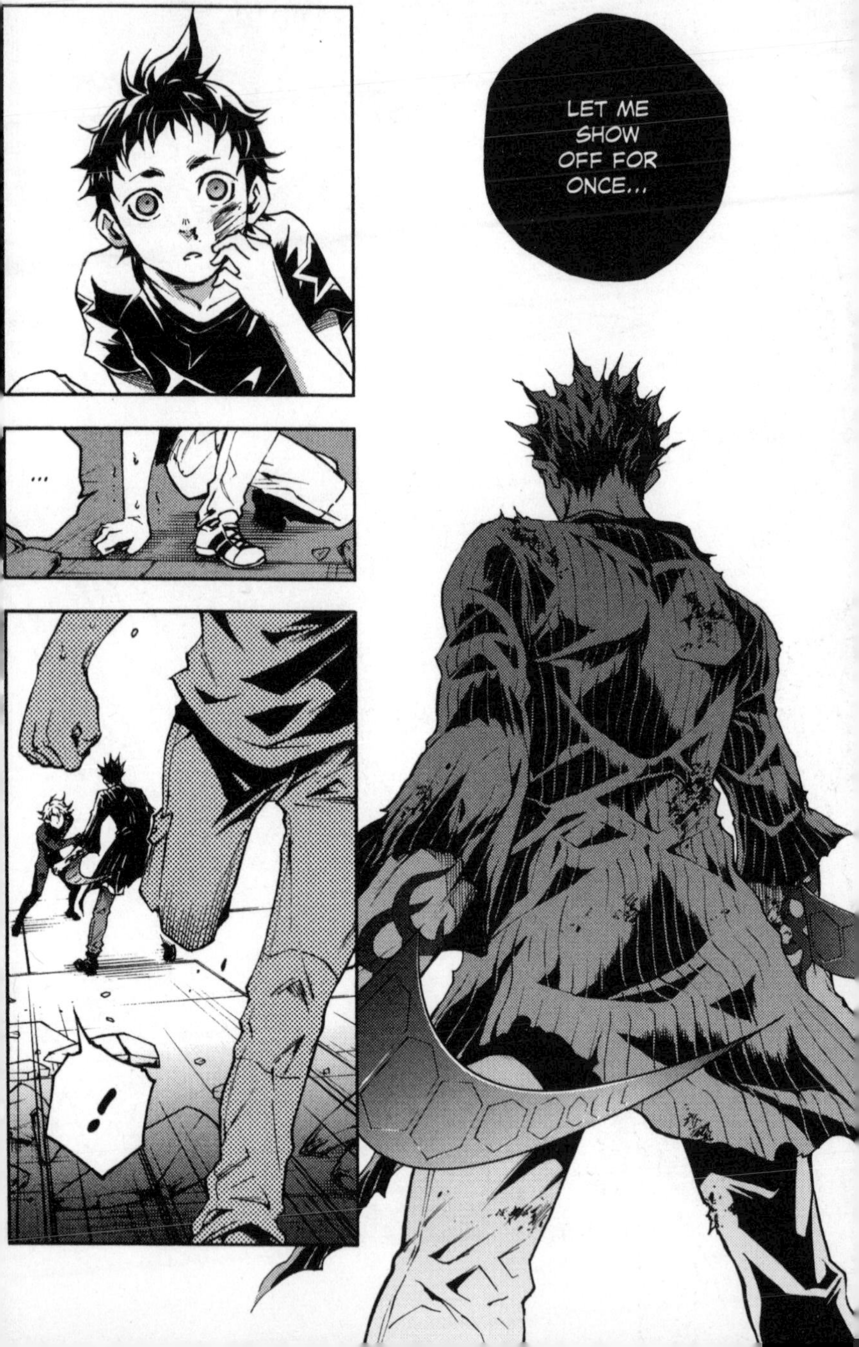
LET ME SHOW OFF FOR ONCE...
...
!

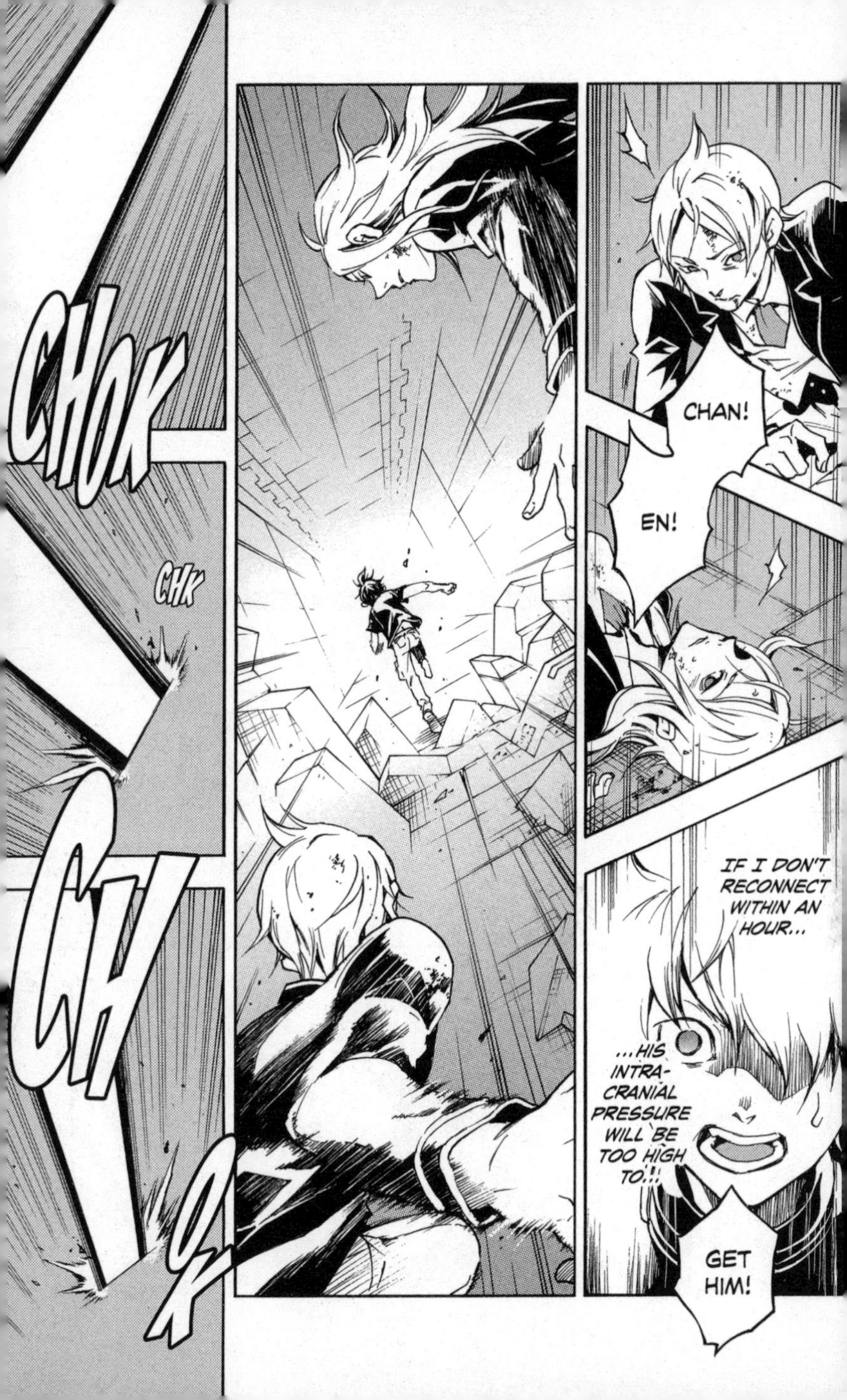
CHAN!
EN!
IF I DON'T RECONNECT WITHIN AN HOUR...
...HIS INTRA-CRANIAL PRESSURE WILL BE TOO HIGH TO...!
GET HIM!
CHOK
CHK
CHOK

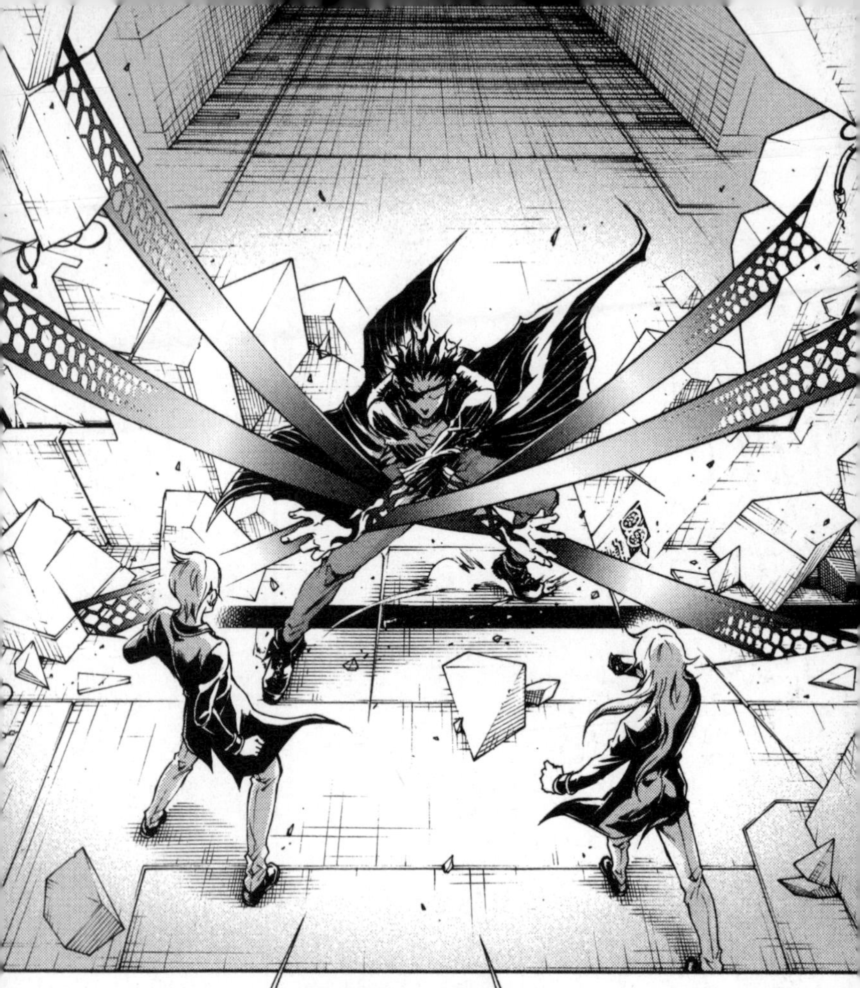

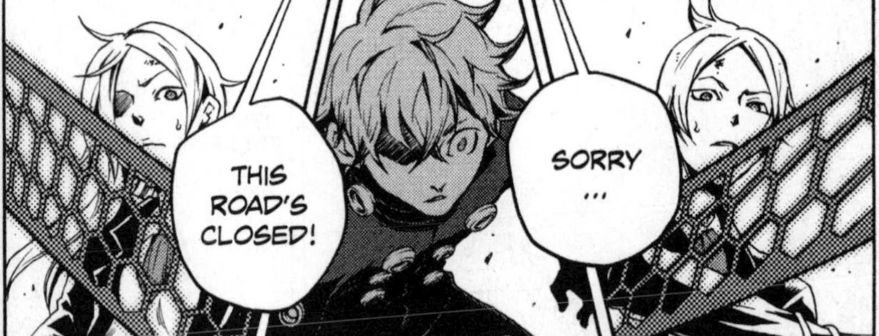
SORRY ...
THIS ROAD'S CLOSED!

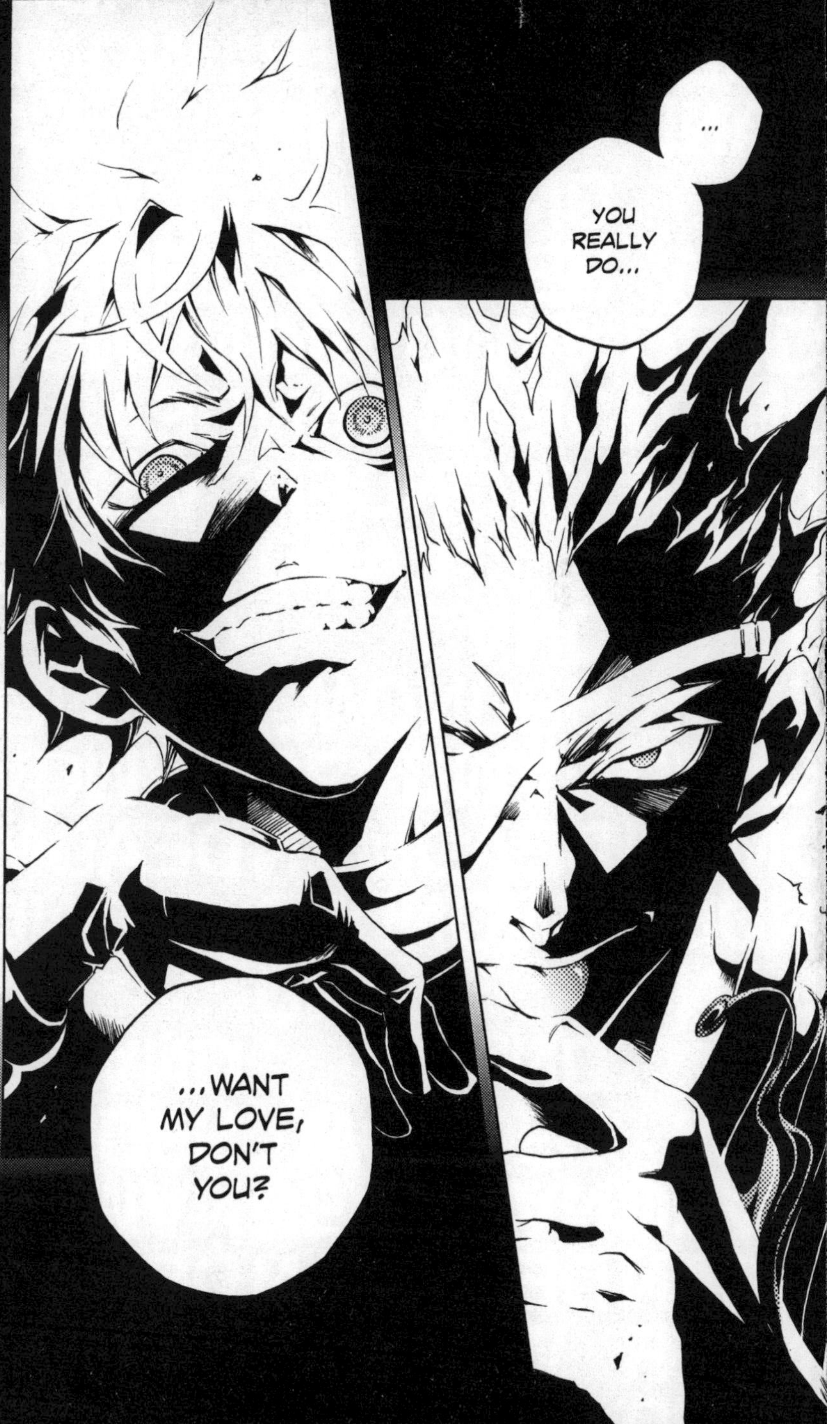
...
YOU REALLY DO...
...WANT MY LOVE, DON'T YOU?

DEADMAN WONDER LAND

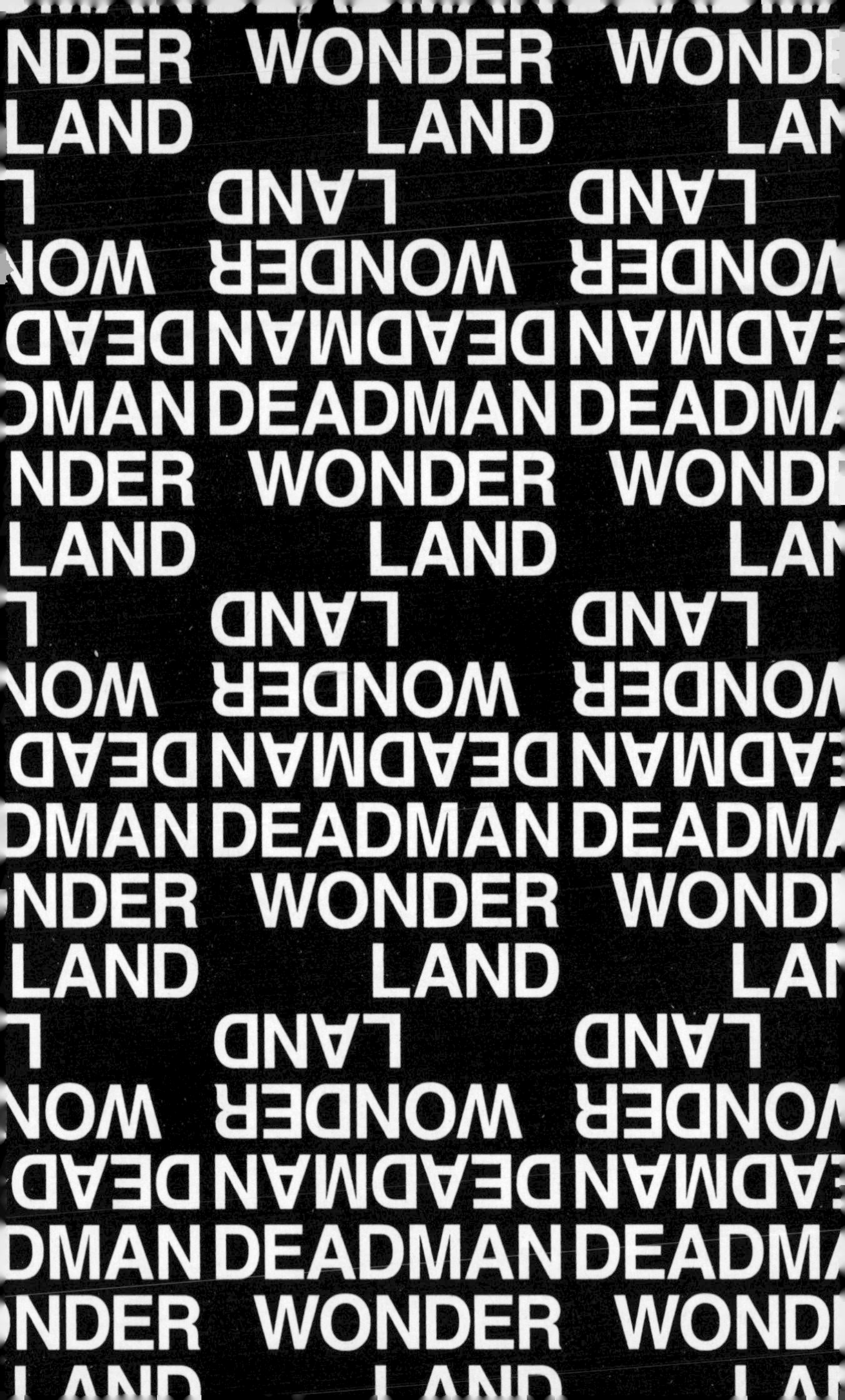

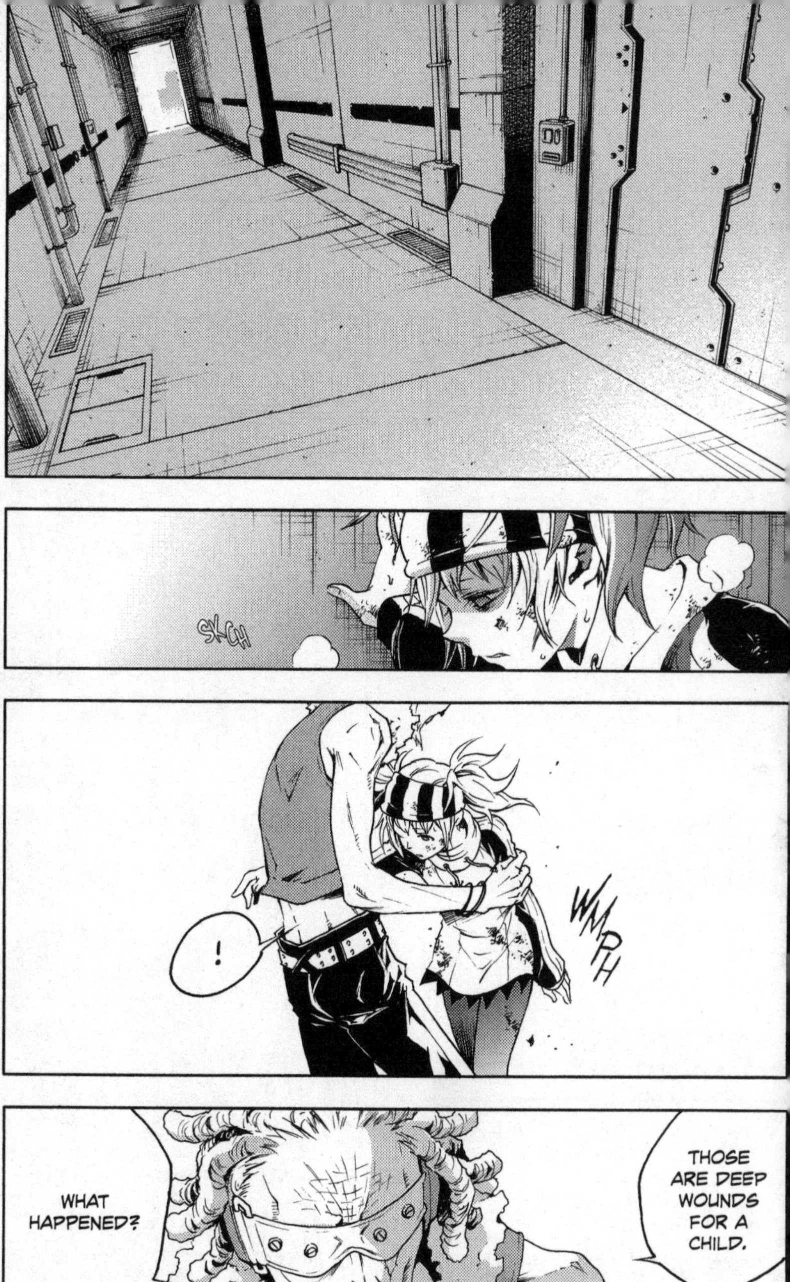
SKCH
!
WMPH
THOSE ARE DEEP WOUNDS FOR A CHILD.
WHAT HAPPENED?

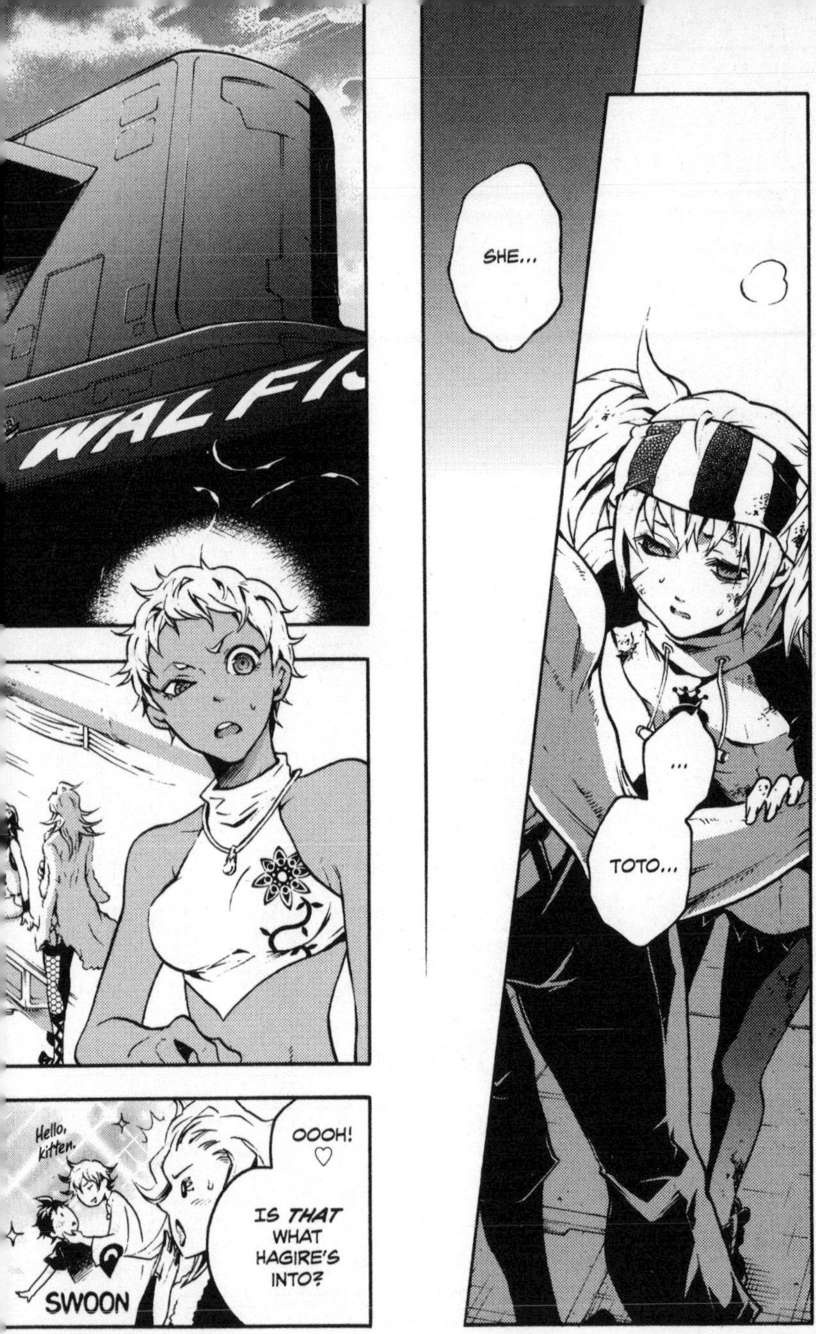
SHE...
...
TOTO...
OOOH! ♡
IS *THAT* WHAT HAGIRE'S INTO?
Hello, kitten.
SWOON

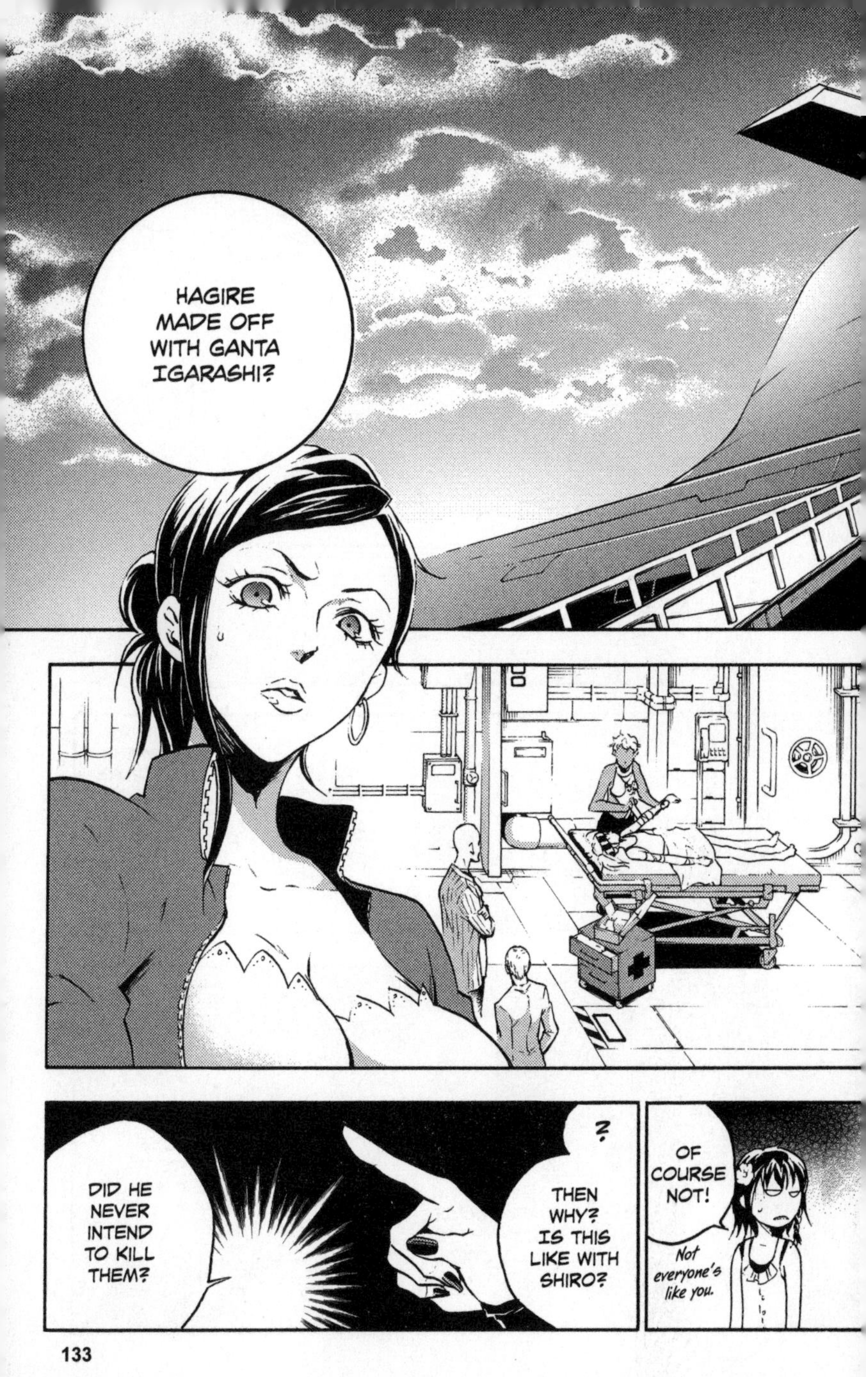
HAGIRE MADE OFF WITH GANTA IGARASHI?
OF COURSE NOT!
Not everyone's like you.
?
THEN WHY? IS THIS LIKE WITH SHIRO?
DID HE NEVER INTEND TO KILL THEM?

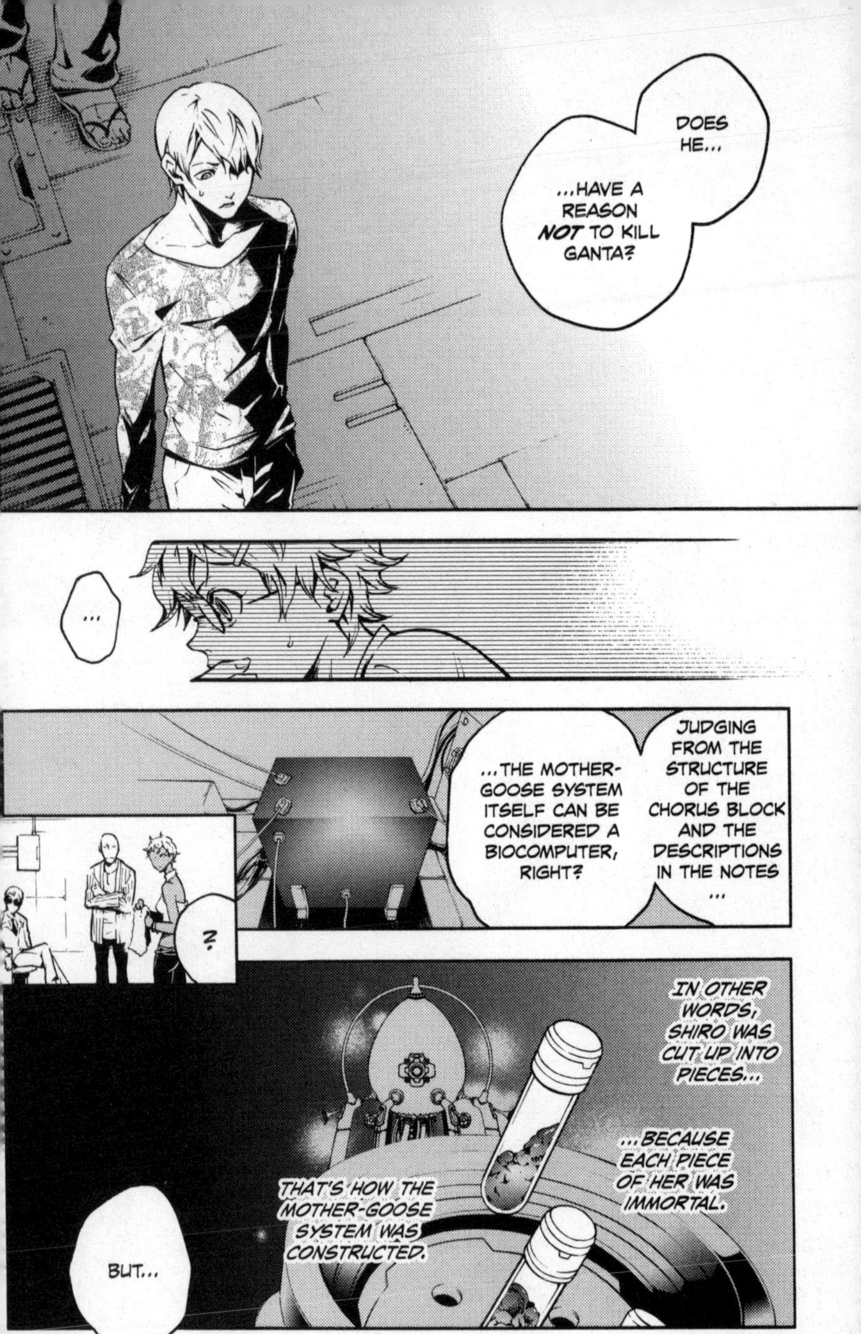
DOES HE...
...HAVE A REASON ***NOT*** TO KILL GANTA?
...
JUDGING FROM THE STRUCTURE OF THE CHORUS BLOCK AND THE DESCRIPTIONS IN THE NOTES ...
...THE MOTHER-GOOSE SYSTEM ITSELF CAN BE CONSIDERED A BIOCOMPUTER, RIGHT?
?
IN OTHER WORDS, SHIRO WAS CUT UP INTO PIECES...
...BECAUSE EACH PIECE OF HER WAS IMMORTAL.
THAT'S HOW THE MOTHER-GOOSE SYSTEM WAS CONSTRUCTED.
BUT...

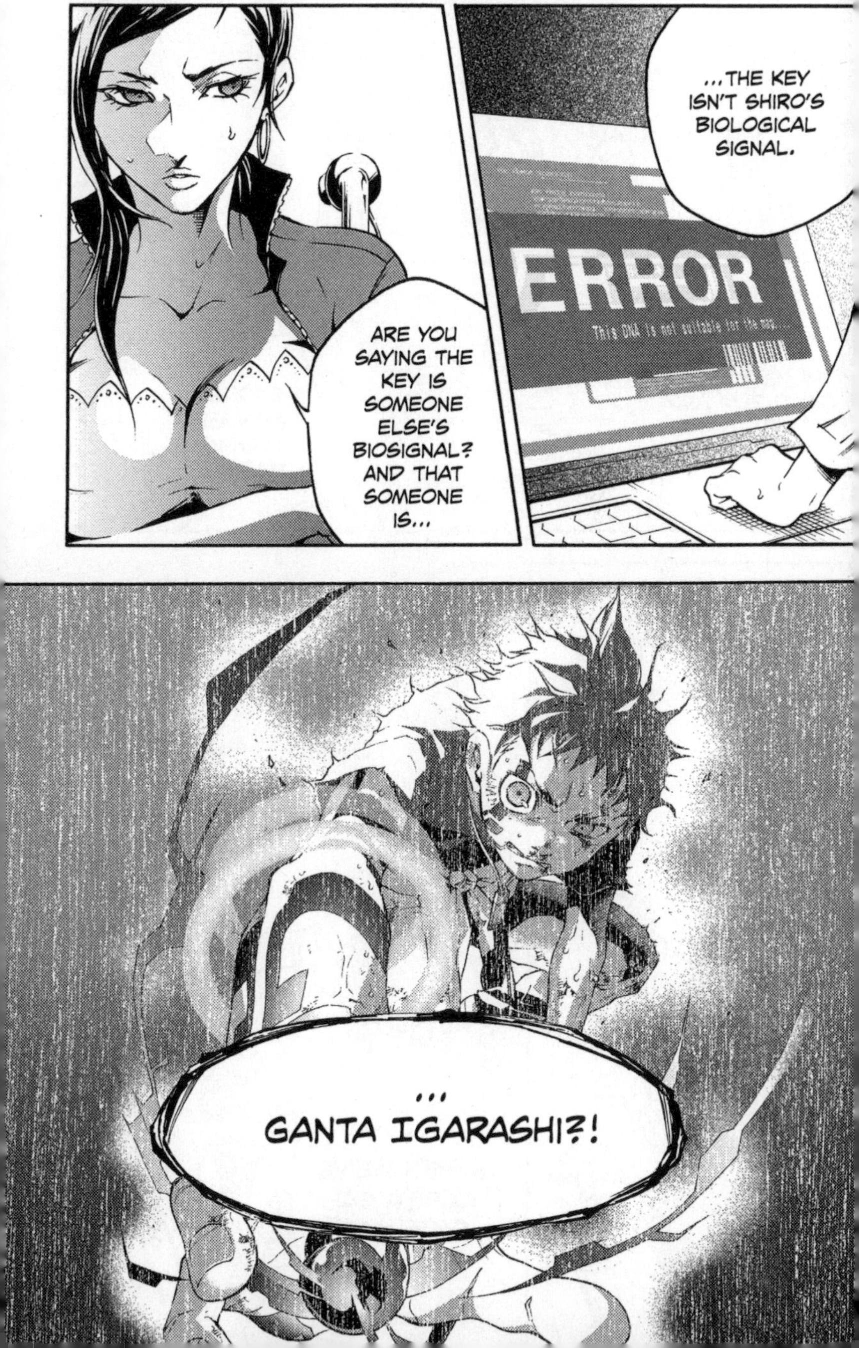
...THE KEY ISN'T SHIRO'S BIOLOGICAL SIGNAL.
ERROR
This DNA is not suitable for the map...
ARE YOU SAYING THE KEY IS SOMEONE ELSE'S BIOSIGNAL? AND THAT SOMEONE IS...
... GANTA IGARASHI?!

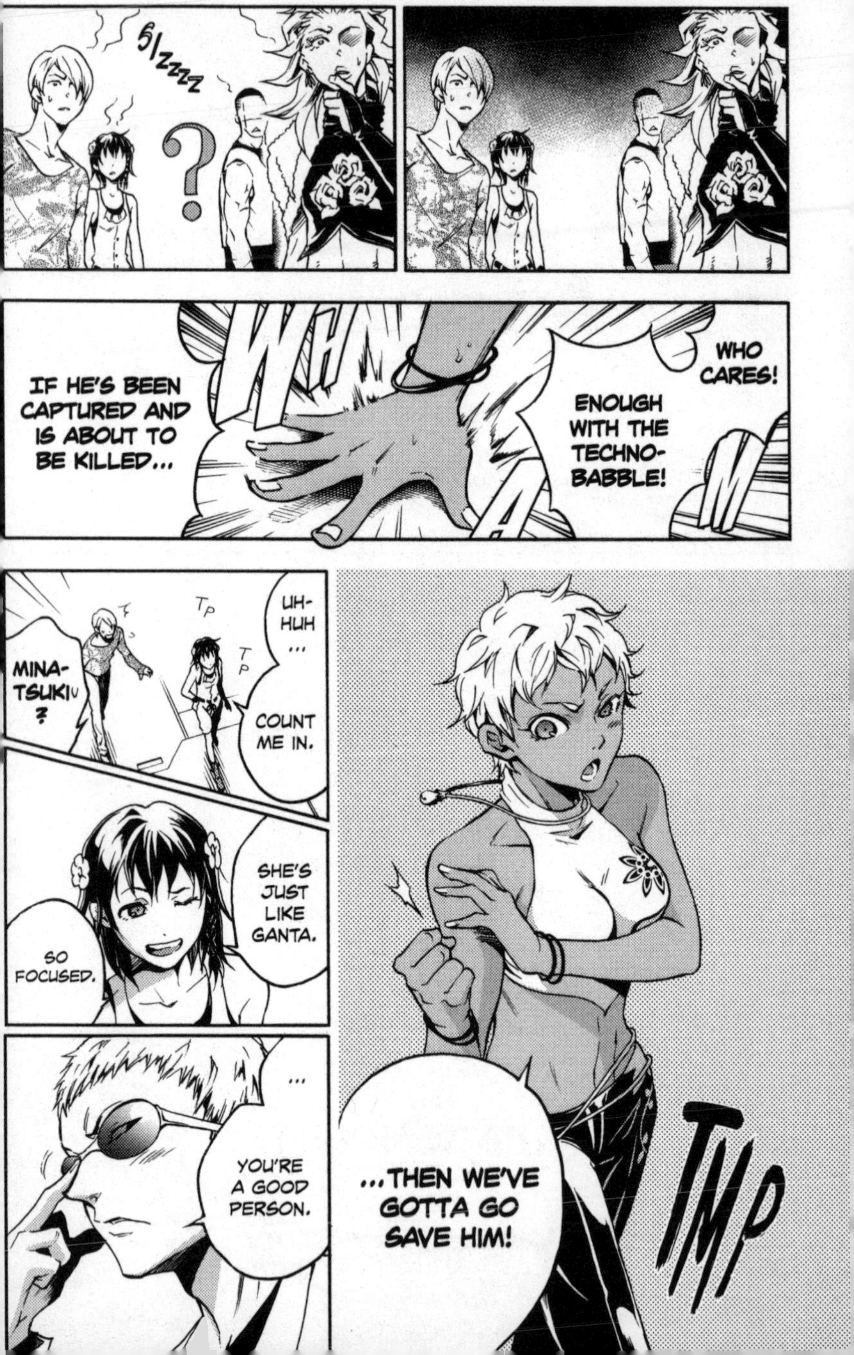
SIZZZZ
?
WHO CARES!
ENOUGH WITH THE TECHNO-BABBLE!
IF HE'S BEEN CAPTURED AND IS ABOUT TO BE KILLED...
...THEN WE'VE GOTTA GO SAVE HIM!
TMP
UH-HUH...
TP
TP
COUNT ME IN.
MINA-TSUKI?
SHE'S JUST LIKE GANTA.
SO FOCUSED.
...
YOU'RE A GOOD PERSON.

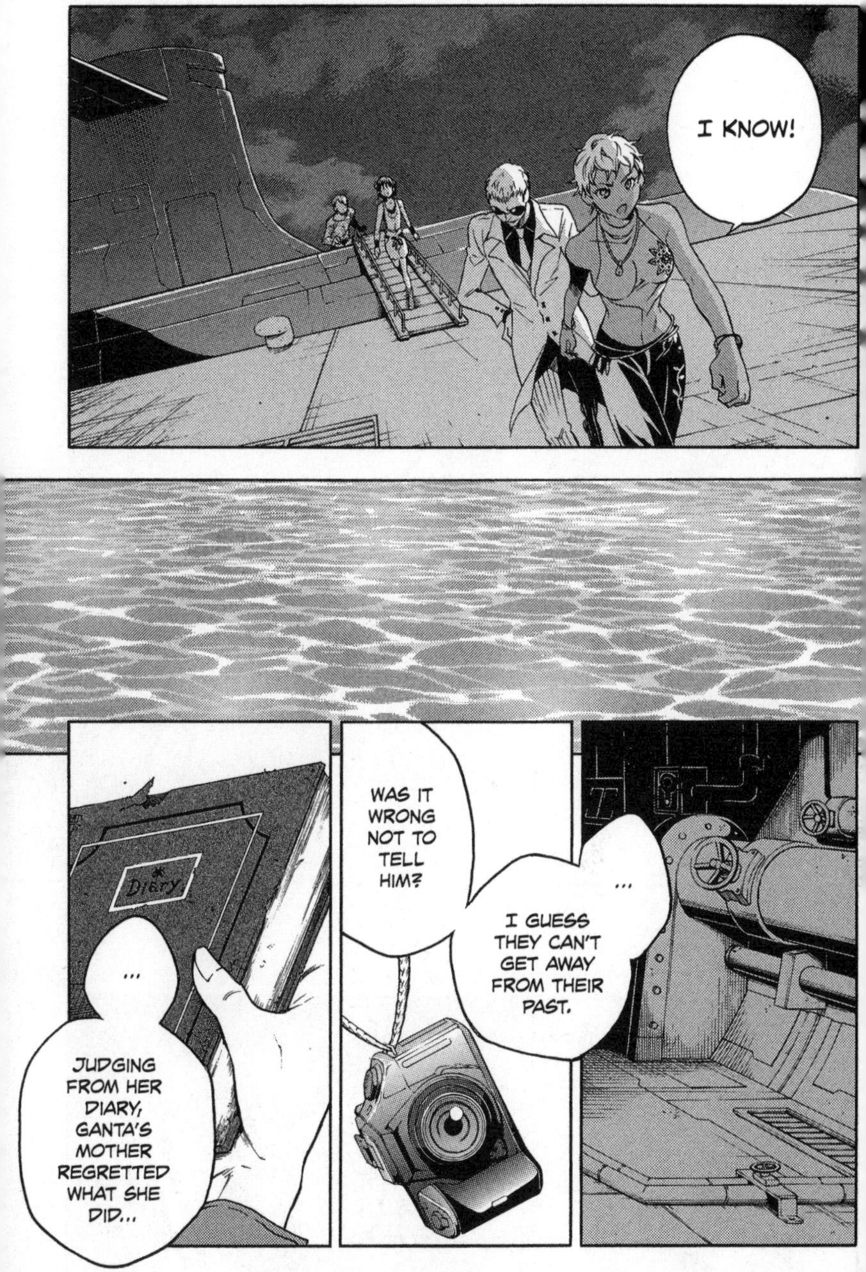
I KNOW!
WAS IT WRONG NOT TO TELL HIM?
...
I GUESS THEY CAN'T GET AWAY FROM THEIR PAST.
Diary
...
JUDGING FROM HER DIARY, GANTA'S MOTHER REGRETTED WHAT SHE DID...

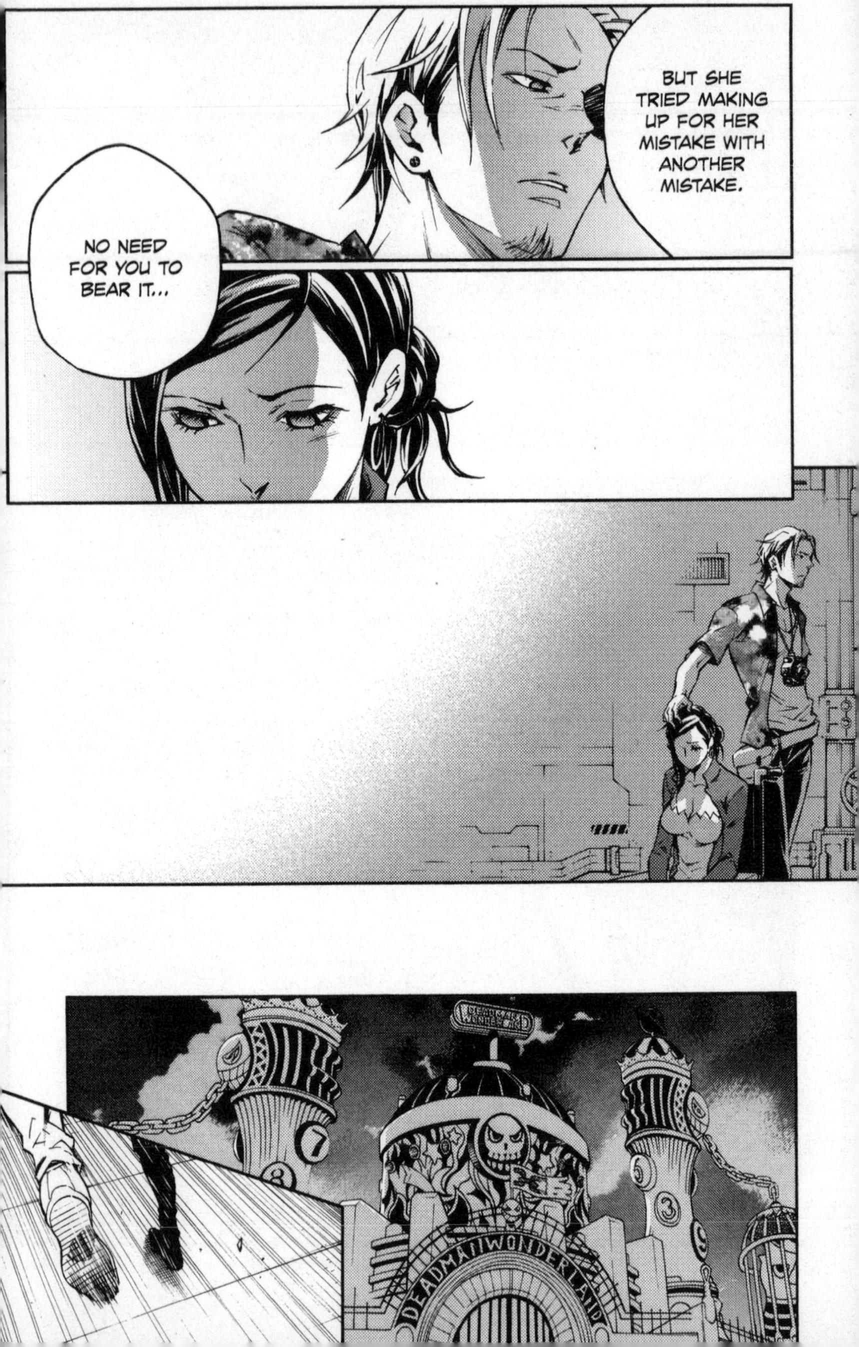
BUT SHE TRIED MAKING UP FOR HER MISTAKE WITH ANOTHER MISTAKE.
NO NEED FOR YOU TO BEAR IT...
DEADMAN WONDERLAND

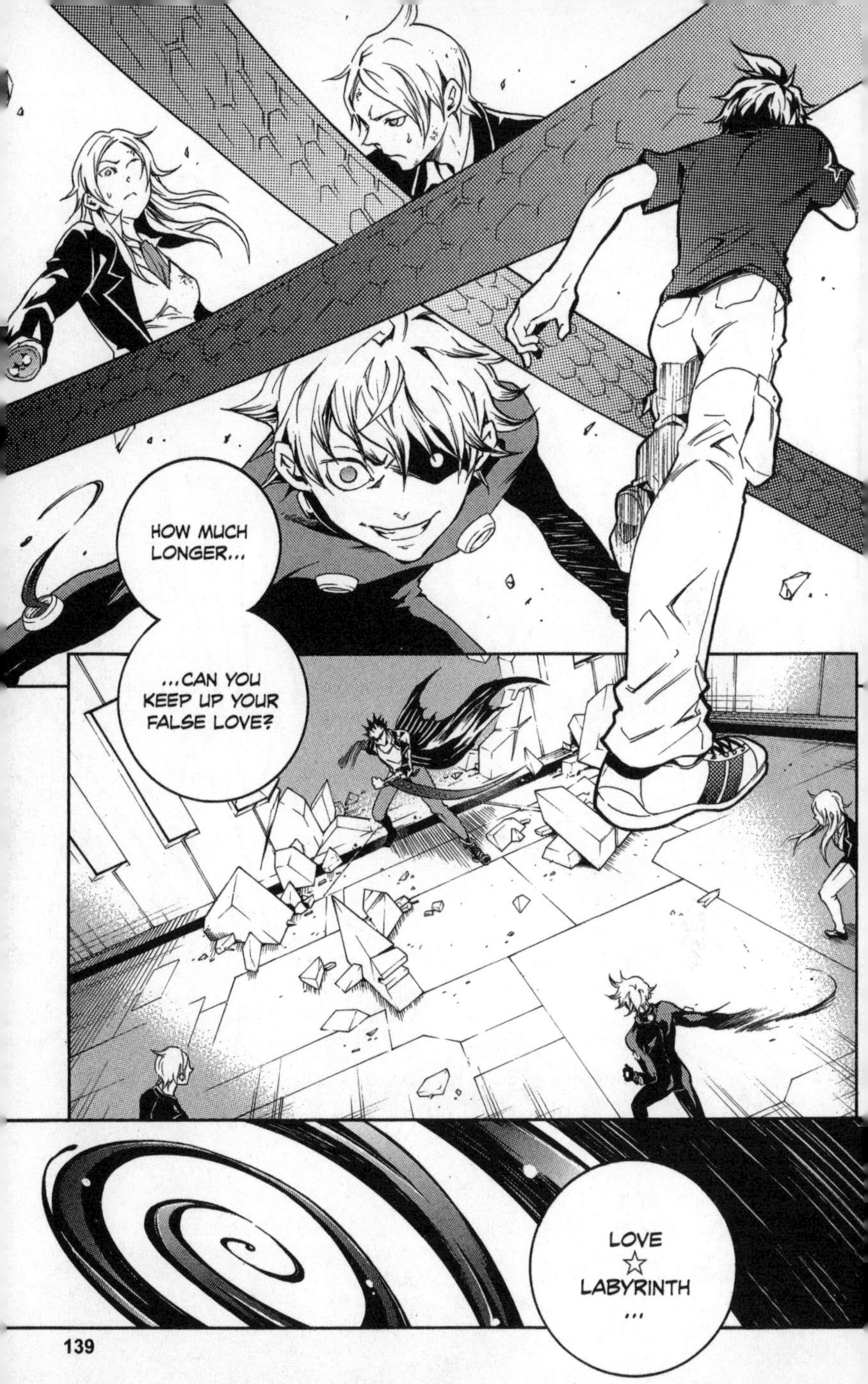
HOW MUCH LONGER...
...CAN YOU KEEP UP YOUR FALSE LOVE?
LOVE ☆ LABYRINTH ...

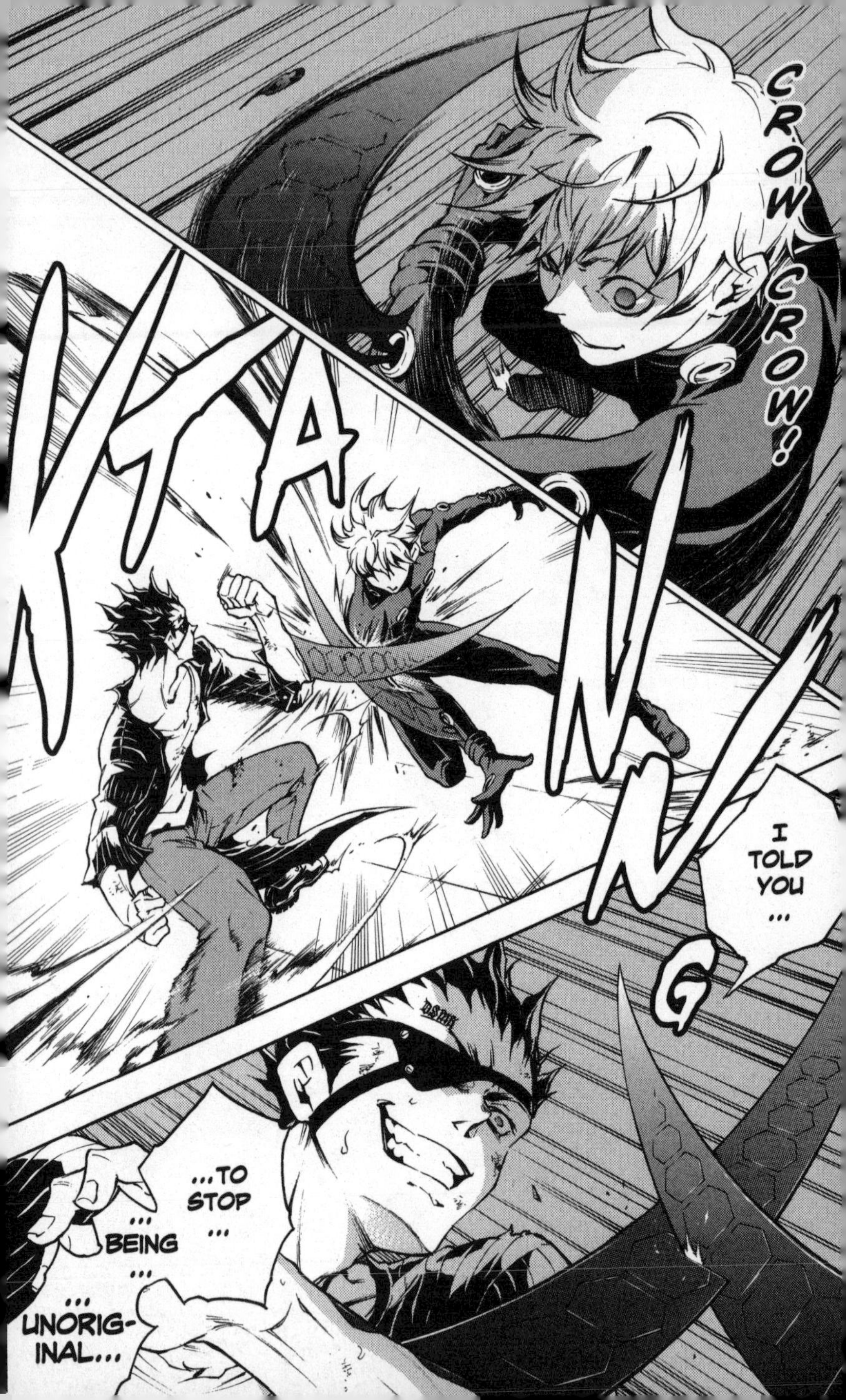
CROW CROW CROW!
KTANNNG
I TOLD YOU ...
...TO STOP ...
... BEING ...
... UNORIG-INAL...

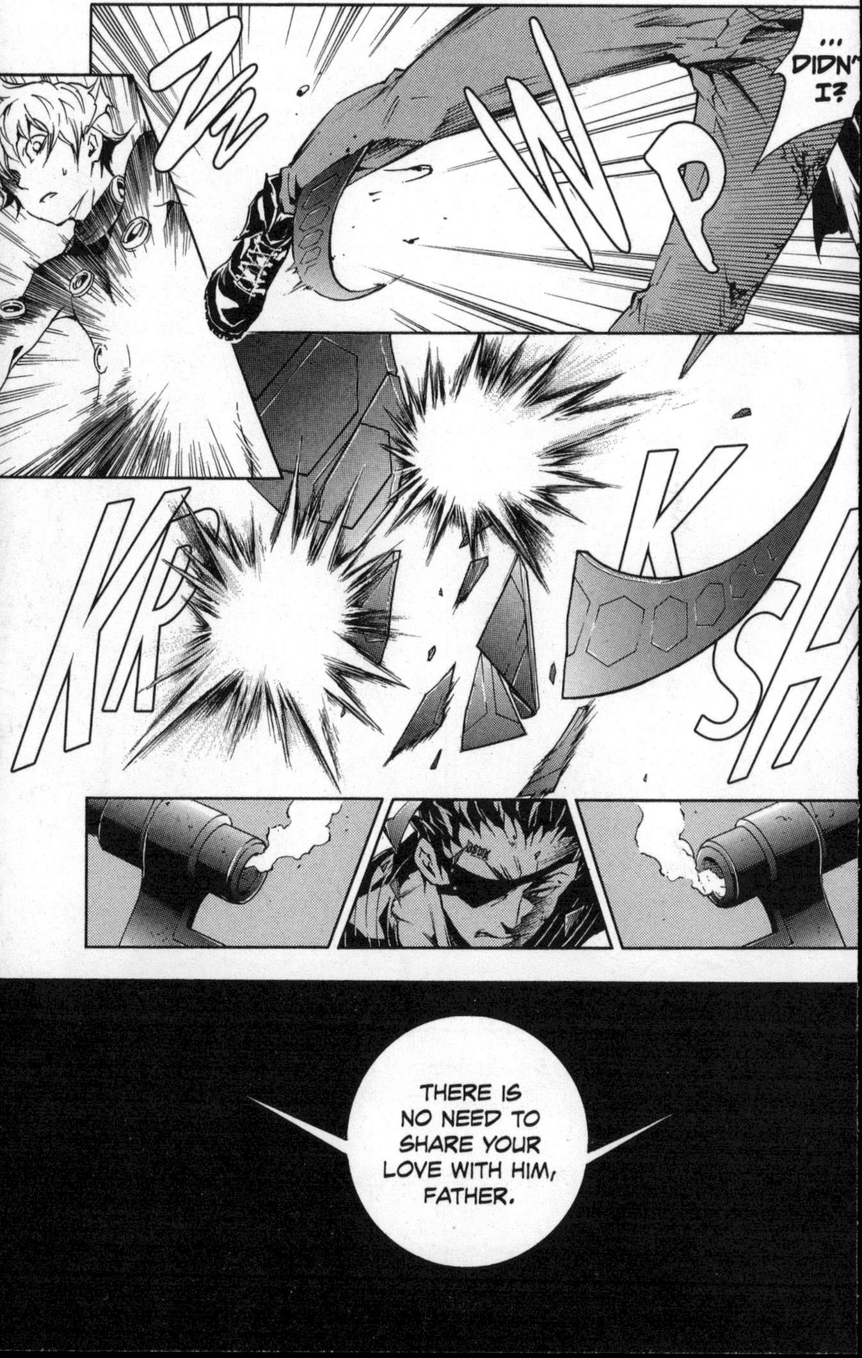
...DIDN'T I?
THERE IS NO NEED TO SHARE YOUR LOVE WITH HIM, FATHER.

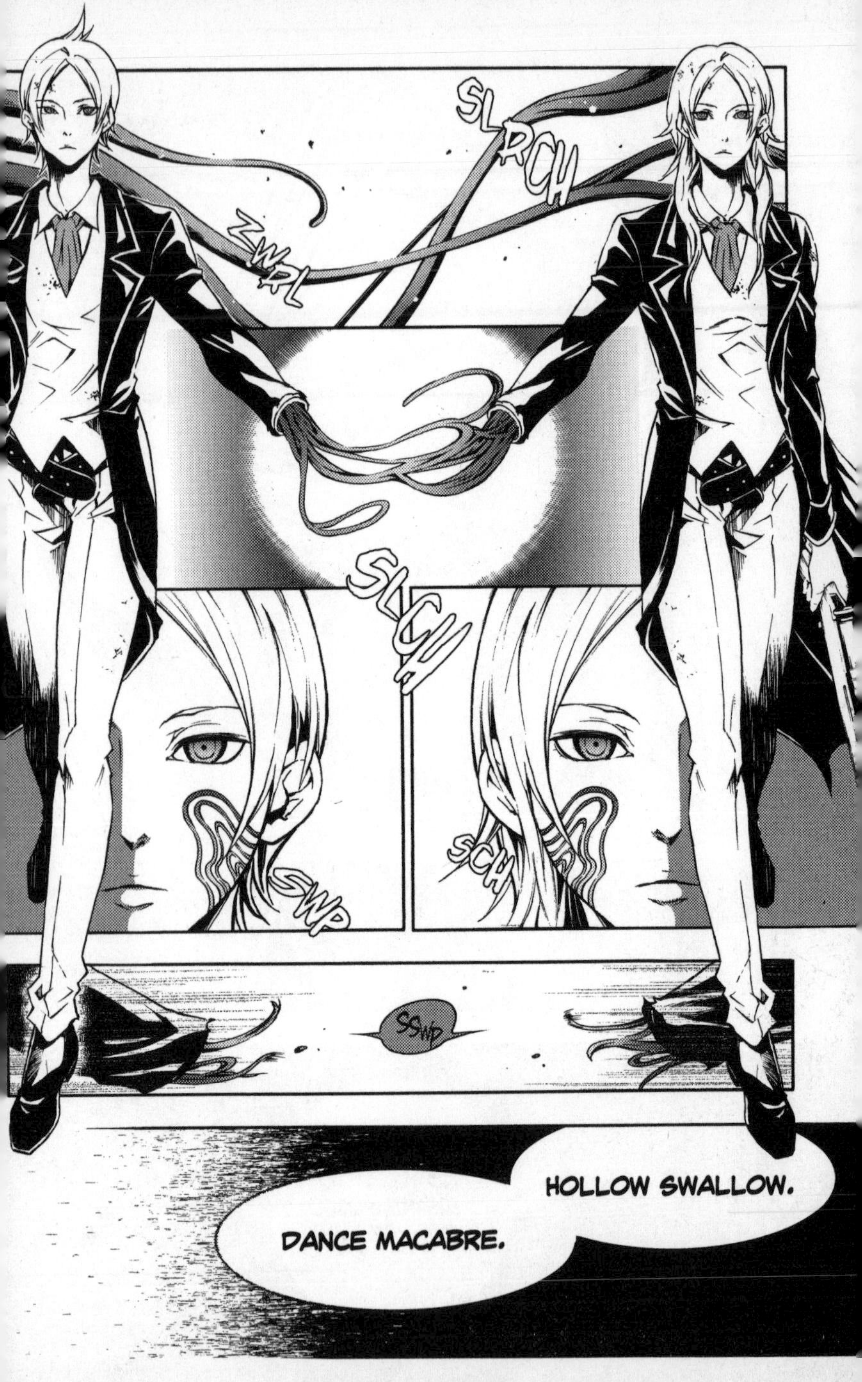
SLRCH
ZWRL
SLCH
SCH
SWP
SSWP
HOLLOW SWALLOW.
DANCE MACABRE.

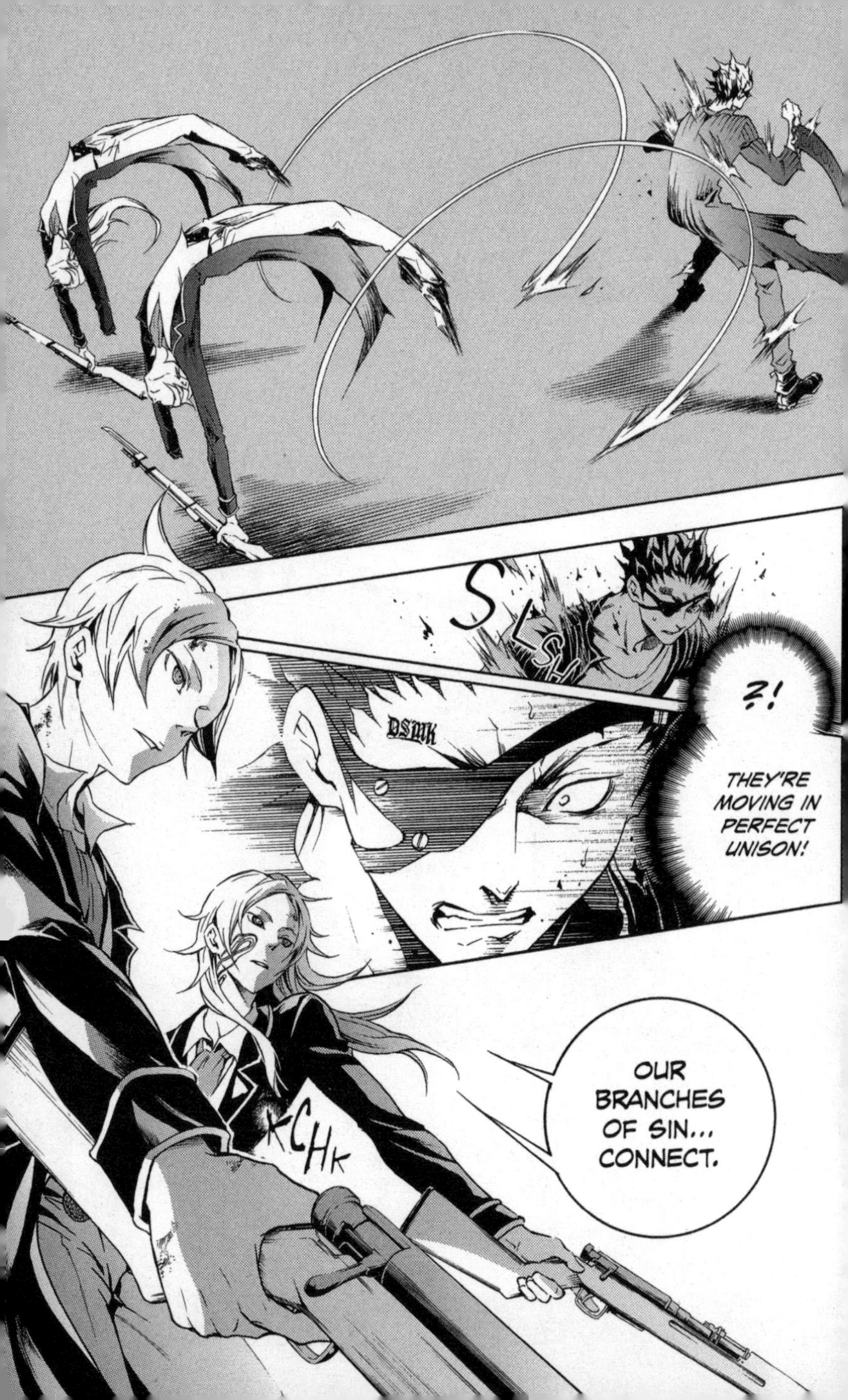
SLSH
?!
THEY'RE MOVING IN PERFECT UNISON!
KCHK
OUR BRANCHES OF SIN... CONNECT.

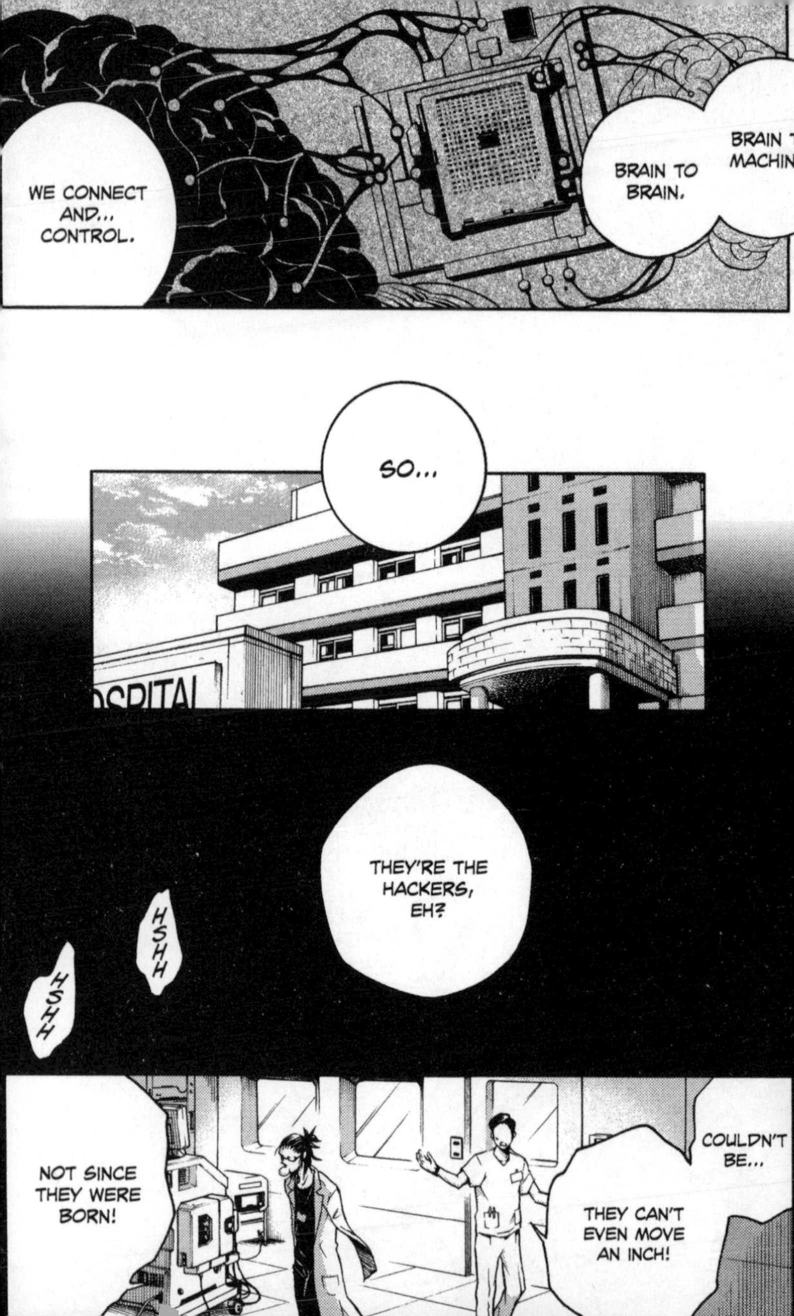
BRAIN TO MACHINE.
BRAIN TO BRAIN.
WE CONNECT AND... CONTROL.
SO...
THEY'RE THE HACKERS, EH?
HSHH
HSHH
COULDN'T BE...
THEY CAN'T EVEN MOVE AN INCH!
NOT SINCE THEY WERE BORN!

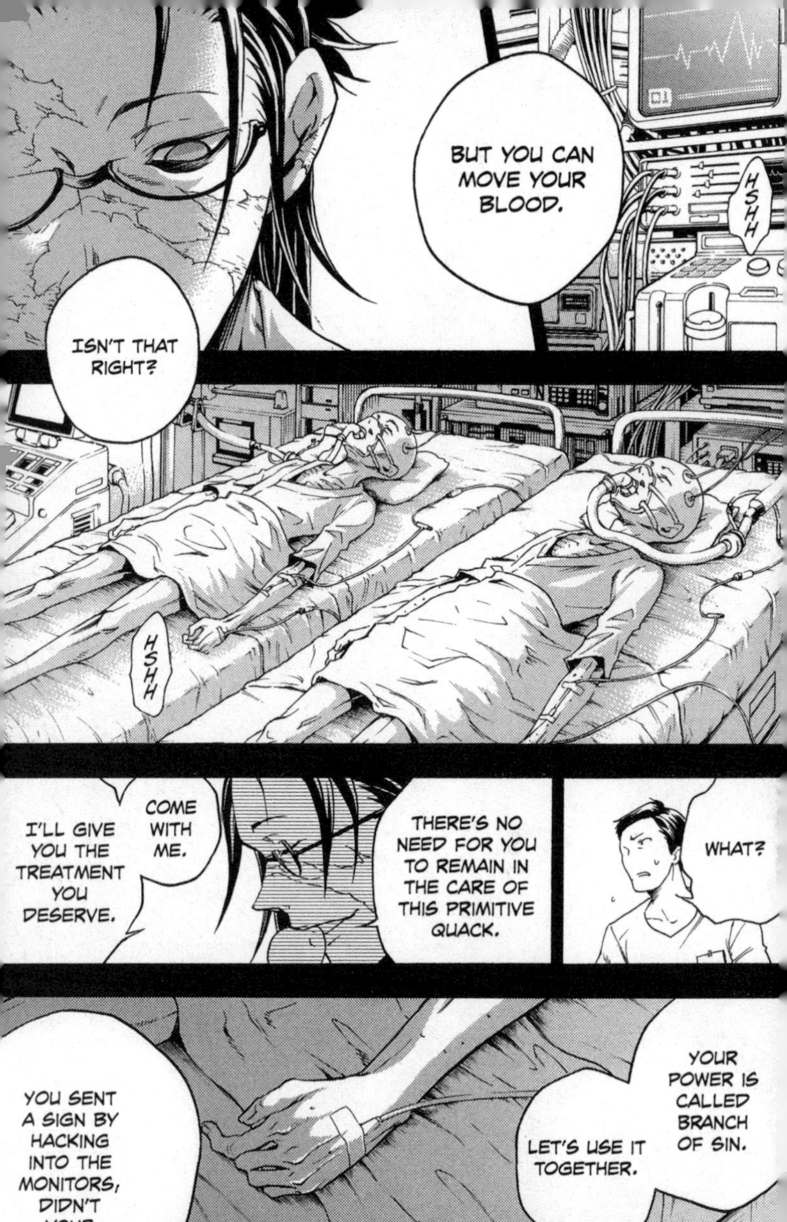
HSHH
BUT YOU CAN MOVE YOUR BLOOD.
ISN'T THAT RIGHT?
HSHH
WHAT?
THERE'S NO NEED FOR YOU TO REMAIN IN THE CARE OF THIS PRIMITIVE QUACK.
COME WITH ME.
I'LL GIVE YOU THE TREATMENT YOU DESERVE.
YOUR POWER IS CALLED BRANCH OF SIN.
LET'S USE IT TOGETHER.
YOU SENT A SIGN BY HACKING INTO THE MONITORS, DIDN'T YOU?

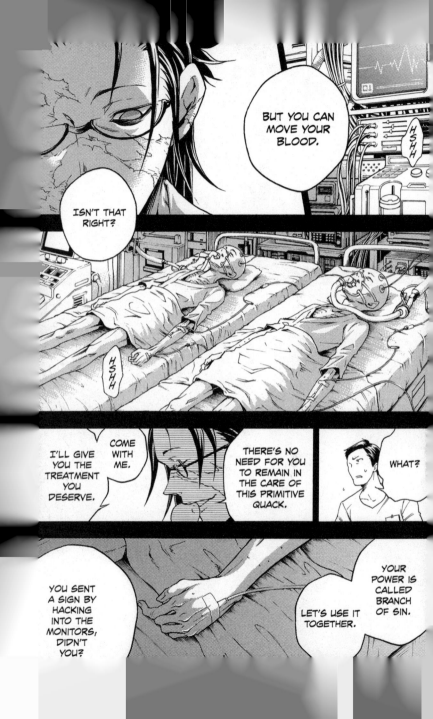

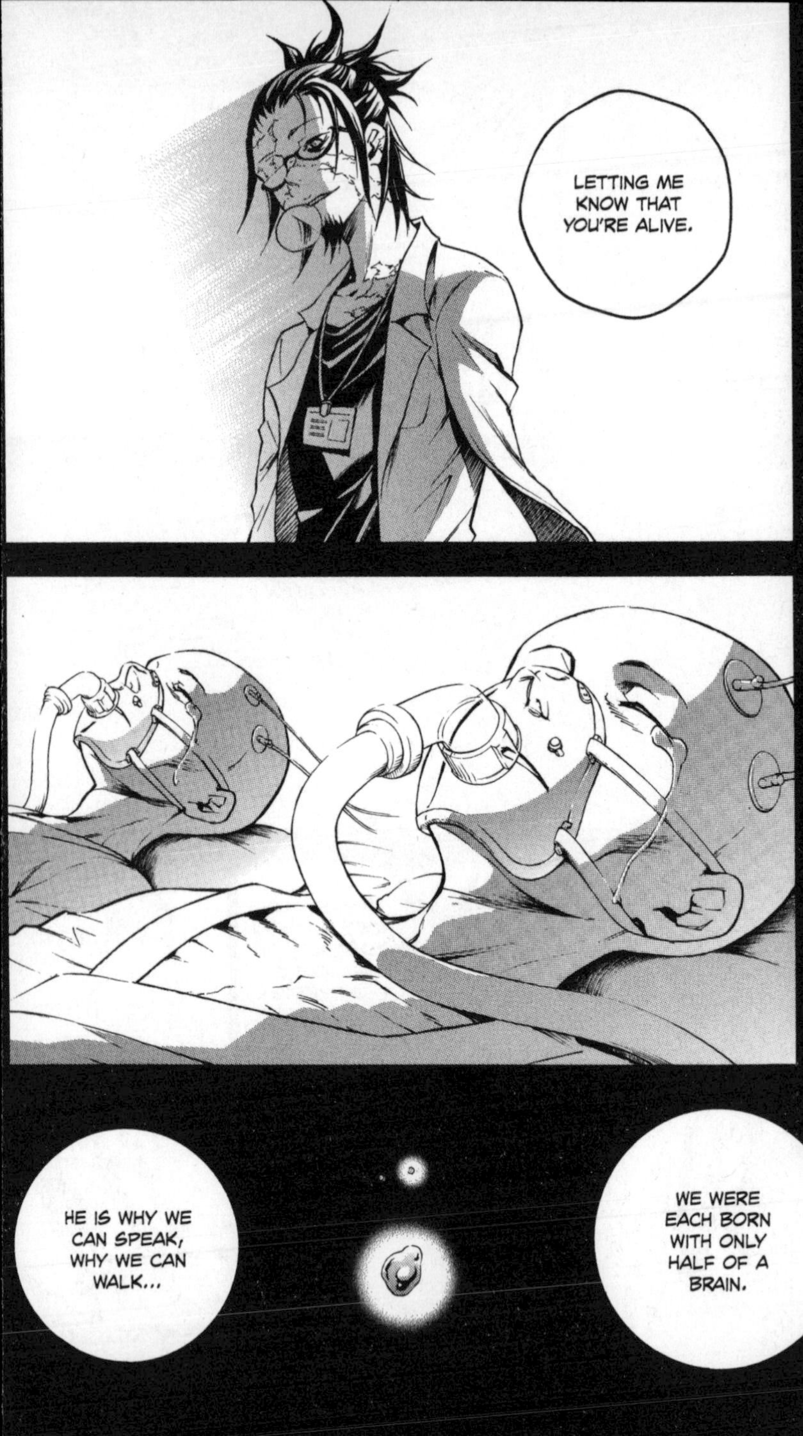
LETTING ME KNOW THAT YOU'RE ALIVE.
WE WERE EACH BORN WITH ONLY HALF OF A BRAIN.
HE IS WHY WE CAN SPEAK, WHY WE CAN WALK...

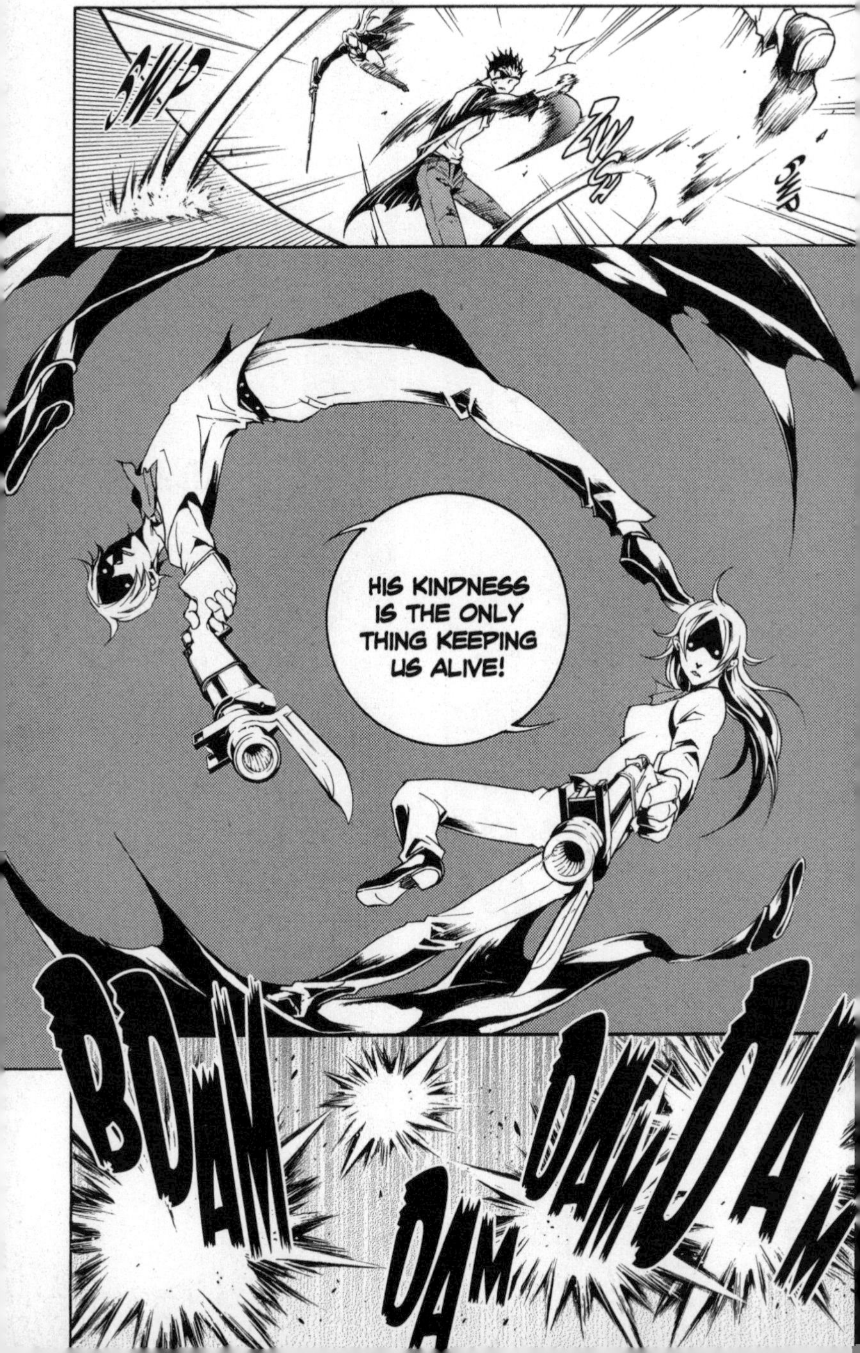
SWIP
ZWCH
SWIP
HIS KINDNESS IS THE ONLY THING KEEPING US ALIVE!
DAM
DAM
DAM
BDAM

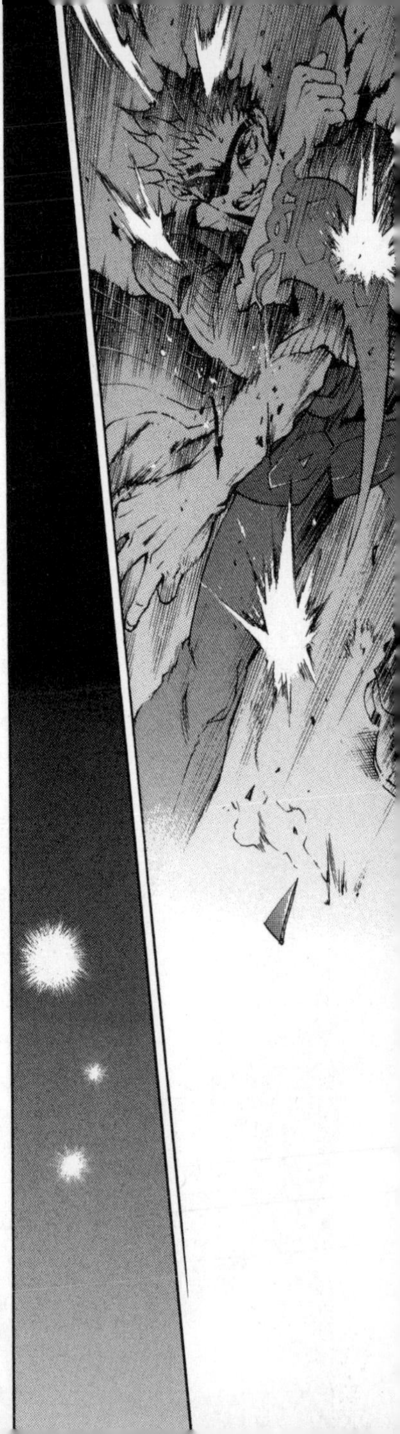
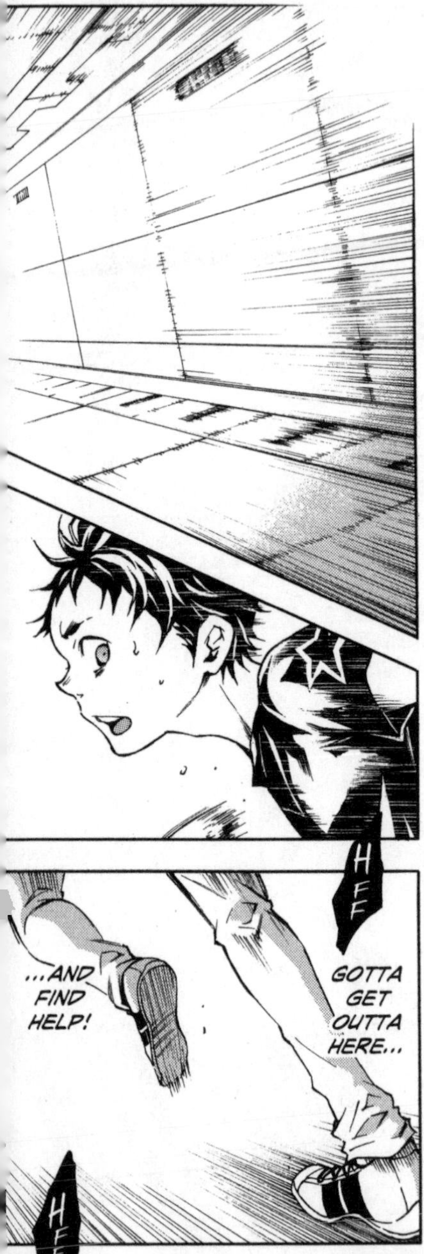
HFF
GOTTA GET OUTTA HERE...
...AND FIND HELP!
HFF

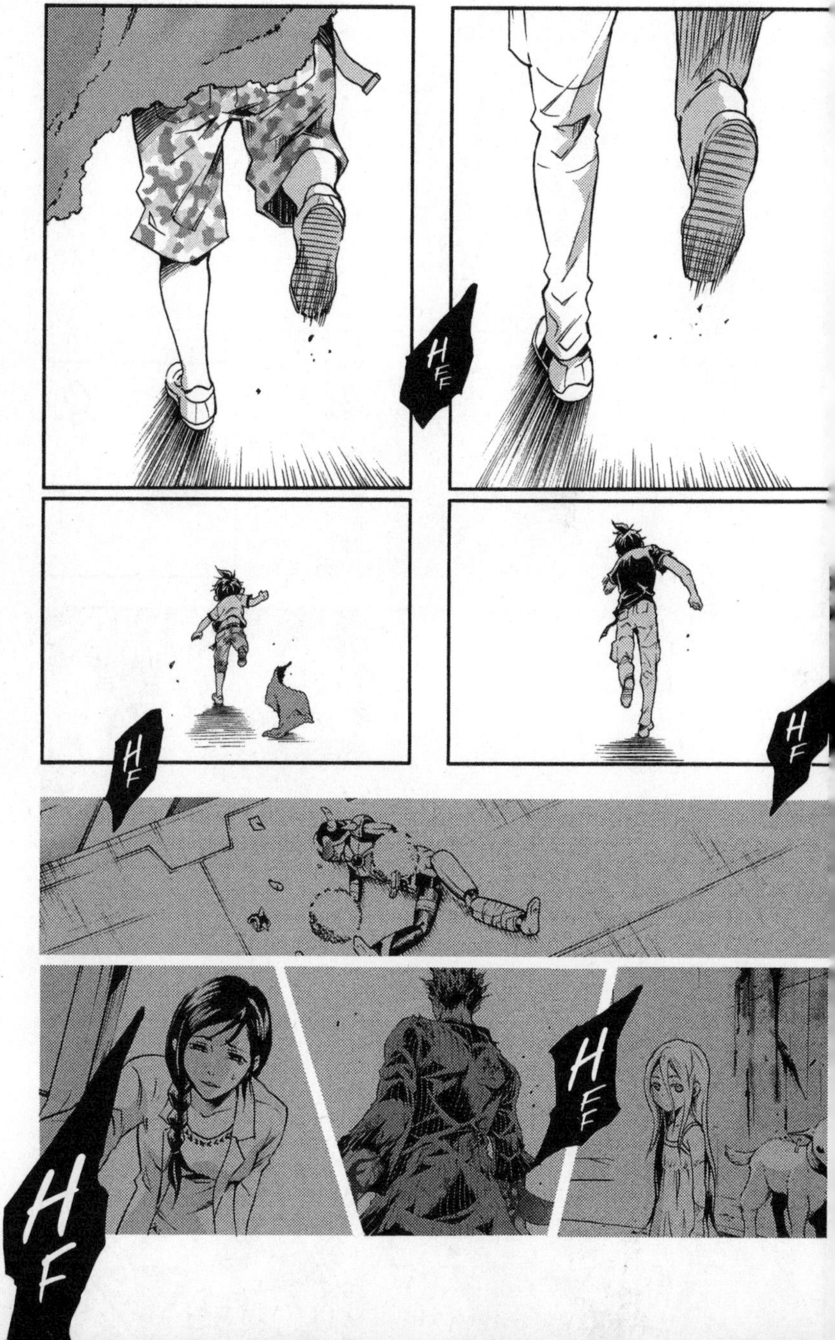
HFF
HF
HF
HFF
HF

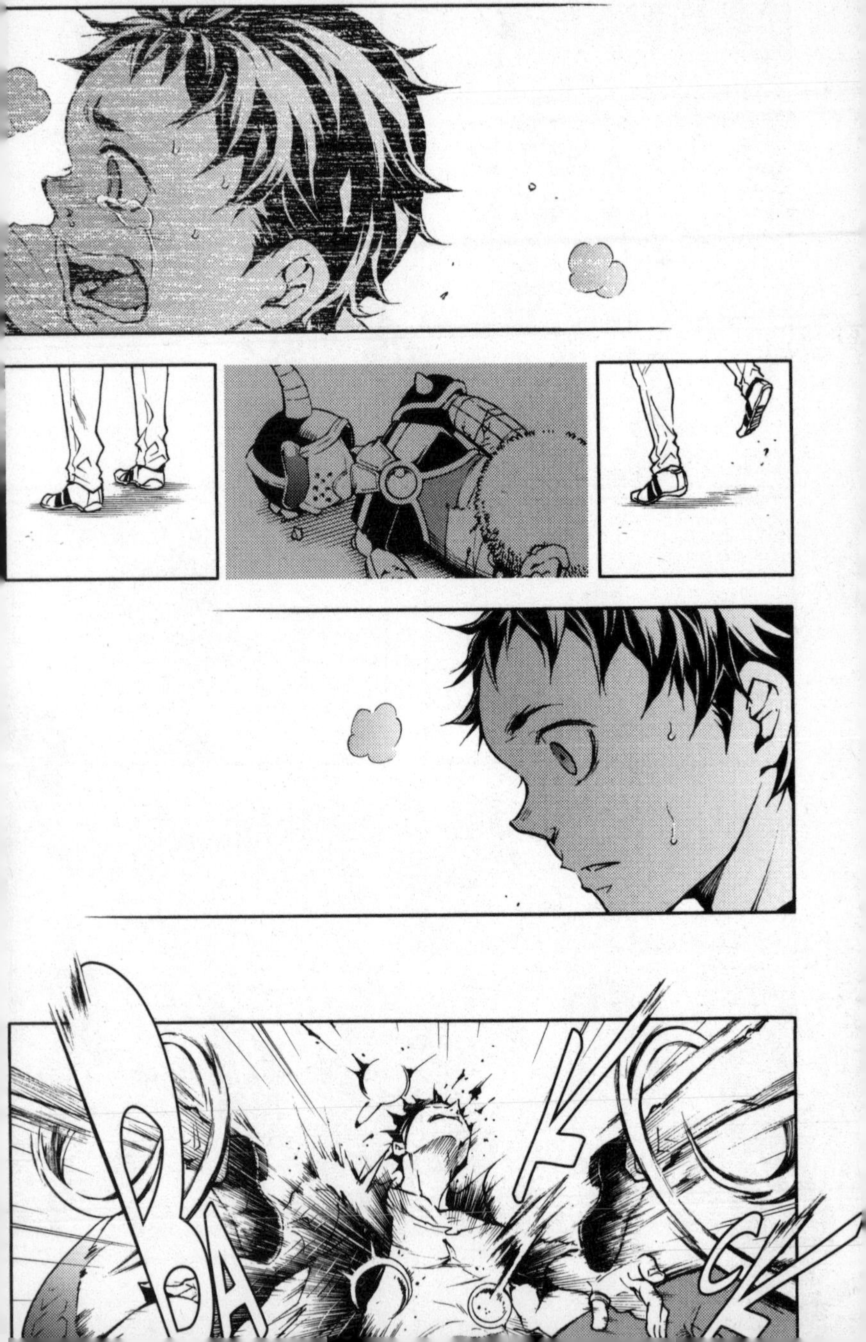

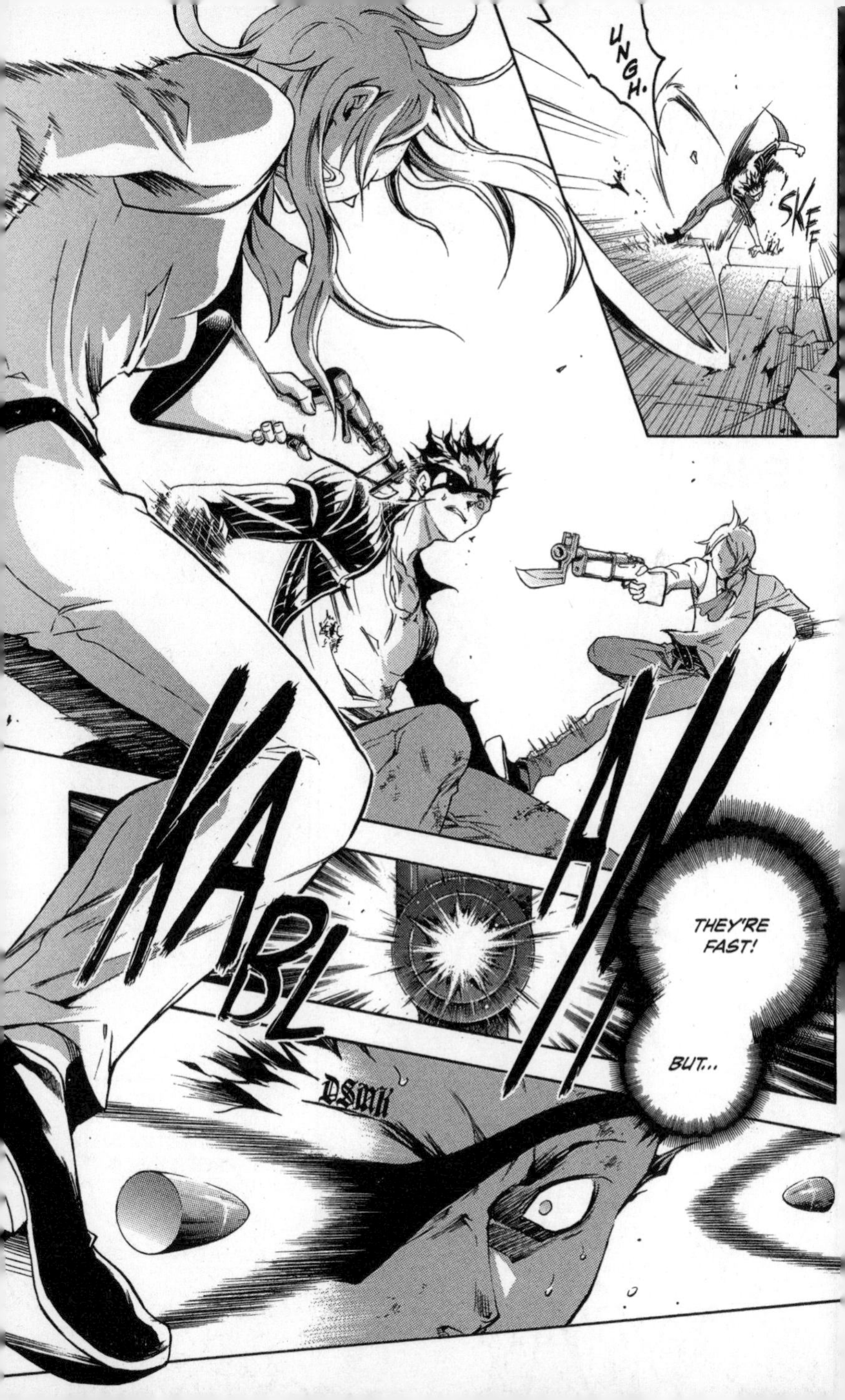
UNGH.
SKFF
KABLAM
THEY'RE FAST!
BUT...

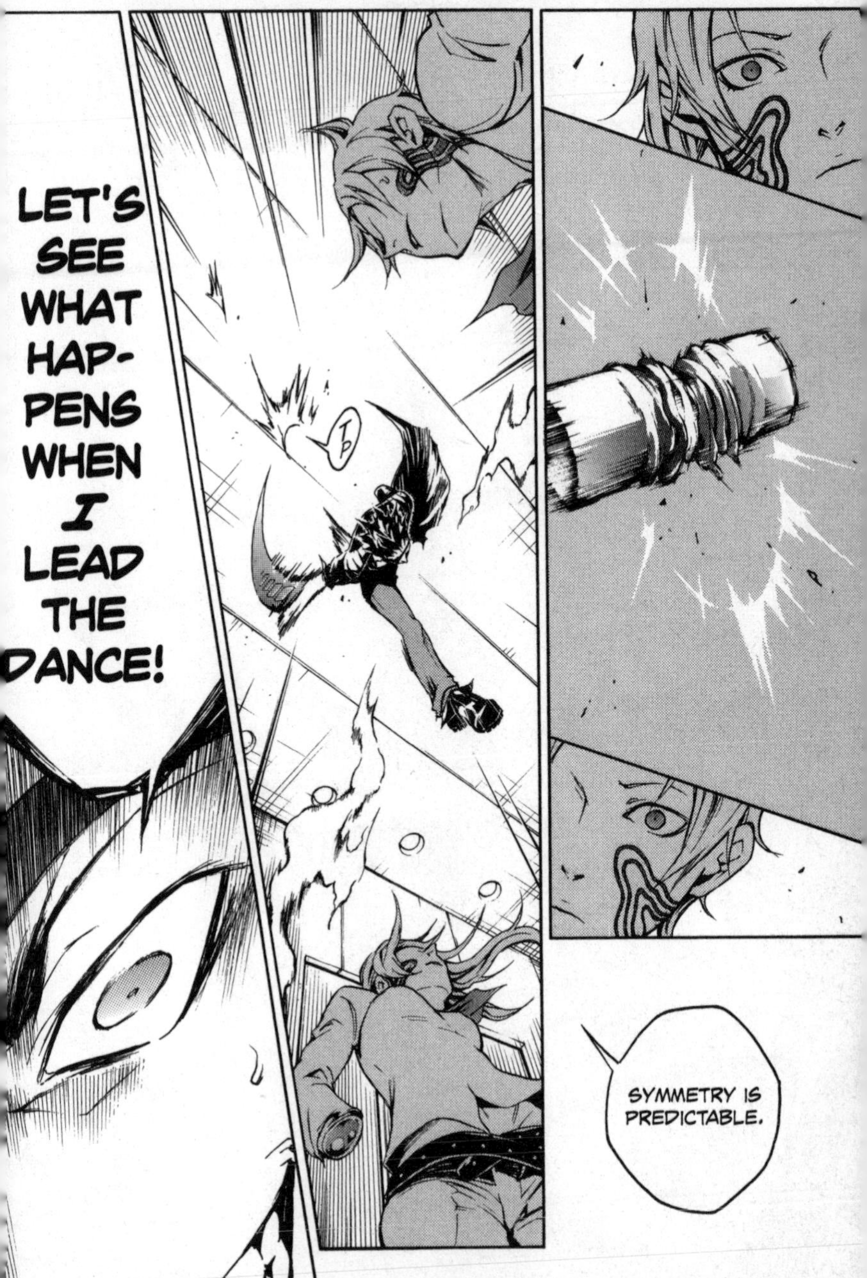
SYMMETRY IS PREDICTABLE.
LET'S SEE WHAT HAP-PENS WHEN I LEAD THE DANCE!

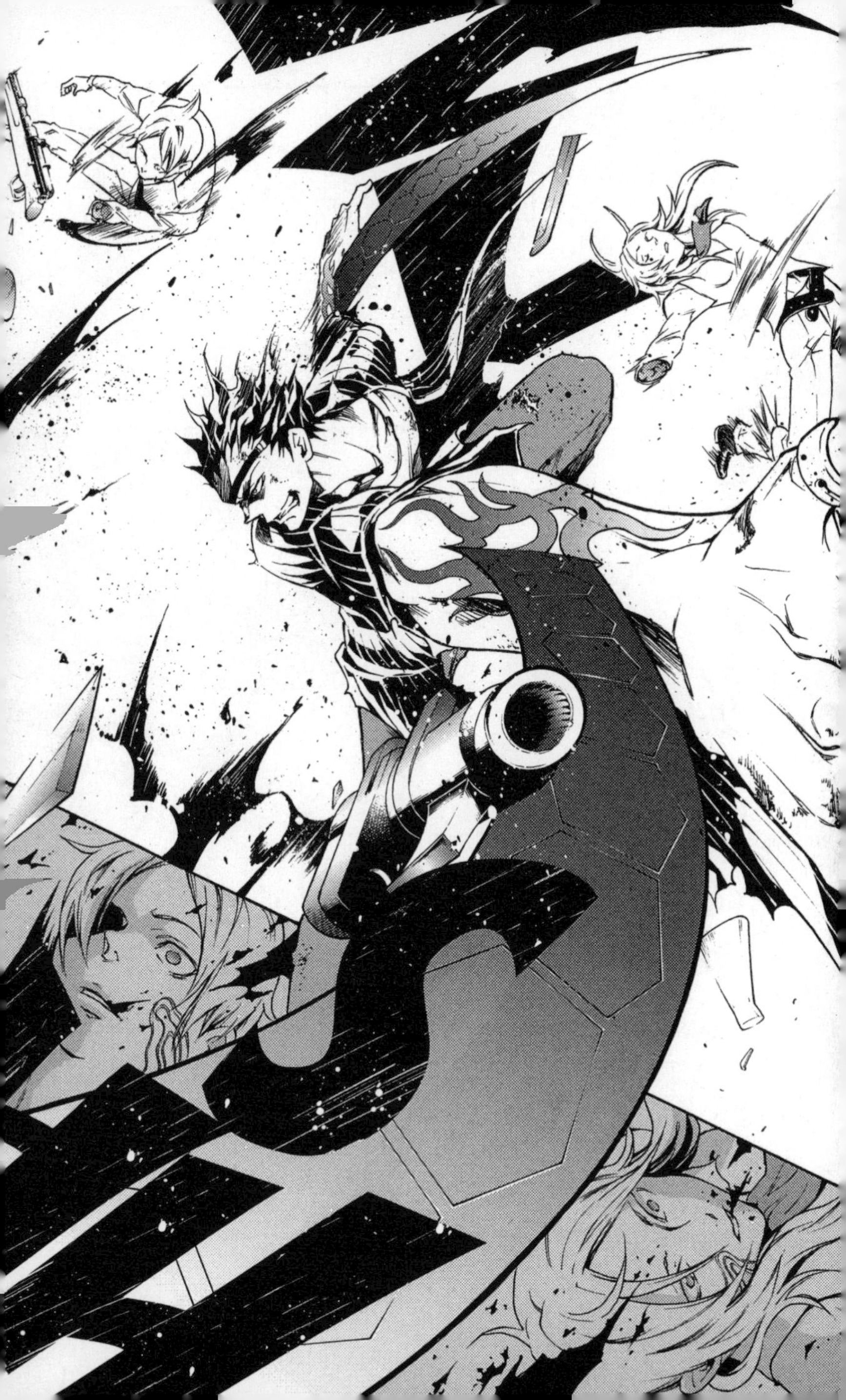

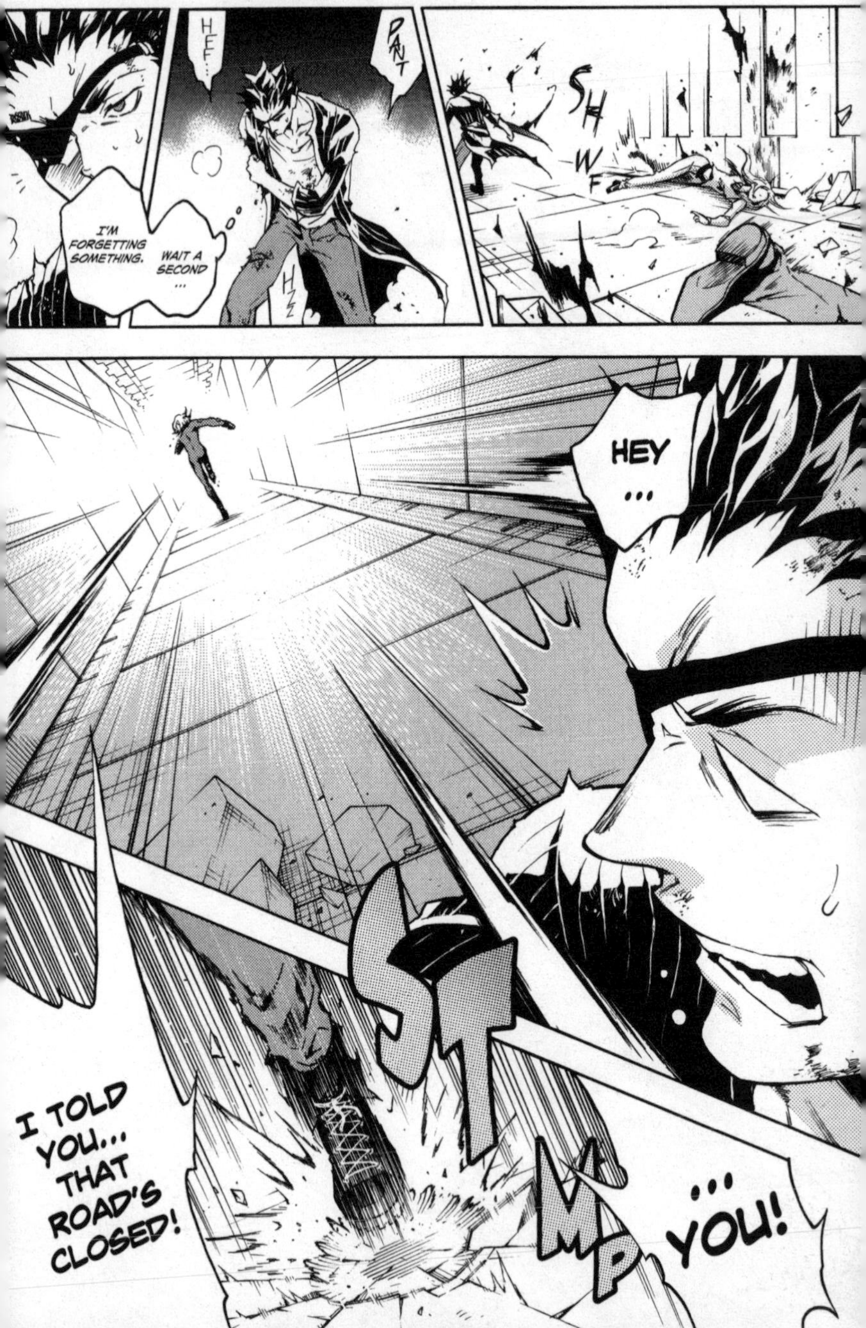
SHWF
PANT
HEF...
HZZ
WAIT A SECOND...
I'M FORGETTING SOMETHING.
HEY...
...YOU!
STMP
I TOLD YOU... THAT ROAD'S CLOSED!

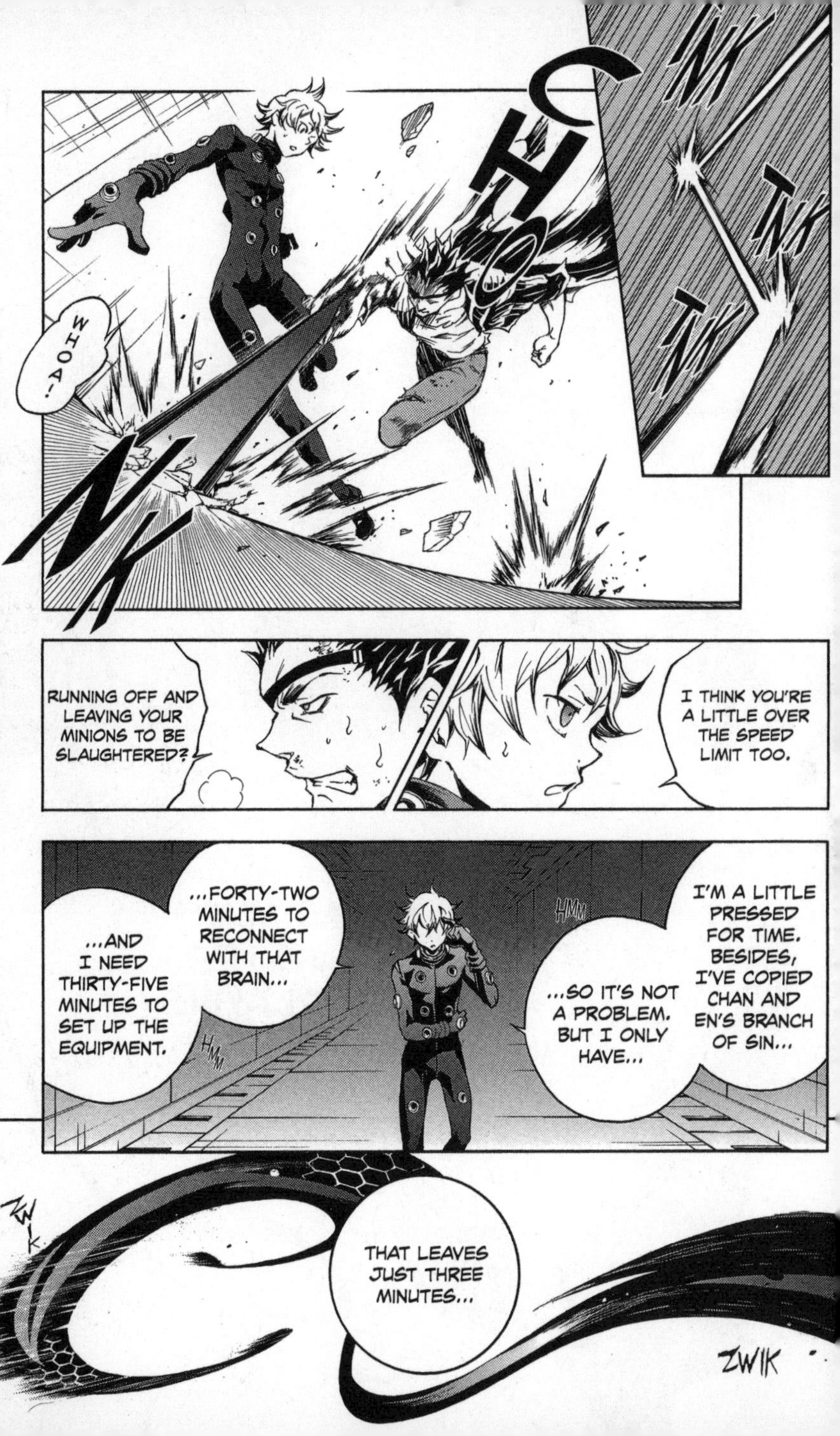
TINK
TINK
WHOA-!
I THINK YOU'RE A LITTLE OVER THE SPEED LIMIT TOO.
RUNNING OFF AND LEAVING YOUR MINIONS TO BE SLAUGHTERED?
I'M A LITTLE PRESSED FOR TIME. BESIDES, I'VE COPIED CHAN AND EN'S BRANCH OF SIN...
...SO IT'S NOT A PROBLEM. BUT I ONLY HAVE...
HMM
...FORTY-TWO MINUTES TO RECONNECT WITH THAT BRAIN...
...AND I NEED THIRTY-FIVE MINUTES TO SET UP THE EQUIPMENT.
HMM
ZWIK
THAT LEAVES JUST THREE MINUTES...
ZWIK

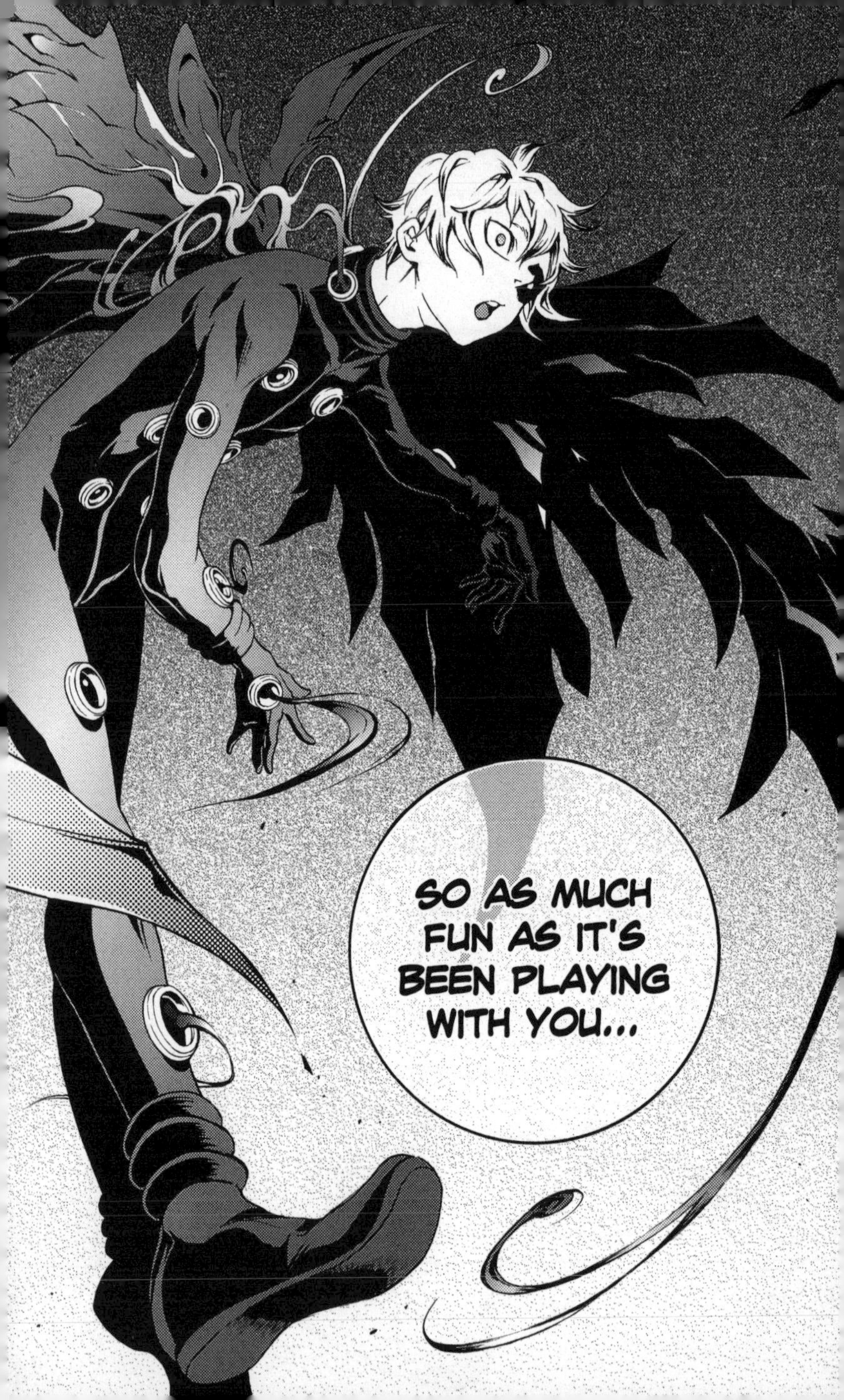
SO AS MUCH FUN AS IT'S BEEN PLAYING WITH YOU...

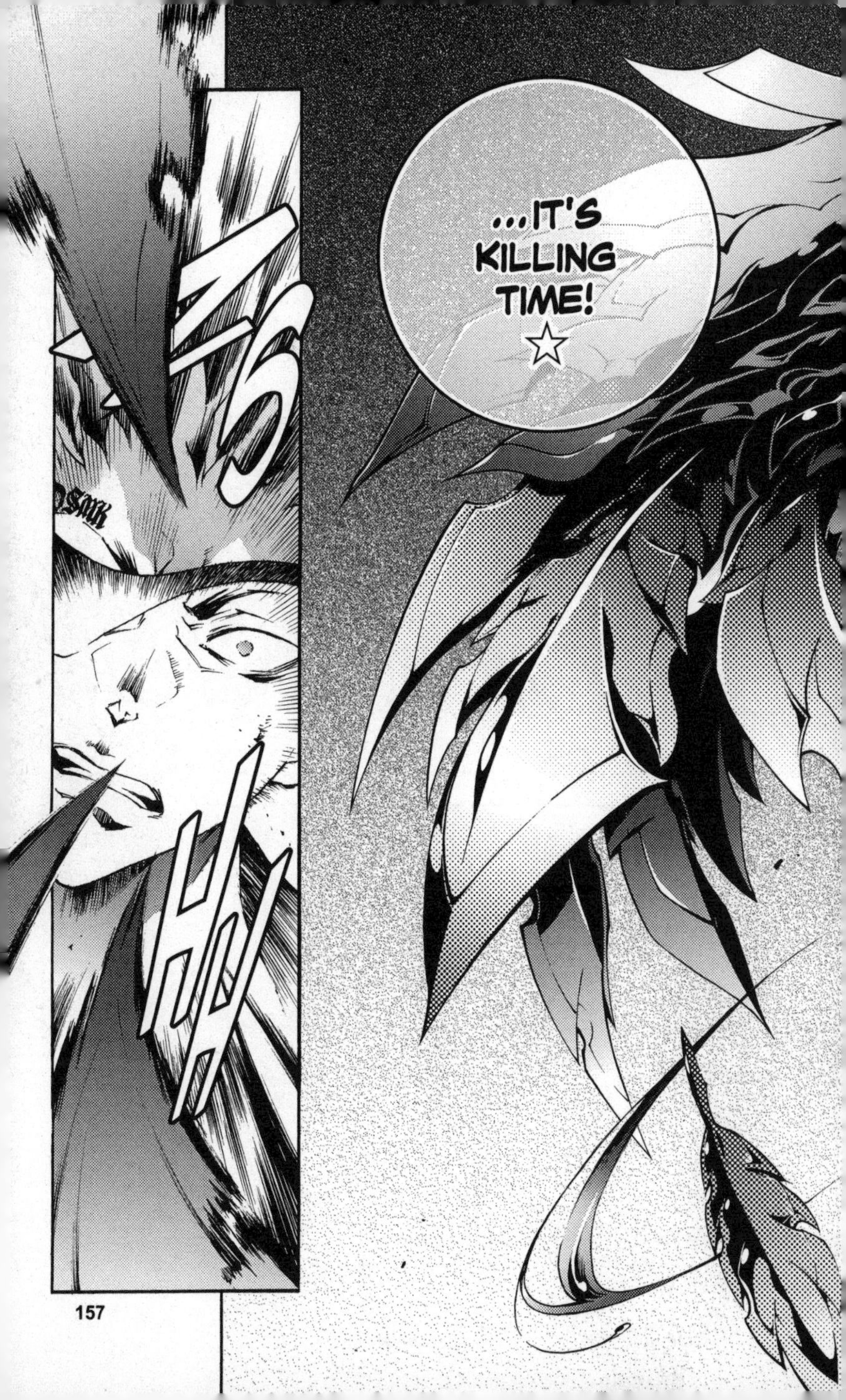
...IT'S KILLING TIME! ☆

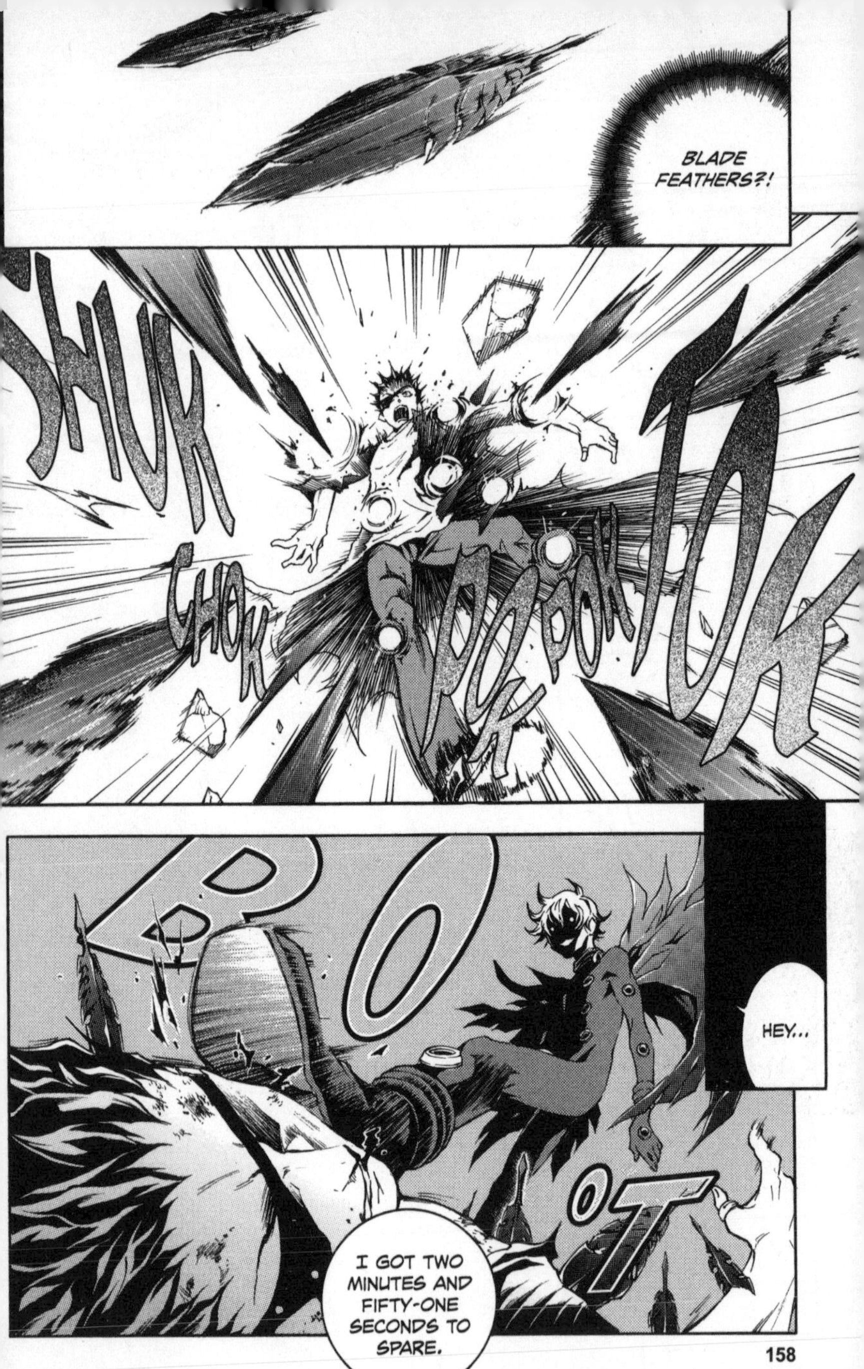
BLADE FEATHERS?!
TOK
POK
POK
CHOK
SHUK
HEY...
BOOT
I GOT TWO MINUTES AND FIFTY-ONE SECONDS TO SPARE.

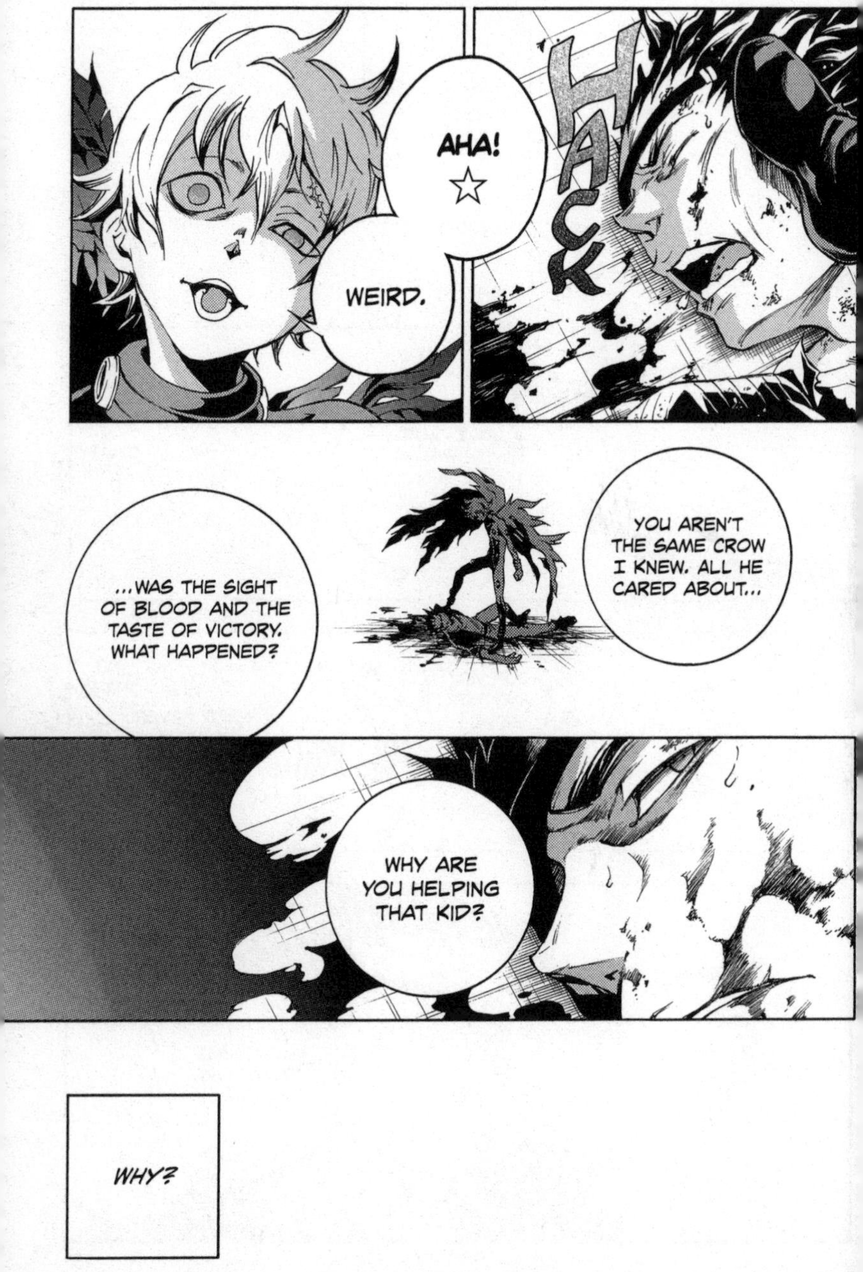
HACK
AHA! ☆
WEIRD.
YOU AREN'T THE SAME CROW I KNEW. ALL HE CARED ABOUT...
...WAS THE SIGHT OF BLOOD AND THE TASTE OF VICTORY. WHAT HAPPENED?
WHY ARE YOU HELPING THAT KID?
WHY?

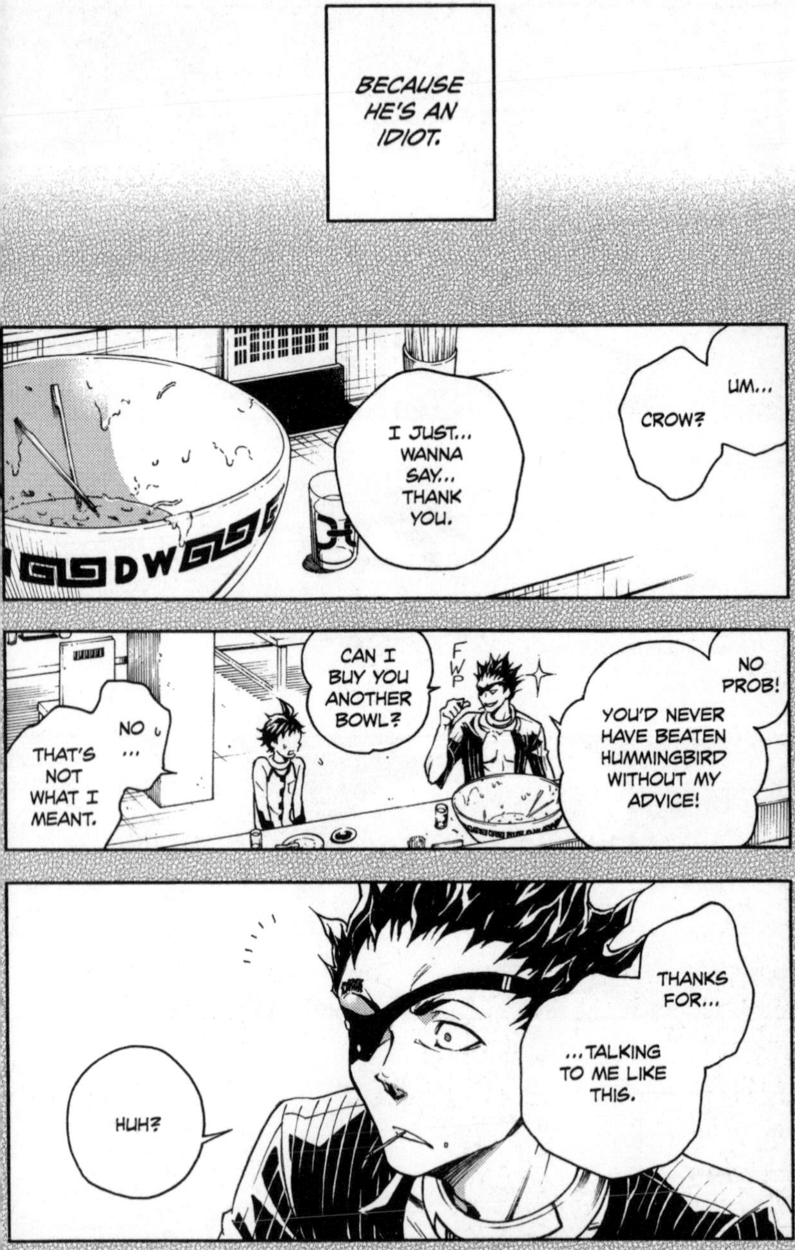
BECAUSE HE'S AN IDIOT.
UM... CROW?
I JUST... WANNA SAY... THANK YOU.
NO PROB!
YOU'D NEVER HAVE BEATEN HUMMINGBIRD WITHOUT MY ADVICE!
FWP
CAN I BUY YOU ANOTHER BOWL?
NO...
THAT'S NOT WHAT I MEANT.
THANKS FOR...
...TALKING TO ME LIKE THIS.
HUH?

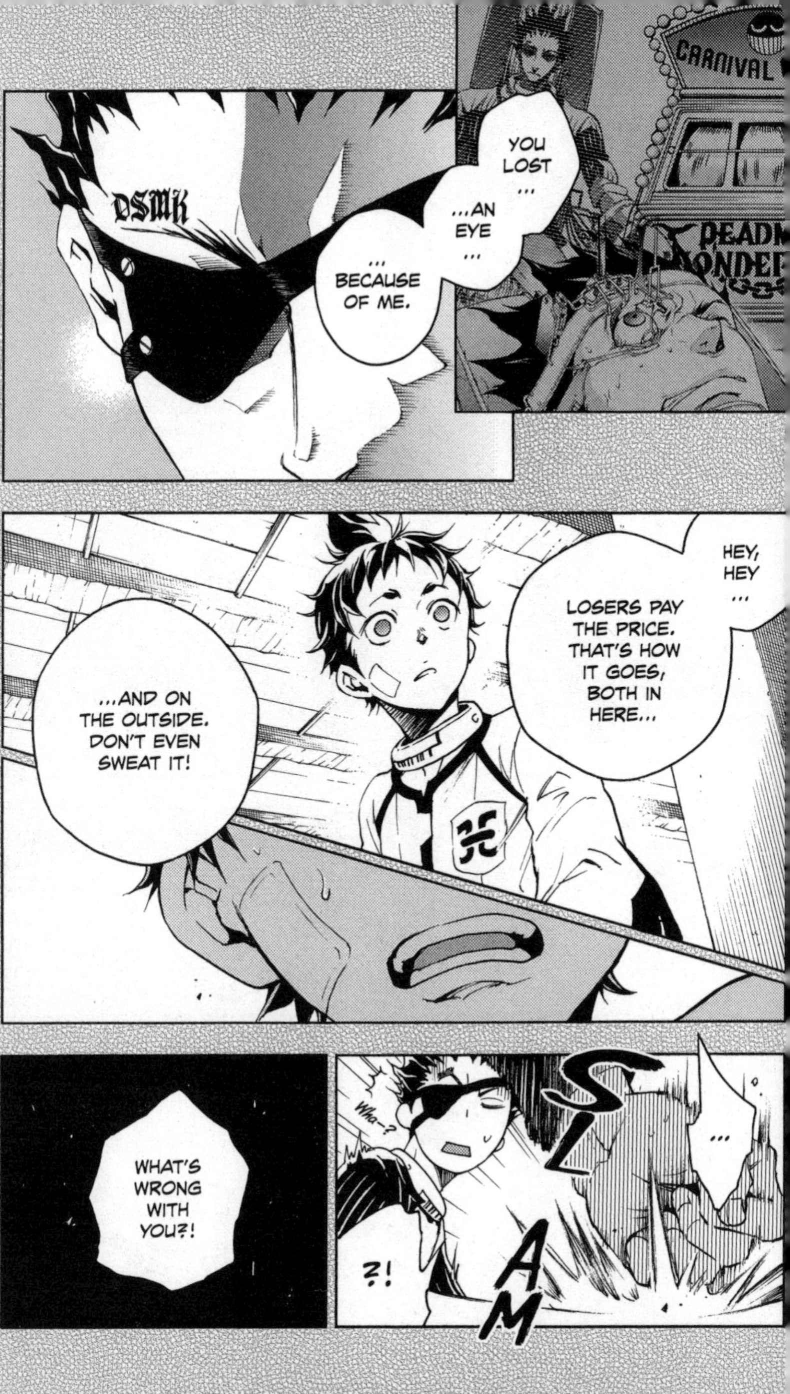
CARNIVAL
YOU LOST ...
...AN EYE ...
... BECAUSE OF ME.
DSMK
HEY, HEY ...
LOSERS PAY THE PRICE. THAT'S HOW IT GOES, BOTH IN HERE...
...AND ON THE OUTSIDE. DON'T EVEN SWEAT IT!
...
SLAM
Wha-?
?!
WHAT'S WRONG WITH YOU?!

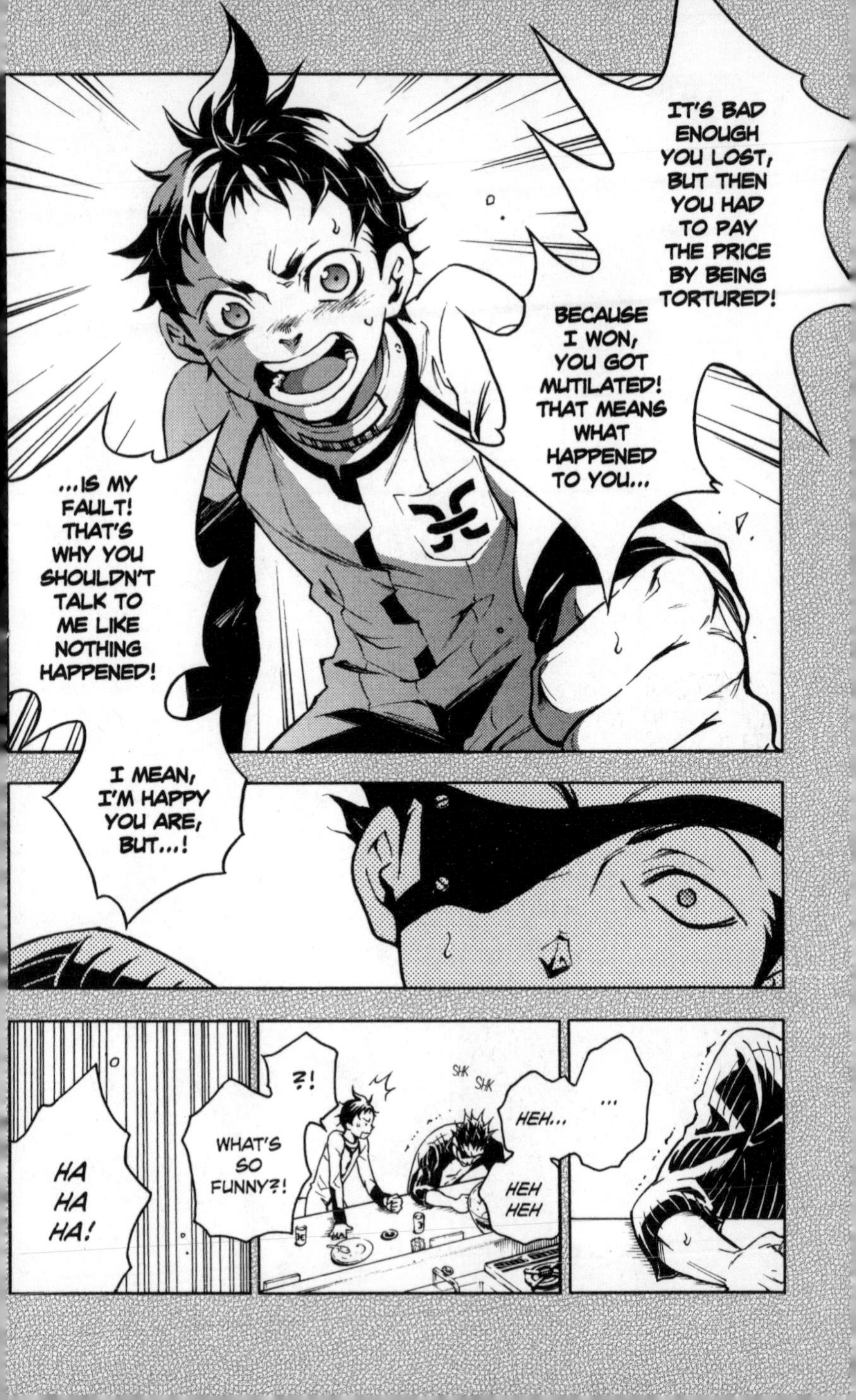

IT'S BAD ENOUGH YOU LOST, BUT THEN YOU HAD TO PAY THE PRICE BY BEING TORTURED!
BECAUSE I WON, YOU GOT MUTILATED! THAT MEANS WHAT HAPPENED TO YOU...
...IS MY FAULT! THAT'S WHY YOU SHOULDN'T TALK TO ME LIKE NOTHING HAPPENED!
I MEAN, I'M HAPPY YOU ARE, BUT...!
...
HEH...
SHK SHK
?!
HEH HEH
WHAT'S SO FUNNY?!
HA HA HA!

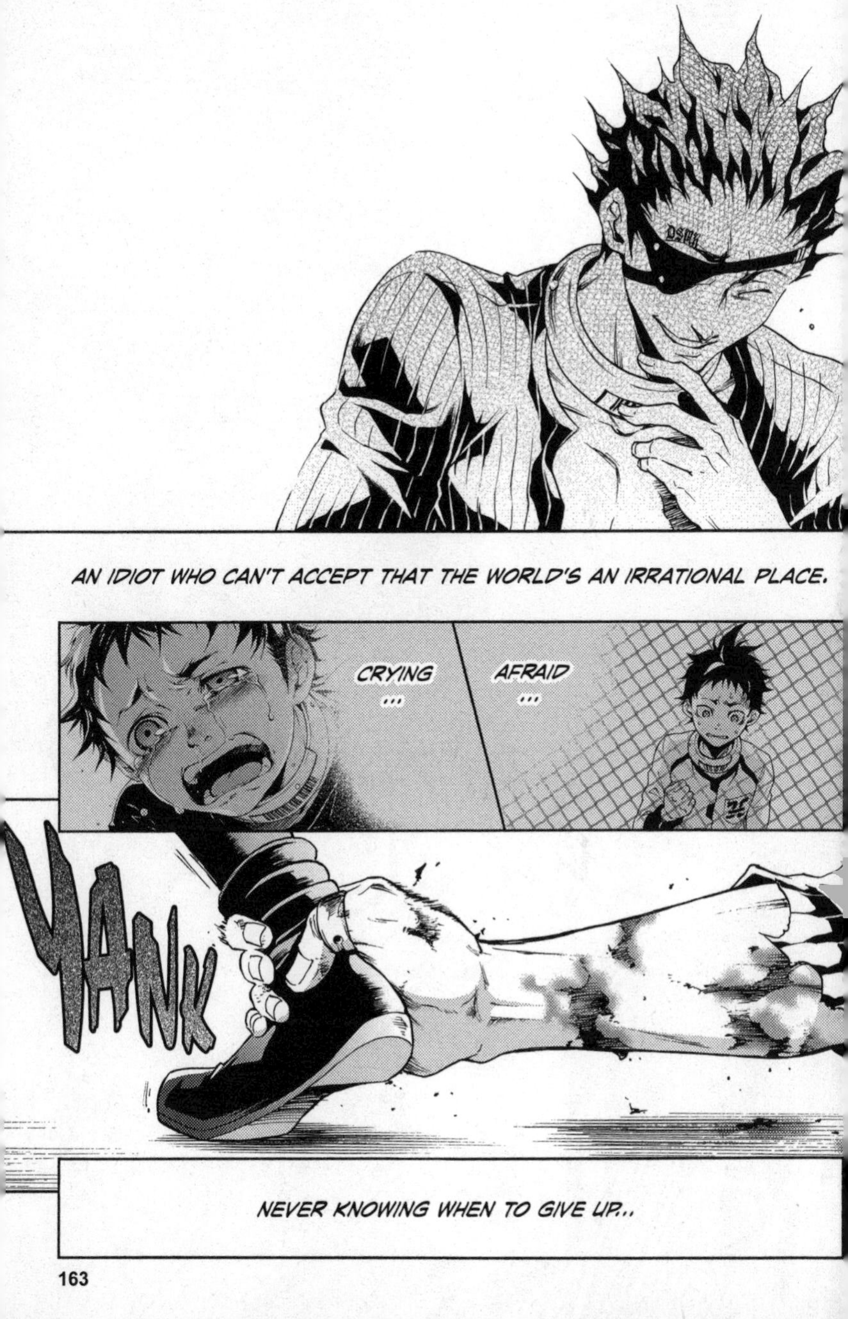
AN IDIOT WHO CAN'T ACCEPT THAT THE WORLD'S AN IRRATIONAL PLACE.
AFRAID ...
CRYING ...
YANK
NEVER KNOWING WHEN TO GIVE UP...

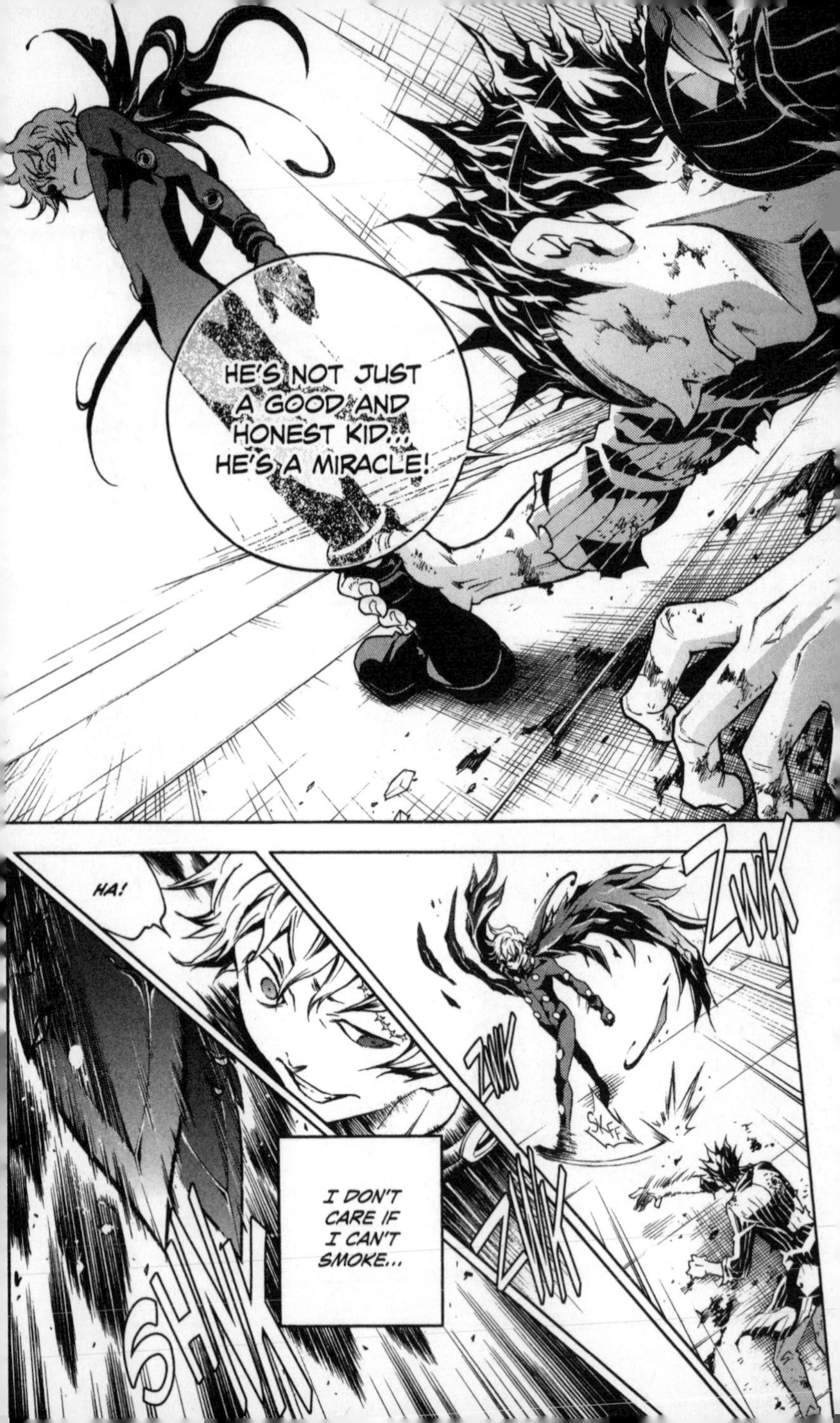

HE'S NOT JUST A GOOD AND HONEST KID... HE'S A MIRACLE!
ZWIK
ZWIK
SKFF
ZWIK
I DON'T CARE IF I CAN'T SMOKE...
HA!

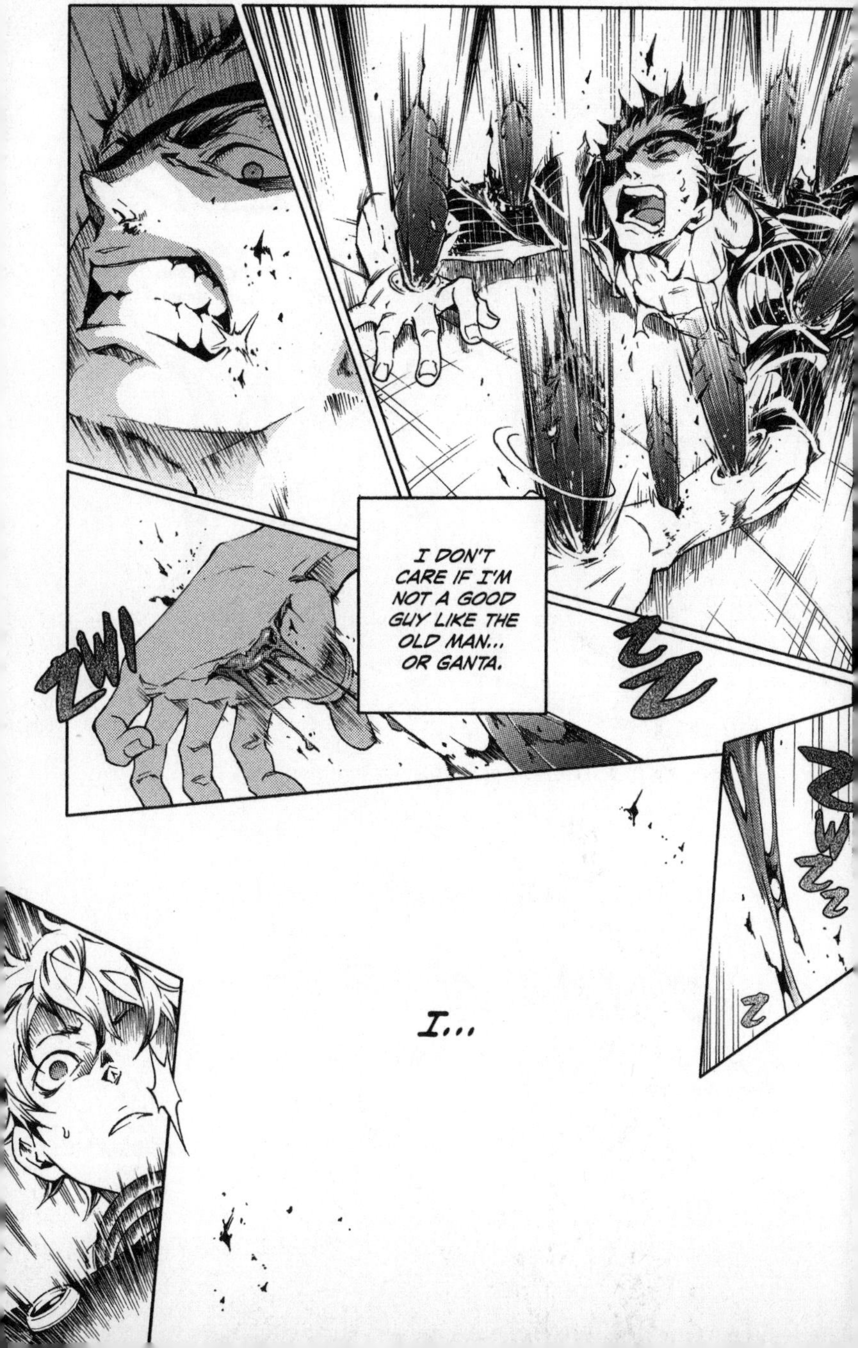

I DON'T CARE IF I'M NOT A GOOD GUY LIKE THE OLD MAN... OR GANTA.
ZN
ZWI
ZWZZZ
I...

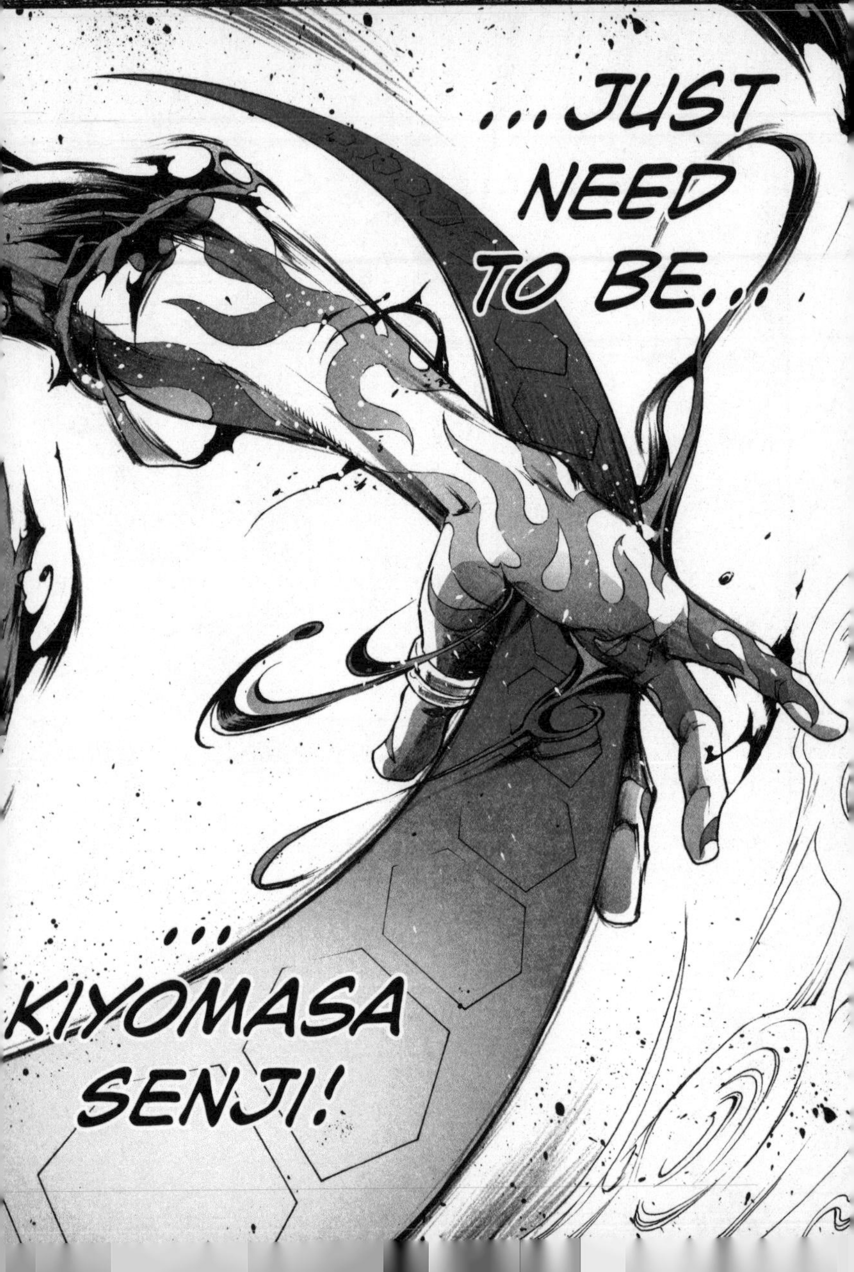
...JUST NEED TO BE...
...KIYOMASA SENJI!

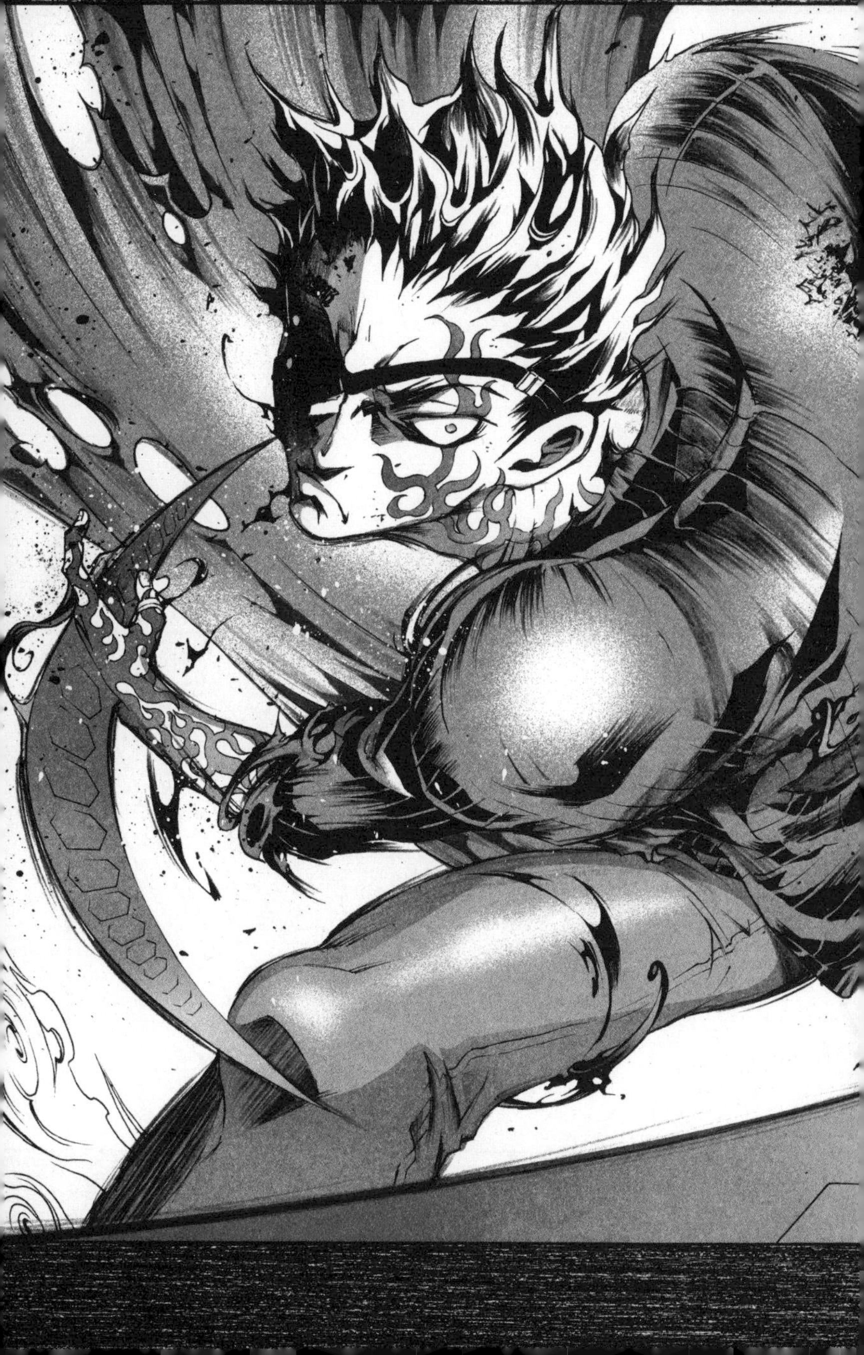

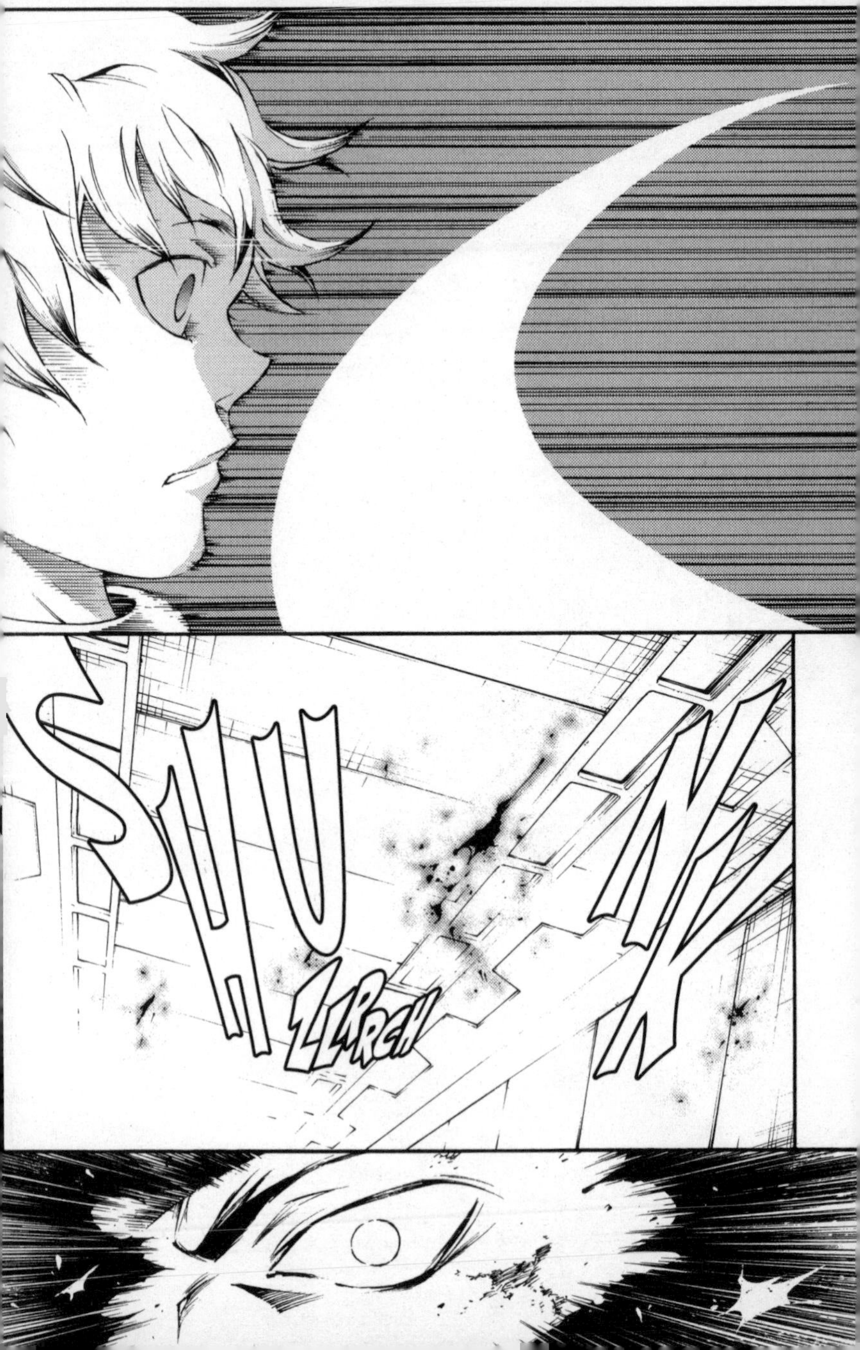
SHUNK
ZLRCH

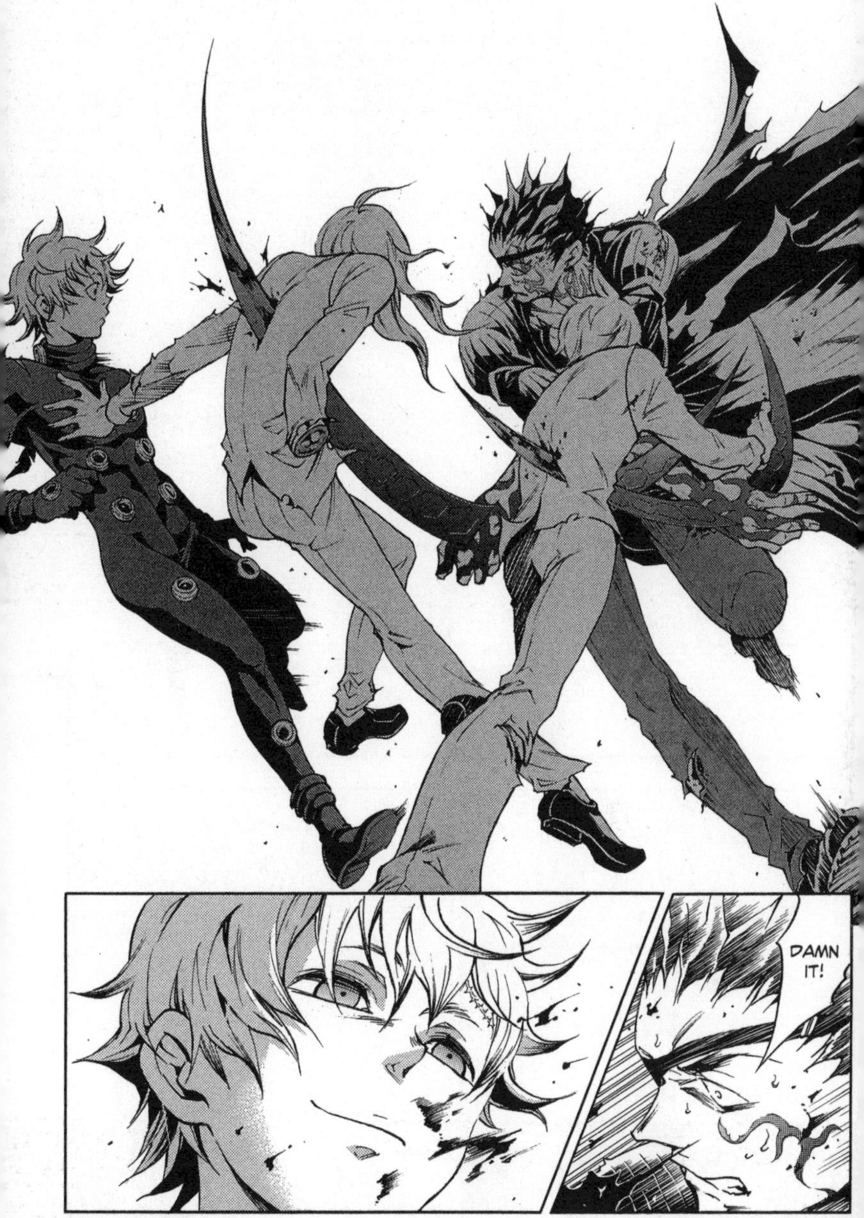
DAMN IT!

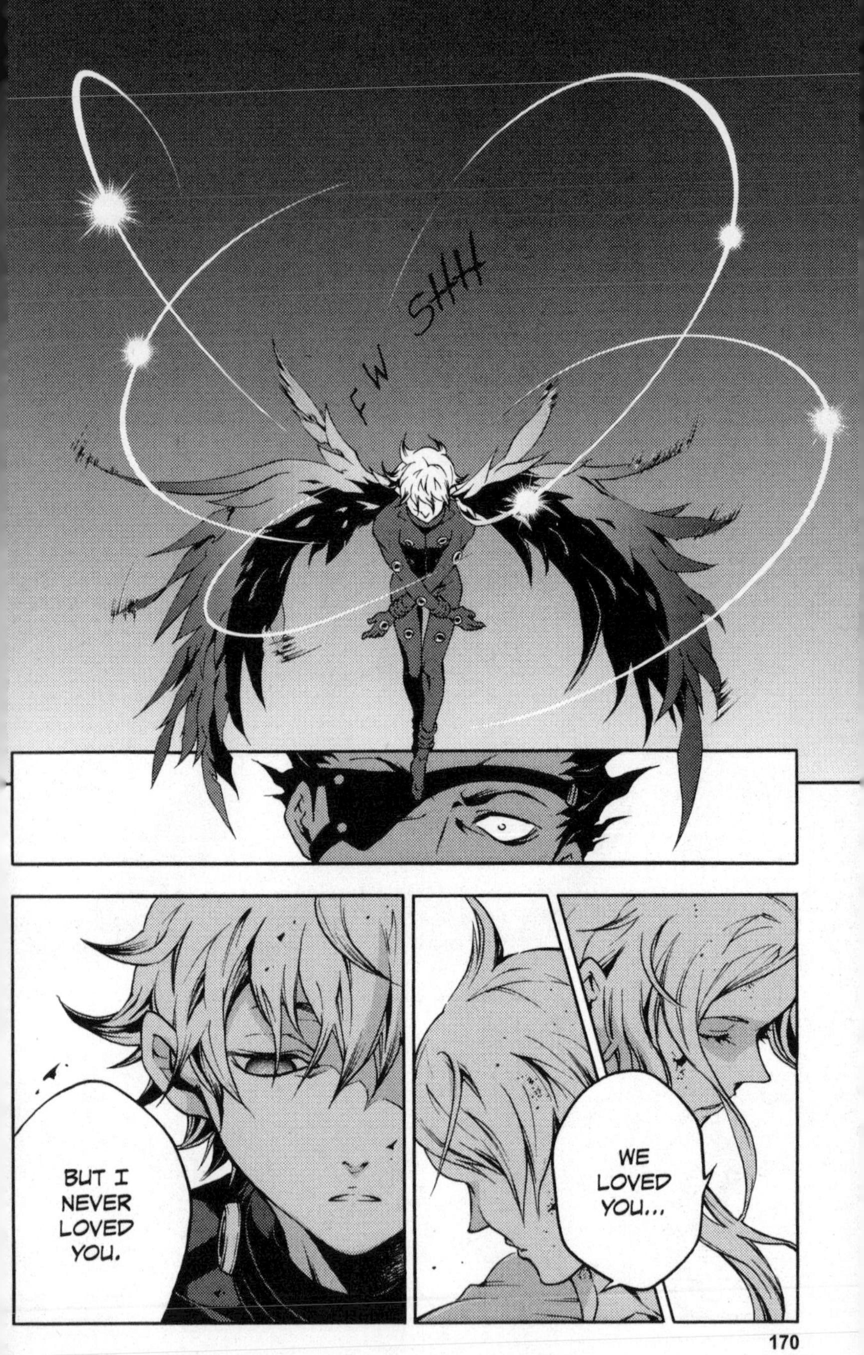
FWSHH
WE LOVED YOU...
BUT I NEVER LOVED YOU.

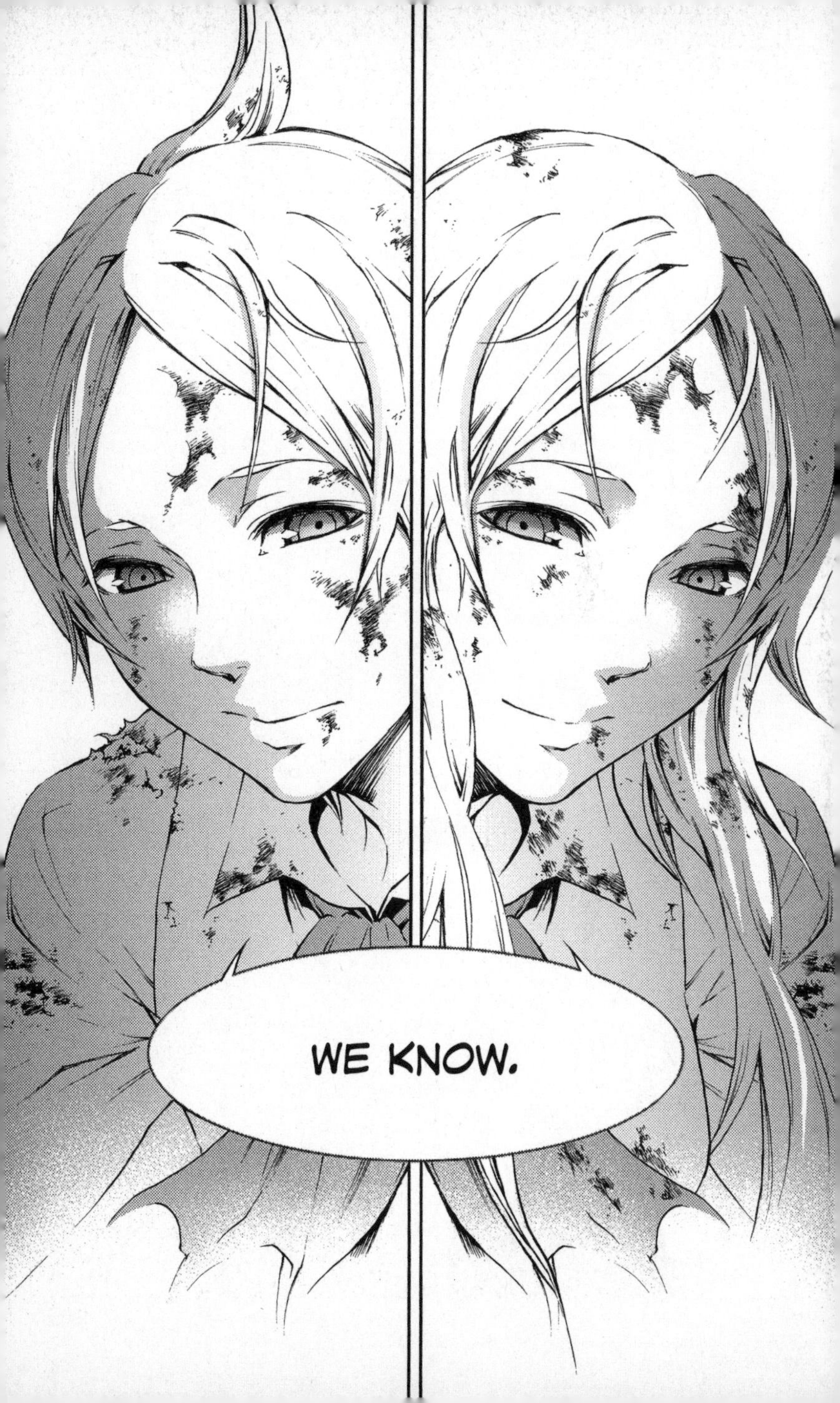
WE KNOW.

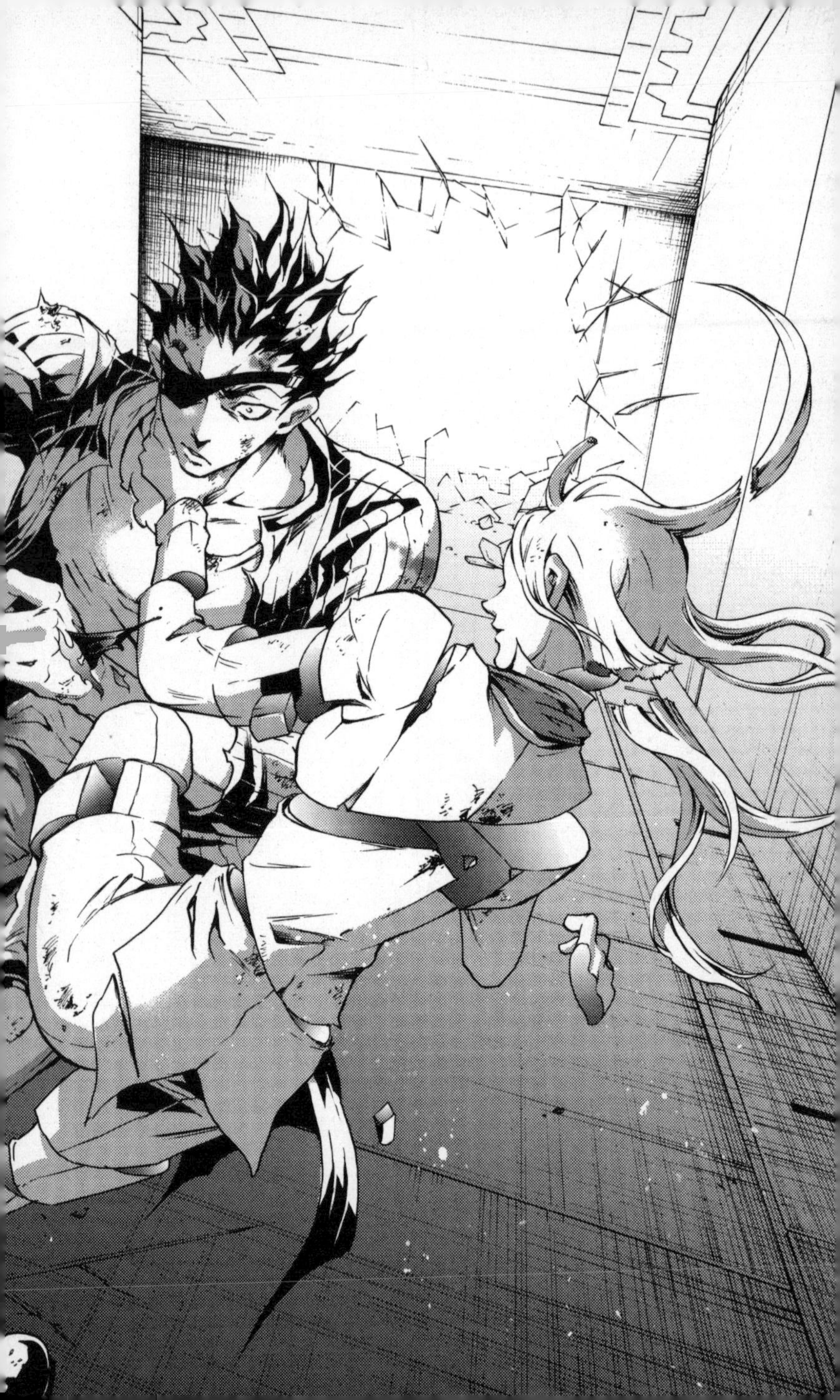

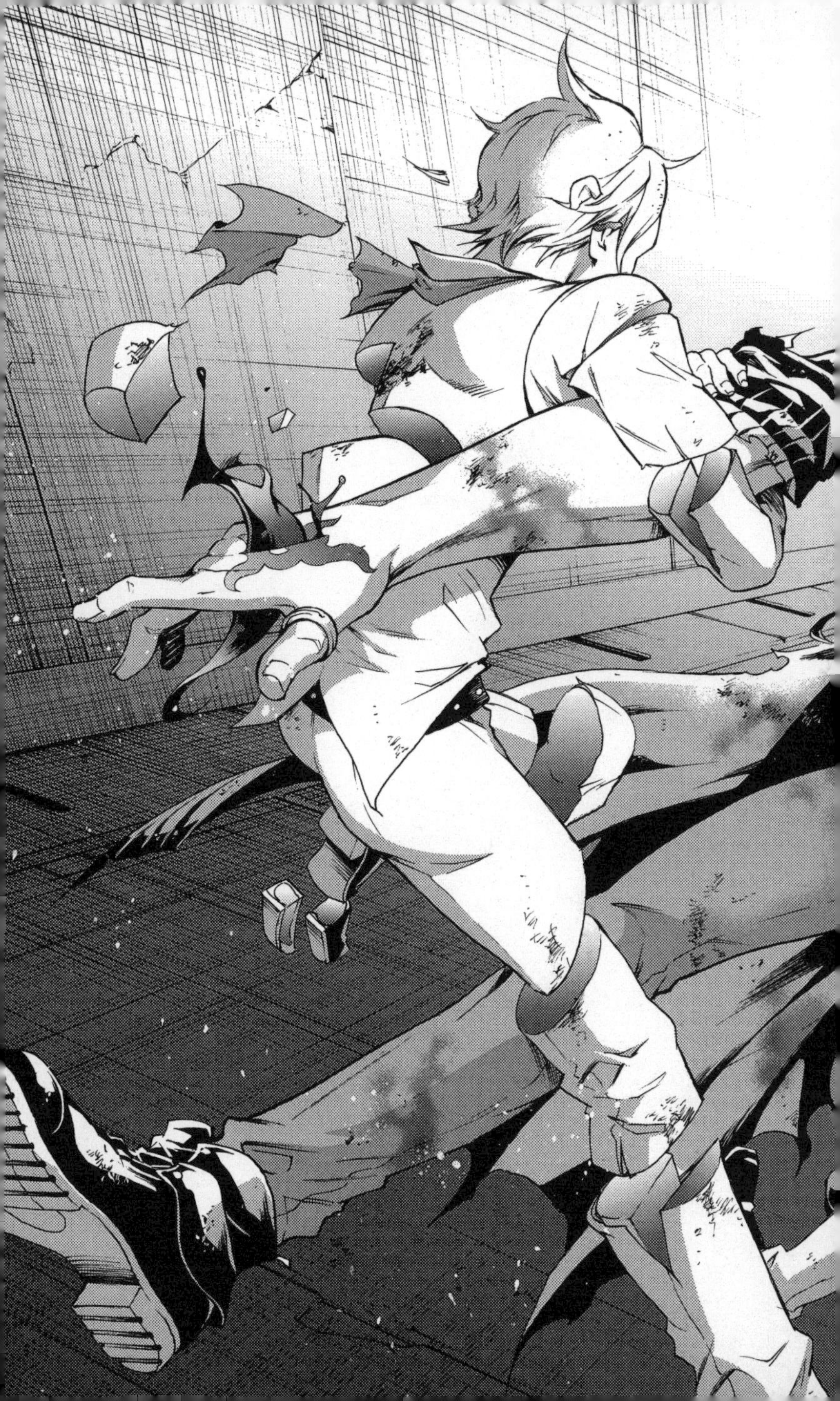

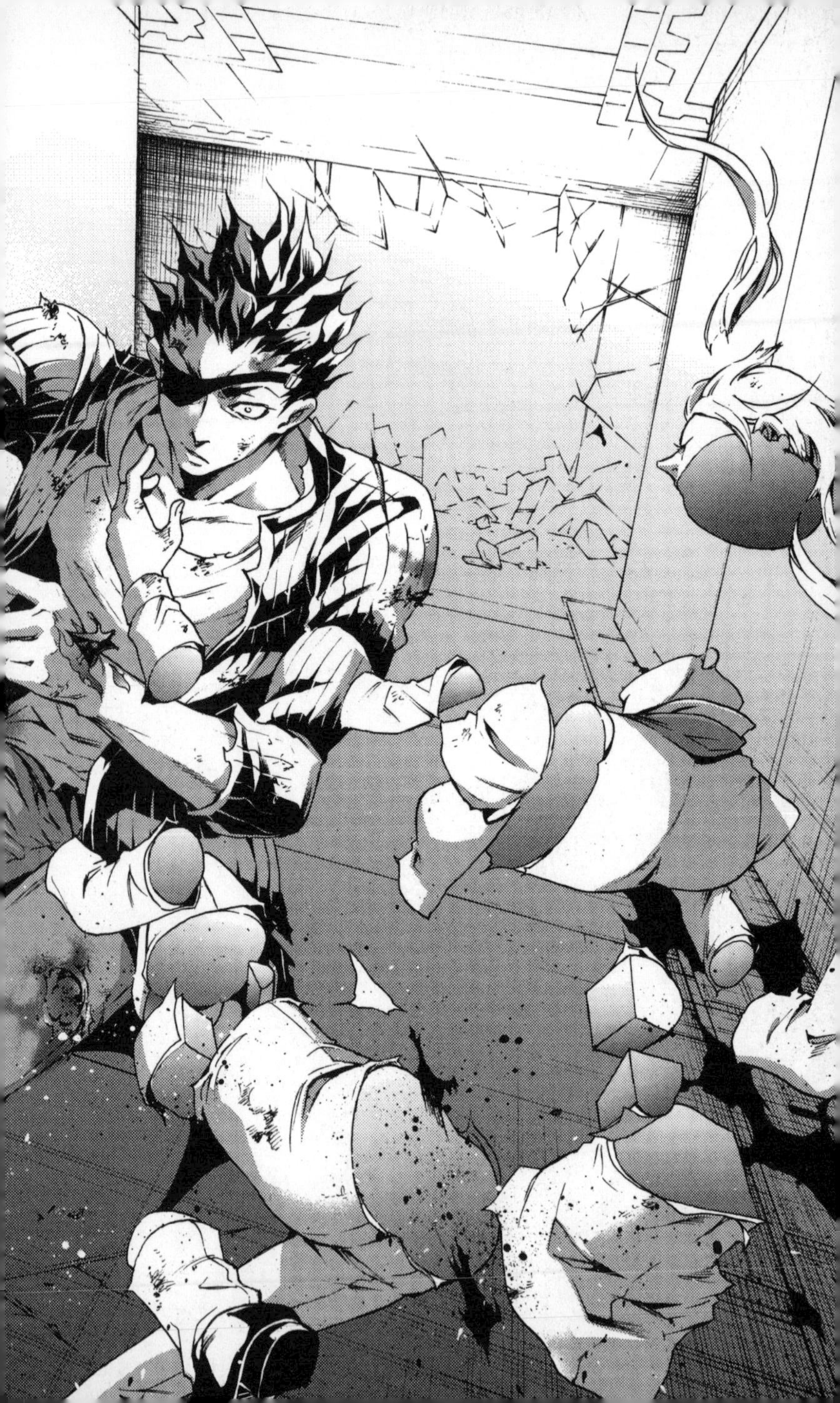

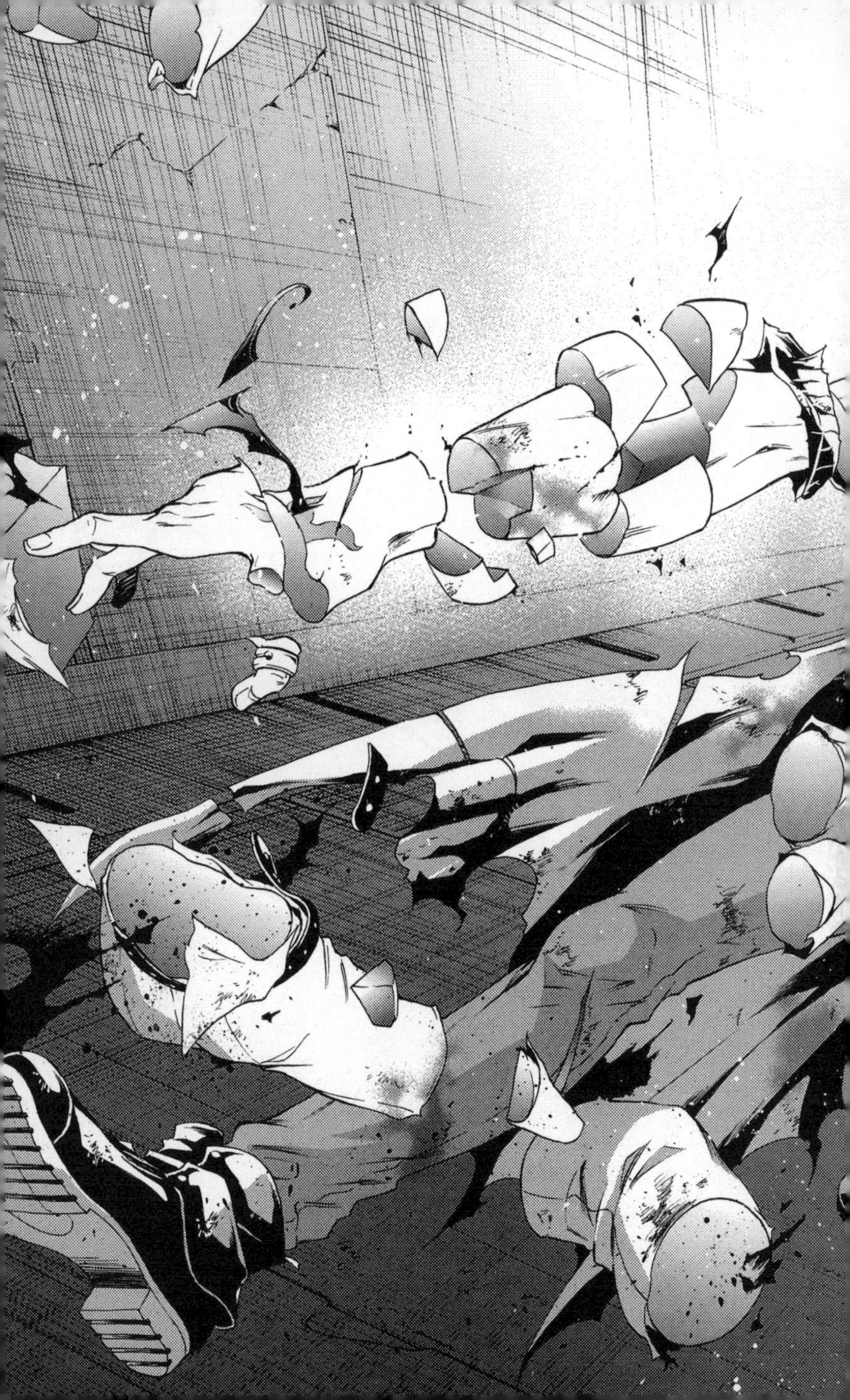

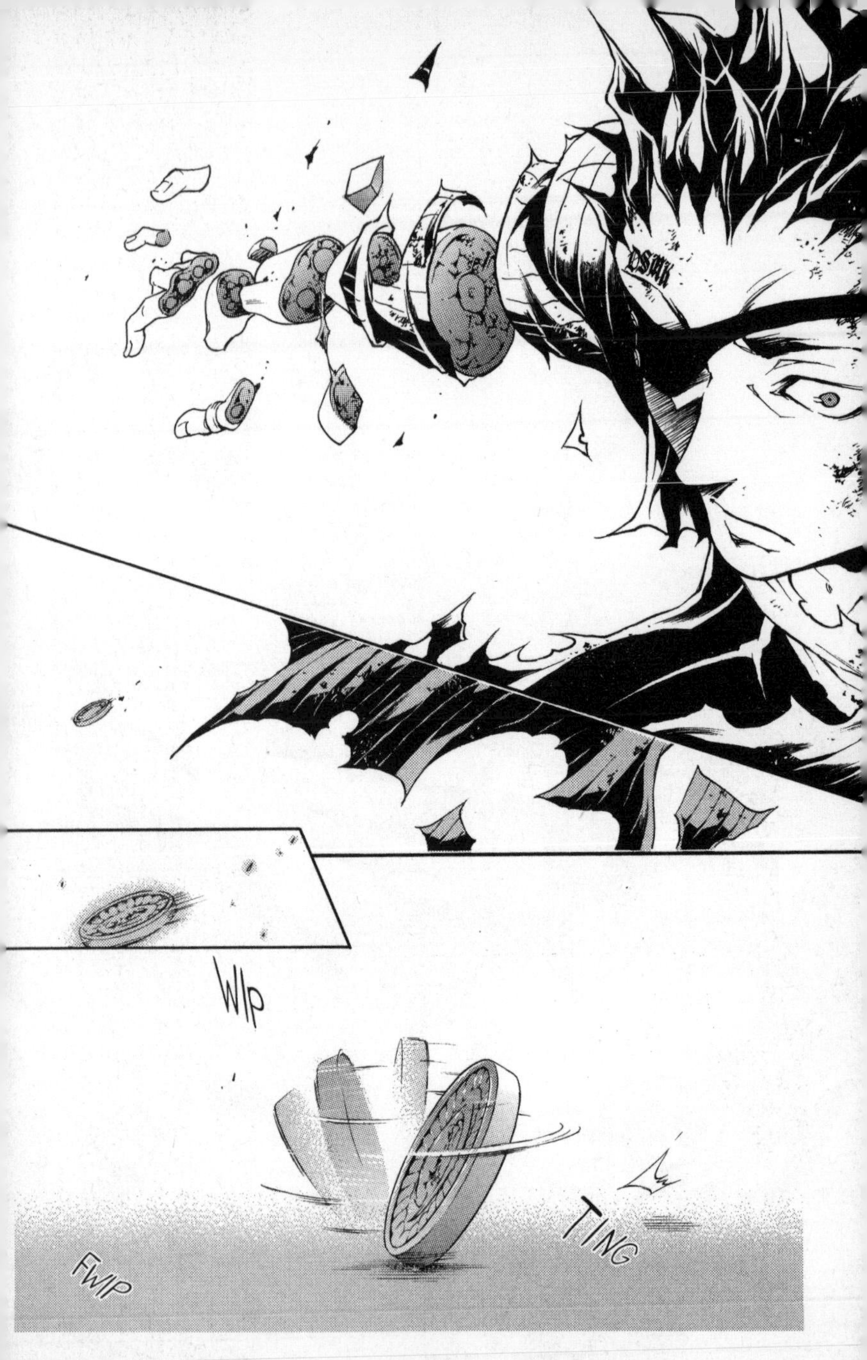
WIP
TING
FWIP

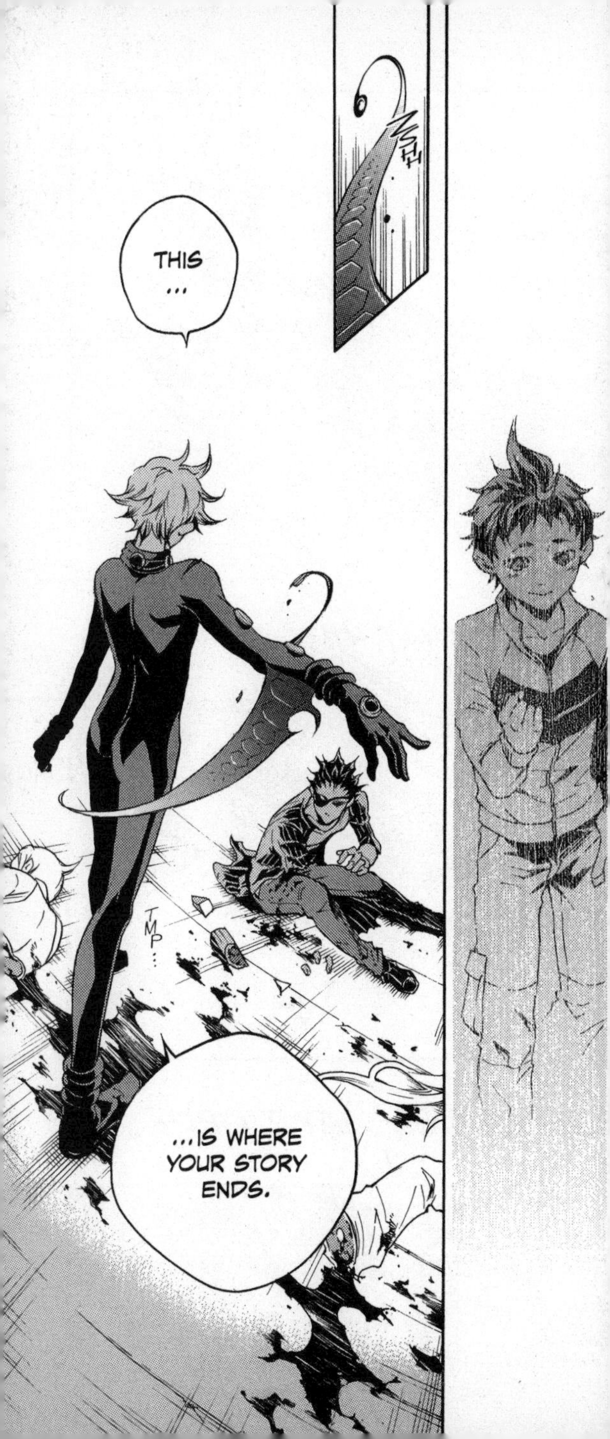
SHH
THIS ...
TMP...
...IS WHERE YOUR STORY ENDS.

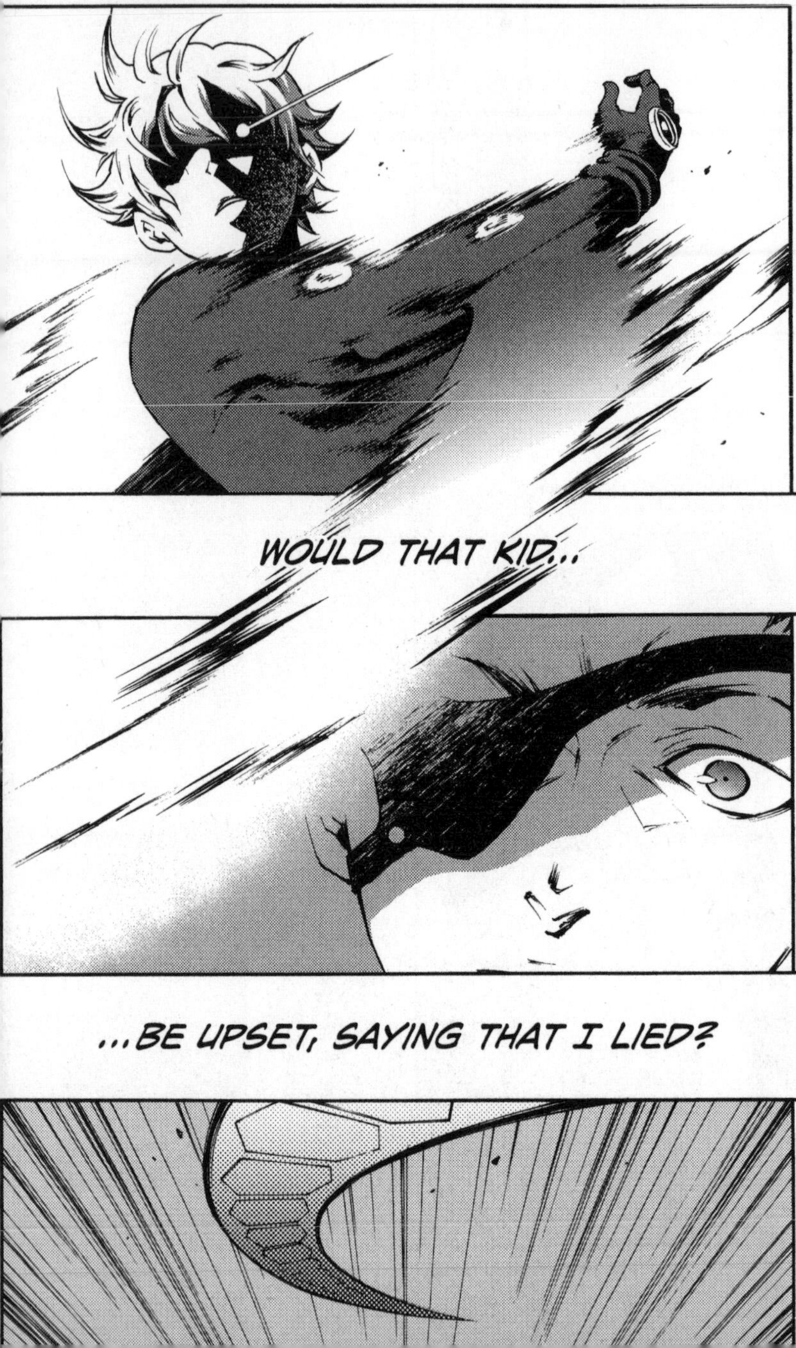
WOULD THAT KID...
...BE UPSET, SAYING THAT I LIED?

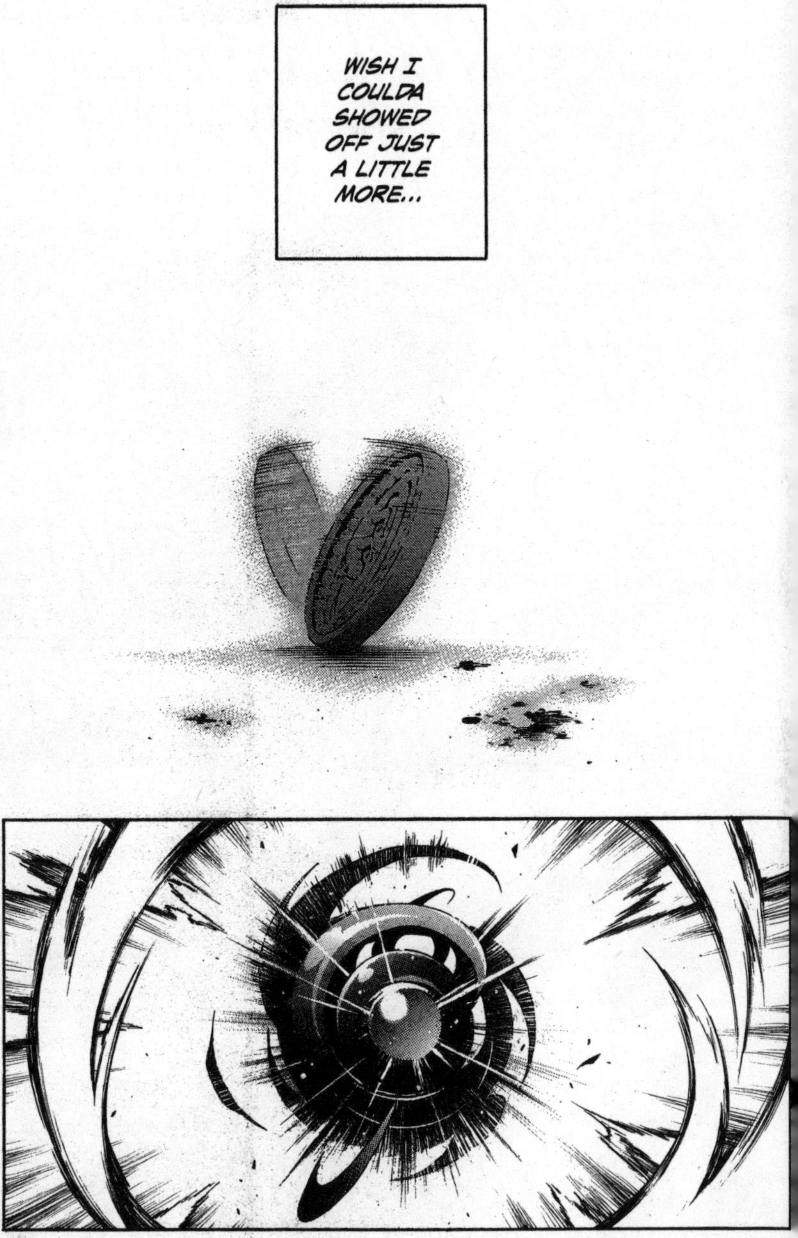
WISH I COULDA SHOWED OFF JUST A LITTLE MORE...

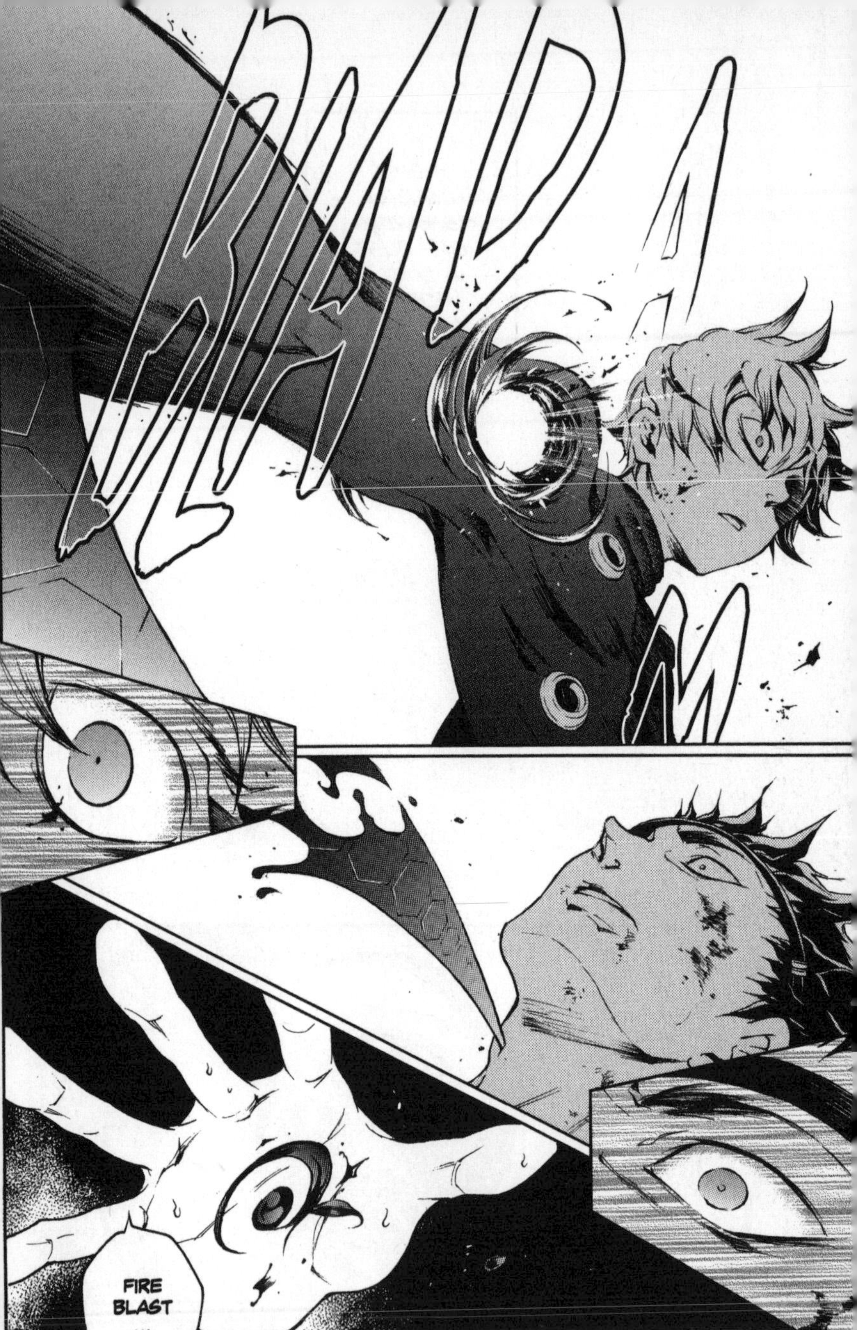
FIRE BLAST ...

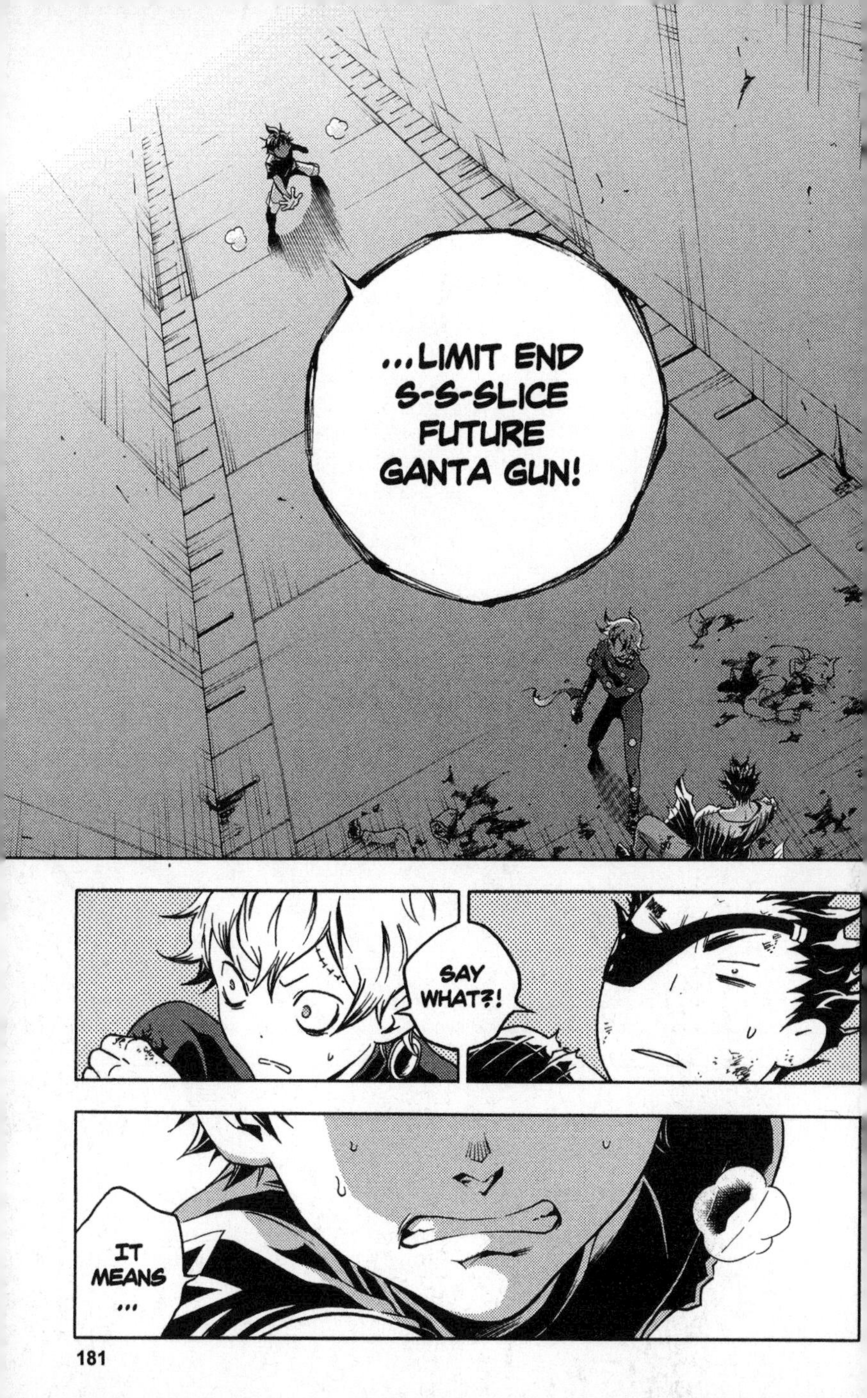
...LIMIT END S-S-SLICE FUTURE GANTA GUN!
SAY WHAT?!
IT MEANS ...

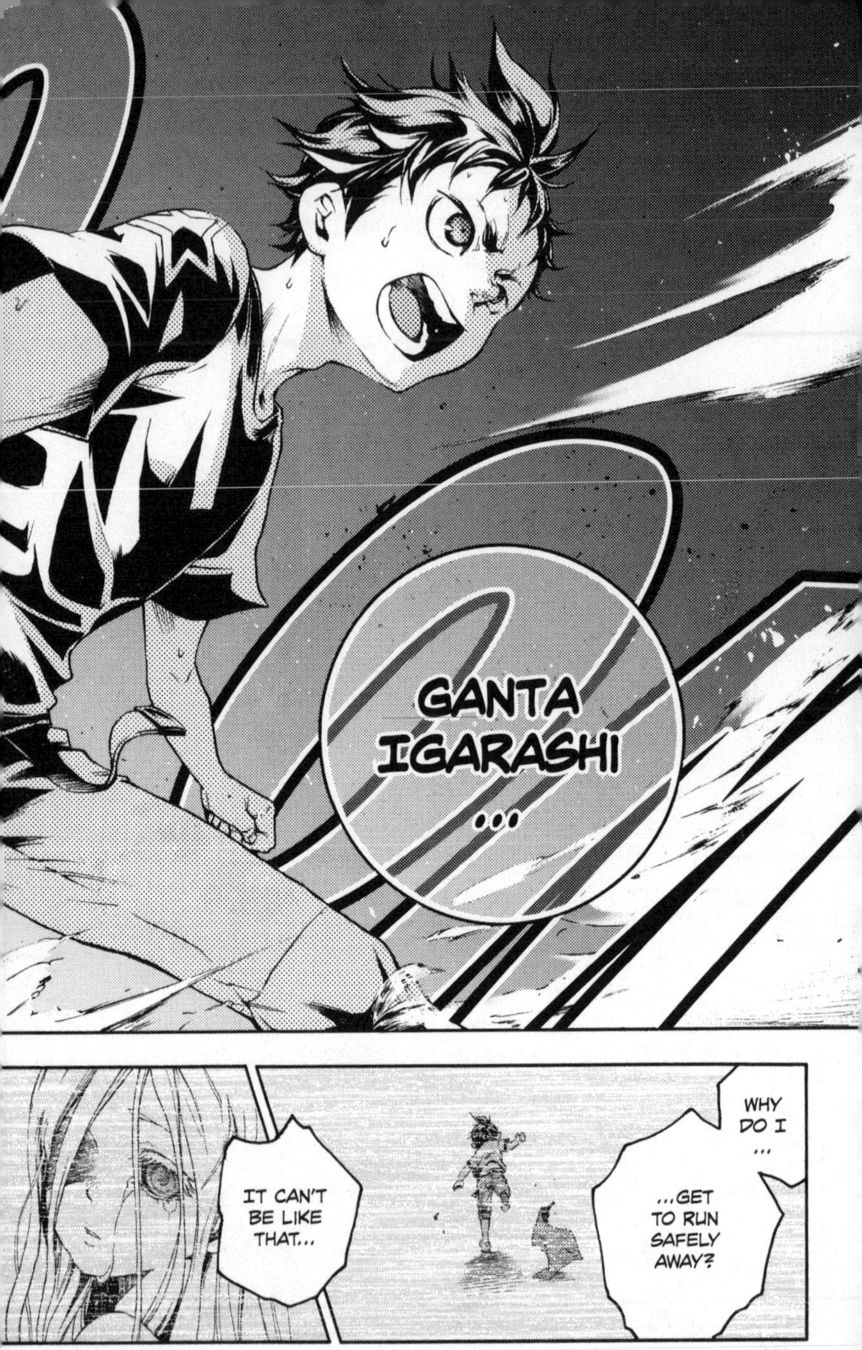
GANTA IGARASHI ...
WHY DO I ...
...GET TO RUN SAFELY AWAY?
IT CAN'T BE LIKE THAT...

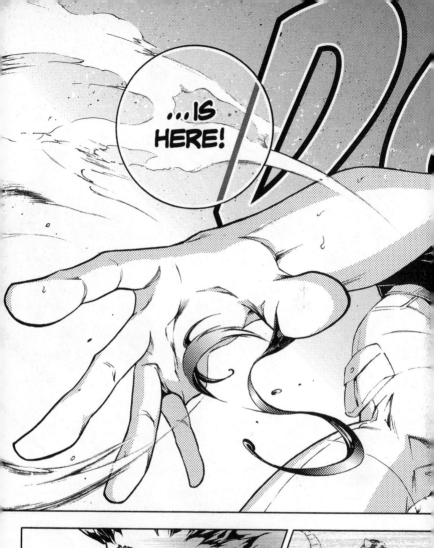

...IS HERE!

I'M NOT A KID ANYMORE.

... NOW.

183

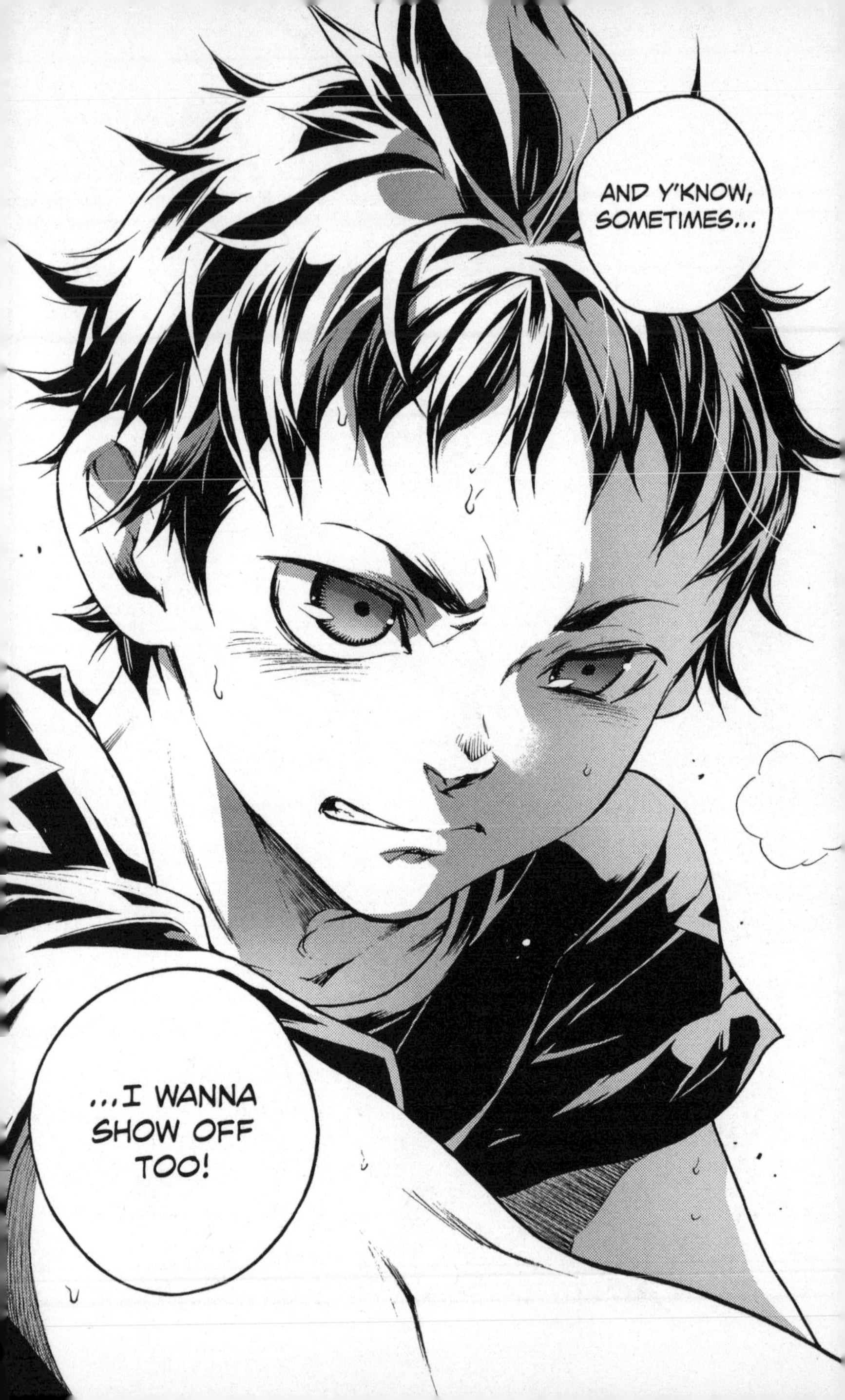
AND Y'KNOW, SOMETIMES...
...I WANNA SHOW OFF TOO!

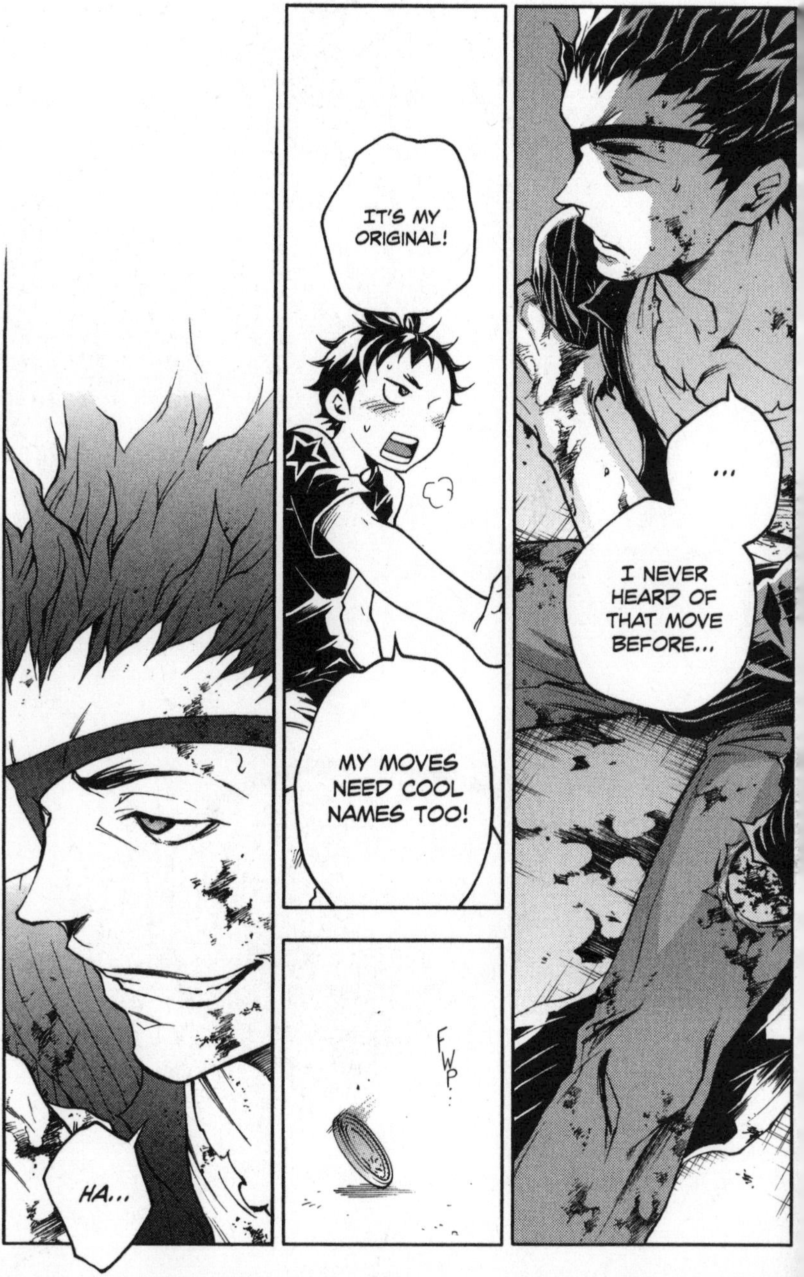
...
I NEVER HEARD OF THAT MOVE BEFORE...
IT'S MY ORIGINAL!
MY MOVES NEED COOL NAMES TOO!
FWP...
HA...

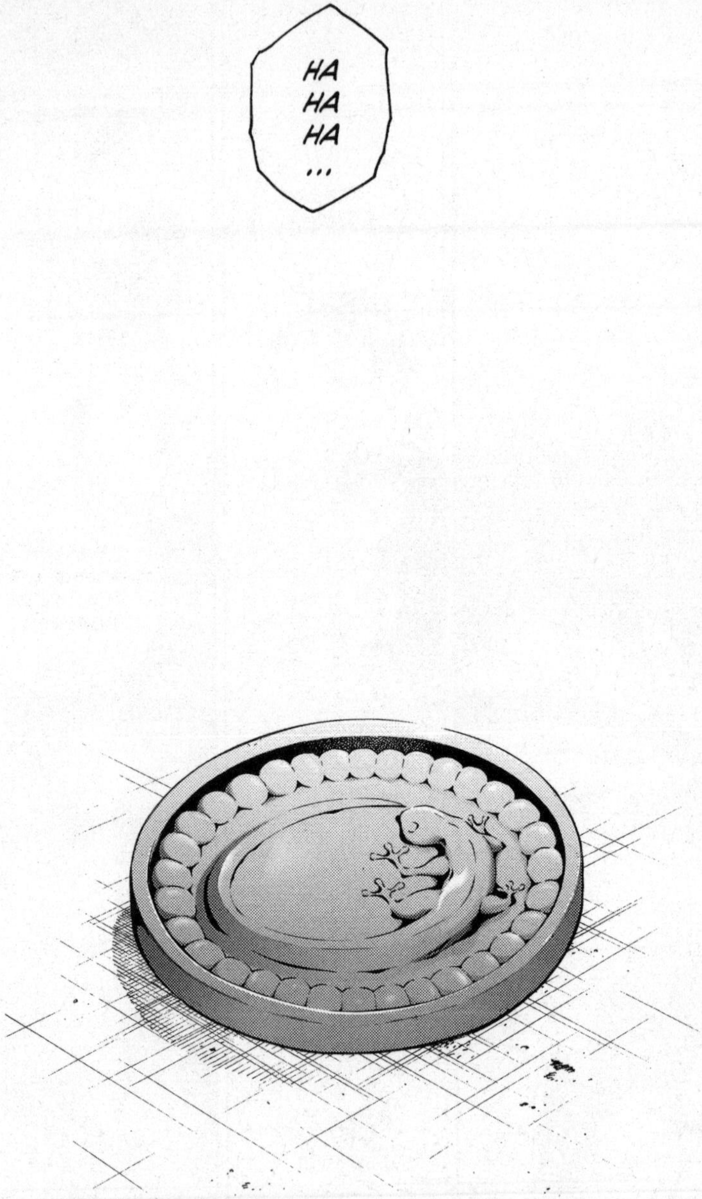
HA HA HA ...

DEADMAN WONDERLAND 11

Jinsei Kataoka
Kazuma Kondou

STAFF

Yukitsune Amagusa

Karaiko

Shinji Sato

Taro Tsuchiya

Taku Nakamura

Toshihiro Noguchi

Wataru Ishikawa

CONTINUED IN VOLUME 12

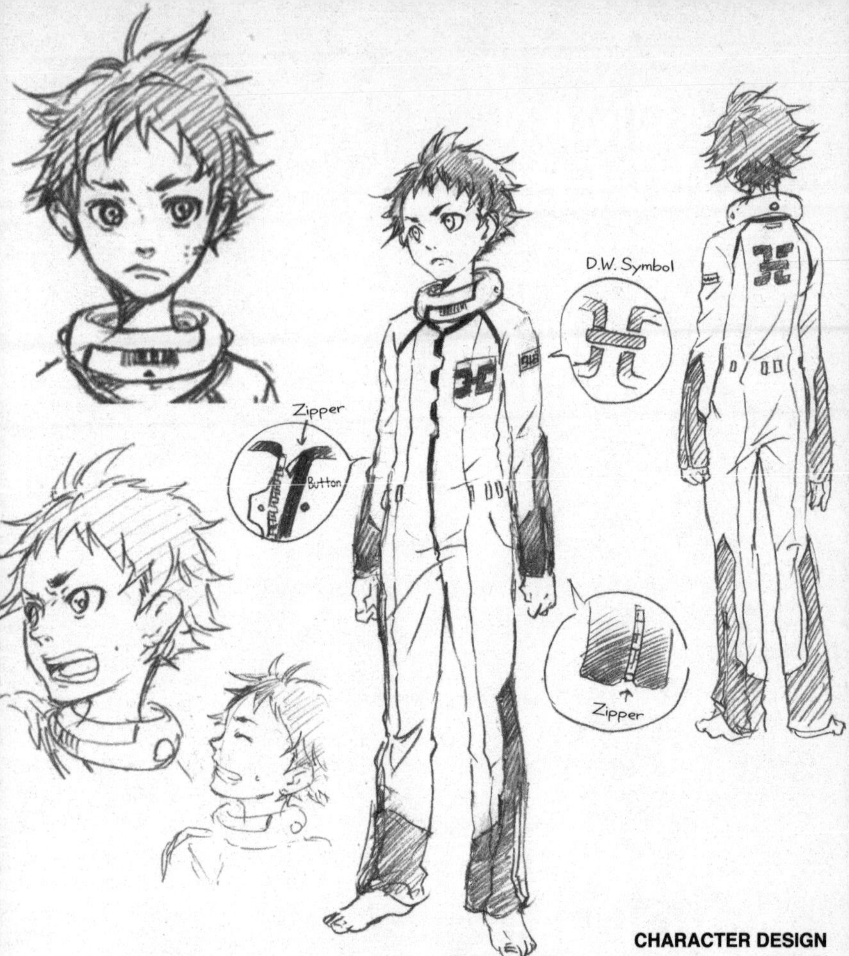
D.W. Symbol
Zipper
Button
Zipper

CHARACTER DESIGN

Ganta Igarashi

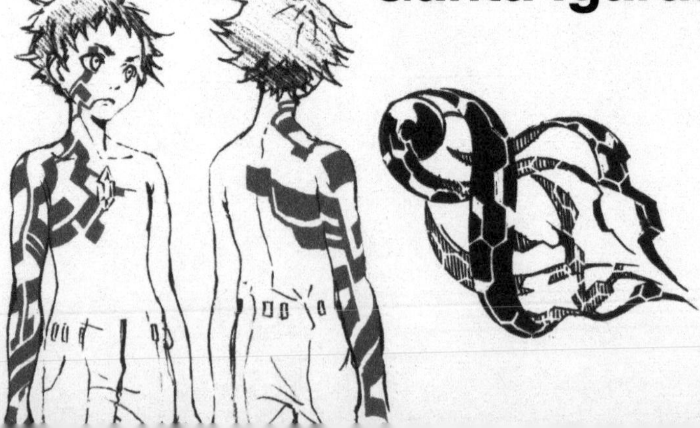

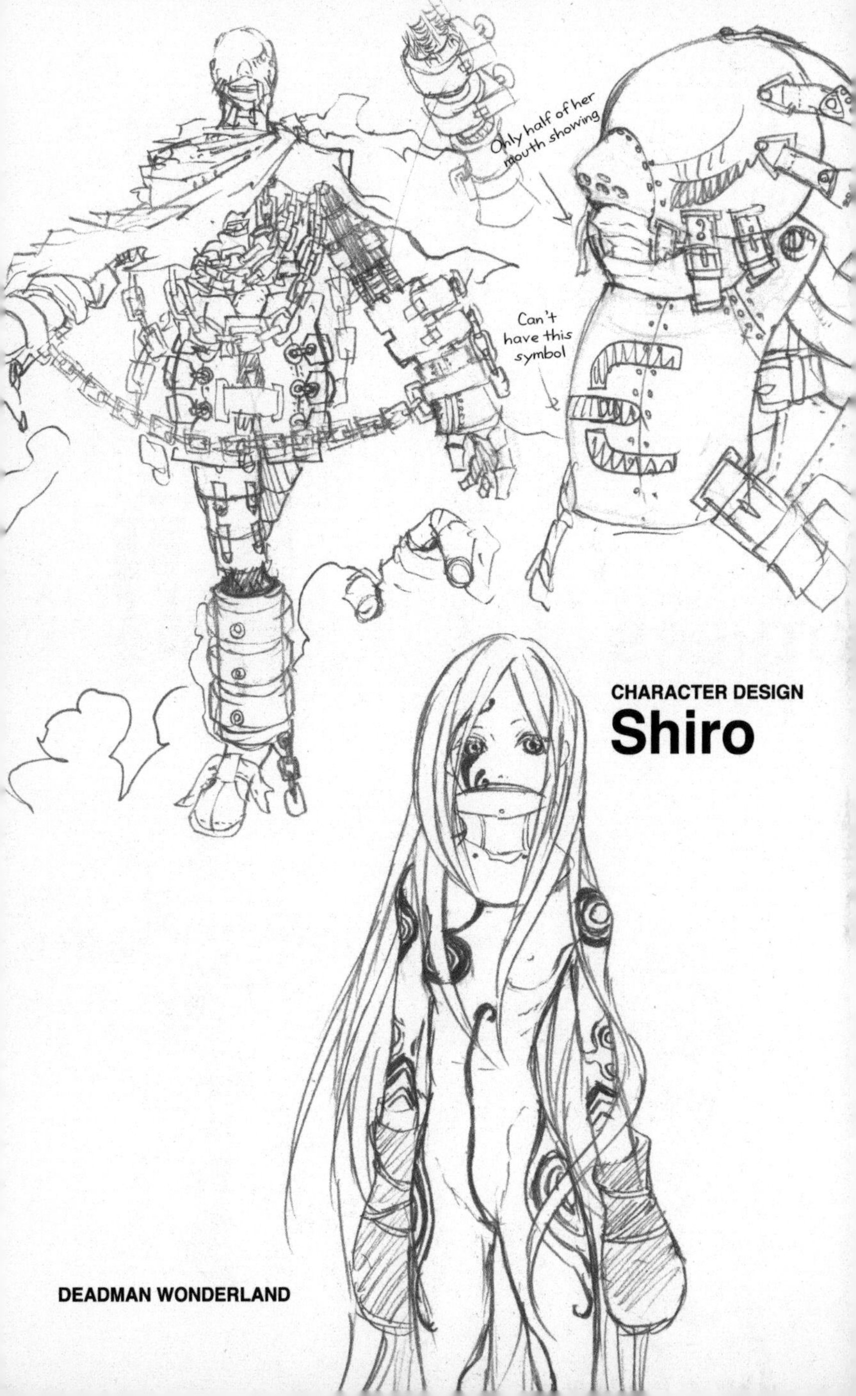
Only half of her mouth showing
Can't have this symbol

CHARACTER DESIGN
Shiro

CHARACTER DESIGN
OTHERS

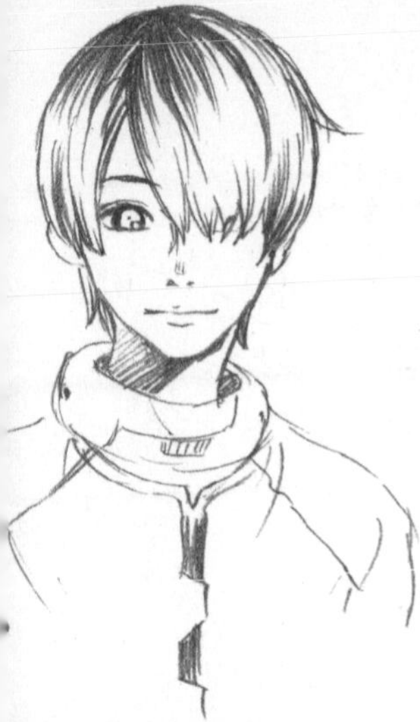

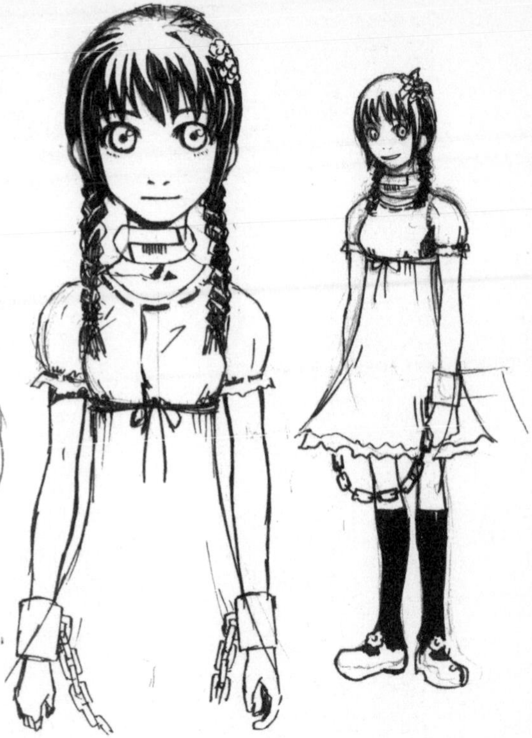

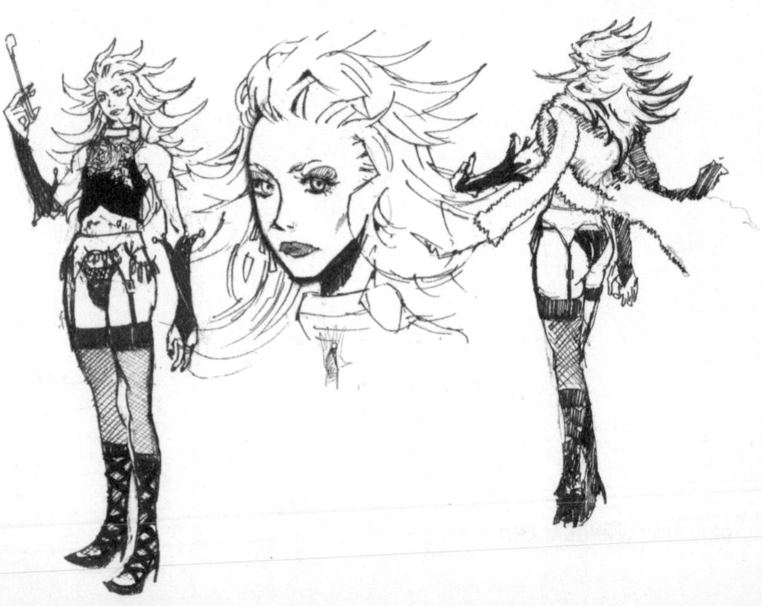

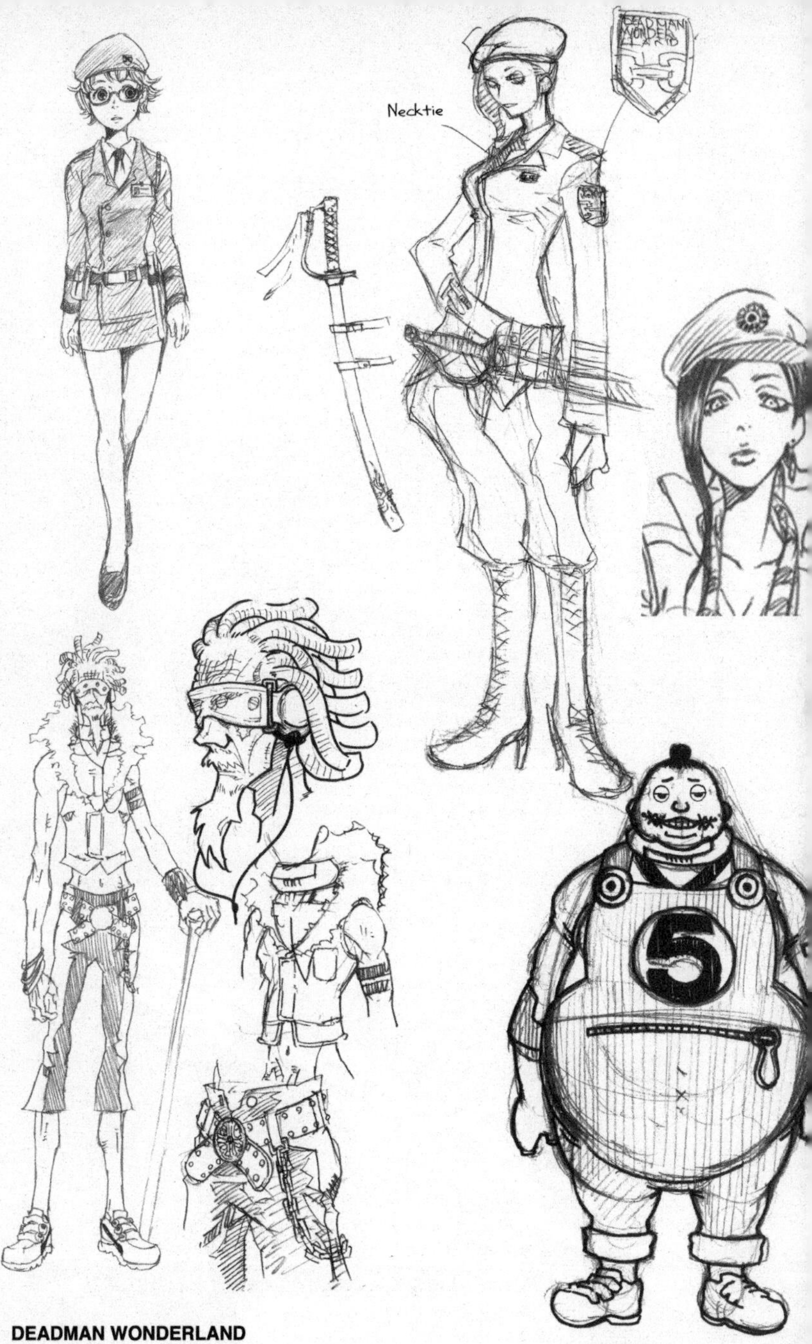
Necktie
5

DEADMAN WONDERLAND

DEADMAN WONDERLAND
VOLUME 11
VIZ MEDIA EDITION

STORY & ART BY
JINSEI KATAOKA, KAZUMA KONDOU

DEADMAN WONDERLAND VOLUME 11
©JINSEI KATAOKA 2011 ©KAZUMA KONDOU 2011
EDITED BY KADOKAWA SHOTEN
FIRST PUBLISHED IN JAPAN IN 2011 BY KADOKAWA CORPORATION, TOKYO.
ENGLISH TRANSLATION RIGHTS ARRANGED WITH KADOKAWA CORPORATION, TOKYO.

TRANSLATION/JOE YAMAZAKI
ENGLISH ADAPTATION/STAN!
TOUCH-UP ART & LETTERING/JAMES GAUBATZ
DESIGN/SAM ELZWAY
EDITOR/JENNIFER LEBLANC

PUBLISHED BY VIZ MEDIA, LLC
P.O. BOX 77010
SAN FRANCISCO, CA 94107

10 9 8 7 6 5 4 3 2 1
FIRST PRINTING, OCTOBER 2015

www.viz.com

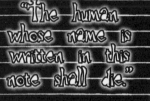

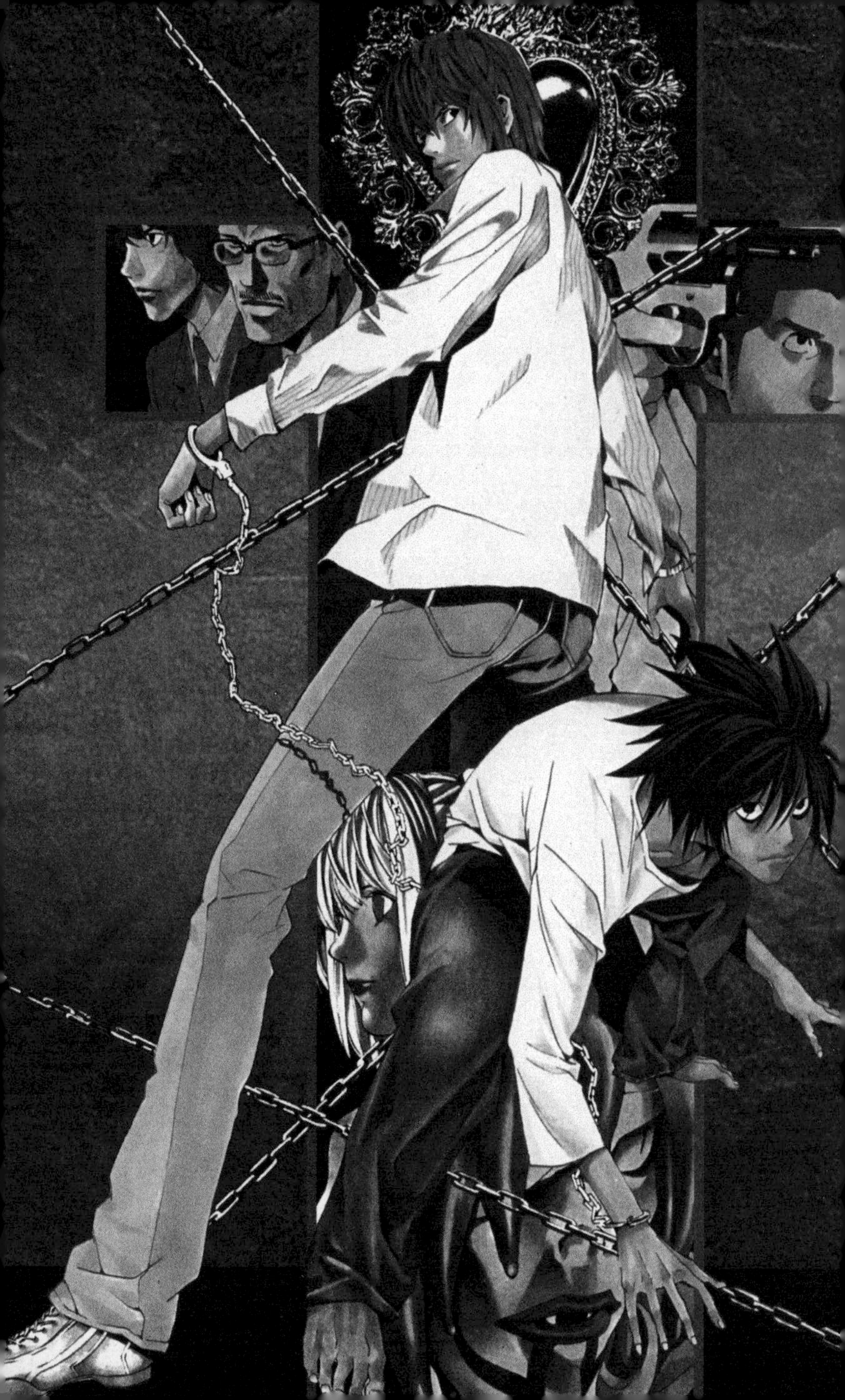

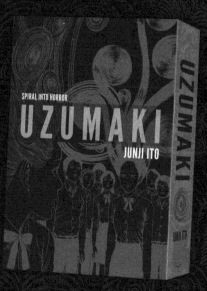